Latino Politics

RACE, ETHNICITY, AND POLITICS
Luis Ricardo Fraga and Paula D. McClain, Editors

Latino Politics

IDENTITY, MOBILIZATION, AND REPRESENTATION

Edited by Rodolfo Espino, David L. Leal, and Kenneth J. Meier

University of Virginia Press | *Charlottesville and London*

University of Virginia Press
© 2007 by the Rector and Visitors of the University of Virginia
All rights reserved
Printed in the United States of America on acid-free paper
First published 2007

9 8 7 6 5 4 3 2 1

LIBRARY OF CONGRESS CATALOGING-IN-PUBLICATION DATA

Latino Politics : identity, mobilization and representation / edited by Rodolfo Espino,
David L. Leal, and Kenneth J. Meier.
    p.   cm. — (Race, ethnicity, and politics)
  Includes bibliographical references and index.
  ISBN 978-0-8139-2651-3 (cloth : alk. paper)
  1. Hispanic Americans—Politics and government. 2. Hispanic Americans—Ethnic
identity. 3. Political participation—United States. 4. Representative government and
representation—United States. 5. United States—Ethnic relations—Political aspects.
6. United States—Race relations—Political aspects. I. Espino, Rodolfo. II. Leal, David L.
III. Meier, Kenneth J., 1950–
E184.S75L36248 2007
324.089′68073—dc22

2007005311

To Chris, John, and Rudy—pioneers in the study of Latino politics

Contents

Contents

Foreword

Rodney E. Hero

A POLITICAL SYSTEM NEEDS to be viewed and understood not only in terms of its strengths but also in terms of its contradictions and/or weaknesses. The study of Latino and "minority" politics brings attention not only to numerically small(er)—if increasingly large and growing—groups but, more important, to groups that are (more or less) disadvantaged and to the problem of how these groups practice a politics that simultaneously draws upon and challenges American political values. Latino politics is well within the American mainstream but has not succeeded in the goals of fuller equality and incorporation and (therefore) often functions in the interstices and/or at the margins of American society and politics. Thus, the study of Latino politics leads us to examine a variety of substantial, yet often-neglected, assumptions and theoretical, normative, and empirical questions in American politics and American political science—and this collection of essays substantially contributes to those endeavors.

How does American democratic theory account for the politically and socially disadvantaged status of Latinos? Do such groups and their circumstances imply a need to question and/or redefine our understanding of democracy, and/or of power? If so, how; if not, why not? Considerable political and social theorizing has focused on African Americans as an exception to the broader embrace of the American "democratic creed." But Latinos (as well as Native Americans and, perhaps, others) may be additional exceptions to African American exceptionalism. African Americans have been the "manifest" and major (if no longer the largest) "minority" group in American history; Asian Americans have been seen as a "model" minority because of general socioeconomic success. Latinos have been a "meso," "in the middle," minority, which has made it difficult to characterize and analyze this group substantively and theoretically; yet the unique history(ies) and forms of inclusion into the American polity, numbers, population growth, and other factors make Latinos a pivotal group to understand.

What does American politics mean for Latino politics? What does Latino politics mean for American politics? And what does Latino politics mean for Latinos? The expansive and insightful collection of essays in this volume helps us grapple with these important issues. Each of the essays touches on these questions to greater or lesser degrees and more or less directly, but each section and the individual essays within speak to the questions with different emphases.

The general contours of the issues addressed and essential findings of the essays are nicely summarized in the introduction (Espino and Leal below). Therefore, here I wish to offer some general comments that parallel that introduction but also depart somewhat, in the spirit of providing one view on "what it all means," and suggest that the essays may be as notable for what is taken for granted as for what is said. I begin by prefacing those comments with a vignette that demonstrates skepticism about the study of Latino and minority politics and, conversely, underscores, in my view, the very significance of such inquiry.

One of the more memorable experiences I've had in my (now many) years in political science occurred at a panel of the American Political Association annual conference in late August 2002. Following the presentation of a paper I coauthored, titled "Political Science, the New Immigration and Racial Politics in the United States: What Do We Know? What Do We Need to Know?" a member of the audience, a very well-known and very highly respected scholar, posed a question of the paper's authors: "Why don't you just study American politics?"

This question was generally interpreted by the paper's authors (myself included) as meaning that identifying and emphasizing race/ethnicity—and particularly Latino politics, because of that element's centrality in the paper—as an orienting focus of study was somehow not "really" the study, perhaps not even (an important) part of the study, or not an entirely legitimate way of thinking about "American politics." Focusing on questions suggesting inequality and contentiousness, rather than on (an assumed) essential commonalities of various groups' social and political situations seemed uncomfortable to the questioner (Smith 1997). Assuming the authors'/panelists' interpretation of the question was reasonably accurate, one wonders how widely that view is shared among political scientists. If nothing else, I think we can safely assume that such a question would not be posed at very many, if any, other panels on American politics.

The editors and the contributors to the present book are surely aware of challenges and even dismissiveness of the sort implied by sentiments of the questioner. Yet, the volume confidently (some critics might say naively) wades boldly into these topics, as exemplified by its very title, which indicates few reservations about the legitimacy of its focus—to the point of simply declaring that Latino politics is "a discipline." And the various essays herein more or less explicitly adopt that orientation. Beyond that, however, what is suggested by the form and content of the essays implies that research on Latino politics is not always easy to situate, or at least to situate fully, within "mainstream" American politics research, much like the condition of Latinos is not always readily situated within practical American politics. But that is precisely much of what makes the topic important and worthy of careful attention.

Research such as that presented here faces (at least) two interrelated challenges. One, as noted, is situating the research within what is often deemed "broader" analyses; the other question has to do with the "value added" of this research. It is easier to do the former than the latter, although the research is ultimately most likely to be judged more by the latter rather than the former. The essays acquit themselves well on both counts and make clear the significance and theoretical benefits of approaching politics through the analytical lens of race/ethnicity; they also demonstrate the incompleteness and inadequacy of research that ostensibly focuses on "just American politics."

The essays, especially those on "identity" politics, on the one hand assume, and on the other hand, also seem compelled to seek to clarify and explain grounds for group formation and maintenance. Broadly speaking, the primary bases social scholars have employed for delineating group bounds in American politics have been race, class, and culture, although the intersection of these (and other) social factors is commonly recognized and integrated into analyses as well. The actual *study of Latino politics* has primarily emphasized a cultural frame, if not necessarily fully consciously so, it seems to me. Culture itself is a complex, at times ambiguous, concept. In some ways it is apparent; in other ways it seems more apparent than real; and in yet other ways it often seems to essentially amount to what is left, the residual, after other social and economic factors are accounted for. Culture may suggest a sense of shared memories and history and notions of community (as Márquez says), and/or a distinct convergence of opinions, if only in the aggregate, about various issues of public concern (as Leal says); it may orient but not necessarily determine affinities in every case all the time. Latinos also have many differences attributable to experience and self-perception as an "ethnic" (or a "minority") group, and as a result of immigration status and/or attachment to one's home country (transnationalism), which complicate and are additional dimensions (see Jones-Correa's essay) of Latinos' group sense or culture.

Culture emphasizes beliefs and norms that are created primarily internally to the group. Whether these norms and beliefs are in part caused by "racialization" and/or social class (material) circumstances, however, is examined and viewed differently from different analytical stances. How and how much those cultural traits are preceded or followed (are cause or effect), or amplified or muted by racial and class factors is not simple, as Márquez demonstrates.

Another dimension of these uncertainties is whether the nature and level of the differences—cultural, class, or racial—are such that they are appropriately understood within the predominant pluralist or the hierarchical interpretation of American politics. Interestingly, research on Latino politics seems to be premised on the notion that there are not only differences—cultural and otherwise—but also some degree of hierarchy in the American political system. Latino politics is then studied, however, with pluralist assumptions and frameworks, although the basic findings of the research do not necessarily affirm pluralist claims. Indeed, as often as not, they contradict such claims. On the whole, however, one might understandably conclude from this section on "identity" that Latino politics is coherent, though not cohesive.

When the discussion turns to "Latino political action," in part 2, the role of culture, perhaps linked to "interests" and other forces, is considered regarding ethnic affinity, voting and vote choice (Barreto), the effect of cultural and historical experiences (which are often intertwined) of different national origin groups (DeSipio and Pantoja), and unique socially and economically induced behaviors that affect political mobilization (Ramírez). These all assume the importance and potential efficacy of political mobilization and engagement, again consistent with a pluralist outlook, although also identifying social and political conditions and context that may enhance or inhibit activity. These articles all demonstrate that social structure(s) matters and matters in unique ways in Latino politics.

Group cohesion and group willingness and ability to form coalition is also a major element of pluralist politics; the third section makes clear that issues relevant to coalitions arise within as well as across groups, that is, may be intragroup, intergroup, or both. Grasping the ostensible internal cohesion and sense of community of groups is one element of analysis typically addressed in interest group/pluralist studies; whether cohesion is based on or leads to "inward-" or "outward-looking," whether they have "bridging" or "bonding," orientations is another matter. The different bridging or bonding orientations of Latino groups is linked to political participation in Manzano's analysis, which draws on, one could say itself bridges to, the influential "social capital" thesis, of which Robert Putnam (2000) is the most visible proponent. A distinct, yet not entirely incompatible concept from social capital, "intersectionality," is offered and is shown to be important in understanding not only Latina/Latino relationships but broader aspects of minority politics and gender politics as well (Fraga and Navarro). The articulation and application of social capital and intersectionality introduce novel perspectives and/or amplify existing theories as they pertain to intragroup aspects of Latino politics. These general arguments illuminate Latino politics, and assessing Latino politics, in turn, modifies and refines the theoretical claims.

Intergroup relations, particularly concerning Latinos and African Americans and including potential coalitions based on public policy preferences, and governing coalitions and policy outcomes in education are thoughtfully engaged in the two essays by Gary Segura and Helena Alves Rodrigues and by René Rocha, respectively. These essays belie any notion of simple intergroup conflict or cooperation, demonstrating that "ideas" and "interests" intersect and possibly conflict but also complement each other; this is clearly evident in the crucible of governance described by Rocha, but its potential fluidity is also suggested by Segura and Alves Rodrigues. Equally important, these studies provide frameworks and, in turn, explain that relationships "depend on" the issues and/or other dimensions of politics and policy at issue and how they do so. The ongoing relationships of these two similar yet different groups (African Americans and Latinos) and their self-construction and social construction that result play major roles in defining the evolving racial/ethnic "order" in American politics.

The interplay of people and institutions—of officials, whether elected or appointed, exercising governmental authority through holding positions in formal governmental bodies—acting on behalf of the citizenry in the complex phenomena we refer to as "representation" rightly occupies a prominent place in the volume. Are most of the concerns of Latinos simply more intense than, or are they (also) qualitatively distinct from those of other elements in society? In either case, can those concerns be adequately subsumed under general indicators of responsiveness or representation? And where, in what formal institutions of governance, is and should representation be considered? The evidence offered in these studies suggest that while there are similarities that can be captured, within general policy indicators there are, indeed, distinct issues and aspects that require attention and that can be discerned only through appropriate, targeted analysis. These are manifested differently in different institutions—legislatures, as thoughtfully discussed by Rodolfo Espino and Jason Casellas, or in bureaucracies, as Eric Gonzales Juenke and Nick Theobald demonstrate—and may only become evident when particular methodological approaches or attention to specific actors and their behaviors are scrutinized.

The representational situation in political and governmental institutions is echoed in another set of institutions—Latino scholarship in political science, Latinos as college/university faculty and as graduate and undergrad students, and among the professional organizations/associations in political science (Martinez-Ebers and Avalos). Strikingly, though not altogether surprising, the conditions and outcomes of Latinos within these institutions seem to largely mirror that of Latinos in the broader political system—some signs of pluralism and inclusion, other evidence of relatively low status within a hierarchy and a minimal presence in certain institutions (such as the most "elite" universities).

Along with their numerous insights, these essays reaffirm in my mind that the study neither of "American politics" nor of "Latino politics" are by themselves sufficient, though both are necessary to understand contemporary circumstances in the United States. The essays in this collection underscore the complexity of Latino and of American politics—which are (to some substantial, albeit debatable degree) part and parcel of one another. However, to say these issues are "complex" says a great deal but also says very little, unless the nature and extent of that complexity is carefully described and analytical approaches and appropriate evidence are brought forth. Learning is advanced by understanding the complexity of ostensibly simple phenomena and, conversely, discerning some of the simplicity of complex phenomena. The essays in this volume have done this admirably; they also make clear that if Latino politics is not seriously considered, an analytical problem for an analytical solution in the broader scheme of American politics and the study thereof stands to be confused. While most valuable in its own right, students of American and Latino politics will also likely hope and wish that this volume represents a crucial building block that has summarized and advanced future research but that will also serve as a precursor and an essential guide for that research.

Latino Politics

Introduction

Latino Politics: The State of the Discipline

Rodolfo Espino and David L. Leal

IN THE NEW CENTURY, the public discussion of Latinos is pervasive. Whether the conversation is about politics, economics, or popular culture, Latinos are an essential part of the story. This discussion often has a positive tone, but sometimes it is more negative. For instance, there are many who talk about attracting Latinos as both voters and consumers. Politicians take Spanish classes, businesses seek to reach the "Hispanic market," and many see Latinos—both citizens and noncitizens—as a key component to a bright future for their political party or business. For others, however, the growing Latino population is more problematic. Some worry about the economic costs of Latino immigration, such as job competition and the educational and medical costs to local governments. Others seem to conflate all Latinos with immigrants in a way that suggests cultural concerns are the real issue.

Often lost in these discussions is a key question: Who are Latinos? Are they immigrants who cross borders in response to the beckoning "invisible hand" of Adam Smith if not always U.S. law—or are they long-standing residents who were living in present-day New Mexico before English colonists arrived in Jamestown? Do they burden local governments by raising the cost of schools and hospitals—or do they serve governments and the public as soldiers, teachers, police officers, and nurses? Latinos are the largest category of undocumented (or illegal) immigrants—but it is also true that the U.S. Border Patrol has the highest proportion of Hispanic employees of any federal government agency. What can we make of this diverse population, and how can social scientists help to understand the political beliefs and behaviors of Latinos in a systematic and scientific manner—and thereby go beyond the sensationalism and stereotyping that often passes for political debate and media coverage?

To familiarize students, scholars, and the general public with this complex population is beyond the ability of any single book. It will require a larger effort that involves political scientists as well as journalists, political activists from across the spectrum, and other observers. Already we see a growing literature in academic libraries and popular bookstores, but not long ago few such titles could be found on the shelves.

The editors and contributors in this volume are political scientists and will address a wide range of political and policy topics that involve the attitudes and actions of Latinos in the American political system. In general, this book is part of a growing interest in the study of Latinos in the discipline of political science.[1] This increased scholarly attention is not an accident, nor was it inevitable. It results, in large part, from the efforts of a handful of scholars who devoted their lives to the study of "Latino voices" (de la Garza, DeSipio, F. C. Garcia, J. Garcia, and Falcon 1992) and "Latinos and the political system" (F. C. Garcia 1988), and the result was the creation of a field dedicated to "Latino politics in America" (J. Garcia 2003). This literature illuminates a long-ignored population, provides a more complete understanding of other political science fields, highlights the exceptionalism of the American political system, and underscores the unique construction of race in America.

Our volume of scholarly work builds on this tradition and serves several purposes. First, it highlights the important contributions made by the study of Latino politics to date. Second, it suggests areas that have yet to be explored in this relatively young and burgeoning field. Finally, and, perhaps most important, this volume demonstrates that the study of Latino politics does not exist in a vacuum.

The overview of the field of Latino politics presented in the essays should be useful to those who study Latino politics and policy as well as those who do not, as it speaks to many of the fundamental debates engaging our discipline. While no project can capture all the scholarship on Latinos in politics, the research presented in this book is fairly representative of such work. We also hope this volume will be of interest to social scientists of all backgrounds, as no field of study can be complete without an understanding of Latinos.

The importance of the Latino politics field is directly related to the significant growth of the Latino population, both in absolute numbers and as a percentage of the American population. As the Latino population continues to grow and the share of the Anglo (non-Hispanic white) population continues to decline, scholars will find it increasingly important to include Latinos in any discussion of "American" politics.

The Latino population numbered 14.6 million in 1980 and subsequently grew to 22.4 million in 1990 and 35.3 million in 2000. These data likely undercount the Latino population, as many Latinos are undocumented and may avoid contact with government census officials. Given the high Latino birthrate in the United States and the significant level of migration from Latin America, such numbers are only likely to increase. By the year 2050, a quarter of the American population may be Latino; by the end of the century, one in every three Americans may be Latino.

Latinos are now the nation's largest minority group. The most recent data from the Bureau of the Census (July, 2005) indicate that Latinos constitute 14.4 percent of the population. Considering that the number of Latinos increased by 1.35 million individuals in just one year (from July of 2004 to July of 2005), the scale of the demographic shift occurring in America is evident.

Taken together, minorities now constitute one-third of the American population,[2] and whites have moved from majority to plurality status in four states (Texas, California, Hawaii, and New Mexico).[3] Even in such states, however, the Latino share of the electorate significantly lags behind the population percentage, as citizenship and demographic factors lower the number of eligible and likely voters. Nevertheless, as the non-white population of the United States continues to grow, it will call into question the utility and meaning of such concepts as "minority" and "majority." Indeed, the traditional black-white racial paradigm in the United States is already outdated and is transitioning into a more complex multiethnic perspective.

One fundamental question—which should be the starting point for all research in this area—is "Do Latinos Exist?" (Domínguez 1994). The familiar agent-structure debate in political science is certainly relevant to Latino politics. Understanding how Latino identities are both ascribed and asserted has been fundamental to the study of Latino politics. Scholars often debate the concept of "Latino," and some have asked if there is "no there there"—the statement by Gertrude Stein about the city of Oakland, but also appropriate to the issue of whether Latino politics is a field worth pursuing. For instance, while Mexican Americans and Cuban Americans are both "Hispanic," how much do they politically have in common, and what does this mean for the study of "Latino" politics? Even if "Latino" is identified on the map of political science, we may still ask whether such a locale serves as a useful guide to points elsewhere. The essays in this volume will address these questions.

The research in this volume will also highlight the exceptionalism of race and politics in America. A fundamental dilemma in American politics has been a racial dilemma—a dilemma grounded in the political experiences of European immigrants and America's African American population. Latinos therefore face a racial context that has been constructed for them by previous experiences, requiring them to negotiate the political system in two ways. First, many Latinos have the status of an immigrant group striving to assimilate yet struggling to maintain some of their culture and identity.[4] Second, Latinos are also members of a recognized minority group that has endured two centuries of discrimination. Just as African Americans have not been allowed to assimilate in the manner of Irish or Italian immigrants, so too Latinos may not become fully assimilated into the American mainstream. Will the Latino experience prove to resemble either of the above, or will it have elements of both? Several of the essays here therefore discuss the political relationships between Latinos and non-Latinos, particularly Anglos and African Americans.

Another unique factor in the Latino experience is the diversity of its population. This not only shapes political outcomes (e.g., Cuban Americans and the Republican Party) but it also influences many aspects of the Latino experience of interest to scholars. Just as Latinos in the American electorate must negotiate a political terrain in which they are not easily classified, so too are scholars of Latino politics required to piece together a variety of theoretical and methodological approaches to do justice to their complex topic. This will be evident in the essays to follow.

In addition, readers of this volume will notice that the study of Latino politics is grounded in the more general study of American politics. This is because "Latinos" do not exist in Latin America; the term only has meaning within the United States. One might expect that those who study Latino politics will analyze the political system that created the context for such a categorization. Such boundaries are not always clear, however. A number of essays in this volume will therefore discuss the interactions of Latinos in the United States with people and institutions in the sending nations of Latin America. This comparative dimension adds to the significance of studying Latinos because it not only expands the scope of American politics scholarship but it also more properly reflects the complex reality in which Latinos in the United States live. While this international aspect complicates the analysis of Latinos, it is necessary to understand the already-complex reality of Latino lives.

This is an exciting time to study Latino politics. For many years, there was little data on Latino political actions and opinions, but this deficit is now being remedied by a number of new surveys and data-collection efforts. A brief examination of the public opinion field illustrates this dynamic. (See the Leal essay for a fuller discussion.)

Although the behavioral revolution in political science began in the 1950s, the first national political survey of even a single Latino national-origin group was the

4

1979 Chicano Survey (Arce 1979). Another decade would pass before the first national sample of Latinos took place, the Latino National Political Survey (de la Garza et al. 1992). Aside from these efforts, very little social science survey data on Latinos were available well into the 1990s. The result was that as public opinion and political behavior research exploded in mainstream political science, it advanced much more slowly in the Latino politics field, and even this progress was only the result of the dedicated efforts of a relatively small number of scholars.

Today, the situation is rapidly changing. While not every survey includes Latino respondents, a growing number do, and many researchers are proactively engaged in survey research and other data-collection efforts that focus specifically on Latinos, both citizens and noncitizens. Latino politics scholars today have more data at their disposal than ever before, and the prospects for the future are bright. A new Latino National Survey completed in 2006 only adds to this.[5] It includes a nationally representative sample of Latinos and a number of large state-level samples — including states where Latinos have a growing but traditionally limited presence. This survey will give scholars a key source of useful data to test any number of theories for years to come.

This volume has five general parts. The fundamental dilemma of Latino politics — identity politics — is the theme of the first. Benjamin Márquez lays out ways in which the identity of Latinos is constructed and used by various political organizations over time. His work causes us to reevaluate the meaning and content of "Latino" activism, as he finds that Latino identities are elastic enough to expand to accommodate virtually any political agenda. Some Latino organizations endorse free market capitalism and accept the inequalities it generates. Conversely, other groups critique market-driven inequalities and believe discrimination plays a central role in maintaining or justifying economic hierarchies. Groups even disagree about whether ethnicity is a legitimate organizing principle. Some organizations recruit members and engage in political actions based on a sense of group attachment and mutual obligation, yet others argue that ethnic loyalties have no appropriate role in the public sphere and work to build multiethnic coalitions.

For the organizations Márquez studied, Latino political identities had little intrinsic meaning and only made sense when understood within the larger universe of their values and goals. While all activists express strong cultural commitments, they come to different conclusions about their political implications and the specific ways culture bound them to other Latinos.

The essay that follows by David Leal moves the focus from the aggregate to the individual. He asks the fundamental question of whether we can speak of a "Latino" public opinion, and therefore how panethnic identifiers can serve to both unify a population and obscure differences within it. Using national survey data, he finds more differences than similarities in the opinions of Latinos and Anglos, with Latinos tending to take more liberal policy and political positions. There are few systematic differences according to Latino national-origin group membership, however. Taken together, this suggests that categories like "Latino" and "Hispanic" have a certain base validity. Some divergent opinions do exist, however, so researchers should be cautious before making broad generalizations.

Michael Jones-Correa then discusses the three major approaches to the understanding of the Latino political experience—the "ethnic," "transnational," and "immigrant" perspectives—including their strengths and weaknesses. He points out the striking absence of communication among scholars who pursue research based on these perspectives. The dominant approach among Latino political scientists is to treat Latinos as participants in an "ethnic politics" in the United States, thereby focusing on Latinos as citizens and emphasizing voting and elections. It is a story of individuals choosing to come to the United States, their incorporation as Americans, and their gradual success.

As Jones-Correa points out, however, Latinos in 2000 constituted 12 percent of the population, 7 percent of the eligible voting-age population, and 5 percent of actual voters. Much of the research in the study of Latino politics looks at those who voted—but what about the political engagements of the many nonvoters? This has led some scholars to study transnational participation that spans borders and enables individuals to sustain multiple social memberships, identities, and loyalties. This approach emphasizes that aspect of the Latino experience that is still closely connected to other nations. Others argue that the Latino experience is best understood not through the immigrant lens but as a story of persistent, if not permanent, racial categorization, difference, and inequality. Jones-Correa therefore concludes that scholars need to better understand how these three dimensions of ethnic, transnational, and immigrant politics interact and influence one another—a challenge for scholars, but one that is necessary to understanding the Latino reality.

Together, the chapters by Márquez, Leal, and Jones-Correa complement each other by demonstrating the methodological and theoretical pluralism that is necessary in the study of Latino political identities, as well as how such study uncovers significant diversity. When one begins to investigate "Latinos" or "Mexican Americans," one quickly finds a number of factors that complicate the easy use of such labels. This field of study is therefore not for those who want simple categories, as complexity and diversity are likely to remain the hallmarks of Latino politics for the foreseeable future.

The next part analyzes the ways in which the identities of Latinos translate into political action. The essay by Matt Barreto examines how the characteristics of candidates, particularly Latino candidates, can affect the choices of Latino voters. His work speaks to the ways political elites can influence the dynamics and construction of racial boundaries. In particular, he studies how Latino voters react when a Latino candidate is on the ballot. While previous research suggests that shared ethnicity is not an important factor in voting, Barreto examines two public opinion surveys and finds that ethnic attachment is an important predictor of vote choice.

Ricardo Ramírez turns the analytical focus in the opposite direction. Instead of studying the characteristics of candidates, he studies how the characteristics of the Latino population shape the strategic choices of candidates and political parties. In an analysis of Latino voter behavior in the 2003 municipal election in Houston, Texas, he discusses how residential mobility plays a role in political mobilization campaigns. Voters who move more often are less likely to report being contacted by a candidate, political party, or political organization, even though they overcame the same voter registration hurdle as those who move less frequently. Thus, lower participation rates among persons who are residentially mobile are not only attributable to institutional barriers or political disinterest, but are also affected by campaigns that choose to ignore the less residentially stable segments of the electorate. This is a particular problem for Latinos, given their relatively low rates of homeownership, and it shows how low socioeconomic status negatively affects Latino political power in a number of ways.

In the final piece in this part, Louis DeSipio and Adrian Pantoja address issues of identity and political participation when they compare the transnational activities of Puerto Ricans with those of Mexicans, Salvadorans, and Dominicans. Puerto Rico's commonwealth status and history of revolving migration suggest that transnational political ties would be strongest among Puerto Ricans. Using a unique survey by the Tomás Rivera Policy Institute (TRPI), however, DeSipio and Pantoja found that such Puerto Ricans ties were not markedly different than those developed by others. Nonetheless, evidence of Puerto Rican exceptionalism is found when it comes to the reasons why different Latino immigrants/migrants engage in the politics of their home countries. This indicates the importance of not only comparing levels of political activity but also examining how such activity may be structured differently across Latino national-origin groups. In this case, it would be a mistake to assume that similar levels of activity indicate similar reasons for such participation. Their work also points out how scholars should be encouraged to blur the boundaries of American and comparative politics.

In this second part of the volume, we therefore see how ethnicity helps determine how political elites mobilize Latinos, how voters choose candidates, and why

Latinos engage in transnational activities. There are very different types of civic engagement, but Latino and national-origin group memberships structure them in ways with implications for Latino influence at home and abroad.

Moving beyond Latino identity politics is the theme of the third part, which discusses coalitional politics. Latinos do not participate in politics in isolation from other groups, so an important question is how Latinos politically interact with other racial and ethnic groups and the potential for future interactions. This question gains in significance as the Latino population continues to grow. The American political future will look very different depending on the level of Latino political engagement with others.

Sylvia Manzano brings some of the assumptions of research on social capital to bear on the study of Latino political behavior. Her essay examines how Latinos employ social capital as they participate in Latino and mainstream political activities, and it tests if social capital works differently for Latinos than it does for Anglos. It explores how the behavior of Latinos has the potential to strengthen their own communities from within as well as to develop bonds with surrounding communities — thus increasing the cumulative social capital and resources upon which Latinos can draw for political action. Her work not only helps to better understand Latino participation in the political system, but it also raises potential lines of inquiry for all scholars of social capital. Her findings show that social capital of the bridging variety has a stronger influence on Latino participatory behaviors than does bonding capital, and that Latinos and Anglos share some similarities in their social capital outcomes. Her work challenges scholars in the future to more extensively compare levels of social capital across racial groups and further consider the ways different groups may draw on different forms of social capital.

The work by Helena Rodrigues and Gary Segura develops a new theoretical framework with which to study interracial relations in American politics, specifically between Hispanic Americans and African Americans. Empirically, they find that Latinos perceive little in common with Anglos or African Americans, while African Americans perceive Latinos as sharing similar circumstances and experiences. Despite such conflicting assessments, policy agreement between Latinos and African Americans is generally high, and it is clearly higher than levels of agreement between either group and Anglos. This research has implications for the prospects of Latino and African American "rainbow" coalitions; while the evidence suggests that coalitions will not be automatic or easy, such efforts have a foundation in similar policy opinions (even if many individuals are unaware of this).

The essay by René Rocha examines black-brown relations with a quantitative analysis of policy outcomes in educational politics. In recent years, several studies have focused on the level of socioeconomic and political competition between the two groups in a variety of arenas. His essay examines African American and Latino competition within the policy domain of education. It therefore builds on public opinion studies of the potential for racial and ethnic coalitions by examining real-world dynamics at a very local level. Specifically, he tests whether the hiring of African American administrators and teachers limits opportunities for Latinos, and vice versa. He also examines whether African American and Latino gains on standardized tests occur simultaneously, or if gains by one group come at the expense of the other.

The results indicate that African American and Latino success are inversely related for administrative and teacher hirings, but gains in student performance tend to be complimentary. As with the Rodrigues and Segura essay, this has both positive and negative implications for coalition building. While the education of Latino and African American children is complementary, there may be a zero-sum game at a more elite political level for the limited number of school district jobs.

The essay by Luis Fraga and Sharon Navarro discusses how Latino politics intersect with gender politics. They demonstrate that the study of Latino politics is advanced when conceptions of identity are broadened to incorporate the intersectionality of the multiple identities lived daily by Hispanics. They not only discuss studies that reveal descriptive differences between Latino men and women, which encompass traditional factors like public opinion and political participation, but they also review literature that addresses prescriptive possibilities. The latter focuses on Latina feminist writings and emerging models of Latina legislative representation. Unlike the first category, these literatures explicitly develop new ways of conceptualizing the interests of Latino communities and develop related strategies of policy advocacy built on Latina intersectionality. For instance, they ask if Latinas, who hold office in legislative bodies in growing numbers, may be able to use their membership in both Latino and women's caucuses to build coalitions and thereby more effectively advocate for legislation that benefit both groups. Fraga and Navarro find such questions to be the most intellectually rich in the study of Latina/o politics, as well as the most likely to affect the future of Hispanic politics.

Taken together, the work in this part moves beyond a specific focus on Latinos themselves and explores the ways in which Latino politics can intersect with other groups and disciplines. Whether this is the unfulfilled potential or the reality of Latino and African American coalitions, and whether gender dynamics lead to closer coalitions between Latino and Anglo legislators, we see that a full understanding of Latino politics must consider Latino interactions with others.

The essays in the fourth part examine the political representation of Latinos. Representation, in particular the representation of minority groups, remains a criti-

cal factor in the assessment of any democratic system. The essays in this part therefore study the concept in a variety of institutional settings, ask whether descriptive
representation matters, and examine the determinants of descriptive and substantive representation.

In his essay, Rodolfo Espino examines representation in the U.S. Congress,
specifically asking whether spatial modeling can determine if there is a "Latino"
dimension to voting in addition to the traditional single liberal-conservative dimension. It is possible, he writes, that Latino interests are best found within the
former than the latter. If not, then perhaps the most direct way to maximize Latino
representation is for Latinos to simply vote for the most liberal candidates, regardless of race or ethnicity. Espino uses new advancements in the estimation of spatial
voting models to uncover a Latino dimension to voting in Congress. This suggests
that Latino representation is more than a left-right issue and that the descriptive
representatives in Congress, who likely best understand Latino policy needs, can
produce important substantive outcomes.

Jason Casellas examines the substantive representation of Latinos in the U.S.
House of Representatives, specifically whether Latino legislators vote differently
than their non-Latino counterparts. Through the use of Poole-Rosenthal ideology
scores, this essay asks whether having Latinos in high places makes a difference in
terms of ideology scores. For the 87th through the 104th Congresses, the results
are different than previous research; Latino representatives have more liberal voting records (a negative, significant effect on the Poole-Rosenthal score) than do
other representatives while controlling for other factors. When the Latino population percentage of the district is taken into account, there is no effect on the
representative-ideology relationship. This suggests that electing Latinos to office
is more important than increasing the Latino population percentage in a constituency—thereby indicating the utility of majority-minority redistricting.

Eric Gonzalez Juenke examines representation in local educational systems, an
arena directly involved in the critical task of creating needed opportunities for Latinos. Instead of asking about voting patterns, he asks about the process by which
Latinos become legislators and bureaucrats. The first possibility is that minority
legislators delegate top-level bureaucratic responsibilities to minority agents, who
in turn appoint more minorities to lower-level positions (a top-down process). The
alternative is that minorities enter the bureaucracy at the lower levels and move
their way up the organization through time, finally gaining access to legislative positions as they acquire organizational influence (a bottom-up process). By examining Latino school board, administrative, and teacher representation in one thousand school districts in Texas across a seven-year period, he finds both processes at

work. As with the Casellas essay, his research suggests a substantive dimension to Latino descriptive representation.

Nick Theobald looks at allocation responsiveness and its association with Latino bureaucrats and the Latino population. He notes that past research on this topic—the relationship between Latino school board representation and bilingual education funding—produced mixed results. By including in his models a neglected key actor, district superintendents, he finds that Latino representation both on school boards and as superintendents leads to more resources for language-minority children. Once again, we see the important substantive benefits of descriptive representation for Latinos, both in terms of elected and appointed office.

The above four essays provide an assessment of the representation of Latino interests, which has been a central dilemma in American politics as the political system has struggled with conflicts over the equal representation of all voices. Collectively, they suggest that Latino descriptive representation has important substantive implications, whether in national or local legislative bodies, and for both elected and appointed officials.

The fifth section in the book contains two essays with implications for the future of Latino politics. The first, by Valerie Martinez-Ebers and Manuel Avalos, examines the presence and influence of Latino scholars and Latino politics scholarship in the political science discipline. Their findings contain both good news and bad news. The bad news is that Latino faculty members and graduate students continue to be severely underrepresented in the discipline. Not only are there problems with the "pipeline" issues of recruiting and retaining graduate students and junior faculty members, but gender disparities have also remained constant over the last three decades. Conversely, the authors are optimistic about the future because "the Latino *community* is stronger in the profession than ever before." The number of scholars in the field is growing, as is the representation of Latinos in leadership roles in professional associations such as the American Political Science Association (APSA) and the Western Political Science Association (WPSA). Martinez-Ebers and Avalos also discuss individual and institutional strategies to strengthen the presence of Latino politics in the political science discipline.

The volume concludes with an essay by Kenneth J. Meier about how to best advance the Latino politics research agenda. He notes that while the field of Latino politics is growing by leaps and bounds, research resources are limited. He argues that scholars should therefore target particular theoretically important questions in order to maximize the research return on investment. In addition, this should be done in a way that not only illuminates Latino politics in particular but American politics more generally. Meier suggests that scholars become missionaries to the political science field by showing, not just claiming, that the study of Latinos can provide important leverage on central questions in political behavior, institutions, and public policy. He uses the example of political representation to show how the study of Latino politics would be useful for specialists in the former who have little current knowledge of the latter: "Scholars can track the evolution of the representation linkages from institutions with no representation to those that have well-established representatives with substantial clout. Latinos provide significantly more variation, and with ongoing immigration will continue to do so, on variables likely to affect the linkages between elites and masses."

Overall, the work compiled in this volume will be of interest to veteran observers of this "road less traveled" as well as to those just starting the journey. As the former understand, and the latter are beginning to glimpse, it is increasingly difficult to understand any arena of American politics (or culture, or economy) without studying the role of the growing Latino population. While this has been said in the past more wishfully than factually, the signs are everywhere today that Latinos are irrevocably bringing "the Americas" into "America."

Yet Latinos have been involved in politics for some time, and if they have been "ignored voices" (de la Garza 1987), the scholarly world was often complicit in this state of affairs. Creating knowledge about Latino politics is therefore a two-part process. First, researchers outside the field will need to commit themselves to exploring how Latinos affect their specialty—whether it is public opinion, political institutions, public policy, or political behavior. It will simultaneously be necessary, however, for those in the field to make the case for the relevance of Latino politics to the wider discipline. The literature is full of questionable references to Latinos as the "sleeping giant" of American politics; we hope our volume will help awaken students, professors, and other political observers to the varied and dynamic research taking place in this field and to the scholars who are writing it.

Notes

1. We will use the terms Latino and Hispanic interchangeably, which is a convention established by the National Council on La Raza, an organization founded in 1968 devoted to improving the life opportunities for Hispanic Americans, and a standard most recently adopted by the Office of Management and Budget on January 1, 2003. We use the terms to collectively refer to individuals in the United States of Mexican, Puerto Rican, Cuban, or other Hispanic backgrounds. In addition, we use the term "Latino" to refer to both Latinas and Latinos. We will use the particular gender specific terms, as appropriate, when making any distinctions on the basis of gender.

2. U.S. Census Bureau. "Nation's Population One-Third Minority." Accessed December 31, 2006 at http://www.census.gov/Press-Release/www/releases/archives/population/006808.html000.

3. U.S. Census Bureau. "Texas Becomes Nation's Newest "Majority-Minority" State, Census Bureau Announces." Accessed December 31, 2006 at http://www.census.gov/Press-Release/www/releases/archives/population/005514.html.

4. Except those who became Americans because of the Mexican-American War.

5. See LNS website: http://depts.washington.edu/uwiser/LNS.shtml.

PART 1

Latino Identity Politics

Latino Identity Politics Research

Problems and Opportunities

Benjamin Márquez

SOCIAL IDENTITY IS our understanding, who we are, who other people are, and, reciprocally, other peoples' understanding of themselves and of others. Political identities distinguish individuals and groups in their social relations with other individuals and groups. They establish similarity and difference in social relations by providing frames of reference through which political actors can initiate and maintain relationships with other groups and individuals (Jenkins 1996; Cronin 1999; Cornell and Hartmann 1998). Because identities influence political behavior and help determine the distribution of power and resources, identities are particularly important in societies like the United States. Asserted ethnic identities are responses to discrimination and exclusion, but they are also political constructions, the result of a process where practical interests, political beliefs, and moral values are brought into the political sphere. They are political projects that emerge from distinct visions of community life and politics. When Latinos create political organizations, they articulate visions of life in the United States that arrange ethnic symbols and reinterpret group history for a specific political purpose.

The content of ethnic identities is an important indicator of discontent and group solidarity. Although a substantial literature has emerged on the role Latino ethnic identity has played in community mobilization and individual behavior, much work remains in unpacking the values and goals underlying identity-based politics. Many questions about political identities remain unanswered. What constitutes a Latino political identity? How does it differ from other political identities? How are ethnic political identities created? Why do they take the form they do? In what ways are they distinct from other aspects of an individual's political identity? How do they change over time? Finally, how and under what conditions do ethnic identities influence political behavior?

To make progress answering these questions, greater attention must be paid to the political goals and values underlying Latino identities. The ideological quality of identity politics greatly complicates our work as social scientists, but the concept of identity goes to the heart of our research. However, it is essential that we understand the political content of Latino identities as well as the conditions under which they emerge. With this goal in mind, I will review some recent developments in Latino identity politics research and suggest ways that identity research can be strengthened to bring greater clarity to the Latino experience in the United States. I will discuss how new debates over the role of identity in social movement organizations speak to how ethnicity informs, interacts with, or operates independently of more conventional variables like class, political ideology, and immigrant status. I will argue for a closer examination of Latino ethnicity and suggest ways that political scientists who study Latino politics can build bridges across subfields and disciplinary boundaries.

Assimilation and Identity Formation

What makes ethnic identities important is their power to influence behavior and attitudes in ways that would not be predicted by an individual's socioeconomic status. Historical memory, a sense of shared fate, and cultural similarities can strengthen a sense of loyalty that binds disparate members of a group to one another. Ethnicity powerfully determines cooperation and solidarity, because it is regarded as biological in origin, is reflected in social stratification, and is frequently institutionalized in religion, language, nationality, residential location, and government policy (Light and Gold 2000).

Identities can be powerful political forces, but they are constantly evolving. A large body of sociological literature predicts the demise of strongly held ethnic identities as discriminatory barriers are broken down and individuals gradually occupy positions in the institutions of the larger society (Dahl 1964; Gordon 1964; Lieberson and Waters 1990). Indeed, there is reason to believe that the process of assimilation is well under way for Latinos, albeit in an uneven manner. The gains of the civil rights movement era created new possibilities for increased assimilation by outlawing most forms of discrimination and moving the dynamics of American politics toward greater inclusion. Subsequent economic mobility allowed Latino politics to encompass new organizations and political expressions that often extend beyond issues of race or cultural distinctions. By breaking a rigid system of racial hegemony based on outright segregation or coercion, Latinos were no longer thrown together along a single axis of racial domination and subordination (Winant 1995). Occupational and income trends reveal that successive generations of Latinos are participating in an increasingly broad spectrum of American life (Melendez, Rodriguez, and Figueroa 1991; Gonzalez 2002).

The difficulty with most models of social assimilation stem from their basis in the experiences of white ethnic immigrants. When applied to Latinos, these models tend to diminish the effect of race or continuing immigration and assume an inevitable movement toward cultural assimilation (Steinberg 2001; Massey, Durand, and Malone 2002). Latinos constitute such a complex array of subnationalities, subcultures, and economic classes that identity formation is likely to take a fractured and less-predictable course than it did for white ethnics. Alejandro Portes and Ruben Rumbaut (2001) found that the process of assimilation and identity formation among the children of Latino immigrants is a murky, less-certain process, one profoundly influenced by differential levels of discrimination, government policy, educational achievement, and family composition. Depending on the circumstances surrounding the arrival of each Latino immigrant group, assimilation can move ahead at a steady clip, or these groups could find themselves marginalized in American society. Ironically, Latinos who have successfully incorporated into American society did so by strengthening their ethnic and familial ties. Although the pressure toward socioeconomic incorporation still serves as a useful master trend when theorizing about Latino identity, the contingencies of a changing social and economic context cautions against pat claims about the direction those identities are likely to take (Alba and Nee 2003).

I argue that the literature on political organizing offers a useful insight into the process of identity formation and its political content. Identities in organizations give existing members ideological reasons for contributing their time and resources to a cause. Identities also serve as an incentive for others to join like-minded individuals in collective action. What the extant literature suggests is that no single ideological thread runs through Latino organizing efforts. Rather, Latino activists have built ethnic identities that span the ideological spectrum and redefine ethnic boundaries to suit their values. For example, the working-class character of the Mexican-American and Puerto Rican populations can spawn labor unions and blue-collar associations designed to defend worker rights. But Latino business owners also have a long history of constructing identities that define ethnic interests and group loyalty in ways congruent with their interests as property owners (Torres 1990; Zweigenhaft and Domhoff 1998). More recently, Latino organizations representing women, immigrants, and professionals have formed, each with its own interpretation of ethnicity and political interests.

Are Latino political identities therefore little more than an expression of individual material and occupational interests, or do they converge in any meaningful way? It is here that the theoretical and research challenges lie. The literature on Latino political organizing is heavily skewed toward the leftist politics of college students, radical community groups like the Crusade for Justice, the Young Lords, and the land grant movement in northern New Mexico (Barrera 1979; Muñoz 1989; I. Garcia 1989; Melendez 2003). Many of the first studies of Latino politics reflected a keen interest in the militancy of the Chicano and Puerto Rican independence movements. Some were written by individuals who were either active participants or sympathetic to the ideals of the movements' demands for ethnic nationalism and autonomy. Part of their scholarly mission was to expose social injustices, challenge stereotypes, and document the persistence of Latino cultural distinctiveness (Colon 1961; McWilliams 1949; Acuña 1972). Contemporary scholarship continues to call attention to the effect radical Latino activists have had through unconventional politics and the ways they gained concessions or precipitated repressive actions (Haney-Lopez 2003; Melendez 2003). This body of research has brought greater clarity to the relationship between Latino identity and political mobilization (Muñoz 1989; Escobar 1999). Interest in radical identities and mobilization remains high as scholars continue to explore the role of cultural nationalism as a challenging identity to American society (Haney-Lopez 2003; Vigil 1999; Torres and Velazquez 1998).

Although few political scientists have tried to unpack the constituent parts of Latino identity, sociologists and historians have uncovered a greater diversity in political values and goals than work on Latino radicalism would suggest. Latino labor organizers often took the lead in community organizing by emphasizing the need for ethnoracial solidarity to improve working conditions, benefits, and wages (M. Garcia 1989; Zamora 1993; Gomez-Quiñones 1994; Pitti 2003). Even within the labor movement there were significant differences in identity-based organizing. Some advocated the need to promote female leadership as well as multiethnic and race-based coalitions (Ruiz 1987). The United Farm Workers Union was built, in part, by creating alliances with Anglo labor unions, community organizations, churches, and the Democratic Party (Jenkins 1985; Mooney and Majka 1995). Latino professionals and business owners, arguably the best-financed and organized of all Latino political activists, have attracted little scholarly attention (Márquez 2003a). There is ample historical evidence of conservative Latino social movement organizations whose activists argued racial equality could only be realized by rewarding individual merit within the framework of free market capitalism. Indeed, equality could be achieved once racism was eliminated so that individual Latinos could find their rightful place in the social hierarchy (Márquez 1993; M. Garcia 1989; Bonilla-Santiago 1988).

Connecting asserted identities to their effect on the political process is another aspect of Latino politics that deserves closer scrutiny. Identity politics played an important role for African Americans during the civil rights movement. The movement of millions of African Americans out of the rural south and the ideological struggle between the United States and the Soviet Union after World War II set the stage for African Americans to press their political demands (Piven and Cloward 1977; Bloom 1987). Changing economic circumstances and state action can generate conditions under which some identities are more likely to foster alliances or facilitate access to political authorities. The principle of equal treatment before the law helped build broad-based support for formal equal rights, but calls for a redistribution of wealth and power floundered (Hamilton and Hamilton 1997; Wilson 1996).

The challenge is to understand how Latino identity politics operate in the current matrix of race, power, and ideology. Are Latinos racially stigmatized to the extent that common themes will emerge as they form new political identities? Or are they forming identities similar to those of white ethic immigrants that stand outside of the black/white racial binary (Ignatiev 1995; Marx 1998; Roediger 1999)? Considerable work needs to be done before these questions can be answered. However, researchers should note that the creative possibilities in the construction of a Latino political identity are remarkable. Activists have defined Latino identity and political interests in such radically different ways that researchers need to carefully examine their working assumptions about Latino boundaries and group ties.

I have conducted field research on Latino political organizations, some of which advocate free market capitalism while others promote racial separatism, liberal feminism, or religiously based identities, often within the same community. They come to different conclusions about the degree of racism practiced against Latinos and the appropriate remedies for racial discrimination. They differ in their understanding of the causes and justification for economic stratification. Finally, cultural practices—a central component of ethnic identity—vary in their importance to Latino activists. Some believe it is a necessary medium for the communication of issues common to the group and mutual recognition. Others scrupulously avoid cultural or racial appeals in their campaigns and assert that Latino interests are best served in nonracially based coalitions (Márquez 2003a).

Disentangling the meaning of these divergent trends will not be easy. Latinos are more likely than whites to perceive high levels of discrimination, although that belief may bind Latinos together only under special circumstances. For example,

English-only campaigns, cases of police brutality, or a bid by a Latino to capture a high-profile public office can generate a show of racial solidarity, but one likely to be a short-lived response to a threat or political opportunity. Given the divergent ways Latino organizations interpret and hope to eradicate racism, community responses during high-profile racial conflicts resemble coalitions more than an expression of a Latino identity. A political identity, in the full sense of the term, is a world view intertwined with beliefs about the causes and intensity of racial discrimination, the fairness of economic hierarchies, and judgments about the politicization of Latino culture.

Some Latino organizations sustain their membership based on an identity that recalls the separatist and nationalist goals of the 1960s. They call for ethnocultural solidarity while exhibiting a deep distrust of Anglo-dominated institutions (Moore and Head 1994; Márquez 1998). These groups exist side by side, however, with Latino chambers of commerce that enhance the profit-making capabilities of their members by fostering close personal relationships with elected officials, financial officers, and other entrepreneurs (Torres 1990; Márquez 2003b). Some of the most active Latino political organizations reject the notion of race-based organizing altogether and work to build alliances across racial and ethnic lines (Wilson 1999; Shirley 1997; Warren 2001). Finally, Latinos have created professional associations, women's groups, business groups, and civil rights organizations (Hardy-Fanta 1993; Pulido 1996; Honig 1996; Pardo 1997, 1998).

A final challenge for Latino research is judging the relative appeal and political power of constructed Latino identities. There is an urgent need for survey research that probes the complexity of Latino identity politics and clarifies the degree to which Latinos are receptive to a given identity construction. As I have argued, nationality does not predispose individuals to embrace a given world view but operates in complex, counterintuitive ways. Qualitative researchers should be mindful of the ways political developments can influence the emergence and visibility of social movement organizations. Radical, disruptive organizations can receive wide coverage by the media, thereby giving them more popular recognition than their resources and organizational base warrants. Conversely, challenging identities with significant community support can fail to manifest themselves because of police repression or lack of resources.

Another problem in the study of Latino politics is the advantage conservative organizations have in advancing their agenda. When building social movement organizations, moderation is rewarded with political access, legitimacy, and financial support. Consequently, the groups best able to project their ideas onto the public sphere are not necessarily those with significant community support but those whose principal activists have been most successful at securing foundation and corporate support (Márquez 2003b).

Emerging Latino Identities?

A common critique of the constructivist approach to identity politics is that ethnic identities have material and cultural foundations that exert a powerful influence on the individual's attitudes and behavior. In other words, they have a shared socioeconomic background cemented by a common language and culture generates emotionally driven loyalties that cut across divisions like class, occupation, and ideology. If this assertion is true, group appeals like Latino ethnicity still have the potential to override self-interested incentives associated with class, income, or occupation. Studies of Asian and Native American identity politics suggest that political activists can create viable social movements based on a perceived common fate that cuts across cultural and national boundaries. Activists hoping to build shared identities encounter tremendous difficulties negotiating new identities among tribes and subnationalities, but common cultural attributes and histories offered real possibilities for political action (Nagel 1996; Espiritu 1992). Researchers have expressed a similar interest in the question of a pan-Latino identity, but the results have been less promising. Comparative research on Latino subgroups reveals considerable similarities in experiences and outlooks, but enough differences exist among those groups to call into question the strength of a pan-Latino identity (Portes and Bach 1985; de la Garza et al. 1992).

Of those who have researched the question of pan-Latino identity formation, John Garcia (1997, 2003) is the most optimistic. He asserts that a growing Latino population, combined with its common language, political interest, and similar culture, bodes well for the formation of a common political identity. Garcia believes political activists can help forge these shared characteristics into a working imagined community to deal more effectively with the problems most Latinos have in common. There is a compelling logic to Garcia's contention, but the evidence for a powerful pan-Latino identity is limited (Jones-Correa and Leal 1996). Latino subgroups have cooperated to achieve political goals, but those alliances exhibit little lasting power (De Leon 1989; Padilla 1985a). The Latino National Political Survey (LNPS) found that Latino subnational groups may share similar socioeconomic profiles, but they have little knowledge of one another and retain significant cultural differences (de la Garza et al. 1992). As Nicholas DeGenova and Ana Ramos-Zaya (2003) found, Mexicans and Puerto Ricans in Chicago construct such radically different ethnic identities that they conflict more than they cooperate in their day-to-day lives.

Even ties within individual Latino subgroups have proven difficult to maintain. The possibility that ethnic ties can bond individuals across national boundaries has sparked several investigations into the persistent strength of ethnicity through transnational ties. Ease of travel, low-cost communication technology, proximity to the homeland, and outreach to immigrant communities by Latin American politicians reinforce group ties in ways that pan-Latino proponents cannot. Transnational identities can profoundly influence an immigrant's attitude toward life and politics in the United States by orienting them to homeland politics and kindling a desire to return (Jones-Correa 1998; Vila 2000; Levitt 2001). Research on transnationalism is intriguing, but other studies reveal that attention to or participation in homeland politics is low and that immigrant organizations are actually more focused on the integration of their members into American society (de la Garza and Hazan 2003; DeSipio et al. 2003).

Other researchers have suggested that the homeland experiences of South and Central American groups can actually inhibit transnational ties and community formation as individuals struggle to overcome the violence and devastation surrounding their immigration to the United States. The trauma of leaving a war-torn country can inhibit institution-building capacity, raise distrust among coethnics, and otherwise act as a demobilizing force. Cecilia Menjivar (2000) found that the trauma of their experiences in their homeland fractures the Salvadoran population in the United States and hobbles the formation of community within their own group. Other studies of Salvadoran and Guatemalan immigrants document the difficulty some Latinos face in building community among people still contending with the legacy of war and violence in their home countries (Mahler 1995; Hamilton and Chinchilla 2001).

The wide-ranging historical experiences of Latinos set them on different social trajectories. For example, the Communist regime in Cuba continues to have an enormous effect on Cuban-American politics (Torres 1999). The continuing importance of exile politics and Cuban-American antipathy toward the Castro regime combined with a higher socioeconomic status distinguishes them from poorer, more liberal Mexican Americans and Puerto Ricans (Torres 1999; Perez-Firmat 2000). By the same token, the political status of Puerto Rico is of enormous importance to Puerto Ricans but of little relevance to Mexican Americans, for whom immigration and citizenship issues loom large (Serrano 1999; Duany 2002). In the end, Latinos may share some general historical and cultural characteristics, but their identities are profoundly affected by the reception each group receives from society at large, government policies, and the group's educational attainment (Portes and Rumbaut 2001).

Conclusion

The study of political identities presents the researcher with some significant challenges and opportunities. In my work on social movement organizations, I argue that Latino identities are elastic enough to expand to accommodate virtually any political agenda. My research uncovered a dynamic in Latino politics that defies traditional understandings of identity and group ties. A sense of ethnic loyalty and bonds, the defining feature of identity, are easily incorporated within a broad spectrum of ideological orientations. Business groups express ethnic attachments and loyalty to other Latinos by increasing entrepreneurial opportunities and training a new generation of business owners. Some community organizations recruit members and engage in political actions based on a primordial sense of group attachment and mutual obligation. Other Latino activists argue that ethnic loyalties have no appropriate role in the public sphere and work to build multiethnic coalitions. For the organizations I have studied, Latino political identities had little intrinsic meaning and only make sense when understood with the larger universe of their values and goals.

The practical demands of research and professional survival make it difficult for individual scholars to incorporate all the conceptual and empirical demands that identity politics research requires. Still, there is clearly a need for more research that disentangles the constituent elements of Latino identity. Mobilization along the lines of race and ethnicity builds on some powerful cleavages in our society, and clarifying the relationship between identity and politics is central to our mission as social scientists. There is a need to ask more probing questions about Latino identity and its relationship to Latino political attitudes and actions. Additional historical and ethnographic field work on Latino identity can produce rich insight into the elements of identity, but it needs to be supplemented with survey data. For example, it is important to understand the way Latinos assess the character of racism in the United States. I have studied organizations whose activists were convinced that the divide between themselves and the white majority was deep, almost insurmountable. Conversely, I have encountered groups whose members were angry about the barriers erected by the white majority but were convinced they would eventually be overcome through institutional means or economic incorporation.

It bears repeating that an understanding of Latino perceptions of social stratification and the means they propose to deal with it are central elements of Latino ethnic identity. I have studied groups that endorse free market capitalism and accept the inequalities it generates as long as racism did not determine the final outcome. Conversely, some Latino organizations critique market-driven inequalities and believe discrimination plays a central role in maintaining or justifying economic hierarchies. The cause of social inequalities and what, if anything, should be done about them calls for closer scrutiny. As noted earlier, liberals tend to favor equal opportunity and civil rights enforcement as the remedy for social inequality. Radicals tend to favor disruptive politics, but often engage in traditional lobbying tactics as the only viable outlets for political activism. Latinos are part of both traditions.

Finally, the potential for Latino cultural distinctiveness to inform attitudes and behaviors needs careful reexamination. All the organizations I have ever studied were run by individuals who expressed a deep attachment to their cultural heritage. However, I found significant disagreement over the role they believe culture should play in the political realm. Some activists assume that one's ethnocultural background encompasses a wide spectrum of an individual's sentiments and defines their political interests. Others take a less expansive approach but believe it is an important medium that can facilitate cooperation between individuals with different political views. Still other Latino organizers express a deep pride in their cultural heritage but do not believe it has an appropriate role in the public sphere. In each case, activists expressed strong cultural commitments but came to different conclusions about their political implications and the specific ways culture bound them to other Latinos. The political arena has changed dramatically over the past two decades, and today's Latino political organizations can and are driven by values and goals they share with other racial and ethnic groups. Ethnic identities are still central to Latino political organizing. Our task as social scientists is to explain how and under what conditions.

Latino Public Opinion

Does It Exist?

David L. Leal

W HILE INCREASING ATTENTION has been paid in the policy, political, and scholarly worlds to Latino public opinion, there is relatively little understanding of whether Latino attitudes are fundamentally different from those of Anglos (non-Hispanic whites). This essay investigates whether Latino political attitudes are distinctive by examining a national data set of Latino and Anglo opinions. In addition, the distinctiveness of Latino nation-origin group opinions will also be tested, which will help in understanding to what degree we can speak of an aggregate "Latino" opinion.

A number of scholars have emphasized the importance of studying Latino opinion in a comparative manner. As Bruce Cain and D. Roderick Kiewiet (1987, 47) noted, "it has been hard to tell from exclusively Latino surveys how unique or similar Latino attitudes and political behaviors are to those of other racial and ethnic groups in the electorate." F. Chris Garcia (1987, 116) similarly commented that,

> Comparative methodology should be the preferred approach to this kind of research. Simply surveying one population without reference to another group in comparable circumstances may leave as many questions unanswered as it answers. Research comparing a Hispanic group with the majority culture, with other distinctive ethnic cultures, and with other Hispanic groups which vary in terms of national origin, geographic location, or socioeconomic cir-

cumstances must be conducted if we are to understand more fully the orientations of Hispanics.

Among the small number of scholars who have tested for distinctiveness in Latino public opinion are Rodolfo de la Garza and Janet Weaver (1985), who examined the spending priorities of Anglos and Mexican Americans in San Antonio. They found differences for only a relatively small number of issues. De la Garza (1985) studied Anglo-Mexican American opinion on a wide range of issues, finding evidence of some but not extensive Mexican American uniqueness, and he concluded that Mexican Americans were not a distinct electorate. Nicholas Lovrich (1974) explored differential Anglo, African American, and Mexican American attitudes toward service provision by local government in Denver, Colorado, finding that Anglos were the most satisfied.

Cain and Kiewiet (1987) used a 1984 California poll to compare the attitudes of Anglos, Latinos, African Americans, and Asian Americans on bilingual education, bilingual ballots, amnesty for illegal immigrants, employer sanctions, partisanship, and voting for Ronald Reagan in 1984. They found that Latinos were the most likely to favor bilingualism and amnesty, they were closer to African Americans than Anglos in terms of partisan identification, and just over a third claimed to have voted for Reagan.

The most prominent aggregate effort is found in *Latino Voices* (de la Garza, DeSipio, F. Garcia, J. Garcia, and Falcon 1992). They concluded that, "On many key domestic issues, significant majorities of each [Latino] group take the liberal position. On other issues, there is no consensus and, depending on the issue, Mexicans may be on the right, while Cubans and many Puerto Ricans are on the left of the nation's current political spectrum. Thus, labels such as liberal or conservative do not adequately describe the complexity of any one group's political views" (15).

As the above quotation indicates, it is important to test whether Latino opinions vary according to national-origin group status. While relatively few scholars have investigated overall Latino opinion, even less work has studied whether the opinions of Latino national-origin groups are distinctive. While *Latino Voices* provided evidence that respondents from these subgroups sometimes express varying opinions, we do not know whether such differences are still present after the passing of a decade.

Latinos and Public Opinion

The political science understanding of Latino public opinion is much less developed than that of Anglo public opinion. One key reason is the historic lack of interest in Latino opinion and the concomitant desultory efforts to include Latino respondents in major polls. This was particularly true in the early decades of postwar public opinion polling, but this situation continued into the 1970s and 1980s and still exists today. The most prominent polling project in political science, the American National Election Study (ANES), does not contain a large and nationally representative sample of Latino respondents and could therefore be renamed the Anglo National Election Study.

It was not until 1979 that an attempt was made to collect national-level survey data on political attitudes for even a single Latino national-origin group. The Chicano Survey (Arce 1979) included 991 Mexican American respondents, of whom 667 were U.S. citizens. The survey focused on respondents' demographic characteristics, employment history, health issues, and social identity, with only a smaller cluster of questions examining political opinions, attitudes, and participation. The sample, representative of an estimated 90 percent of the Mexican American population living in the United States at the time, was drawn from five states (California, Texas, New Mexico, Colorado, and Arizona) and the city of Chicago.

It was not until 1989 that political scientists would survey a national sample of Latinos. This project, the Latino National Political Survey (LNPS), included respondents from the three most prominent national-origin groups: Mexican Americans, Puerto Ricans, and Cuban Americans. It gathered information on a wide range of political activities, preferences, and behaviors among Hispanics in the United States. Unlike the 1979 Chicano Survey, the focus of the LNPS was expressly political. The survey population, randomly selected from forty Standard Metropolitan Statistical Areas (SMSAs) across the United States, was representative of 91 percent of the nation's Latinos (de la Garza et al. 1992, 7).

These efforts notwithstanding, by the end of the 1980s (the so-called "Decade of the Hispanic"),[1] only scattered data on Latino opinion existed. This largely consisted of uneven exit polls conducted by news organizations and occasional state and local surveys conducted by academics.[2] This situation caused de la Garza (1987, 1) to lament:

> For whom did Latinos vote in the 1984 elections? What were their views on
> the issues and candidates in that election? Surprisingly, reliable answers to
> these and related questions are unavailable. No independent source — not the

national press, not the nation's leading public opinion pollsters, no one — systematically asked Latinos their views or monitored their participation in the 1984 election.

Why is such inattention by the field of public opinion consequential? As de la Garza (1987, 4) further argued, "Polls can and do influence candidate selection and issue resolution. By not having their views regularly reported in polls, Latinos are effectively excluded from influencing both of these outcomes. In a fundamental sense, because of the role that polls play in our political life, being excluded from them is tantamount to partial disenfranchisement."

Political scientists today have more polls at their disposal, but the situation is far from ideal. Foundations and media organizations are more involved in devising quality surveys, although not always with input from the scholarly community. Many of these polls are therefore not devised with key political science questions in mind, and scholars are therefore limited in the types of questions they can investigate.

This lack of commitment by the political science discipline to Latino opinion is sometimes justified by the cost and technical difficulty of surveying Latinos. This argument points to the need for Spanish-speaking interviewers, the variety of Latino national-origin groups, the difficulties encountered in reaching Latino respondents, the citizenship issue, the need to represent respondents according to generational status, as well as a number of purported challenges best described as cultural (See I. A. Lewis 1987).

This essay does not deny that some complexities exist, but there is more to the story than affordability. When political scientists decided that the study of Senate elections was unduly neglected, the ANES responded with the 1988–1990–1992 Senate Study, which was not a costless undertaking in terms of time and (taxpayer) dollars. Why was the Senate chosen for special consideration and not Latino opinion? In many ways, this is a political issue. As Benjamin Page (1987, 45) suggested, "If you want oversampling, organize!" This implies that a professed interest in Latino politics from political scientists and political science institutions may not be enough. Just as in the real world of politics, Latinos must continue the struggle to reach positions of power to ensure that the needs of their community are met.

Despite these challenges, a number of authors have gathered data on Latino public opinion and have sought to understand it systematically. Sometimes Latino opinion is explored by itself and sometimes in comparison with Anglo and African American opinion. Because of a lack of data, many scholars have designed or used surveys that encompass a specific population or locale. As Cain and Kiewiet (1984, 315) noted in their study of the election of Marty Martinez in the Thirtieth California congressional district, "Although national election surveys do not sample a sufficient number of Mexican Americans to permit adequate analysis of their attitudes and political behavior, there have been many excellent regional studies."

For example, Lawrence Miller, Jerry Polinard, and Robert Wrinkle (1984) surveyed Mexican Americans in Hidalgo County, Texas, about the perceived benefits and problems associated with undocumented immigration. De la Garza, Polinard, Wrinkle, and Thomas Longoria (1991) surveyed Mexican Americans in Travis and Hidalgo counties, Texas, finding that "Mexicanness" and contact with the undocumented were associated with support for immigration.

Carole Uhlaner and Garcia (2002) analyzed a number of surveys to better understand a wide range of Latino attitudes toward political and policy topics. They found that "Latinos share many of the same attitudes, beliefs, and values as non-Latino Americans," and that "Latinos overall have very much the same policy agenda as most Americans" (99). They also noted that there is considerable diversity of opinion by national-origin group as well as by socioeconomic class, region, and immigration status.

Latinos, African Americans, and Political Ideology

On the issue of political ideology, there is some debate as to just how liberal or conservative Latinos and African Americans are. According to aggregate data, members of both groups are, on the whole, less politically conservative than Anglos. Latinos are much stronger supporters of the Democratic Party than are Anglos in terms of both partisan identification and voting in presidential and congressional elections. Latinos are also more likely to support an activist government and to differ on language and ethnic issues, such as bilingual education, making English the official language, requiring English in the workplace, providing public services in Spanish, and affirmative action (de la Garza, DeSipio, F. C. Garcia, J. Garcia, and Falcon 1992). African Americans are even stronger supporters of the Democratic Party, are more likely than Anglos to favor an activist government and redistributive programs, and are more liberal on economic issues and affirmative action (Swain 1995, 11; Whitby 2000, 8).

This is not to imply that Latinos or African Americans are monolithically liberal. There are well-known conservative issue positions within the Latino community; Latinos in the aggregate have been reported as less likely to support abortion and are often reported to be well disposed toward faith and family issues, and Cuban Americans are more likely to oppose diplomatic relations with Cuba and to support the Republican Party. Latinos are also more likely to identify themselves as conservatives than liberals. Carol Swain (1995, 11) similarly found that "a strand of social conservatism runs through black America. More African Americans than whites disapprove of abortions on demand (41 versus 28 percent). Fewer African Americans than whites approve of married women working (70 versus 76 percent) or like the idea of female politicians (65 versus 75 percent)."

In sum, there are some conservative elements even in populations that have voted in the liberal direction for decades. This suggests we should not simply test for whether populations identify as simply liberal or conservative. Stances may vary by issue, which means that scholars must study opinions on a wide range of political questions.

Nevertheless, the Republican Party is worried about a future in which an expanding Latino population augments Democratic political power. Some Republicans, however, have used aggregate data to suggest their party might successfully compete for a large share of the Latino vote. For instance, some point to evidence that Latinos are socially conservative. The most prominent evidence is abortion attitudes, but school vouchers are another issue that Republicans hope will bring minority voters closer to their party. According to one analysis from the 2000 campaign, "Bush thinks his support of vouchers will score points among usually antagonistic minority voters . . ."[3]

Ideological self-identification also provides some hope for Republicans. In the LNPS, 36 percent of Mexican Americans considered themselves conservative and 29 percent liberal. In the Kaiser survey almost a decade later, a similar 35 percent identified as conservative and 24 percent as liberal. Nevertheless, James Gimpel and Karen Kaufmann (2001) found few reasons to think Republicans could attract a significant number of Latino voters, largely because "the Democrats are in line with Latino policy preferences on education, health care, and social services" (9).

De la Garza and associates (1992, 3) noted that the claims of both parties about Latino opinion were suspect because they were often built on unrepresentative samples or unreliable data. Republican claims about Latino conservative views and "traditional" values, for instance, were either extrapolations from the Cuban American community or were based on the opinions of affluent Latinos who lived in mixed or majority-Anglo areas. Furthermore, much of the data on Mexican Americans derive from surveys overrepresenting liberal respondents from regions such as Southern California and South Texas. They concluded that, "Taken together as a Hispanic population, then, they do not fit neatly within either the Democratic or the Republican parties. Nonetheless, if it were necessary to locate Hispanics as a single population within the party structure as it currently exists, their policy preferences would better fit under the Democratic umbrella" (16).

The issue of distinctiveness is also related to the debate about the political future of Hispanic Americans in the United States, as some suggest that any distinctiveness in their opinion has implications for their political incorporation. According to de la Garza (1985, 236), "Another factor that will influence the effect of Mexican-American participation on the political process is the nature of the demands Mexican-Americans make. If their demands differ radically from those of the general public, an increased Mexican-American presence could destabilize regional and national political processes."

He concluded that Anglos and Mexican Americans "do not constitute distinct electorates." While Mexican Americans held unique opinions on government spending on minority-related issues, education, welfare, and space, they did not uniquely favor or oppose spending on crime, drugs, defense, foreign aid, and urban problems. This essay will also help assess whether and in which ways Latinos are distinct electorates and thereby provide some insight into how Latinos will influence the political system in the future.

Data and Models

This essay uses the 1999 Washington Post/Henry J. Kaiser Family Foundation/Harvard University National Survey on Latinos in America (NSLA). This is a nationally representative sample of 4,614 respondents, including 1,802 Anglos and 2,417 Latinos.

It is the most appropriate survey for the purposes of this essay because it contains a large number of policy and political questions as well as a large Latino sample. Most national surveys of American political opinion, such as the American National Election Studies, do not include a sufficient Latino sample to confidently assess this large and complex population. The NSLA, however, not only includes respondents from the three largest Latino national-origin groups (Mexican American, Puerto Rican, and Cuban American), but also those of Caribbean and Central/South American heritage.[4]

We will therefore examine respondent opinions by ethnic groupings (Latinos and Anglos) as well as by national-origin groups (Mexican Americans, Cuban Americans, Puerto Ricans, and Central/South Americans). Scholars have argued that such analysis is critical because of the many Latino subgroup differences. Enrique (Henry) Trueba (1999, 33) noted that, "we cannot trivialize the ethnic, social, racial, and economic differences of Latino subgroups." Rodolfo de la Garza and Louis DeSipio (1994, 3) argued that the study of the overall Latino population:

confuses rather than clarifies our understanding because of the characteristics that distinguish the national-origin groups thus subsumed (Bean and Tienda 1987; de la Garza, Fraga, and Pachon 1988; Pachon and DeSipio 1988; Fuchs 1990). This approach fails to assess differences in political culture associated with the distinct socialization experiences within the United States and the countries of origin and neglects the link between those differences and political behavior.

Lastly, some surveys are problematic because they do not use bilingual interviewers. This dramatically underrepresents Spanish-dominant respondents and generates a Latino sample that is biased in a number of important ways. In the Kaiser survey, 49 percent of the Latino respondents chose to be interviewed in Spanish, which indicates the importance of this option.

Policy and Political Questions

The political opinion questions are grouped into several related categories: (A) policies; (B) moral (sometimes referred to as "social") issues; and (C) government and partisan opinions.[5]

The first set of policy questions involves health care and gun control. The former include HMO reform and government-provided health insurance. Previous research suggests that Latinos support government health care and social insurance programs (Martinez-Ebers, Fraga, Lopez, and Vega 2000). Research in several cities has found that Latino violence rates are generally higher than those of Anglos while lower than those of African Americans (Block 1993; Martinez 1996; Bradshaw et al. 1998). This suggests that minority respondents may favor crime-prevention plans, such as gun control.

Two of the policy questions are of particular concern to Latinos: bilingual education and immigration policy. Bilingual education is considered by most Latino activists to be of critical importance to the Latino community for both educational and cultural reasons.[6] There has been some debate, however, about whether Latinos favor bilingual education.[7]

Latino attitudes toward immigration have been more complex than is commonly understood. While Mexican Americans today generally recognize the ties than bind them to new immigrants from Mexico, there has historically been concern that additional immigration would undercut their fragile economic position and stir up nativist sentiment among Anglos (Gutierrez 1995).

The next set of questions involves attitudes toward moral issues with political

34

implications. Latinos, according to some observers, are particularly conservative on such questions and therefore somewhat uncomfortable in the relatively liberal Democratic Party. Some Republicans hope to attract Latino votes by emphasizing such issues to this largely Catholic population.[8] Indeed, some Democratic elected officials have recently been criticized for their pro-choice positions by Catholic bishops.

We therefore examine attitudes toward abortion, the death penalty, and assisted suicide—the three policies addressed by Pope John Paul II's Encyclical Letter *Evangelium Vitae* (Paul 1995). Republicans typically mean abortion when they discuss Latinos and morality. It is possible, however, that Latino morality is consistently "pro-life" in light of Catholic Church teaching by including not just antiabortion but also anti-death penalty and anti-assisted suicide stances. If so, this could work to the disadvantage of Republicans, who are stronger death penalty proponents than are Democrats.

In addition, the survey asks three questions that involve traditional morality: the acceptability of divorce, homosexual/lesbian sexual activity, and bearing children out of wedlock. Such issues sometimes arise in politics and might benefit Republicans if Latinos have particularly conservative views.

Three attitudes about the U.S. government are also examined. The first asks whether Washington or the individual should be responsible for solving problems, the second solicits opinions about the size of government, and the third asks about trust in government. If Latinos look to Washington, favor a larger government, and trust government in general, this would suggest a liberal political orientation. Previous aggregate research has found that Latinos have higher levels of trust in the U.S. government than do Anglos (de la Garza et al. 1992), so this essay will similarly check for differences.

To further test where Latinos stand politically, we include two questions about party support and two about presidential evaluations. The former ask about the respondent's party affiliation and which party best looks out for the interests of Latinos. The latter ask whether the respondent anticipated voting for Al Gore or George W. Bush and for an evaluation of outgoing president Bill Clinton.

Results

Anglo-Latino Opinions

Table 2.1 reports the responses of Latinos and Anglos to the full range of policy and political questions. The following sections will analyze the results by type of question, as categorized above.

TABLE 2.1
Latino-Anglo opinion variation

Question	Latinos	Anglos	Question	Latinos	Anglos
HMO reform			**Divorce**		
1=more regulation necessary	67%	56%	1=Acceptable	57%	67%
0=not necessary	23%	33%	0=Unacceptable	41%	32%
Government-provided health insurance			**Washington solve problems**		
1=support	83%	61%	1=Yes	64%	52%
0=oppose	14%	34%	0=No	32%	42%
Guns			**Size of government**		
2=Harder to buy	71%	65%	1=Larger	67%	28%
1=Current laws right	18%	28%	0=Smaller	28%	65%
0=Easier to buy	9%	5%	**Trust government**		
Bilingual education			4=Always	19%	4%
1=Favor instruction in	59%	35%	3=Most	27%	19%
native language			2=Some	51%	71%
0=Favor instruction in	40%	64%	1=Never	2%	5%
English			**Party affiliation**		
Immigration			2=Democrat	51%	35%
2=Increase	28%	7%	1=Independent/Other	21%	20%
1=Keep the same	50%	51%	0=Republican	24%	45%
0=Decrease	17%	39%	**Which party supports Latinos**		
Abortion			2=Democrat	44%	29%
4=Legal in all cases	12%	19%	1=No difference	38%	51%
3=Legal in most cases	27%	29%	0=Republican	10%	7%
2=Illegal in most cases	24%	34%	**Clinton evaluation**		
1=Illegal in all cases	33%	14%	1=Approve	82%	53%
Assisted suicide			0=Disapprove	12%	41%
1=Support	38%	57%	**Gore vs. Bush (anticipated vote)**		
0=Oppose	58%	38%	1=Gore	40%	31%
Death penalty			0=Bush	45%	56%
1=Favor	54%	76%			
0=Oppose	41%	20%			

Note: Bold print indicates a difference of at least 10 percentage points. Some responses do not add to 100 because of rounding or the "don't know" option.
Source: 1999 National Survey on Latinos in America.

Question	Latinos	Anglos
Gay/lesbian sexual activity		
1=Acceptable	24%	31%
0=Unacceptable	73%	66%
Children out of wedlock		
1=Acceptable	50%	48%
0=Unacceptable	48%	51%

POLICY OPINIONS   The first policy questions ask about health care reform and gun control. We see that Latinos were 11 percentage points more likely than Anglos to favor government-provided health insurance and 22 percentage points more likely to support HMO reform. By a 10-point margin, Latinos were less likely than Anglos to believe that current gun control laws were adequate.

The next two items include policy variables of specific interest to Latinos. Again, we see substantial differences between Latino and Anglo opinion. Latinos were over 20 percentage points more likely to favor bilingual education and to support increased immigration. This was not unexpected, as such polices affect large numbers of Latinos.

OPINIONS ON MORAL ISSUES   First, we see that overall record abortion opinions differ only slightly by ethnicity. While Latinos are 19 points more likely than Anglos to oppose abortion in all cases, they are 12 points less likely to believe it should be illegal in most cases. The percentage of Latinos and Anglos who think abortion should be legal in all or most cases is 39 percent and 48 percent, respectively—which is less than a 10-point difference.

The survey also asked respondents whether they thought gay and lesbian sexual activity was acceptable or unacceptable, and the results reveal few differences. While both groups were more likely to disapprove than approve, there was only a single-digit opinion difference. Similarly, the respondents did not differ on the issue of whether having children out of wedlock was acceptable. In fact, contrary to stereotype, Latinos were 2 percentage points more likely to report that it was acceptable.

There was more substantial variation on the issues of divorce, assisted suicide, and the death penalty, but the results do not point in a single ideological direction. While Latinos were more likely to oppose divorce (10 points) and assisted suicide (19 points), they also expressed more negative views about the death penalty (22 points).

GOVERNMENT AND PARTISAN OPINIONS   Table 2.1 also shows that Latinos have a more positive view of government than do Anglos. They are more likely to look to Washington to solve problems (12 points), more likely to favor a larger federal government (39 points), and more likely to always trust government (15 points).

The next questions ask about political orientations. Given the previous results, it should be no surprise that Latinos are more likely than Anglos to identify themselves as Democrats (16 points) and to see the Democratic Party as more favorable to the interests of Latinos (15 points). In addition, Latino respondents are more likely to favor Gore over Bush (10 points) and to positively evaluate Clinton (29 points).

SUMMARY OF RESULTS   These data show substantial opinion differences across a wide range of policy issues. Of the fourteen policy opinions examined, there were Latino-Anglo differences of 10 percentage points in eleven cases. Ideologically, Latinos were more likely to support liberal policies. In comparison to Anglos, they supported more government spending, more immigration, more gun control, more bilingual education, and more government regulation of HMOs; they also expressed less support for the death penalty. The only issues where Latinos were clearly more conservative were divorce and assisted suicide. Latinos did not have distinct opinions about having children out of wedlock and support for gays and lesbians, and opinions about abortion were not on the whole distinct — which shows that Latinos are not more conservative on all "moral" issues.

In terms of partisanship, Latinos were more likely than Anglos to identify as Democrats, more likely to think that the Democratic Party was more concerned with Latino interests, more likely to approve of President Clinton, and less likely to anticipate voting for Bush.

Latino National-Origin Group Opinion

A key question for the Latino politics literature is whether it makes sense to discuss an aggregate "Latino" opinion, or whether there are important differences by subgroups. Table 2.2 therefore analyzes whether opinions vary according to Latino national-origin group.

POLICY OPINIONS   Latino opinion does not substantially vary on HMO reform, government health insurance, and gun control; Latinos were consistently in favor of all three policies.

For policy issues of particular relevance to Latinos, there were both similarities and differences. First, there was consistent agreement with bilingual education. Group support varied only from 60 to 63 percent. Conversely, there were substantial differences of opinion about immigration policy. While Mexican Americans and Central/South Americans expressed similar views, Puerto Ricans were less favorable about increasing immigration while Cuban Americans were more supportive. As all Puerto Ricans are citizens, immigration is likely a less important issue to them, and Latino immigrants could be perceived as a source of economic competition. However, as most Cuban Americans were shaped by the immigration experience following the Cuban Revolution, they may be more sympathetic toward immigrants.

OPINIONS ON MORAL ISSUES   For the six social issues, we find some differences by national-origin group, but no consistent patterns. No one group is the most conservative or the most liberal across the items. For instance, while Cuban Americans are the most supportive of the death penalty, they are also the most supportive of assisted suicide. Mexican Americans are the most opposed to divorce, but the groups

TABLE 2.2
Latino opinion variation by national origin group

Question	Mexican	PR	Cuban	C-SA
HMO Reform				
1=more regulation necessary	65%	73%	68%	71%
0=not necessary	24%	16%	21%	20%
Government health insurance				
1=support	83%	84%	87%	86%
0=oppose	14%	15%	11%	11%
Guns				
2=Harder to buy	70%	72%	75%	75%
1=Current laws right	20%	16%	12%	10%
0=Easier to buy	8%	9%	10%	11%
Bilingual education				
1=Yes, in native language	60%	61%	62%	63%
0=No, in English	40%	38%	37%	36%
Immigration				
2=Increase	30%	17%	44%	28%
1=Keep the same	49%	44%	41%	57%
0=Decrease	15%	35%	12%	10%
Abortion				
4=Legal in all cases	9%	27%	25%	36%
3=Legal in most cases	27%	40%	19%	20%
2=Illegal in most cases	25%	19%	25%	28%
1=Illegal in all cases	36%	20%	24%	38%
Assisted suicide				
1=Support	36%	48%	52%	34%
0=Oppose	60%	46%	45%	64%
Death penalty				
1=Favor	52%	54%	70%	42%
0=Oppose	43%	38%	27%	48%
Gay/lesbian sexual activity				
1=Acceptable	22%	31%	25%	19%
0=Unacceptable	75%	63%	73%	77%
Children out of wedlock				
1=Acceptable	47%	52%	54%	56%
0=Unacceptable	51%	47%	45%	44%

Question	Mexican	PR	Cuban	C-SA
Divorce				
1=Acceptable	51%	64%	58%	68%
0=Unacceptable	47%	34%	38%	31%
Washington solve problems				
1=Yes	63%	73%	59%	58%
0=No	34%	20%	35%	36%
Size of government				
1=Larger	69%	63%	59%	70%
0=Smaller	26%	26%	33%	26%
Trust government				
4=Always	21%	15%	21%	20%
3=Most	25%	41%	32%	25%
2=Some	52%	40%	42%	53%
1=Never	2%	3%	2%	0%
Party affiliation				
2=Democrat	49%	57%	37%	57%
1=Independent/Other	22%	18%	17%	20%
0=Republican	25%	19%	41%	18%
Which party supports Latinos				
2=Democrat	42%	52%	33%	45%
1=No difference	39%	34%	37%	39%
0=Republican	11%	6%	19%	9%
Clinton evaluation				
1=Approve	81%	89%	69%	90%
0=Disapprove	12%	6%	23%	5%
Gore vs. Bush (anticipated)				
1=Gore	37%	50%	32%	47%
0=Bush	49%	34%	57%	39%

Note: Bold print indicates at least one difference of at least 10 percentage points. Some responses do not add to 100 because of rounding or the "don't know" option.
Source: 1999 National Survey on Latinos in America.

do not vary on children out of wedlock, and it is Central/South Americans who are most opposed to gays and lesbians. The issue with the most intergroup variation is abortion: for the position of allowing abortion in all or most cases, we see support range from 36 percent (Mexican Americans), 44 percent (Cuban Americans), 56 percent (Central/South Americans), and 67 percent (Puerto Ricans).

Opinions about the Government   There are also no consistent differences about government. While Puerto Ricans are most likely to believe that Washington should solve problems and to trust government "just about always" or "most of the time," they are only the third most likely group to favor increasing the size of government.

Conversely, there are consistent partisan differences according to national-origin group. Cuban Americans are the most likely to affiliate with the Republican Party, to believe that the Republican Party supports Latinos, the least positive about Clinton (although he nevertheless received 69 percent support), and the most likely to anticipate voting for Bush (57 percent). This indicates a population that is more Republican than other Latinos but is not more conservative in terms of the policy issues described previously.

Summary of Results   The results in table 2.2 indicate that the opinions of Latinos from the four national-origin groups either do not differ or do not differ in a consistent manner. First, for a number of issues, there was no significant variation. This includes the questions of HMO reform, government provision of health insurance, bilingual education, and having children out of wedlock. Second, there were some issues in which just one national-origin group differed from the others. These include gun control, gays and lesbians, divorce, the size of government, and the role of Washington. There was no consistent pattern to such variation, however. For instance, while Puerto Ricans were the most likely to believe that Washington should solve problems, they did not have distinctive attitudes about the size of government. In addition, Central/South Americans were the most tolerant of divorce, but they were the least supportive of gays and lesbians. Third, a few policy issues see respondents from two groups differing from other respondents, but again there are no consistent patterns.

Taken together, the above results suggest that any opinion difference between Latino national-origin groups may reflect random variation, idiosyncrasies, or socioeconomic differences rather than deep-seated cultural differences (testing the SES hypothesis is the next iteration of this research project). In addition, some of these differences would disappear if the threshold were raised from 10 to 15 percentage points. This lack of consistent findings broadly parallels the conclusions of de la Garza et al.: "On many key domestic issues, significant majorities of each [Latino] group take the liberal position. On other issues, there is no consensus and, depending on the issue, Mexicans may be on the right, while Cubans and many Puerto Ricans are on the left of the nation's current political spectrum. Thus, labels such as liberal or conservative do not adequately describe the complexity of any one group's political views" (1992, 15).

The one exception is partisanship. Mexican Americans, Puerto Ricans, and Central/South Americans are more likely than Anglos to favor the Democratic Party, believe the Democratic Party promotes Latino interests, positively evaluate Bill Clinton, and anticipate voting for George W. Bush. Conversely, Cuban American opinion is not particularly distinct in the policy opinion regressions, thus confirming previous, aggregate-level analyses indicating that domestic policy is not the source of Cuban American partisan distinctiveness.

Conclusions

As the Latino population grows both numerically and proportionately, it is increasingly difficult to understand public opinion and political participation in America without reference to this group. This essay therefore investigated whether and how contemporary Latino opinion is distinct. This allows us to better understand to what degree we can speak of an overall "Latino" perspective on political and policy questions, or whether substantial differences exist across Latino national-origin groups. Although these groups are sometimes assumed to think and act in similar ways, there are a number of socioeconomic, demographic, cultural, and other differences that cannot be overlooked.

The first table examines whether Latino and Anglo views differ across a wide range of policy and political questions. When taken together, the results suggest that Latinos have unique policy orientations, although not in every instance. First, they favor policy issues of particular relevance to their communities, including immigration and bilingual education. Second, they are generally supportive of "big government": they would like to see HMO reform and government-provided health insurance, and they express a high level of trust in government and look to Washington to solve problems. In addition, Latinos are less supportive of the death penalty. These orientations are in the liberal direction, and Latinos are relatively conservative only in their relative opposition to assisted suicide and divorce.

Latinos also uniquely support the Democratic Party and Democratic politicians. Aggregate polling data and election returns have often indicated this, and as DeSipio, de la Garza, and Mark Setzler (1999, 7) noted, "Much of the talk of Latino conversion by Republican leaders is more rhetoric than reality"—a sentiment this essay largely supports.

When the data are examined according to Latino national-origin group (table 2.2), we see either no opinion differences (four issues) or differences that are substantively small or do not suggest any clear ideological pattern. While the number of differences cannot be ignored, we may not be seeing anything beyond random noise. What is clear is that more research is needed on the political orientations of Latino national-origin groups, especially as there are a growing number of Latinos who have a heritage other than Mexican, Cuban, or Puerto Rican.

The one consistent pattern in the data involves Cuban American partisanship. This population is unique in its support of the Republican Party and its candidates, although it does not particularly differ from other Latinos on domestic policy questions.

Given these findings, it seems that scholars should have some license to discuss "Latino" opinion. While such a label will inevitably prove less useful when discussing some issues than others, the data do not reveal the sort of interethnic similarities or intra-Latino differences that would cause scholars to pull the "emergency stop" cord on the Latino Politics Express.

Notes

1. According to David Maciel and Isidro Ortiz (1996, x). "Civil rights, affirmative action, bilingual education, job-training programs, financial aid, and immigration came under constant attack during the 1980s, years ironically characterized by the print media and political establishment as the 'Decade of the Hispanic.' As the decade evolved, it became apparent that it would be many things, but certainly not the 'Decade of the Hispanic.' Instead of being years when a consolidation of earlier achievements and successes occurred, the 1980s threatened to become a period of retrenchment and regression in conditions that had taken decades to change for the better."

2. Although Armando Valdez (1987, 193) in the mid-1980s identified 220 Latino public opinion data sources constructed at an estimated cost of over thirteen millions dollars, he noted that "the quality of the data is so uneven that a considerable amount of effort remains ahead. The truly adequate data resources are few."

3. *Business Week*, April 20, 2000. "The ABC's of Vouchers and Politics."

4. The survey includes 818 Mexican Americans, 318 Puerto Ricans, 312 Cuban Americans, and 593 Central/South Americans. The data were "weighted to the national Latino population, so that nationalities are represented in their actual proportions (as estimated by the Census Bureau's Current Population Survey)." From "National Survey on Latinos in America: Questionnaire and Toplines," iii.

5. For the exact wording and coding of all dependent variables, as well as the aggregate responses by Latinos, African Americans, Anglos, and the Latino national-origin groups, see: http://www.kff.org/kaiserpolls/3023-index.cfm. This information is not included in the paper because of space considerations.

6. When describing the strategies of Latino political activists, Guadalupe San Miguel Jr. (1987, 215) found that, "After 1975 bilingual education came to be viewed as the most appropriate instrument for attaining equality in society. Bilingual education was considered the key for ameliorating historic problems in schools with large numbers of Spanish-speaking children. . . .

This comprehensive approach of instructing Spanish-speaking children implied a fundamental reassessment of the support, governance, administration, and content of the public schools as well as an increase of state and federal intervention on their behalf and a call for greater participation by the community in educational matters."

7. The issue was brought to the fore during the debate over Proposition 227, the 1998 California ballot initiative to end bilingual education. Some early polling suggested that many Latinos supported the proposition, but ultimately 63 percent of the Latino vote was negative (Pyle, McDonnell, and Tobar 1998).

Although not all students enrolled in bilingual education classes are Latino, they constitute three-quarters of limited English proficiency (LEP) students (Congressional Research Service 1999).

8. Although with a growing Protestant component. The most recent estimates are that approximately 30 percent of Latinos are Protestant.

Fuzzy Distinctions and Blurred Boundaries

Transnational, Ethnic, and Immigrant Politics

Michael Jones-Correa

MUCH OF THE GROWTH in the Latino population in the United States over the last thirty years has come about as a result of immigration from Latin America. First-generation immigrants make up 41 percent of the total Latino population and slightly more than 60 percent of all Latino adults. First- and second-generation immigrant Latinos—immigrants and their children—make up more than two thirds of all Latinos.

Despite these figures, there's been a striking absence of conversations or communication among scholars studying Latinos through the lenses of ethnicity and race, those pursuing studies of immigrant assimilation or incorporation, and scholars taking transnational approaches to Latino immigration. For example, scholars looking at immigration through assimilationist or ethnic lenses (like Nee and Alba 2003, for example, and most political scientists working on immigrant politics and political behavior) spend very little time looking at transnational networks and organizations, but they have analyzed the processes of immigrant incorporation into receiving country societies.

Conversely, Alejandro Portes (2003) points out (as others have as well—Kasinitz, Mollenkopf, and Waters 2003 in their second generation study, for example) that only a minority of immigrants are engaged in regular transnational behavior. A large majority do not, or do so only occasionally. But the significance of these findings is only rarely acknowledged or explored in the literature on transnational immigration. While ostensibly addressing the same population, these literatures rarely speak to one another. Yet, it's curious that more attention isn't paid to how the practices and experiences implied by the terms transnational, immigrant, and ethnic relate to one another. How do they intersect, overlap or compete?

Ethnic Politics

The dominant approach among Latino political scientists (as reflected in the contributions to this volume), and among scholars of Latino politics more generally, is to treat Latinos as participants in an "ethnic politics" in the United States. This approach emphasizes the role of Latinos as actors in American politics, particularly in formal American political institutions, exploring their experiences with such phenomena as registration, voting, electing candidates, and representation. Ethnic politics focuses on Latinos as *citizens,* albeit citizens whose attachments may be to their own coethnics.

In its pure form (though it is at least partly historical fantasy), ethnic politics is a story of individuals choosing to come to the United States, of their incorporation as Americans, and of their gradual success, if not for themselves, then for their children and children's children. In this narrative the focus is on individual struggle rather than structural barriers, and on voluntary rather than forced migration or colonization. As a part of this story, ethnic politics is seen as a largely transitory phenomenon, one containing the seeds of its own demise. In an unfamiliar and sometimes hostile environment, immigrants may rally at first in support of their own, but with their social, economic, and political incorporation over time, this support becomes more symbolic than real—endorsing politicians who march in once-a-year parades or who have had their photos taken in immigrants' "home" countries. The increasingly symbolic role ethnicity plays in American politics is seen as the very sign of the incorporation of ethnic groups (Dahl 1961). This is echoed in some narratives of the Latino political experience in the United States (de la Garza 2004, 123; Skerry 1993).

In the study of American politics, the primary competitor to this immigrant narrative is the race narrative, which is centered on the story of African Americans and slavery, but which has been expanded to include other "others" as well, and which hinges on the difference between whites and these others. Both the categories of "white" and "other" may change over time, but the critical aspect of this narrative is that the differences between whites and others are largely decided by and imposed by whites for their own benefit, are structural in nature, and are expressed in almost every aspect of social life in the United States. That is, these differences are reflected not just by law (formal segregation), but also in informal social relations (residence, marriage patterns), culture (music, literature, and so forth) and economics (occupations, employment, income, and wealth). The race narrative, then, is a story of persistent, if not permanent, racial difference and inequality.

During the last great wave of immigration, in the nineteenth and early twentieth centuries, the race and immigrant narratives were still seen as largely separate. Immigration at the time was overwhelmingly from Europe, while the "race problem" in the United States was African American. The racial prejudice suffered by blacks and the hardship undergone by immigrants had their similarities, but also their own trajectories: African Americans were caught in a web of institutionalized racism, while immigrants, even if initially seen as distinct "races," "became white," allowing them incorporation into the larger American society (and in so doing, participating in the oppression of African Americans) (Jacobson 1998; Ignatiev 1995; Lieberson 1980).

Nonetheless, even in the midst of the last great wave of European immigration, these narratives were already becoming blurred. The immigration of other "nonwhite" immigrants at the time complicated the stories of both immigration and race. The Supreme Court ruling clarifying the Fourteenth Amendment's birthright citizenship clause dealt not with African Americans but with Asian Americans (*United States v. Wong Kim Ark* 1898), and many of the cases that traced the line between potential citizens and permanent aliens were those brought to the court by Asian immigrants who claimed that they too were white and so should be allowed to naturalize as U.S. citizens (*Ozawa v. United States* 1922; *United States v. Bhagat Singh Thind* 1923). Mexican Americans in the southwestern states were incorporated as foot soldiers in local political machines but simultaneously treated as second-class citizens, or at times not as citizens at all—being deported when the economy turned sour.

If the immigrant and race narratives were already becoming intertwined by the beginning the twentieth century, they have become inextricably linked at the turn of the twenty-first century. In the political arena, this was the result in no small part of the effect of two pieces of legislation, the 1965 Voting Rights Act and the Immigration Act of the same year. The Voting Rights Act was the culmination of a half century of carefully calibrated challenges by African American activists to segregation policies implemented across the country, but primarily in the South, that marginalized African Americans in all public arenas. Coming on the heels of the early Civil Rights Act of 1964, which ended federally sanctioned segregation, the Voting Rights Act was designed, most immediately, to rid states of obviously onerous and arbitrary formal barriers to registration and voting. The act was initially targeted largely at the practices in seven southern states, and at African Americans in those states. When the act was renewed in 1975, however, its focus was expanded to include "linguistic minorities" in the United States—at the time, mostly native-born Hispanic and Asian Americans. If a locality met the criteria for inclusion under the expanded Voting Rights Act, then not only would it have to provide dual-language ballots for those citizens who requested them, but its electoral laws would also fall under the scrutiny of the Justice Department. Because the criterion for coverage was language, areas receiving immigration were more likely to be covered under the act.

Immigration to the United States was already on the upswing in the post–World War II period when Congress passed its immigration reform bill in 1965. The Hart-Cellar Act abolished the national origins quota system that had been in place since 1921 (and that had dramatically favored immigrants of European origin) and placed a new emphasis on family reunification for the purposes of allocating residency visas. These two provisions together radically (if unintentionally) changed immigration flows to the United States. The abolition of national quotas allowed immigration from Asia, and family reunification preferences abetted continued immigration from Latin America and elsewhere. By 2000 there were 28.4 million immigrants in the United States—10.4 percent of the total population. Whereas previously most immigration had come from Europe, 80 percent of immigrants arriving to the United States from 1970 to 2000 were from Latin America and Asia, with only 15 percent hailing from Europe. This most recent wave of immigration has transformed the Latin American and Asian-origin populations in the United States.

By 2000 the Asian American population had shifted from being largely native born to being overwhelmingly foreign born. While the shift was not as dramatic among Hispanics, by 2000, 41 percent of Latinos in the United States were foreign born and two-thirds were either immigrants or the children of immigrants. Immigration has also had an effect on the African American population in the United States, with almost 10 percent being foreign born by 2000, and up to 30 percent in gateway cities like New York and Miami.

After 1964 Hispanic and Asian Americans were covered under the nation's civil rights statutes as racial minorities and after 1975 by its voting-rights provisions as linguistic minorities. Under civil rights and voting rights legislation, the 22 million immigrants of Asian and Latin American origin who had entered the United States as legal residents up through 2000 were, upon their arrival, also considered to be racial and linguistic minorities. In this way, the race and immigration narratives, which had been seen as largely distinct through much of American history, were by the end of the twentieth century, while not identical, at least very much linked. For the 85 percent of immigrants now meeting the definition of racial or linguistic minorities, their incorporation into American life is no longer seen simply as a tale of instrumental ethnic solidarity and individual struggle. Instead, their experience is compared to that of native-born whites, and their segregation, whether residential, occupational, or institutional, is seen against the backdrop of a history of racial exclusion.

The ethnic approach to Latino politics combines elements of these immigrant and racial narratives. However, even within the boundaries of this paradigm, contemporary immigration raises questions of how Latino experiences—both immigrant and native born—play out against the difficult history of race relations in the United States. As race and immigration intersect, how does this, in turn, shape contemporary ethnic politics? Furthermore, is the "ethnic" approach sufficient to describe what's going on in Latino politics today?

The answer to the first question is what drives much of the research in the field of Latino politics, but it also tends to obscure the appropriate response to the last question, which I believe is clearly "no." The ethnic approach plays down the implications of the figures I cited at the beginning of this essay—that 41 percent of Latinos are foreign born (with 60 percent of Latino adults foreign born) and that two thirds of all Latinos are either first- or second-generation immigrants. It also ignores the figures Louis DeSipio and others have pointed out: that the numbers of Latinos participating in electoral politics are a minority of all Latino adults, with about a third eligible to vote, a third as permanent residents, and another third as undocumented migrants (DeSipio 1996). To put it another way, in 2000 Latinos made up 12 percent of the population, 7 percent of the eligible voting-age population, and 5 percent of actual voters. Much of the research in this volume and in the study of Latino politics more generally looks at the 5 percent—but what are all those other Latinos doing?

Transnational Politics

A large majority of that first generation—those 60 percent of all Latino adults—are engaged in some form of participation in transnational networks—social connections that span borders, enabling individuals to sustain multiple social memberships, identities, and loyalties. Immigrants remit money, travel, maintain their interest in sending country affairs, keep up with media from their country of origin, and may take part in organizational life, politics, and social events linking the sending country with expatriates in the receiving country. It is pretty much taken as a given among immigration scholars that these transnational networks and practices are prevalent in the first generation.

For the most part, I have been critical of the overemphasis among certain immigration scholars on the phenomenon of transnationalism (Jones-Correa 2003).

After all, the large majority of first-generation immigrants arriving in the United States choose to stay, and of course so do their children. The long-term trend seems to be toward engagement in some form of ethnic politics. But it is also the case that transnational behaviors are common among the first generation and persist among at least some portion of the second generation. At least some of the children of immigrants, for instance, maintain some knowledge of their parents' native language, travel back and forth to their parents' country of origin, and even send remittances back to extended family. (See the contributions to Levitt and Waters 2003.) What should we make of the persistence of transnational behaviors and practices, and what influence might they have on Latino politics?

Conversely, while transnational behaviors persist, larger survey studies find that even occasional transnational practices (travel, remittances, language retention) are rarer by the second generation, with those responding positively accounting for fewer then half the sample. Those with regular, repeated transnational behaviors account, on the whole, for only a small percentage of their second-generation respondents (about 10 percent in surveys conducted in New York City and San Diego, for example). If the first generation often still maintains some ties to their countries of origin, an overwhelming majority of the second generation is deeply rooted in the United States.

In one San Diego survey, for example, by their twenties, 88 percent of respondents consider the United States their home, 84 percent are U.S. citizens (even among young adults of Mexican origin this figure is still 81 percent), 66 percent say they prefer using English (an additional 32 percent say they are equally comfortable in English and their parents' native language). A total of 72 percent have never sent remittances, and 75 percent have visited their parents' country not more than twice in their lives (Rumbaut 2003). Philip Kasinitz and associates' New York study had similar findings on language (56 percent prefer English), travel (73 percent have traveled to their parent's home country three times or less), and remittances (71 percent have never remitted money).

In New York City, 78 percent of the second generation are U.S. citizens (including 58 percent of those not born in the United States). A total of 70 percent are registered to vote in the United States, with 53 percent voting in 1996. Respondents were more interested in New York City politics than in the politics of their countries of origin. For at least some of the groups examined, transnational practices seem to decrease with age (for South Americans and West Indians), and for Dominicans the more likely immigrants are to have U.S. citizenship, the less likely they are to exhibit transnational behavior (Kasinitz et al. 2003).

On the whole these findings confirm what we can glean from other sources, suggesting that immigrants and their children in the United States are here to stay, and that they are increasingly incorporated in the social and political life of this country. Other national survey data indicate, for instance, that:

- Immigrants are no more likely to return to their countries of origin today than they were a century ago, and their children, not surprisingly, are even less likely to do so (Immigration and Naturalization Service 1992, table 2). The increasing incidence of dual nationality may have the opposite effect than expected: research shows that Latin American immigrants from countries recognizing dual nationality have significantly higher rates of naturalization as U.S. citizens, and once naturalized also have higher rates of participation in electoral politics in the United States. Why would this be? Dual nationality decreases the costs immigrants face in becoming U.S. citizens. If U.S. citizenship is presented as an either/or choice, many immigrants will prevaricate, staying in the United States as permanent residents but unwilling to sunder their official standing with their countries of origin. Dual nationality allows immigrants to retain recognition of these ties, making it easier for them to fully incorporate into American political life (Jones-Correa 2001a).
- Immigrants increased their rates of citizenship acquisition over the last ten years, and relatively few immigrants (and even fewer of their children) actively acquire dual nationality, or take advantage of provisions for voting abroad (Jones-Correa 2001b).
- Although total immigrant remittances to sending countries in Latin America have been increasing (they were over $30 billion in 2003), we should keep in mind that the total purchasing power of Hispanics in the United States in 2003 was estimated at $653 billion—which is to say that total remittances only make up between 4 and 5 percent of Latino household income (Hispanic Market Facts 2003).
- Research indicates that, for individual migrants, remittances peak in the first decade in the United States and fall thereafter, as family ties are diminished by the toll of death and distance or as other family members migrate in turn to the United States. (Orozco 2003; Lowell and de la Garza 2000; DeSipio 2000).
- Immigrants are increasingly homeowners, settling as stable residents in neighborhoods across the United States (Joint Center for Housing Studies 2001).
- Immigrants and their children learn English; indeed, their children become English dominant (Portes and Rumbaut 2001; Rumbaut and Portes 2001).
- The children of immigrants have high rates of outmarriage: at least a quarter of Asian and Latino immigrants marry outside their broad ethnic/racial categories (as defined by the census) in the first generation; half do by the second generation (Farley 1998). Keep in mind that these figures are certainly higher for those mar-

rying out of their national origin (rather than racial/ethnic) group, so that in New York City, for instance, increasing numbers of pairings are seen among Latinos of different national origins (Puerto Rican/Mexican, Colombian/Dominican, etc.)

Despite evidence of the existence of transnationalism among the first generation, and to a lesser extent their children, taken overall these data provide evidence for the assimilation of immigrants—that is, evidence that immigrants are further incorporated into society over time and with each succeeding generation. The debate about transnationalism is not, as some conservative policy analysts have pitched it, about whether immigrants and their children "Americanize." Clearly they do. Rather the question is, what is "Americanization," and what does transnationalism mean within the context of Americanization?

If regular transnational practices appear among most immigrants, but at most among only a small percentage of their children, what significance will these behaviors, attitudes, and identities have on their political engagement? Will transnational ties have any long-term, widespread effect? Among first-generation immigrants, one can readily point to economic remittances, political participation, and social networks that have unmistakable effects on their home countries, and by implication, on immigrants' opportunities for participation in the United States. Given the relatively miniscule proportion of regular transnationalism apparent among the second generation, we might be tempted to dismiss the longer-term influences of transnationalism and to accord it little or no significance over the longer run.

However, there are good reasons to reflect before passing judgment. There are at least six ways in which transnationalism could continue to have longer-term effects after the first generation: for the second generation itself, for the United States, and for their parents' countries of origin:

- The success of Americanization does not necessarily imply that most children of immigrants will *never* take up in transnational behaviors. Transnationalism may be occasional or sporadic, with the children of immigrants engaging in transnational behaviors in response to life events (like births, marriages, and deaths) or in response to crises in their parents' country of origin or in the immigrant community. This kind of sporadic transnationalism may escape notice, or be underplayed, in survey results and may only be adequately captured by qualitative fieldwork. Moreover, transnationalism may continue to play an important role in the second generation and beyond because its manifestations may very well vary over an individual's life cycle, with transnational activities rising and falling as individuals have the time, inclination, and resources to pursue them (Levitt 2002; Jones-Correa 2003).

- Although transnational actors in the second generation may be quite a small minority among their peers, they may still be quite large in number. This is to say, even if only 10 percent of the 23 million strong second generation currently in the United States have regular patterns of transnational behavior, that 10 percent translates into 2.3 million people—not an insignificant number. If these couple of million young adults remain actively engaged in their transnational networks (or if as they drop out, others come in to replace them), then they could conceivably continue to have a considerable influence on both their communities in the United States and their countries of origin.

- The consequences of immigrant transnational behavior may be exaggerated, for better or worse, by immigrants' relative wealth and influence. For instance, immigrants living in the United States can have a disproportionate effect in diaspora politics, just by virtue of having more resources to contribute than their compatriots in their countries of origin. Examples might include the relationship between the Irish and the Irish Republican Army, or American Jews and Israel. Benedict Anderson worries that this disproportionate influence may lead to all kinds of irresponsible meddling by immigrants in their home countries' ethnic, religious, and political feuds (1994). In a less sinister light, second-generation transnationalism can mean continuing to play a significant role in the economy of their country of origin, either as sources of investment and economic development (see Kapur 2001), or if only because their remittances act as a secondary social safety net.

- Transnationalism is almost certainly unevenly distributed within the United States and among immigrant populations in the United States. This has in part to do with the overwhelming concentration of migrants within a handful of states, but also with the concentration of immigrants within those states, as well as the clustering of particular country of origin groups within these immigrant populations. For example, one of the findings reported by Philip Kasinitz, John Mollenkopf, and Mary Waters is that second-generation Dominican immigrants are more likely than, say, their Chinese counterparts to have regular contacts with their parents' countries of origin. Because Dominicans are heavily concentrated in the northeastern United States, and in New York City in particular, the transnational behavior of second-generation Dominicans may continue to have important consequences both for the Dominican Republic and for New York City (2003). In addition, because most transnational behaviors (remittances and travel for instance) tend to be directed at very specific localities in the home country, transnationalism is also likely to have uneven effects in immigrants' countries of origin. Even quite limited transnationalism, if it is concentrated in these ways, might have significant local effects.

- Latent transnational identities can be triggered by crises in the country of origin: war, for instance, and other forms of political instability, or famines and natural disasters. The mobilization of these networks need not only be focused on the country of origin. Indeed, one of the most persistent debates on immigration and international relations has been on the possible biases introduced by ethnic lobbying on the conduct of U.S. foreign affairs. (See, for example, Ahrari 1987; DeConde 1992). It may even be the case that the *option* of transnationalism, of having alternative networks of social ties that are potentially available, even if they are never taken up, might have a significant effect on people's identities and choices. Knowledge of transnational possibilities, even if they are the "road not taken," may affect an individual's life choices. These effects, however, are subtle, and their effects difficult to measure beyond individual biography.

- Some speculate that transnationalism could continue, or even be rejuvenated and reinforced, among the second generation because of the continued influx of first-generation immigrants from the home country (some of whom will be of the same age as they are, and so with whom they are more likely to form a single cohort). The second generation will be constantly exposed to language, media, and culture from their country of origin in ways that were not true for the second generation at the turn of the last century, when immigration was largely curtailed after 1921. However, this hypothesis relies on at least two assumptions: that immigration will continue indefinitely at its current rate and that new immigrants in the future will be arriving into the same context as that experienced by current immigrants. There is no guarantee, however, that current patterns will continue indefinitely into the future.

In sum, the persistence of transnationalism depends very much on the "unevenness" in the distribution of this transnationalism, since this unevenness in time and space may translate into very different consequences for different immigrant Latino populations and the communities they have ties to. But it would be a mistake, again, to dismiss transnationalism, or its possible influence on Latino politics, out of hand.

Immigrant Politics

A focus on ethnic politics emphasizes the incorporation of immigrants into American society; "transnational" politics emphasizes continuing ties with the home country. Elsewhere I've proposed the existence of a third possibility, of "immigrant politics"—a liminal state of disengagement from the politics of both sending or receiving countries, even if not from politics entirely (Jones-Correa 1998). This liminal politics comes about as an escape from what immigrants see as the irreconcilable demands placed on them by their countries of origin and the country in which they reside. For sending countries, citizenship taken on in another country can be seen as a betrayal, triggering loss of citizenship; for receiving countries, the acquisition of citizenship carries with it an implicit or explicit pressure to renounce memberships and loyalties in other countries. However, immigrants often resist institutional pressures to make irrevocable decisions about membership in political communities. So immigrants avoid taking on a new citizenship in the United States, while also strategically distancing themselves from the demands of the state they have abandoned (by not taking part in elections in which expatriate residents can participate, for instance). In this view, much of the political life of Latin American immigrants in the United States is a matter of finding a compromise, balancing between two mutually exclusive polities. To find this balance, immigrants construct a politics in which they have some autonomy of action without making any irrevocable choices.

Pundits of all political persuasions often see a correlation between the absence of sustained immigrant engagement in American politics and their presumed focus on their countries of origin. The reason, they say, we don't see immigrant participation in the United States is that they must be engaged elsewhere, and this engagement siphons away their energies so that they have neither the time nor the inclination for politics in the United States. This ties in well with the transnational perspective outlined above. But the fact is that Latino immigrants are likely to stay away from formal politics in both their countries of origin *and* the United States. Immigrants are no more likely to be involved in formal politics in the home country than they are to be involved in the United States. Given the opportunity to vote in home-country elections, the overwhelming majority stay at home. Staying away from electoral politics in both countries is consistent with an overall policy of avoiding partisanship and controversy — immigrants try not to pick sides.

Immigrant politics might be seen as aggressively *anti*-political, rather than political, but this is only somewhat true. For the most part the "politics of in-between" is expressed most overtly in the space opened by events like parades and festivals, where immigrants can broadcast multiple (and at times seemingly conflicting) identities, without being forced to make choices among them. Parades, for instance, allow immigrant Latinos simultaneously to display signs of their attachments to their hometowns, to their countries of origin, and to the United States and to signal transnational, ethnic, and panethnic ties all at once. (See the description of an Ecuadorian parade in Queens, for instance, in Jones-Correa 1998, chapter 8.) At times, however, when immigrant communities feel under threat, immigrant organizations can use their latent resources for social mobilization, resulting in interventions in the larger public sphere. Often these appearances, for the most part reactive in nature, are triggered by specific issues—concerns about their children's schooling, the quality of life in their neighborhood, or perhaps even broader issues about the erosion of immigrants' rights and benefits. The mobilizations of millions of Latinos in immigrant rallies in dozens of cities across the United States in the spring of 2006 were a dramatic example of this kind of mobilization. Latino immigrants *do* make forays into formal politics. From the outside, immigrant mobilization appears to be sporadic or episodic, but is, in fact, consistent within a framework of a politics of in-between, that is, of avoiding any rupture between their loyalties to their countries of origin and their country of residence.

Again, as with transnationalism, it might be tempting to dismiss immigrant politics as a transitional phenomenon. But there are two reasons why I think this would be mistaken. The first is that the organizations constructed by the second generation both reflect and perpetuate the social networks of the first generation. But more important, I think, is that the attitudes and behaviors of the first generation—their mistrust of formal political institutions and practices—may very well be passed on to their children. I don't think we know very much about immigrant political socialization, but there is the real possibility that the liminality of the first generation is reflected in the subsequent electoral nonparticipation of the second and subsequent generations.

Layered Organizations: Complementary or Competitive?

Each of the forms of Latino politics discussed above—ethnic, transnational, and immigrant—has its own form of social organization. Ethnic politics is often studied through Latino participation in associations like political parties, interest groups, or neighborhood associations or through the behavior and attitudes associated with this participation. Transnational politics is examined through hometown associations, the parties and consulates of sending countries, and role of media, whether print or electronic. Immigrant politics might look at the local associations—religious, civic, social—organized by Latino immigrants in their receiving context. None of these short descriptions is meant to do anything more than trace the outlines of the forms of social organization in these three forms of Latino politics. But it should be clear that studies of these three forms of social organization need not overlap—in fact, each of these three arenas of organizational life might be described as "layered." A focus on ethnic politics might touch hardly at all on the extensive networks of hometown and regional associations that exist in first generation communities; from the perspective of ethnic politics, these organizations are largely invisible or irrelevant. Likewise, for many immigrants engaged in immigrant churches, social clubs, sports organizations, and the like, the structures of American electoral politics are often simply avoided. One could imagine these three organizational layers as alternate social universes. Are they? And are they complementary or competitive?

One of the underlying assumptions among many transnationalists is that transnationalism will continue as long as immigration continues, and so will be continually replenished. The primary assumption of students of ethnic politics is that, ultimately, participation in the institutions and practices of electoral politics is what really drives Latino political life. And finally, those adopting the perspective of immigrant politics see the possibility of continued marginality from both transnational and ethnic politics and the participation of immigrants in a distinct organizational sphere. So, are these approaches mutually exclusive? And are their organizational universes really distinct?

The answers to these questions are most likely "no," but we do not really understand how these three organizational universes overlap or how they might affect one another. At least some scholars have begun to argue that ethnic incorporation and transnationalism should not be seen as opposites and that there are multiple ways that immigrants and their children can combine transnationalism and assimilative strategies, leading to diverse outcomes, both in the United States and immigrants' countries of origin. (See Fouron and Glick Shiller 2003; Levitt and Glick Shiller 2004.) Kasinitz and associates (2003) find that the children of West Indian immigrants who are most engaged in regular transnational practices are also actively participating in New York City politics. Rumbaut finds that homeownership, which in other contexts signals a commitment to settling permanently in the United States, is also correlated, among second generation immigrants, with sending back remittances (2003). This complementarity works the other way too: elsewhere I have argued that the option of dual nationality facilitates acquisition of American citizenship, so that transnationalism in this case leads to political incorporation (Jones-Correa 2001a and 2001b).

These examples, then, point to ethnic incorporation and transnationalism as complementary processes, each having their own social networks, and immigrants can participate in both without contradiction. Neither of these networks contains every immigrant, but because most immigrants are linked to at least some of the individuals in each network, these social networks are able to reach almost the full extent of the immigrant population. Most immigrants are thus at least potentially transnational, even as they are also incorporated into American society. Even quite assimilated second-generation Americans might be tempted at times to reengage in the issues and problems of their ancestral countries and hometowns.

However, the argument for complementarity underplays the extent to which there are real disagreements and tensions among immigrants, and even within immigrant families, regarding both ethnic incorporation and transnationalism. Immigrants disagree, among many other things, on how to raise a family, whether to learn English or retain their language of origin, whether or not to return, and where to focus their energies and commitments. Just as there are some immigrants who feel very strongly about being transnational, there are some who want nothing to do with it. These divisions and disagreements can lead to participation in very different social networks, which not only may not overlap, but also may actually be in competition with one another.[1] Thus, though ethnic incorporation and transnationalism may be going on simultaneously, they are not necessarily complementary. Nor it is the case that these networks are necessarily equally influential. The second generation, in particular, has ties to the broader receiving society through language, education, friendships, work, marriage, and children that their parents may not have. If the children of immigrants are more likely to be engaged in these receiving society networks than in transnational ones, and the processes of transnationalism and assimilation are competitive rather than complementary, then assimilation will eventually drive transnationalism out.

Nor will the continual flow of new immigration necessarily keep transnational practices alive in the second generation and beyond. The presence of a more-established, rapidly assimilating second generation may well result in the more-rapid incorporation of new immigrants rather than resulting in the transnationalization of immigrants already in the United States. On arrival to a new setting, first-generation immigrants set up social networks and organizations, many of which can be described as "transnational." But as this generation ages and the second generation comes into its own, the second generation will create its own networks or take over those of the first.

So, new immigrants coming in will have two options: they can be covered under the organizational umbrella of the second generation or create their own networks. Both alternatives could take place. But given the costs of setting up new organizational networks and the benefits of membership in established networks, older immigrant organizations are likely to be dominant. Future immigrants will not be arriving to an organizational blank slate, but rather to a previously organized social space that will shape and channel their mobilization and incorporation. For examples of how this might play out, we need only look at the situation in Miami after the influx of Cuban refugees—Marielitos and balseros—in the 1980s and 1990s, and at the arrival of Russian Jews to New York City during the same period. In both cases new immigrants were drawn into well-established ethnic communities that played a crucial role in their adaptation and incorporation.

And what happens if there is no continual flow? Second-generation transnationalism was less apparent among immigrants in the previous immigration wave a century ago because of an emphasis on assimilation into American life and values and because any incipient transnationalism was, in any case, curtailed by a number of factors: restrictions in immigration beginning in 1917, the Great Depression and then the Second World War. (See Ueda 2002 on Asian Americans in Hawaii, for instance.) The current immigration wave beginning in the 1960s has arrived to a very different context, when mobilization and display of ethnic and racial identities became part of the accepted repertoire of American politics. However, there is nothing to guarantee that this period of acceptance will continue; indeed, following the destruction of the World Trade Center in September of 2001, there have been some indications that this acceptance has diminished, with a resurgence of an emphasis on "American" identity, restricted movement across borders, and calls for reduced immigration, as evidenced by the very restrictive bills that passed the House of Representatives in 2005 and the somewhat less punitive version that passed the Senate in 2006. How do these shifts in national contexts play out for Latinos, and for the political incorporation of Latino immigrants?

It is a very real possibility that, over time, ethnic politics will eventually drive out transnational politics among Latinos living in the United States. But the devil is in the details, and the landscape of transnational and immigrant politics may have lasting effects on the organizational makeup of Latino ethnic politics. One example I have touched on already is the effect of immigrant socialization on Latino participation in electoral politics: if first-generation immigrants are alienated from formal political institutions in the United States, in the absence of any outside mobilization, isn't there a likelihood their children will be as well? Another example might be the role of hometown associations, often pointed to as the epitome of transnational political organization among Latin American immigrants living in the United States. Historically, there has been little contact between the organizational layers of ethnic and transnational politics. But there are some signs that this may be changing, as umbrella groups of hometown associations seek to have greater contact and influence on Latino elected officials and issues in the United States. Chicago-area hometown associations are a good example of this process. For their part, elected officials are increasingly eager to tap into the organizational membership and resources of hometown associations. Because of the relative absence of well-organized grassroots actors in Latino politics, it may be that "transnational" hometown associations will end up playing a critical role over the longer run in Latino ethnic politics. But this remains to be seen.

Conclusions

This essay suggests, first of all, that there actually three dimensions to Latino politics (ethnic, transnational, and immigrant), second, that these three dimensions are likely to be persistent (in some form and among some subsets of the population), and third, that these three dimensions interact with one another and are likely to continue doing so into the foreseeable future.

If we accept these suggestions, then three conclusions naturally follow:

- Given the demographic make up of the Latino population in the United States today, we cannot pretend to understand Latino politics only through the study of electoral politics. Ethnic politics is a necessary but not sufficient component of the study of Latino politics as a whole. Much of the current study of Latino politics focuses on Latinos as assimilated immigrants and racial minorities, to the detriment of any understanding of their transnational and immigrant dimensions. We need research in all three areas to grasp the full complexity of Latino politics in the United States.
- To appreciate the complexity of Latino politics, scholars also need to better understand how these three dimensions of ethnic, transnational, and immigrant politics interact and influence one another. If initially these three dimensions are somewhat separate, over time their boundaries blur. In short, the importance of these interactions is only likely to increase with the passage of time.
- The historical assumption has been that immigrant and transnational politics eventually, and inevitably, lead to ethnic politics. But this probably is not true, at least in any simplistic way. Apart from the fact that facets of transnational and immigrant politics are likely to continue, it is far from clear that there is only a single kind of ethnic politics. More probably, ethnic politics takes different shapes and forms at different times and among different groups. But if so, why? It is also the case that there are probably alternative pathways of mobilization and participation. Among these are some that might lead Latinos to nonethnic, non-Latino forms of political mobilization. Labor union politics, or religious mobilization might be examples of these (though they might also be examples of the different forms ethnic politics can take).

Note

1. "Competition" here may be direct, be driven by ideological or other disagreements, or simply be the result of competition over scarce resources, like time or money. Given the scarcity of resources, the second generation may only be able to commit to one network or the other, or may only be able to commit to them both unequally.

PART 2

Latino Political Action

The Role of Latino Candidates in Mobilizing Latino Voters

Revisiting Latino Vote Choice

Matt A. Barreto

A T LEAST SINCE Robert Dahl's seminal theory of ethnic politics (1961), scholars of minority politics have wondered what effect ethnicity has on political
behavior. Distinct from Dahl's research on "ethnic politics," research on race was
prominent among political scientists interested in the African American political incorporation. Harold Gosnell (1935), Gunnar Myrdal (1944), and V. O. Key (1949)
all investigated the extent to which African American political participation differed
from whites and noted that race was an important variable to consider. While research on African American voting trends finds that race can matter, work on Latino voting has generally not found this to be the case. This essay seeks to provide
an answer to the question of whether or not ethnic identification influences Latino
voting behavior. Specifically, does the presence of Latino candidates mobilize the
Latino electorate, resulting in strong support for the coethnic candidate?

In 2001, 2003, and 2005 mayoral elections in several of the nation's largest
cities witnessed Latino candidates running vigorous and competitive campaigns
that seemed to generate political excitement among Latino voters. In New York,
Los Angeles, Miami, Houston, Denver, San Francisco, and San Antonio high-
profile Latino candidates for mayor made headlines by running strong campaigns.
In the fall of 2002, viable Latino candidates were garnering national media attention in the New Mexico and Texas governors' races. Elsewhere, Latino candidates
surfaced in mayoral elections in Bloomington, Indiana, and Las Vegas, Nevada,
and for the first time Latinos were elected to city councils in Georgia and others

to state legislatures in North Carolina and North Dakota. Nationwide, the National Association of Latino Elected Officials (NALEO) reported that nearly one thousand more Latinos hold public office now than ten years ago. Simply stated, cities and states across the nation are witnessing both an increase in Latinos candidates and an increase in Latino electoral success. While the rise in Latino candidates might be seen as the inevitable consequence of gains in Latino population, Latino candidates allow a political environment to surface that may result in higher rates of voting and strong support for Latino candidates by Latino voters, a proposition that was previously untestable. The aim of this work is not to explain the success of Latino candidates for office,[1] but rather, to examine what influence these candidates have on the voting behavior of Latino voters.

As evidenced by Biliana Ambrecht and Harry Pachón (1974) and John Garcia and Rodolfo de la Garza (1985), previous research on Latino political behavior has played down the role of shared ethnicity. Attempts to understand the comparatively lower rates of turnout among Latinos have often focused on lower levels of resources (DeSipio 1996), and lower levels of civic skills (Verba, Scholzman, and Brady 1995) leaving much room for improvement in explaining the Latino vote. This essay presents two improvements in modeling Latino political behavior: (1) accounting for the presence of Latino candidates; and (2) introducing a measure of ethnic identification. *I argue that the electoral context surrounding the campaigns of Latino candidates is a mobilizing factor that leads to strong levels of support for the coethnic candidate.*[2] Further, this effect should hold after controlling for standard predictors of political participation as well as for election-specific issues.[3] Thus, my basic argument rests on two theories: first, ethnic candidates increase the level of psychological engagement and interest in the election among ethnic voters (Tate 1993, 2003; Garcia and Arce 1988) and second, ethnic candidates direct more resources to mobilize voters in ethnic communities (Leighley 2001). While not all ethnic candidates are publicly running "ethnic campaigns," for those who are, the argument is quite clear and for those who aren't, it is still likely that their campaigns will reach out to minority voters and that their candidacy will resonate with some minority voters.

However, the effect may not be the same for all Latino voters, and therefore it is necessary to include a measure of the degree of ethnic identification. Building on theories of minority empowerment and racial incorporation, I make the case that for Latino voters with high levels of ethnic identification, coethnic candidates increase their level of political awareness and interest in the election, increase the opportunity to be contacted and asked to vote, generate a sense of psychological engagement with the political system, and strengthen feelings of shared group consciousness (e.g., Uhlaner 1989; Leighley 2001)

FIGURE 4.1
Shared ethnicity model of Latino political behavior

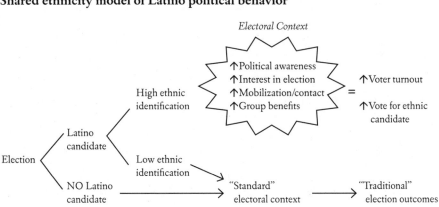

While a handful of studies have examined the connection between ethnicity and political participation, they have repeatedly concluded that no direct link exists for Latino voters. In articles published in *Social Science Quarterly*, Cain and Kiewiet (1984) and Graves and Lee (2000) both show that in explaining candidate preference, partisanship—not ethnicity—is the deciding factor for Latinos, and in his book, *Counting on the Latino Vote*, Louis DeSipio observes that, "ethnicity will come to play less of a role in [Latino] political decision-making than will other societal divisions" (1996). The project proposed here is important in that (1) it brings a variety of new, experimental evidence to bear on this question, and (2) it provides an alternative mechanism for measuring ethnic identification that better captures the effect of shared ethnicity.

Ethnic Identification and Latino Voting

Before undertaking this analysis, the case must be made why Latinos might have a sense of shared ethnic identity, and second, why ethnicity is more likely to matter in future elections. While an individual may have multiple identities, there often exists a group of people with whom an individual may share many identities, such as language, cultural practices, religion, and race. "Peoplehood" then is roughly "coterminous with a given rural land space; political government, no matter how rudimentary, a common culture in which a principal element was a set of religious beliefs and values shared more or less uniformly by all members of the group, and a common racial background ensuring an absence of wide differences in physical type" (Gordon 1964). This sense of peoplehood is best described as the individual's ethnicity (from the Greek *ethnos,* meaning "people") that may encompass his or her race, religion, national origin, language, and more. Although ethnic identity is fluid, a society may develop seemingly fixed categories for identification that serve to reinforce each identity as separate and unique and that reinforce group members' attachment to their ethnic identity. As Will Herberg notes, "The way in which one identifies and locates oneself ('Who, what, am I?') is closely related to how one is identified and located in the larger community ('Who, what, is he?')" (1955). The social constructions of group identification, whether real or not, guide individuals to take their place in a group and act as a member of the group. The extent to which they act congruently on political issues is the question being considered here.

For Latinos, there are four characteristics that are common to all Hispanic Americans regardless of their background: Latin American heritage, the immigrant experience, Spanish language, and Spanish colonial influence. These four traits are stronger for some Latinos than others and may be altogether dormant at times, but their existence cannot be easily refuted. Building on these four components, an additional component, ethnic discrimination, augments the relationship of these characteristics and may bring Latinos together when one of these components of ethnic identity is culturally under attack. With this in mind, the shared ethnic identification argument can be made that provides the foundation for this essay, that is, ethnicity is an important component of Latino political behavior. Further, given the decline of party control over campaigns and candidate centered elections (Wattenberg 1994), a growing interest in candidate qualities over issues (Popkin 1991), and the reliance on ethnic-based outreach and mobilization by candidates of both major parties (Segal 2003), it may not be surprising that ethnic identification is now salient.

This research builds on the theories advanced by Carole Uhlaner (1989), Jan Leighley (2001), and Lawrence Bobo and Frank Gilliam (1990), among others. Uhlaner refines a theory of group relations to demonstrate that political participation is rational, despite high costs, because in-group members receive additional benefits from a sense of shared group consciousness. She argues that groups with more unified support for a candidate or issue have a stronger sense of group identity, which they can use as a bargaining chip to collect additional in-group benefits. Leighley proposes a new model for examining Latino and African American political participation that takes into account the shared group consciousness, minority empowerment, and geographic racial context to improve on traditional socioeconomic models. In particular, she makes the argument that ethnic candidates direct more resources to mobilizing ethnic communities and deserve more attention in understanding Latino voting behavior.

According to Bobo and Gilliam, minority elected officials empower minority communities, resulting in higher levels of voting and block voting. In particular, African American mayors are found to empower African American voters through feelings of shared group consciousness and in-group benefits. I expand this to Latino voters and Latino mayors to test whether or not the effect is the same. More important, Bobo and Gilliam provide a framework that envisions minority candidates and office holders as instrumental in explaining minority participation. Finally, from a practical perspective, Lionel Sosa, a media consultant and presidential campaign adviser, notes that in his experience conducting focus groups and targeting Latino voters, positive ethnic identification with the candidate is an important factor. Specifically, Sosa argues that, "issues also work, but only *after* Hispanic voters like and trust the candidate" (emphasis in original, 2004).

Beyond the inclusion of two new and interesting data sets, I also propose an alternative mechanism for measuring shared ethnicity that may account for its lack of relevance in previous research. Earlier attempts to include ethnicity in a model of Latino political behavior considered it to be an all or nothing issue in which all Latinos are considered to have the same level of ethnic identification. Instead, this project proposes a sliding scale, similar to the measure of party identification, that place Latinos on a spectrum from low to high levels of ethnic identification. This scale should include both direct and indirect measures of ethnic identification. With a more accurate assessment of their degree of shared ethnicity, it becomes clear that for Latinos with higher levels of ethnic identification, ethnicity does play a central role in their political decision making.

The data employed here are from two recent public opinion surveys of Latino registered voters. The first is a survey conducted by the Latino Issues Forum (LIF) in 2000 regarding vote choice among hypothetical candidates (one Latino, one non-Latino) and the second is a Tomás Rivera Policy Institute (TRPI) survey from 2002 for California and New York, which explores cross-over voting tendencies among Latinos. My argument is that after controlling for partisanship and issue preference, ethnic attachment will lead Latino voters to support an ethnic candidate, even across party lines.

The Argument

During the 1990s, the Latino electorate grew faster than any other segment of American voters. Increasing from 3.7 million in 1988 to 5.9 million in 2000, Latino voters received national media attention and were courted heavily by both parties in the 2000 presidential election. While Latinos have generally favored Democratic candidates, scholars and pundits have characterized the Latino community as heterogeneous and fluid as an electorate (Pachón 1999). As stated above, earlier efforts to test the connection between ethnicity and vote choice for Latinos have found partisanship to be an intervening variable of greater weight, leading scholars to conclude that ethnicity has only an indirect effect (Cain and Kiewiet 1984; Graves and Lee 2000). That is, ethnicity predicts party identification, which predicts vote choice, but no direct tie between ethnicity and candidate preference is said to exist. Recognizing areas of difference on policy issues among Latino voters, I nonetheless argue that ethnic identity unites them, both explicitly and implicitly.

I argue that three trends have made it possible for ethnicity to persist as a central component of Latino politics in the twenty-first century. First, the Latino community has witnessed an increase in ethnic-based discrimination, making it more likely that ethnicity will have a distinct influence on the political behavior of Latinos. Anti-immigrant ballot measures, the rollback of affirmative action, and attacks on bilingual education have alienated and angered Latino voters in many states (Ramírez 2002b; García-Bedolla 2000; Pachón 1998; Segura et al. 1997). What's more, public opinion data suggests that Latinos are increasingly feeling like targets of ethnic discrimination.[4] Second, the number of viable Latino candidates for public office has increased dramatically over the past decade (Hero et al. 2000; Pachón and DeSipio 1991), creating the *opportunity* for ethnic identity to emerge in the political sphere. Third, rapid growth in naturalization, registration, and voter turnout among Latinos has given legitimacy to the size and significance of the Latino electorate (Sierra et al. 2000). The convergence of these three trends during the past ten years has produced an environment where ethnic attachment may remain a principal component of the Latino vote.

Because the survey data presented here is based on experimental design and not on a national sample, actual election results from across the country were gathered and examined that support the primary finding in this essay. This evidence comes from four large city mayoral elections in 2001. Los Angeles, Houston, Miami, and New York all had viable Latino candidates running for office in nonpartisan elections. The summary results presented in table 4.1 detail the percentage of the Latino vote won by the Latino candidates according to exit polls.

Los Angeles is interesting because Latino candidates of somewhat differing ideologies—liberal mayoral contender Antonio Villaraigosa and politically moderate city attorney candidate Rocky Delgadillo—both captured over 80 percent of the Latino vote. In Houston, the Cuban-born candidate Orlando Sanchez, a registered Republican, received over 70 percent of the Latino vote from the predominantly Mexican American community with ties to the Democratic Party. In Miami, second-generation Cuban American Manny Diaz emphasized his strong ties

TABLE 4.1
Latino candidate preference nationwide in 2001 mayoral elections

City →	Los Angeles	Houston	New York	Miami
Candidate →	Villaraigosa	Sanchez	Ferrer	Diaz
% Latino vote	82%	72%	84%	70%

Source: *Los Angeles Times, Houston Chronicle, New York Times, Miami Herald* exit polls, 2001

to the Cuban community and also won over 70 percent of the Latino vote despite being a registered Democrat in a community where most Latino voters are loyal Republicans. In New York City, Puerto Rican candidate Freddy Ferrer garnered over 80 percent of the diverse Latino vote, bringing together Puerto Rican, Dominican, Colombian, and Mexican American segments of the Latino community in New York in the Democratic primary. Each of these four elections represents an instance in which ethnic identity seemed to play a primary role in candidate preference.

Voting Preference Models

In an information-rich environment, voters are able to identify the policy platforms of all candidates and pick the one who best represents their own political interests. In the model, a set of candidates can be placed at various points along an ideological spectrum and people are expected to vote for the candidate who is closest to their personal views. The first modern application of this spectrum can be found in Harold Hotelling's 1929 economic analysis of business competition. Adapting this model to politics, Hotelling examined political parties to explain why Democrats and Republicans often align themselves near the center of the left-right spectrum to attract votes. Later, Anthony Downs, in his classic work, *An Economic Theory of Democracy,* expanded this model of one-dimensional political competition, arguing that voters have ordered and stable preferences that allow them to be placed on a one-dimensional issue spectrum. In fact, Downs conceptualizes a "linear scale running from zero to 100 in the usual left-right fashion," and "assume[s] that the political preferences can be ordered from left to right in a manner agreed upon by all voters" (1957, 115). These early attempts to describe voter preference characterize voters as rational decisionmakers, for whom issue positions served as the key determinant of their vote choice.

Scholars also contend that partisanship is a critical predictor of vote choice (Campbell et al. 1960). Similar to issue position, this theory suggests that voters will sometimes overlook misaligned issues and support the candidate of their same party. At least since the *American Voter,* this theory has been accepted, and party identification continues to be one of the best indicators of vote preference today. However, some research suggests that a voter's partisanship may not be as "stable" as previously thought and that the role of the party is on the decline. Kent Tedin and Richard Murray (1981) argue that voters can be persuaded by campaign appeals and that the media's focus on *candidate characteristics* does matter. Additional support for candidate-centered elections comes from Martin Wattenberg (1994) and Alan Abramowitz (1989), who argue that voters pay attention to candidates, not parties. Despite differences in conclusions, both scholars reveal that voters are paying more attention to candidates these days, providing an opportunity for the race and ethnicity of the candidate to play a central role. With regard to minority voters, Abramowitz finds such strong support for Jesse Jackson among African Americans (as does Tate 1993) that they do not conform to his other theories of vote preference. The same may be true for Latino voters.

Candidates seek to capitalize on voter calculations of personality and symbolism. Popkin (1991) has argued that savvy candidates know the importance of symbolic politics and will often make religious, racial, and ethnic appeals during campaigns. Popkin extends Dahl's theory of "ethnic politics," which found immigrant communities beleaguered by home-country campaign appeals in Italian and Irish boroughs as far back as 1900. Popkin was writing in the 1990s when he noted that campaign strategists will have their candidate photographed eating tamales in Mexican American communities to gain support of Latino voters, then Governor George W. Bush and Vice President Al Gore must have read his book before the 2000 presidential election, because both candidates spent millions of dollars on Spanish-language advertising and tried to one-up each other in wooing Latino voters. Al Gore, for example, boldly stated, "My first grandson was born on the Fourth of July, and I hope that my next is born on *Cinco de Mayo,*" before a crowd of Latinos in Denver.[5]

The reason non-Hispanic candidates take such actions is because voters may rely on such demographic characteristics of candidates as their race, ethnicity, gender, religion, or social origin as "information shortcuts" in estimating the policy stands of competing candidates. Similarly, Tate draws our attention to the power of shared ethnicity between office holders and voters in her analysis of the evaluations African Americans provide of their representatives in the U.S. Congress. Comparing politics to athletics Tate asks, "is the race of the players salient and important to the many Black spectators in the stands?" (2003, 20). She finds the racial group membership of the legislators matters and that it is one of the most important factors in candidate evaluations along with party identification. As Popkin aptly notes, voters may be more likely to head to the polls wondering, "How does he look to me lately?" rather than "What has he done for me lately?" (1991).

Latino Political Behavior

While there has been some growth in the number of articles investigating Latino political behavior, relatively few have dealt directly with candidate preference. Most studies of Latino politics continue to focus on the perceived low levels of participation among Latinos vis-à-vis non-Latino voters (Garcia and Arce 1988; Hero 1992; de la Garza, Menchaca, and DeSipio 1994; Verba, Schlozman, and Brady 1995; DeSipio 1996; Arvizu and Garcia 1996; Shaw, de la Garza, and Lee 2000; Pantoja et al. 2001; Cassel 2002;). However, a handful a studies do exist that specifically address theories of Latino vote choice and candidate preference that are important in guiding this argument. First, DeSipio (1996) contends that while ethnicity was found to have no statistically significant effect in his model of vote choice, there is the chance that it could emerge under "unique circumstances" or in response to "ethnic-based discrimination." Based on the findings of existing data sets at the time, he concludes that such a scenario is unlikely as Latinos achieve greater assimilation into society.

More recently, Graves and Lee (2000) tackle this question in their examination of voting preference in the 1996 Senate election in Texas. Previously, Cain and Kiewiet (1984) examined the relationship between ethnicity, issue positions, and candidate evaluations in a 1982 congressional election in Los Angeles. Despite evidence of distinct patterns of voting behavior by Latinos in the voting rights literature (Engstrom and Brischetto 1997; Engstrom 1992; Grofman and Handley 1989; Grofman 1993), aside from these two studies, little empirical attention has been directed toward theories of ethnic voting among Latinos in academic journal articles.

Graves and Lee find that ethnicity did play a key role in the Morales-Gramm 1996 Senate election in Texas, but that its influence was mediated by partisanship. Building on the theories advanced by Donald Kinder and David Sears (1985), they argue that ethnicity influences the primary determinants of vote choice such as partisanship, issue positions, and candidate evaluations, but not vote choice outright. Latino identity may influence the "manner in which individuals are brought into and engage the political system," because it places them in a particular social and cultural milieu that shapes their worldview (Graves and Lee 2000, 229). Their findings go far to support these claims. While being Latino is not a significant predictor of candidate evaluation, it is significant in models accounting for partisanship and issue position. In the final model predicting vote choice, Latinos do not behave significantly different from Anglos, but partisanship is the best predictor of vote preference for Morales, and being Latino is the best predictor of Democratic partisanship. Thus, Graves and Lee conclude that "ethnicity exerts a substantial *indirect* influence on voting preference," for Latinos (2000, 234).

Much of what Graves and Lee posit and find is based on a similar analysis conducted by Cain and Kiewiet (1984). In their earlier study of Mexican American voting preference, Cain and Kiewiet find that ethnicity is associated with party identification and perceptions about the candidates, but not directly with vote choice. Controlling for party identification, they found no statistical support that ethnicity affects vote choice. While both of these analyses point to a role for ethnicity in the political behavior of Latinos, they ultimately rely on traditional models of vote choice, where partisanship, issue position, and candidate evaluation take center stage (Aldrich, Sullivan, and Borgida 1989).

This is consistent then with DeSipio's (1996) argument that conventional predictors of participation and behavior are important in understanding Latino voting and that ethnicity may play only a minor role. However, both previous studies examined voting preference in a general election that pitted a Latino Democrat against an Anglo Republican. Because of this scenario and historic ties to the Democratic Party among Latinos, it is natural to expect Latino voters to prefer a Latino Democratic candidate in a general election of this nature. However, the stakes might be different in nonpartisan or primary elections where partisanship is less relevant, or in an election where the Latino candidate is a Republican.

While previous studies have speculated that ethnicity is "all or nothing," it more likely has varying degrees of salience for voters (similar to partisan strength). Thus, while all Latinos may not share a strong attachment to their ethnicity, for those who do, ethnicity is likely to be the guiding force in their political behavior, equal to or possibly surpassing traditional factors, such as issue position and party identification, that may explain vote preference. More specifically, in an election with a Latino candidate of an opposing party or with some inconsistent policy positions, shared ethnicity may propel some Latinos to choose ethnicity over party or policy.

Measuring Shared Ethnic Identity

With a total of more than 35 million people, Latinos surpassed African Americans as the largest minority group in the United States in 2000. However, many political analysts argue that they do not have the same strength in numbers that the African

American community has. They say they lack an equally strong collective sense of ethnic identity because their ancestry is rooted in more than twenty countries. While national origin may remain important, there are two reasons why shared group or pan-Latino identity might play a significant role in the political behavior of Latinos. First, overlapping ethnic and cultural bonds exist that unite Latinos and allow for a shared ethnic identity to emerge. Second, national origin groups tend to be geographically segregated in the United States, making the pan-Latino identity less politically vital in elections where, for example, a Mexican American candidate is running for office. With respect to California, Pachón concludes in a series of articles that ethnic identity has increased, emerging as a mobilizing force in the political participation of Latinos (Pachón 1998, 1999; Pachón, Barreto, Marquez 2004).

However, we should not proceed from the assumption that ethnic identification is equally strong among all Latinos. In fact, the main objective of this essay is to provide a range of ethnic identification for Latinos and to determine if those with high degrees of ethnic attachment are more likely to vote along ethnic lines. With this in mind, it is possible to identify the roots of a shared ethnic experience among Latinos.

Shared group identity for Latinos is strongest at the national origin and generation level, but this does not preclude a shared identity across these boundaries (García-Bedolla 2000). There are four characteristics that are common to all Hispanic Americans regardless of their background: Latin American heritage, the immigrant experience, Spanish language, and Spanish colonial influence.[6] While some Latinos are more strongly connected to these traits than others, they do provide a common background for Latinos of all ancestry.

While there are distinct differences between Latinos of Mexican, Puerto Rican, Cuban, Dominican, and Colombian ancestry, they do share a common Latin American heritage that brings them together (Padilla 1985b). First and foremost, all Latinos (minus the small percentage from Spain), can trace their ancestry to Spanish America. The North, Central, and South American territories occupied by Spain provide a shared homeland for all Latinos living in the United States. With this, comes a common cultural heritage. Setting aside linguistic ties, important cultural, religious, and social similarities exist throughout Latin America that provide Latinos of different national origins with a common point of reference. The strong role of the family, in particular as it relates to holiday and family traditions, is shared throughout Latin America (Moore and Pachón 1985; Williams 1990; Santiago and Davidow 1998). Catholicism and its practices are still overwhelmingly supported and followed (by a two-to-one margin), and the community is often embraced ahead of the individual. While differences exist from country to county, in the United States the shared aspects of Latin American heritage are highlighted for Latinos living as a minority in an Anglo-Protestant environment.

Building on Latin American heritage, the immigrant experience is a second characteristic common across different Hispanic national origin groups (Portes and Rumbaut 2001). According to the 2000 Census, 44 percent of all Latinos were born in Latin America and migrated north to the United States, and an additional 30 percent have parents who were foreign born. Thus, three-quarters of the Latino population closely share this immigrant experience and the social and cultural issues that accompany it. Of the remaining segment of the Latino population, about 15 percent have immigrant grandparents, leaving only about 10 percent of Latinos without an immediate family connection to the immigrant experience.

As Michael Jones-Correa (1998) notes, immigrant families confront unique challenges in their interaction with the public sphere and rely on immigrant-based networks within their community for assistance. Whether facing challenges related to naturalization, visa status, employment, housing, access to health care, or public education, the common experiences and struggles of immigrants provide bridges for Latinos of different nationalities (Portes and Rumbaut 1996).

A strong part of the immigrant experience that also unites Latinos is language. Regardless of the country of ancestry, Spanish provides a collective communication resource for the Latino community. While not all Latinos are completely fluent in Spanish, a recent nationwide survey by the Kaiser Foundation (2000) found that only 5 percent of Latinos speak no Spanish at all, and nearly nine of ten Latinos speak and understand Spanish well. With the numeric growth of the Latino community, Spanish media outlets have become important advertising venues for Latino and non-Latino candidates for public office.

The final pan-Latino characteristic is perhaps the most difficult to identify because it is the least tangible. The Spanish colonial experience is important nonetheless because it represents an underlying psychological attitude within the Latino community. While Spanish colonial occupation has a history of almost two centuries (one century for Puerto Rico and Cuba), it left a lasting legacy of domination, oppression, struggle, and liberation. For two hundred years, Spanish occupation led to constant conflict between the colonizer and the colonized. Descendants of Spain's empire in Latin America, the Southwest, and the Caribbean have been victim to savage conquest and domination and had to fight for freedom and respect. While hard to pinpoint, shared historical traits are considered important components of shared identity among minority groups (Linz and Stepan 1996; Robinson 1999).[7] Just as there is an enduring "American spirit" 225 years after the Revolutionary War, the Spanish colonial influence is still present, to some degree, among Latinos.

While these four characteristics provide a basis for a shared ethnic identity, perceived discrimination against the group can strengthen and solidify the group identity (Dawson 1994; Tate 1993). Discrimination against the Latino community has come in both structural and attitudinal varieties. While the legal discrimination is not as widespread or severe as against African Americans during the post-construction and pre-civil rights eras, discrimination has and does exist based on language and immigration rights (e.g., Propositions 187, 227 in California). In addition, attitudinal discrimination against Latinos has existed for many years. Latin American immigrants have been blamed for job loss and economic problems and considered a drain on social welfare programs. Latinos are often associated with drug trafficking, crime, gangs, and the general deterioration of inner cities. With these stereotypes has come discrimination in the workplace, in public schools, and in the political arena (e.g., gerrymandering and polarized voting).

As anticipated, Latinos perceive group-based discrimination. In the National Survey on Latinos in America, 82 percent of Latinos responded that discrimination against "Latinos" is a problem in society (Kaiser Foundation 2000). Further, when asked if they or their family had personally experienced discrimination because of their ethnicity, a large plurality Latinos reported that they had. While the 40 percent figure for Latinos is lower than the 54 percent of African Americans who have felt discrimination, it is considerably higher the 14 percent of whites who claim to have experienced discrimination. Thus, based on the four characteristics described here and coupled with perceptions of ethnic-based discrimination, we can say that the ingredients for pan-Latino identity exist. Evidence of this can be found again in the National Survey of Latinos in America, where 84 percent of respondents reported that all Latinos would be better off if various Latino groups worked together politically (Kaiser 2000).

Michael Dawson has called this connection between race and identity "linked fate" and argues that it is an important heuristic for the political participation of African Americans (1994). The main contention of the "black utility heuristic is that the more one believes one's own life chances are linked to those of blacks as a group, the more one will consider racial group interests in evaluating alternative policy choice . . . [and] evaluating candidates and parties" (1994, 75). Similarly, studies of Latino politics can be improved by borrowing Dawson's notion of linked fate as it relates to decision-making shortcuts in the political arena. Latinos who tie their self-interest to ethnic group interests should be expected to use ethnicity as a heuristic device when they find themselves in the polling booth deciding between Hernandez and Smith. Dawson concurs that a strong sense of ethnic identity goes far to influence political behavior of minorities, calling this group consciousness the "political building blocks for analyzing perceptions of racial group interests," such as party and candidate preference (1994, 84).

Based on these underlying beliefs, contextual factors, campaign tactics, and issue salience are the key forces behind a collective Latino identity and, hence, a central component in the vote choice of Latinos. Coupled with a high sense of ethnic attachment, notions of political underrepresentation may drive Latinos to follow ethnic cues when voting, rather than issue alignment. DeSipio maintains that for ethnicity to become a salient mobilizing force, a link beyond just culture must exist to unite Latinos politically (1996). While he points to a distinct perspective on policy issues, the presence of a viable Latino candidate may also be one such condition. Given the preceding discussion on vote choice and the role of ethnicity in elections, there are competing theories of candidate preference: the influence of issues/partisanship vs. the influence of ethnic identity. Thus, we can test the following hypothesis:

H_1: Controlling for party identification and issue preference, the level of ethnic attachment of Latino voters will increase the probability of supporting a Latino candidate

Data and Methodology

Using registered voters as the unit of analysis, I test whether or not Latino identity is an important predictor of vote choice. Survey data collected in California[8] by the Latino Issues Forum (LIF) in 2000 and in California and New York by the Tomás Rivera Policy Institute (TRPI) in 2002 permit the examination of whether or not Latino voters having a strong "ethnic identity" prefer coethnic candidates or whether issue position and partisanship dictate candidate preference.

Specifically, the LIF 2000 survey offered respondents the chance to "vote" in a hypothetical election between "Smith" and "Hernandez." Respondents were informed of each candidate's stance on the issues, with Smith portrayed as a traditional Democrat and Hernandez as a traditional Republican, without party labels being given.[9] The absence of party labels corresponds to nonpartisan local elections typical in most states. In addition, because issue positions were given for each candidate, it provides an optimal environment to test the classic Downsian model that voters prefer the candidate who is spatially closest to their preferences (Downs 1957). The TRPI 2002 data asked partisan identifiers how they would vote in an election that pitted a non-Latino partisan versus a Latino nonpartisan to assess the probability of cross-over voting when Latino candidates are present. While no information about the candidates was given, more than a quarter of all respondents immediately picked the Latino nonpartisan over a non-Latino party member.

The LIF survey was conducted in February 2000 before California's presidential primary election on March 2, 2000, and interviewed 750 Latino registered voters (Arteaga 2000). The TRPI survey was conducted in October 2002, before the November 2002 midterm elections in California and New York. Although many surveys have recently been conducted of Latino voters, these data are unique, because they asked registered voters to decide in a hypothetical election between a Latino and non-Latino candidate.

Rather than giving party cues, the LIF survey described the platforms of each candidate, allowing voters to decide based on the issues. Given that most Latinos are registered with the Democratic Party (Cain, Kiewiet, and Uhlaner 1991), LIF offered the challenge of a Latino-surname candidate with a Republican-oriented platform versus an Anglo-surname candidate with a Democratic-oriented platform. This method provided an optimal environment to test whether issues and partisanship or ethnic identity influenced Latino candidate preference. The anti-immigrant, anti-Latino ballot measures in California endorsed by the Republican Party drove Latino voters away from the GOP and into the waiting arms of the Democrats. What's more, because the issue platforms of each candidate were provided, it meets Downs's hypothetical example of perfect information. If Downs's thesis is correct, voters will align themselves with the candidate with which they share common issue positions, regardless of race or ethnicity.

The TRPI survey asked each registered voter which party they were registered with and, among independents, which party they were closer to. Then, after determining the partisanship of each voter, it asked them a follow-up question to get to the heart of the debate on partisanship versus ethnicity. For Democrats, it asked, "In an election between a non-Latino Democrat and a Latino Republican, which candidate would you prefer?" and vice versa for Republicans. While the LIF survey purposely does not cue partisanship, the TRPI survey does, and together, the data provide a complete portrait of Latino vote choice and the role of ethnic candidates.

Ordered-probit and probit regression techniques are employed to accurately predict the trichotomous and dichotomous dependent variables. Postestimation analysis is offered to assess the changes in predicted probability of a vote for the coethnic candidate (Long 1997; Long and Freese 2001).

Dependent Variables

This research seeks to uncover the reasons why Latino voters might prefer one candidate over another, given that one of the candidates is Latino. The LIF survey specifically asked respondents to pick which statement about two candidates for public office came closer to their views:

A. Smith says state and local governments can do a great deal to improve the quality of life for Latinos in California. Smith believes in HMO reforms, improving public education and providing more affordable housing.

B. Hernandez says state and local governments have too much power to regulate individuals and community life for Latinos in California. Hernandez believes in traditional family values, reducing taxes and increasing job opportunities and reducing crime.

Respondents gave a range of five answers to this question: Smith, Hernandez, neither, combination, and don't know.[10] The answers were sorted in two ways, yielding the two dependent variables analyzed here. First, those voters who said "neither," "combination," or "don't know" were grouped together as an "undecided" category (representing about 28 percent of the sample). Second, voters who did not state a preference for either Smith or Hernandez were dropped, and only those with a clear preference for one candidate or the other were analyzed.

Because a large number of respondents — more than a quarter — fall into a category without clearly stated preferences, I kept them in the analysis. Before an election, it is not surprising to find a segment of the electorate still undecided or torn between two candidates. Thus, these undecided respondents represent a real portion of the electorate common to American elections.[11] However, because the undecided respondents have not articulated a clear preference, they may be blurring the results. Since we are interested in candidate preference, and ultimately voters will have to choose between only two options (or abstain), the second dependent variable includes only those who indicated a preference for Smith (0) or Hernandez (1). In short, both models produce the same results with regard to the key independent variables of policy preferences and ethnic attachment.

The TRPI data yield almost the same dependent variables, with respondents being asked to choose between a Latino nonpartisan and a non-Latino copartisan.[12] Republicans were asked who they would prefer in an election between a Latino Democrat and a non-Latino Republican, while Democrats were asked the inverse: who would they prefer in an election between a Latino Republican and a non-Latino Democrat. As with the LIF survey, many voters responded that they were unsure, and two variables were created similar to above, with a trichotomous measure leaving undecided voters in the model (at the midpoint) and a second dichotomous variable that only examines voters with a stated preference.

The Findings

Three general themes are apparent after examining the results of the data analysis. First, policy preferences do matter in determining candidate preferences. Second, ethnic attachment is an important determinant of vote choice among Latinos. And third, a latent predisposition for the coethnic candidate exists among Latino voters that cannot be explained by self-reported ethnic attachment or policy preferences. Before exploring the first two themes in the multivariate probit analysis, I briefly review the survey results with respect to the underlying preference for the Latino candidate.

Generally, there was modest support for cross-over voting in the TRPI survey, as evidenced in table 4.2. Overall, 26 percent of the sample indicated that they would vote for a Latino of the opposing party instead of a non-Latino party member. Given that no information was provided about the potential candidates, this estimate seems high and lends support for the hypothesis that Latino candidates can attract Latino votes independent of their partisanship. As a point of comparison, the TRPI survey also asked respondents how they planned to vote in their coming congressional elections. By matching the voter's party ID to their stated vote preference in the congressional election, we can examine what effect the Latino candidate has on changing vote preference. Table 4.2 reports the results for both the congressional election and the hypothetical cross-over election and tabulates the differences. For the congressional election, 84 percent of respondents picked the candidate of their party, 8 percent were undecided, and 8 percent crossed over. In the example featuring a Latino candidate, only 40 percent chose the candidate of their same party, 34 percent were undecided, and 26 percent favored the cross-over Latino candidate. Not only does the presence of a Latino candidate immediately command cross-over appeal, but it also creates more uncertainty in the electorate, suggesting that even more voters might vote for the Latino candidate if more infor-

TABLE 4.2
Impact of Latino candidate on cross-over voting

	Partisan	*Undecided*	*Crossover*
How vote for Congress	84	8	8
Vote w/ Latino candidate	40	34	26
Difference	−44	26	18
Percent difference	−52%	325%	225%

Source: Tomás Rivera Policy Institute survey of Latino voters in CA and NY, 2002

TABLE 4.3
Issue preference and candidate preference

| | Candidate preference | | | |
Issue variables	Smith	Undecided	Hernandez	(n)
Overall sample	25	28	48	750
Reduce crime	25	28	47	678
Family values	22	28	50	638
Public education	26	28	47	687
Affordable housing	25	29	46	516
Democratic voter	28	23	48	333
Republican voter	27	22	52	155

Source: Latino Issues Forum survey of Latino voters in California, 2000

mation was provided. No immediate party difference was recognizable with both Democrats and Republicans willing to cross over at the same rate (26 percent).

These descriptive results are consistent with the LIF survey, where Latino voters preferred Hernandez over Smith by a two-to-one margin. Overall, 48 percent of voters picked Hernandez, 25 percent picked Smith, and 28 percent were undecided between the two. Democrats and Republicans alike preferred the more conservative Latino over the more liberal non-Latino. Table 4.3 provides a number of detailed breakdowns of vote choice by issue position and partisanship. In addition to these characteristics, the survey directly asked Latinos if they would vote for various ethnic and partisan candidates. Respondents who said they would vote for a white Democrat in an election actually preferred Hernandez, not Smith, 50 to 25 percent, and respondents who said they *would not* vote for a Latino Republican also preferred Hernandez over Smith, 52 to 25 percent. While party labels were not given in the hypothetical candidate matchup, policy platforms were attributed to each candidate, giving voters an opportunity to learn more about each. Thus, it is noteworthy that such high percentages of Latino voters preferred the described "Republican" Hernandez even as they stated previously in the survey they would not.

While the descriptive results presented above are informative and interesting, they do not fully test the mobilizing influence of Latino candidates. For this analysis, multivariate probit and ordered-probit regression were employed to derive two sets of estimates presented here (found in table 4.4). While the variables in the models remain constant, there are two versions of the dependent variable tested. First, where it takes on a trichotomous distribution, ordered probit estimates are presented, and second, when the "undecided" voters are removed and the dependent variable is dichotomous, standard probit measures are presented. In addition,

TABLE 4.4
Determinants of Latino vote choice (LIF)

Independent variables	O-probit	Pr chg.	Probit	Pr chg.
Smith issues	−.1664 **	−.2071	−.2174 **	−.2921
	(.0660)		(.0925)	
Hernandez issues	.1807 **	.1765	.2757 **	.4184
	(.0786)		(.1066)	
Democratic voter	−.0599	−.0159	−.1944	−.0706
	(.1157)		(.1625)	
Republican voter	−.0183	.0049	−.1596	−.0588
	(.1386)		(.1878)	
Ethnic mobilization	.0509 **	.1322	.0753 **	.2824
	(.0254)		(.0356)	
Ethnic attachment	.0418 *	.1730	.0636 **	.3721
	(.0222)		(.0312)	
White Democrat	−.0931 *	−.0985	−.1171	−.1644
	(.0555)		(.0733)	
Latino Republican	−.0302	−.0321	−.0395	−.0572
	(.0484)		(.0662)	
Low sophistication	.1035	.0275	.1377	.0493
	(.1101)		(.1501)	
Female	−.0108	−.0029	−.0375	−.0136
	(.0976)		(.1334)	
Mexican origin	.1424	.0377	.1600	.0591
	(.1157)		(.1634)	
Foreign born	.1344	.0357	.1937	.0690
	(.1173)		(.1592)	
Age	.0201	.0534	.0443 *	.1568
	(.0180)		(.0248)	
Education proxy	−.0489	−.0518	−.0574	−.0839
	(.0326)		(.0437)	
Less than $20,000	−.0279	−.0074	−.1915	−.0711
	(.1521)		(.2133)	
$20,000–$39,999	.2102	.0558	.1592	.0567
	(.1393)		(.1963)	
$40,000–$69,000	−.0960	−.0254	−.2349	−.0872
	(.1440)		(.2029)	
More than $70,000	.2330	.0618	.1810	.0634
	(.1877)		(.2550)	
Registered 1995–98	.0769	.0204	.1724	.0628
	(.1057)		(.1436)	
Spanish at home	−.0553	−.0293	−.0828	−.0605
	(.0685)		(.0912)	
LA County	−.0872	−.0231	−.1096	−.0401
	(.1048)		(.1434)	
Constant			−1.4296	
	n/a		(1.012)	
N	587		429	
Chi²	38.20 **		42.59 **	
Log likelihood	−598.54		−254.46	
PPC			68.76%	
PRE (Lambda-p)			52.48%	

*** p< 0.01   ** p< 0.05   * p< 0.10

for both models, postestimation analysis is used to present the changes in predicted probability.

Table 4.4 reports the full results for the ordered probit and probit models predicting vote choice for Hernandez. The analysis results confirm both the "issue position" and the "ethnic attachment" hypotheses, suggesting that for Latino voters a more complicated (nuanced) theory that incorporates both may be appropriate. As the issue preference hypothesis speculates, those respondents who have the same stance on the issues as a candidate are more likely to prefer that candidate. In this example, the variable *Smith Issues* has a significant and negative relationship with a vote for Hernandez, while *Hernandez Issues* is significant and positive as expected.[13] Interestingly, there is no support for the partisanship theory, because neither the registered *Democrat* nor registered *Republican* variables have a significant effect on vote choice. Although there has been a strong issue-based attachment to the Democratic Party in California among Latino voters in the 1990s, this attachment does not influence vote choice for Smith, the more liberal candidate. This suggests that despite previously stated preference for candidates of a given party, this does not carry over into an election when a Latino candidate is present. This finding fits nicely with Martin Wattenberg's work (1987, 1994), which finds that campaigns are becoming candidate centered and political parties are losing their stronghold on voter decisions.

Further, when a coethnic candidate is present, the candidate focus of the campaign may be augmented for Latino voters. Studies of the 2001 Los Angeles mayoral campaign, a nonpartisan election, revealed that Latino voters were eager to elect a Latino candidate mayor, and exit polls found overwhelming support for the Latino candidate among Latino voters (Sonenshein and Pinkus 2002; Sonenshein 2003). Indeed, the results in Table 4.4 seem to confirm the ethnic attachment hypothesis. Both variables *ethnic mobilization*[14] and *ethnic attachment*[15] demonstrate a significant and positive effect on voting for the Latino candidate. This indicates that Latinos who identify with ethnic themes in mobilization and candidate characteristics are in fact more likely to vote for a coethnic candidate, regardless of partisanship. This finding is consistent with the empowerment theory, because it suggests that those voters who view ethnicity as an important mobilizing force, are likely to prefer a coethnic or coracial candidate (e.g., Lublin and Tate 1992).[16]

In addition, individual voter characteristics have no statistically significant effect in the multivariate analysis. Foreign born, Spanish household, and Mexican origin respondents are no more likely to prefer Hernandez over Smith, all other things being equal. Income, which is generally associated with voting Republican, also has no effect. Interestingly, registration date is also not significant. Because of the three seemingly anti-Latino propositions passed in 1994, 1996, and 1998, Ricardo

Ramírez (2002b) has noted that Latinos who first registered during these years are more likely to be sensitive to "Latino issues." However on its own, registration date has no influence on candidate preference in this hypothetical election.

On their own, the probit coefficients reveal little other than which variables are significant and their directional effect. Using postestimation analysis developed by Scott Long (1997, Long and Freese 2001), we can more precisely determine the specific contribution that each independent variable has on vote choice. The "Pr Chg" columns in table 4.4 report changes in predicted probability for the dependent variable, when the independent variable is moved from its minimum to its maximum value. Generally, issue preferences and ethnicity carry similar predictive capacity in explaining vote choice.

By dropping undecided voters, it is easier to assess the influence an independent variable has on changing one's vote from Smith to Hernandez. Voters who rate both *Hernandez Issues* "very important" are 41.8 percent more likely to prefer Hernandez than those who rate both issues "not important at all." Likewise, those who rate *Smith Issues* positively are 29.2 percent less likely to prefer Hernandez than those who do not resonate with Smith's issues. Because of the potential latent predisposition in favor of Latino candidates, it is not hard to imagine that Hernandez Issue voters find it easier to prefer him, while issue salience may have less of a draw for Smith.

Both ethnicity variables also show considerable influence on vote choice. While Latinos who respond to ethnic-based mobilization are 28.2 percent more likely to prefer Hernandez over Smith, voters who react favorably to Latin candidate characteristics and who have a high degree of *ethnic attachment* are 37.2 percent more likely to prefer the coethnic candidate. Taken further, if the predictive powers of these two ethnic identification variables are combined, a voter who holds both viewpoints is over 60 percent more likely to prefer Hernandez,[17] resulting in ethnic identification as the key determinant of vote choice.

The results from the TRPI survey for cross-over voting show many similarities. This is important, because the TRPI data is from California and New York and for the 2002 election, suggesting that the findings above are not an artifact of the data set alone. Given the consistency in the findings, I will review the results briefly rather than detail each independent variable. Overall, issues (coded similarly as above) did not seem to drive or hinder cross-over voting, however partisanship did play a role. Latinos who had stated a preference for voting Democrat in their congressional race (*Democratic Voter*) were significantly less likely to side with a Latino Republican in both the ordered probit and probit models. Registrants who identified as strong partisans were also far less likely to prefer the ethnic cross-over candidate. These results are straightforward and are what we might expect.

TABLE 4.5
Determinants of Latino cross-over voting (TRPI)

Independent variables	O-probit	Pr chg.	Probit	Pr chg.
Democratic issues	−0.151	−0.106	−0.098	−0.037
	(0.112)		(0.160)	
GOP issues	−0.006	−0.004	−0.034	−0.013
	(0.156)		(0.228)	
Democratic voter	−0.269 *	−0.190	−0.444 *	−0.173
	(0.148)		(0.264)	
GOP voter	−0.008	−0.006	−0.035	−0.013
	(0.176)		(0.291)	
Strong partisan	−0.168 **	−0.237	−0.240 **	−0.186
	(0.069)		(0.104)	
Ethnic commonality	0.116 **	0.242	0.198 **	0.217
	(0.053)		(0.079)	
Latino representation	−0.047	−0.067	−0.112	−0.087
	(0.082)		(0.113)	
Ethnic attachment	0.041	0.086	0.066	0.077
	(0.078)		(0.108)	
Discrimination	−0.015	−0.031	−0.019	−0.022
	(0.047)		(0.066)	
Female	−0.001	−0.001	0.023	0.009
	(0.099)		(0.142)	
Mexican origin	0.084	0.059	0.132	0.050
	(0.146)		(0.206)	
Puerto Rican origin	0.053	0.037	0.065	0.025
	(0.143)		(0.206)	
Foreign born	0.092	0.065	0.178	0.068
	(0.126)		(0.172)	
Third generation	−0.131	−0.091	−0.189	−0.070
	(0.161)		(0.240)	
Age	0.002	0.074	0.000	−0.003
	(0.004)		(0.005)	
Education	−0.080 **	−0.280	−0.139 **	−0.256
	(0.039)		(0.056)	
$25,001–$34,999	0.195	0.138	0.267	0.104
	(0.151)		(0.198)	
$35,000–$49,999	0.136	0.096	0.204	0.079
	(0.159)		(0.224)	
$50,000–$79,999	0.167	0.119	0.213	0.083
	(0.158)		(0.229)	
Over $80,000	0.283	0.202	0.390	0.153
	(0.211)		(0.342)	
Income missing	0.149	0.106	0.213	0.083
	(0.149)		(0.221)	
Married	0.065	0.045	0.120	0.046
	(0.109)		(0.149)	
Church attendance	0.002	0.007	−0.009	−0.018
	(0.031)		(0.044)	
Influence	0.031	0.066	0.055	0.062
	(0.059)		(0.083)	
Interest	0.017	0.036	0.003	0.004

TABLE 4.5
(continued)

Independent variables	O-probit	Pr chg.	Probit	Pr chg.
	(0.063)		(0.088)	
Language (Spanish)	−.008	−0.012	0.016	0.012
	(0.079)		(0.110)	
California	0.025	0.017	0.042	0.016
	(0.149)		(0.205)	
Constant			−0.019	
	n/a		(0.681)	
N	594		396	
Chi²	44.12 **		41.58 *	
Log likelihood	−621.10		−244.28	

*** p< 0.01   ** p< 0.05   * p< 0.10

Even controlling for issues and partisanship, there is also support for ethnicity as an important predictor of vote choice. The *ethnic commonality*[18] variable (how much in common) demonstrated a positive and significant relationship with voting for the Latino cross-over candidate. In fact, among the variables discussed, ethnicity had a substantive effect equal to that of strong party identification. Latinos who had a high degree of ethnic commonality were 24.2 percent more likely to prefer the Latino cross-over candidate, all other things being equal, while strong party identifiers were 23.7 percent less likely to go against their party and pick the cross-over Latino candidate. However, there was a difference from the LIF data presented above. The *ethnic attachment* scale (which combined four similar "ethnic" variables to LIF) did not have a significant relationship with vote choice. We might expect that when partisanship is cued (as in the TRPI survey) that ethnicity may play less of a role. However, the ethnic commonality variable does suggest that when voters know both the partisanship and ethnicity of the candidates, ethnicity and ethnic identification can influence vote choice. Finally, the results indicate that education has an inverse relationship with cross-over voting, which may also be a result of level of political information. While candidate ethnicity might serve as an important information shortcut or heuristic device, the most educated voters may rely more on issue position, partisanship, and campaign promises in making their decision.

While these results are limiting because the two elections were hypothetical, some real evidence for support of Latino Republican candidates was found in the 2002 election. In the California State Assembly, four Latino Republicans were reelected to office with strong support from Latino voters in their districts, while Republican Gary Mendoza, a statewide candidate for insurance commissioner, received the highest level of support of any Republican candidate for statewide office among Latinos and even outpolled the Anglo Democratic challenger in some heavily Latino precincts (California Secretary of State 2002; Los Angeles County Registrar 2002). In addition, in nonpartisan contests, Latinos have shown strong support for Latino candidates despite differences in ideology as in the 2001 Los Angeles mayoral and city attorney elections (*Los Angeles Times* exit poll, 2001).

Discussion

To this point, previous scholarship has failed to find that ethnicity is politically salient among Latino voters. While it has been considered an indirect influence by some (Graves and Lee 2000), other studies using the LNPS found no statistical evidence of a direct effect. In the conclusion to his book, *Counting on the Latino Vote,* DeSipio suggests that, "while there is currently no politically salient basis for Latino ethnicity, the roots are there among a sufficient share of the population. Given the right circumstances, Latinos regardless of ancestry, can shape a common political space" (1996, 178). While DeSipio finds no evidence that ethnicity is politically important, this research has suggested that the presence of a viable Latino candidate may represent a circumstance in which shared ethnicity becomes a salient factor in Latino political behavior.

The results presented here have shown that traditional theories of candidate preference need to be augmented for Latino voters when a coethnic candidate is present. That is to say, issue position, partisanship, and candidate evaluation may not tell the full story for why Latinos vote as they do. Instead, we can refine our understanding of vote choice by including measures of ethnic attachment in the model. Specifically, I have found that Latinos with a high degree of ethnic attachment are more likely to prefer a Latino candidate, absent party labels. Even when controlling for issue positions and party preference, ethnicity matters to vote choice. While previous scholars have found evidence of an indirect influence of ethnicity on voting (Cain and Kiewiet 1984; Graves and Lee 2000), here a direct influence is found. This is in part because of a more sophisticated measure of ethnicity. While previous research looked to a two-stage, indirect model after not finding evidence of a direct influence, this research has established no need to pursue the indirect model. Rather than conceptualizing ethnicity as an "all or nothing" factor, variable scales of ethnic identification are introduced that account for the relative strength of ethnicity to an individual. It is possible still that ethnicity holds *both* a direct and an indirect influence on vote choice. That is, not only does ethnic attachment directly influence which candidate a Latino voter may choose, but ethnic attachment may also influence their partisanship and policy preferences, which, in turn, influence vote choice. This research has tested the former of these propositions and found it to be the case. Had the two ethnicity variables introduced here not achieved statistical significance, we would have rejected the direct link hypothesis and likely sided with the existing literature. However, this was not the case.

Pan-Latino ethnic identity is rooted in four shared characteristics common to all Hispanic Americans. These are Latin American heritage, the immigrant experience, Spanish language, and the colonial influence of Spain's empire. Coupled with these shared cultural characteristics, ethnic-based discrimination continues to exist (and perhaps grow in areas of new Latino population growth such as Iowa and North Carolina), which strengthens the connection with ethnicity. Further, there is a relatively moderate-to-high level of ethnic attachment among all Latinos, and more research is needed to explore what characteristics might influence ethnic attachment.

With more Latinos running for office than ever before, a new paradigm is emerging that challenges traditional notions of political behavior. This research is important, because it has demonstrated that shared ethnic identity does exist among Latinos and that beyond partisanship and issues, ethnicity constitutes an important determinant of vote choice when a Latino candidate is on the ballot.

Notes

I would like to thank Luis Arteaga of the Latino Issues Forum, and Harry Pachón of the Tomás Rivera Policy Institute for kindly granting me access to their data for this project. In addition, I received considerable feedback and input from Gary Segura, Katherine Tate, Bernard Grofman, and Leo Chavez on an earlier draft of this essay. Finally, I am indebted to Rodolfo Espino, David Leal, and Ken Meier for the opportunity to be involved in the *Latino Politics* conference and this larger project.

1. An implicit argument though is that Latino candidate can win public office. If every Latino who ran for office lost, there would be no reason to suspect that their candidacy would "energize" the Latino community.

2. This electoral context may include endorsements by prominent Latino leaders, more in-depth coverage of the election by Spanish-language media, increased registration and mobilization drives by Latino civic organizations, and numerous campaign appearances by the Latino candidate at Latino churches, union halls, and schools.

3. Rather than replace existing models of voter turnout and candidate preference, I use them as a base and introduce additional explanatory variables. Standard predictors will remain in the models: age, education, income, gender, marital status, political efficacy/interest, partisanship, mobilization, and more.

4. A 2003 survey of Latinos in California by the Tomás Rivera Policy Institute found that

a majority of Latino registered voters picked Latinos as the most discriminated-against group, ahead of African Americans, Asian Americans, and Arab Americans.

5. Gore undoubtedly learned this tactic from his boss, President Bill Clinton, who declared before a crowd of African Americans in Atlanta, "I may be white on the outside, but I'm black on the inside," in 1996.

6. Hispanics or Latinos are typically considered to be people who can trace their ancestry to Spanish-speaking Latin America, thus excluding Brazil and parts of the Caribbean. In this study, I rely on a self-reported measure of ethnicity that was used as a screening question on the LIF survey instrument: "Do you consider yourself Hispanic or Latino?" (Arteaga 2000).

7. Robinson argues that one hundred and fifty to two hundred years after slavery was abolished, African Americans are still haunted by the socialpsychological implications that the institution of slavery had on African American–white power relations.

8. It should be emphasized that the survey data are for California Latinos only, which are predominantly of Mexican origin. Among survey respondents, 77 percent self-identified as being of Mexican ancestry. To determine the differences among Latino subgroups I include a dummy variable for Mexican origin in the models below.

9. Unfortunately, the survey did not follow a strict experimental design. A better approach would have been to switch the names "Smith" and "Hernandez" for half of the respondents to more accurately determine the effects of ethnic attachment on vote choice. However, because Hernandez is portrayed as the Republican candidate and California Latinos have strong ties to the Democratic Party, it provides considerable insight into the role of ethnicity in Latino vote choice.

10. The full results for question 13 were: Smith 25 percent; Hernandez 48 percent; neither 5 percent; combination 16 percent; don't know 7 percent (Arteaga 2000).

11. The trichotomous dependent variable takes a value of 0 when Smith is preferred, 1 when voters are undecided, and 2 when Hernandez is preferred. The neither, combination, and don't know voters can all be considered to be undecided between the two candidates and placed in between the options on the three-point index, as opposed to taking a value of zero.

12. The combined results for Democrats and Republicans to this question were: 26 percent Latino; 40 percent partisan; 29 percent depends on the candidates; 5 percent don't know.

13. Elsewhere in the LIF survey, respondents were asked a series of issues questions and the salience of each issue was determined. On each issue, respondents were asked if it was very important, somewhat important, not too important, or not at all important. The salience indicators for, "improving public education," and "increasing affordable housing" were combined and recoded as *Smith issues*. Similarly, "preserving family values," and "reducing crime" were combined and recoded as *Hernandez issues*. Each variable ranges from 2 to 8.

14. The variable *ethnic mobilization* is based on a set of three questions asking respondents whether certain electoral circumstances would increase or decrease the likelihood that they might cast a ballot. Latino registered voters were asked, "Would you be more or less likely to vote in an election where . . . (1) there was a viable Latino candidate; (2) issues important to Latinos had been discussed in depth over the course of the election; and (3) Latino organizations and community leaders were urging Latinos to vote." Although the variable specifically addresses mobilization, it also taps the underlying importance of ethnicity with regard to political behavior (Lien 1994; Pantoja and Woods 1999). Using Cronbach's alpha, we can determine the internal consistency of the scale, based on the average inter-item correlation. The variable

ranges from a low of 3 to a high of 15. Overall, the test produces an alpha reading of .7799, which is quite high for a four-item scale.

15. The variable *ethnic attachment* combines the responses to four questions about candidate characteristics. Respondents were asked a series of questions to determine whether different ethnic-based characteristics would attract support among Latino voters. For example, the survey asked, "would you vote for a candidate who _____, or would the information make no impact on your decision to vote?" I combined the following four characteristics in compiling the *ethnic attachment* variable: (1) is bilingual in English and Spanish; (2) has a Latino surname; (3) is endorsed by a Latino organization or group; (4) is Latino and speaks Spanish as his/her native language. The variable ranges from 4 to 20. Unlike the previous variable, this measure directly addresses the role of ethnic identity in candidate preference. If the ethnic association hypothesis is correct, both variables should reveal a significant and positive relationship with voting for the coethnic candidate, Hernandez. For this measure, the Cronbach Alpha is .7758, again a high degree of reliability.

16. The specific candidate attributes in this hypothetical election are not as important. Voters who stated a preference for a white Democrat are less likely to prefer Hernandez in the ordered probit analysis, but this relationship, which is only marginally significant, dissolves in the probit analysis.

17. In fact, when the two variables are combined into one broad "ethnicity" scale and the models are reestimated, the predictive capacity of the new ethnicity variable in forecasting a vote for Hernandez is 62.3 percent. Additional results are available from the author upon request.

18. Respondents in the TRPI survey were asked, "Just thinking about groups living in the United States, how much do you think you have in common with other Latinos? Is it a great deal, a fair amount, only a little, or do you think you have nothing in common?" The *ethnic commonality* variable ranges from a low of 1 to a high of 4.

Residential Mobility and the Political Mobilization of Latinos in Houston

Ricardo Ramírez

THE PERCEIVED POLITICAL RELEVANCE of Latinos in the United States has increased dramatically since the 2000 presidential election. In that election, a record amount of money ($3.2 million) was spent by presidential campaigns on Spanish-language advertisements targeting messages to Latinos. During the midterm elections of 2002, the amount of money spent on Spanish-language advertisement grew by nearly 500 percent to $16 million (Segal 2003). Despite the fact that Latinos largely lived outside of the swing states, $8.7 million were spent during the 2004 presidential campaign (Segal 2006). The significant increase in political advertisements targeting Latinos has led pundits, scholars, and the national, state, and local media to depict Latinos as a major emerging political force in American presidential elections that should be courted (Segal 2003; Marbut 2004; Ramos 2004).

There are three principal explanations for this increased attention. First, the mainstream media's sudden realization that Latinos matter demographically results largely from the fact that Latinos have concurrently become the nation's largest minority population and the fastest-growing segment of the citizen voting-age population.[1] Second, the political fascination with Latinos as the new "soccer moms" can be traced to the combination of geographic concentration in some of the most populous states (as well as a few "battleground" states), their growth as a segment of the electorate, their rumored increased partisan independence,[2] and the recent variability of their voting behavior.[3]

Third, increased party competition at the national level further explains why the 2000 elections represented the first time both major party candidates for president and their campaigns paid significant attention to Latinos. Not only did Al Gore and George W. Bush speak more Spanish in public, but each candidate's campaign also organized major events in California and Texas, the two states with the largest numbers of Latino voters. These increased efforts to woo Latino voters may indicate a change in attitudes regarding Latino voters.

Growing media attention and campaign-related outreach to Latino voters, however, should not be confused with voter mobilization efforts. It is well established that Latinos are among the least targeted groups in the electorate (Leighley 2001; Wong 2006; Verba et al. 1995; de la Garza et al. 1992). In fact, Latinos report being asked to participate at a lower rate (25 percent) than African Americans (40 percent) and whites (56 percent) (Verba et al. 1995). Driving this disparity are both individual-level and contextual sources. The Latino population is younger and has lower levels of education and income, all characteristics that are negatively associated with partisan mobilization efforts (Gershtenson 2003; Leighley 2001; Verba et al. 1995; Rosenstone and Hansen 1993). Historically, political parties have helped to reduce the costs of participation, thereby promoting the electoral inclusion of immigrants and segments of the population with less income, education, and politically relevant resources. The declining rate of participation among all segments of the population, but especially those with lower socioeconomic status, can be partially attributed to the waning involvement of political parties in the direct mobilization of voters (Wong 2006).

Moreover, the geographic concentration of Latinos in the most populous states is a double-edged sword. While political parties could maximize their efforts to mobilize Latino voters by focusing on the largest states with sizable Latino populations (e.g., California, New York, Texas, and Florida), they do not have an incentive to do so, because—with the exception of Florida—these states are rarely competitive (de la Garza and DeSipio 2004). Regardless of election cycle, it is not an overstatement to say that most Latinos live in states dominated by one party or another.[4] While Latinos do live in highly competitive states like Florida and New Mexico, these are the exception to the rule. Even in these competitive states, political parties rely largely on "air war" campaigns consisting of television and radio advertising, because they lack the organizational capacity to run the type of "ground war" campaigns that historically were used to motivate people to vote.[5]

This decreased capacity of parties has theoretical and normative implications for the participation of all voters, and Latinos in particular. The future of participatory democracy and civic engagement in the United States will depend on partisan and nonpartisan political elites looking beyond short-term electoral goals. These short-term electoral goals frequently neglect low-propensity voters, populations with low levels of politically relevant resources, and those who reside in noncompetitive jurisdictions (ranging from precincts and electoral districts to states). They need to use personalized mobilization efforts similar to those successfully used by political machines in the past.

It is a tall order to ask that political elites move away from the "air war" campaigns and expend resources on activities that do not have an immediate payoff, and to do so in a cost-intensive, personalized manner. Despite this initial perceived hurdle, technological innovations now allow for the incorporation of consumer data with political data; this allows for the more-precise targeting of voters with more personalized direct voter mobilization efforts that have been shown to be effective. Given this increased capability, there is a growing sentiment that mobilization efforts on the "ground level" will gain more prominence in future political campaigns (Meyerson 2004).[6] Clearly, this renewed interest and these innovations in targeting voters have the potential to influence voter turnout as well as existing theories of voter mobilization.

In this essay I revisit the mobilization literature and consider whether the conventional wisdom regarding the determinants of mobilization should be revisited, given the changes mentioned above. Moreover, I emphasize the role of residential mobility and stability on the incidence of Latinos' self-reported mobilization efforts and propose that existing and future studies of mobilization consider the significance of this factor in their analyses.

The remainder of this essay is divided into five parts. First, I review the extant literature on mobilization generally and as it pertains to Latinos in the United States. Second, I consider why scholars of political mobilization have paid little attention to the role of residential mobility despite its likely relevance to partisan and nonpartisan voter mobilization efforts. I then discuss the data used and the proposed measurements of residential mobility and stability. The fourth section presents the results, and the final section concludes with a look at the possible implications of residential mobility for elite mobilization efforts of Latinos and non-Latinos in the United States.

The Personal and the Political

Who votes? This is the fundamental question in political participation research. The proliferation of surveys has allowed scholars to identify compelling explanations for differing levels of political participation based on the characteristics of voters, such as their income, education, age, and partisanship (Wolfinger and Rosenstone 1980; Teixiera 1992; Rosenstone and Hansen 1993; Verba, Schlozman, and Brady 1995). Steven Rosenstone and John Hansen (1993), however, suggest that a person's resources and personal characteristics only explain half the story. The other half of the story is political—being asked to participate.

Such a parsimonious theory, based on the personal and the political, is useful in that it helps to structure necessary questions about differences in political participation in the general population and among subgroups. The consensus is that "parties target individuals who are more predisposed to activity by their individual characteristics" (Gershtenson 2003, 294). Given the strong relationship that has been identified between voting and mobilization, it makes sense that individual characteristics that have been shown to affect participation are also included in models predicting mobilization. As such, the dominant approach in the political mobilization literature focuses on the relationship between participation and mobilization.

Despite the general agreement of these and other studies of voter mobilization regarding the correlation between voting and mobilization (Caldeira, Clausen, and Patterson 1990; Caldeira, Patterson, and Markko 1985; Crotty 1971; Huckfeldt and Sprague 1992; Kramer 1970), it is difficult to fully disentangle the relationship between mobilization and participation because the factors that predict one predict the other. It is probable that voter mobilization efforts disproportionately target likely voters. Therefore, to the extent that there is a relation between contact and turnout, the apparent causal relation may be spurious if contact is endogenous. As such, scholars concerned with this endogenous relationship between mobilization and participation suggest that the best way to delineate the magnitude of the effect of mobilization is through randomized "Get Out the Vote" field experiments (Gerber and Green 2000; Green and Gerber 2004).

Efforts to determine whether direct mobilization is as relevant for Latino participation as it has been found among other populations have largely drawn on three methodologies: aggregate analyses of case studies, public opinion surveys, and field experiments. Adrian Pantoja and Nathan Woods (1999) used aggregate analysis to consider whether individual turnout increased among Latinos living in Los Angeles County cities where Southwest Voter Registration and Education Project (SVREP) conducted GOTV efforts in 1996 and 1998. They do not find a link between the cities where SVREP conducted GOTV efforts and increased turnout among individuals in those cities. The problem with this method is that the authors expected to find an increase in participation even among those living in SVREP-targeted precincts who may not have received contact.[7] Simply living in an area where GOTV efforts were conducted does not mean that they were necessarily contacted. Other case studies of municipal elections largely focus on candi-

93

date campaigns and local mobilization efforts to determine how receptive racial and ethnic groups are to mobilization (Hardy-Fanta 1993).

Using postelection surveys, Daron Shaw, Rodolfo de La Garza, and Jongho Lee (2000) and de la Garza and Marissa Abrajano (2002) found that self-reported contact by a Latino group can positively affect Latino turnout. While both studies use validated postelection surveys, they depend on the accuracy of self-reported contact. Regardless of which of the above methodology was used (case studies vs. surveys), the above studies share two commonalities: (1) they focus on the relevance of mobilization by coethnic groups for Latino participation, and (2) they are unable to concretely determine the size and scope of effect that particularized contact has on Latino turnout.

The third methodology used to determine the relevance of mobilization for Latino participation draws on the field experiment tradition of Harold Gosnell (1927) and Samuel Eldersveld (1956), as well as on the more contemporary methods for more accurate measurement proposed by Alan Gerber and Donald Green (2000). Both Melissa Michelson (2002) and Ricardo Ramírez (2005) used randomized field experiments to measure the effect of mobilization on Latino participation. In rural California, Michelson (2002) found that coethnic mobilization and mode of contact are important mobilizing forces in local elections.[8] The positive effect of Latino coethnic contact and the relevance of mode of contact are validated in the analysis of the largest mobilization field experiment of Latinos to date, consisting of over four hundred thousand Latinos nationally (Ramirez 2005).

General Theories of Mobilization and Latinos

General theories of mobilization have implications for our understanding of Latino mobilization. Rosenstone and Hansen (1993) argued that political elites selectively determine whom to target because of efficiency and outcome-driven concerns: "Once political leaders decide to pursue a mobilization strategy, they want to get the most effective number involved with the least amount of effort" (30–31). While not directly addressed by the authors, self-reported mobilization by Latinos is positively related to the extent that they fall into one or more of the four categories[9] of citizens leaders are likely to target.[10] Joseph Gershtenson (2003) considers the mobilization strategies of partisan elites between 1956 and 2000 and finds that the four categories identified by Rosenstone and Hansen (1993) consistently predict the targets of mobilization by both Democrats and Republicans during the time period in question.[11]

Sidney Verba, Kay Lehman Schlozman, and Henry Brady (1995), conversely, contend that the level and nature of institutional mobilization of individuals is contingent on the levels of politicization of the institution that conducts the mobilization (e.g., church, job, or other voluntary associations). It is notable that Verba, Schlozman, and Brady, unlike most mainstream studies of mass participation and mobilization, systematically consider how race structures who is asked to participate. Accordingly, mobilization of Latinos depends not only on individual-level civic skills but, more important, it also is contingent on the presence of politicized institutions with the necessary resources to engage in mobilizing activities.

Thus, according to general theories of mobilization, only a small number of Latinos can be characterized as likely candidates for mobilization. This is particularly true of Latinos living in majority-Latino districts. In what is perhaps the most comprehensive assessment of the individual and institutional factors that affect mobilization of Latinos, Jan Leighley (2001) found that when Latinos in Texas "make up the largest proportion of the population, they tend to reside in counties in which party chairs engage in fewer mobilization activities—and especially those oriented toward reducing the cost of participation" (66). This leads to a vicious cycle that often excludes Latinos, because mobilization increases turnout, and parties focus on likely voters and ignore low propensity voters.

It is unclear whether parties intentionally neglect Latinos. To ascertain whether or not parties intentionally neglect Latinos and other racial/ethnic minorities, Leighley uses an innovative approach. Using a survey of county party chairs in Texas as well as Verba, Schlozman, and Brady's Citizen Participation Study (CPS) data, she concludes that color-blind considerations structure the patterns of mobilization efforts. She cites ideology, group size, and prior voter turnout as "important factors in elites' decisions about whom to mobilize, as well as perceptions among some minority leaders that, due to these factors, minorities may be overlooked in the mobilization process" (61).

Her study is unique in that it uses data of elite self-reports of mobilization efforts *and* individual's self-reported recruitment, and she considers the ways in which the *nature* and *level* of political mobilization of racial and ethnic minorities vary. Ultimately, Leighley's findings in Texas concur with Verba and colleagues' general observation that Latinos are mobilized significantly less than are Anglos. One paradox in her findings is that for Latinos (in Texas) an increase in Latino group size does not positively influence partisan mobilization efforts, yet increasing Latino population is associated with increased party competition. One would expect that increased party competition would result in increased mobilization activities of the potentially swing vote, in this case Latinos.

Residential Mobility, Participation, and Mobilization Strategies

To date, most of the literature on mobilization has been focused on the effects of residential mobility on political participation. Political participation scholars concur that moving depresses several forms of civic and political participation (Squire, Wolfinger, and Glass 1987; Jackson 1996; Brians 1997; Highton 2000; Highton and Wolfinger 2001; Bowers 2004). Mobility-related factors that depress participation can be categorized as either institutional or social. First, the institutional provisions that require reregistration following a move pose an entry barrier to participation. Second, moving may disrupt "rootedness" in existing social networks that might help reduce the costs of participation (Highton 2000).

Jake Bowers (2004) further delineates the effects on social networks by considering the impositions of costs in three ways: "1) by disrupting the conduits for mobilization (knowing people), 2) by requiring individuals to gather new information and understandings about their new political environments, and 3) by imposing costs of time and money that are higher than normal due to the process of getting from one residence to another" (p 528). Benjamin Highton (2000) suggests that it is not just the act of moving that matters, but the type of movement as well. Interestingly, he finds that the negative effect of residential mobility (movement within a community) is comparable to the negative effect of community mobility (movement across communities). Rather than focus on the negative effects of mobility, Robert Jackson (1996) finds that residential stability has positive effects on voter registration and turnout. The negative effects of residential mobility (or positive effects of residential stability) on participation are assumed to hold true for all segments of the population, yet there is only one existing exploration of such effects among Latinos (Johnson, Stein, and Wrinkle 2003). They conclude that, among Spanish-speaking Latinos in the Rio Grande Valley in Texas, residential stability helps overcome other individual-level barriers to participation.

One problem with studies of mobilization and participation has to do with how mobility is measured and operationalized. When considering the determinants of participation, the concepts of mobility and stability are used interchangeably without a clear standard for the conditions that make someone residentially mobile or stable. Ordinarily, surveys will ask respondents how long they have lived at a particular address. Those who have lived at their current address for less than five years are considered to be more mobile than those who have been at their address longer.[12] While Highton (2000) focuses on distance of movement, Bowers (2004) considers the immediate disruptive effects on participation by identifying whether moving in a particular year influences different forms of participation during the same year. Jackson (1996) uses the square root of the number of years at current residence as a measure of stability. Still others will at times use homeownership as a proxy for stability. The lack of a clear standard for determining who is residentially stable or mobile hinders comparability across studies cited above.

Because residential mobility depresses participation, it would follow that residential mobility should depress mobilization. Parties and other political groups, in an attempt to use their resources in the most effective manner, might be expected to target their mobilizing resources at those with more social connections and the strongest ties to their communities. This includes those with stable community connections, as evidenced by living in the same community for a significant period of time, and those with a deep community connection, as evidenced by owning one's home. Homeowners and those who have lived in a community for a substantial period of time are assumed not only to be easier to contact but also to be more likely to yield indirect benefits through their mobilization within a denser web of community contacts (Rosenstone and Hansen 1993, 166–67). It is therefore unsurprising that Rosenstone and Hansen find that those who own their homes and have lived in a community for a number of years are more likely to be contacted by parties in presidential and midterm elections than nonhomeowners or newcomers to the community (164–65). Rosenstone and Hansen (1993) also found that those who have lived in the same residence most of their lives are more likely to be asked to participate than more recent arrivals. The following analysis builds on this past research to examine whether mobility affects mobilization among Latinos in particular.

Data and Measures of Residential Mobility and Stability

I use data from a municipal postelection survey of registered voters conducted between November 11 and November 26, 2003, using a listed sample of registered voters in Houston, Texas. The total sample consists of 555 registered voters, with an oversample of 269 Latinos. Measures of residential mobility and stability were later added, using a combination of consumer data, voter registration rolls, and trust deed data.

Why restrict the study to registered voters? Most parties and other organizations focus their mobilization efforts on those who are most likely to vote—people who are already registered. The rationale for targeting existing voters consists of two factors. First, it is less costly to remind those who have voted in the past to vote in a coming election than to convince someone who has never voted to participate for the first time in the electoral process. The second factor has to do with the use

FIGURE 5.1
Revised Leighley model of Latino participation

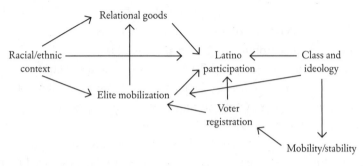

of registered party affiliation as a cue for potential supporters of candidates or ballot initiatives. Partisan and nonpartisan elites are more likely to target people if they are registered and they have registered party preferences. Thus, as was the case with participation, the presence of electoral mobilization is contingent on overcoming the institutional barriers (i.e., voter registration) to electoral participation.[13] Residential mobility therefore needs to be more explicitly considered as a key determinant not only of successful voter registration and participation and mobilization, but also of mobilization. Figure 5.1 incorporates this logic into Leighley's (2001) model of Latino participation.

This revised model of Latino political participation highlights the direct and indirect effects of residential mobility on participation. The primary and more direct effect, as discussed earlier, has to do with the institutional barrier to participation that arises when someone moves and needs to register or reregister to vote. The indirect effect of mobility on participation has to do with the effect on propensity to be targeted for mobilization. Bowers (2004) and Craig Brians (1997) make reference to the negative effects on social networks and an implied effect on propensity to be mobilized, yet they do not test for this directly. I test for this explicitly by considering the role of residential mobility and stability on levels of self-reported mobilization.

The analysis highlights two forms of residential mobility, *recency* and *frequency*, and two forms of stability, *homeownership and household electoral engagement*. *Recency* is captured by focusing on the last of a five-year stability period. *Frequency* focuses on the number of addresses where the respondent has resided within this five-year span. These measures are interrelated in that those with only one address during this period could be coded as having lived at their address five years or more, whereas those with more than one address will have lived at their current address for less than five years. *Residential mobility* focuses on the number of addresses

TABLE 5.1
Number of addresses by homeownership among Latino registered voters, 1998–2003

	1	2	3
Renter	66.70%	22.60%	10.70%
Homeowner	73.30%	21.40%	5.30%

Source: Houston 2003 Postelection survey, University of Southern California

where respondents have lived during the past five years. In effect, I capture both *frequency* and *recency* of mobility, using only one variable because of the number of moves that took place during the five-year stability period designation.[14]

The two measures of social and political stability are very straightforward, as are the expectations for their contribution to participation and mobilization outcomes. The *homeowner* variable is drawn from validated trust deed information, and the *household electoral engagement* consists of a count of the number of household members who are registered to vote. Granted that being registered to vote does not mean the household is fully engaged in the electoral process, but at the very least it allows for the opportunity be engaged. Again, the expectation in the literature is that homeowners participate at higher levels and are targets of mobilization. One would also anticipate that this also applies to households with multiple registered voters.

Among the general population, homeowners are assumed to be more likely to be residentially stable than renters, and more likely to vote. However, it is unclear whether this disparity persists once individuals have overcome the institutional barrier to participation by registering to vote.

As demonstrated in table 5.1, two-thirds of renters and nearly three-quarters of homeowners were at the same address over the five-year span. While renters were more likely than homeowners to have moved three times within the previous five years, the difference is not as large as one might expect. It is important to note that these are mobility patterns of Latino registered voters in Houston, which are quite distinct from the general Latino population in Houston. The pattern that emerges in Houston should serve to caution political behavior scholars. Any empirical models regarding the determinants of mobilization could be critically misspecified if the data used is drawn from the general population, as opposed to registered voters. This is even more likely when considering the effects of homeownership or residential mobility, because the differences are likely greater when comparing renters and homeowners who are not registered to vote.

Ricardo Ramírez

Residential Mobility and Future Efforts to Mobilize Latinos

The results of the analysis of predictors of Latino mobilization are presented in table 5.2. Model 1 incorporates variables found by extant research to increase electoral participation and the propensity to be mobilized. Education, marital status, and attentiveness to politics are positively associated with self-reported mobilization. Also consistent with previous research, Latinos living in areas with high concentration of Latinos are less likely to be targets of voter mobilization (Leighley 2001). Model 2 is the full model that includes measures of residential mobility and stability. Once these variables are included, the role of marital status on reported mobilization is no longer statistically significant, while the other variables remain statistically significant. Not surprisingly, homeowners are more likely to be targeted by mobilization efforts. Also, those who are more residentially mobile are less likely to report being contacted.

Clearly, mobility and homeownership represent key factors in determining whether or not parties and other groups outreach directly to Latinos. It is also important to note two key variables whose effects on mobilization were not statistically significant: marital status and the number of registered voters in the household. Being married is often seen as a significant life-cycle event that can help to encourage participation. While this may be true, it did not increase the likelihood of being contacted for Latinos in Houston, once residential mobility and stability were considered. It is surprising to find that controlling for other factors, an increase in the number of registered voters in the household does not appear to have an effect on likelihood of being contacted. Candidates for political office may not be using one of the key efficiency tools at their disposal—identifying active Latino households. If this is the case, they may be missing an opportunity to maximize their efforts to mobilize Latino voters by focusing on households with the greatest number of voters.

The direction of these effects conforms to what we would expect given prior research on the effects of residential mobility and stability on participation. Clearly, the innovation in the findings and analysis is not in identifying that there are similarities between the determinants of participation and mobilization. Instead, the unique contribution of this essay lies in testing whether existing assumptions regarding the effects of residential mobility are applicable to Latino voters and delineating the indirect effects of mobility on participation through the conduit of elite mobilization.

TABLE 5.2
Logistic regression results for predicting Latino mobilization

Variables	Model 1	Model 2
Age	−0.000	−0.005
	(0.009)	(0.010)
High school graduate	0.668 **	0.696 **
	(0.309)	(0.315)
Women	0.080	−0.134
	(0.265)	(0.271)
Married	0.361 *	0.363
	(0.299)	(0.308)
Naturalized	0.377	0.365 *
	(0.330)	(0.337)
Supermajority Latino precinct	−0.562 **	−0.397 *
	(0.304)	(0.322)
Efficacy	−0.140	−0.148
	(0.155)	(0.157)
Political attentiveness	0.505 ***	0.533 **
	(0.185)	(0.189)
# registered in household		0.095
		(0.108)
Residential mobility		−0.292 *
		(0.231)
Homeowner		0.565 **
		(0.314)
Constant	−1.650 ***	−1.813 ***
	(0.653)	(0.777)
PPC	63.94%	67.66%
Sample size	269	269

*** $p < 0.01$ ** $p < 0.05$ * $p < 0.10$ (one tailed tests)

Source: Houston 2003 Postelection Survey, University of Southern California

Conclusion

I began this essay with a discussion about the perception that Latinos are becoming a powerful force in American politics. Despite the hype, Latinos are not often the targets of mobilization, because they do not fit the demographic profile of likely voters. Unfortunately, Latinos depend on mobilization to help overcome barriers to participation. If we are to understand the changing dynamics of contemporary elite mobilization strategies, we must pay attention to factors not directly related to politics that can nevertheless influence Latino recruitment to politics—including mobility and homeownership. Theories that take these factors into account have direct implications for better and more efficient recruitment efforts that can lead to more participation for Latinos, and thereby potentially greater levels of political incorporation.

There are also other policy implications related to the low rates of Latino homeownership and their patterns of residential mobility. The findings from this study suggest that programs to increase homeownership among Latinos will not only improve Latino economic well-being but also increase their political mobilization and participation. Those who move frequently are also less likely to be mobilized. If an inclusive democracy is the goal, both partisan and nonpartisan elites should revise their mobilization strategies. One possibility is simply to expand existing mobilization efforts at nonresidential places in Latino neighborhoods like supermarkets and community centers. These and other changes would be a first step to more fully acknowledge that the strategic decisions of elites can have very real consequences on the decision of voters to make it to the polls.

Notes

1. There has been an increase in both the number of adult Latino immigrants who have attained U.S citizenship and native-born youths who are reaching voting age.

2. For a contrary view on Latino partisanship in presidential elections, see David Leal, Matt Barreto, Jongho Lee, and Rodolfo de la Garza (2005).

3. Latino voters increased from 2.5 million voters nationally in 1980 to 6 million in 2000, a 136 percent increase. For more on Latino partisan and ideological independence, see Zoltan Hajnal and Taeku Lee (2006). The variability in voting behavior that I allude to refers to the increased willingness to vote for individual Republican candidates at higher rates than historic patters in states where Democrats have historically dominated among Latino voters (e.g., gubernatorial elections of George W. Bush in Texas, George Pataki in New York, and Arnold Schwarzenegger in California).

4. Over two-thirds of all Latinos live in six noncompetitive states: Arizona, California, Illinois, New Jersey, New York, and Texas.

5. The reported increased ground efforts during the 2004 presidential election cycle, while significant, were largely, if not exclusively, confined to a handful of swing states with few Latino voters.

6. A related article in the *New York Times Magazine* refers to the increased precision of targeting subpopulations based on consumer data as "microtargeting" (Bai 2004).

7. Given that contact rates are much lower than 100 percent for all phone and personal can-

vass efforts, it is very likely that many people in the random sample never received treatment. This is even more the case if only certain neighborhoods received treatment but the analysis is on citywide turnout.

8. Precinct walking and person-to-person calls have been shown to be more effective than direct mail or automated calls.

9. These include (1) people they already know; (2) those centrally positioned in social networks; (3) influential individuals; (4) those likely to respond to mobilization.

10. One can also infer how other mainstream studies of mobilization and participation would explain differing levels of mobilization among racial and ethnic minorities. We can infer, for example, from Robert Huckfeldt and John Sprague's (1992) work that level of minority mobilization depends on their previous voting patterns, their partisanship, and the extent to which the local political structure where they live is conducive to the partisan mobilization.

11. He does not distinguish between Latinos and non-Latinos in terms of their propensity to be contacted. Instead, he finds a significant relationship between race and mobilizations through the inclusion of a dichotomous race variable intended to capture the effects for African Americans. It is problematic to lump together whites, Asian Americans, and Latinos because this likely dilutes the effects of race if Latinos and Asians are contacted at lower rates than both African Americans and whites.

12. At times, the cut-off measure of stability is ten years.

13. Several scholars do take the need to register to vote as vital to understanding participation. However, most of these works have focused on institutional mechanisms that reduce the costs of registration, such as later closing dates, same-day registration, and the presence of motor voter. Less has been done to understand why voters facing similar institutional barriers still register or reregister at different rates.

14. I was able to match consumer data information to the survey respondents (all of whom were drawn from registered voter lists). The consumer database allowed me to code for number of addresses held during the last five years.

Puerto Rican Exceptionalism?

A Comparative Analysis of Puerto Rican, Mexican, Salvadoran, and Dominican Transnational Civic and Political Ties

Louis DeSipio and Adrian D. Pantoja

THE FLUIDITY OF MIGRATION and the relative ease of access of citizenship rights of Puerto Ricans in the United States often necessitate an asterisk or a footnote in studies of Latino immigrant adaptation. Since 1917, Puerto Ricans born in Puerto Rico have enjoyed the unique status of being U.S. citizens at birth and having the option of participating politically in both Puerto Rico and the United States (Cámara Fuertes 2004). Puerto Ricans can migrate to the United States without restriction and can exercise the rights of citizenship in the United States on arrival. (Their exercise of U.S. citizenship in Puerto Rico is somewhat more circumscribed just as is their exercise of Puerto Rican citizenship when residents on the mainland.)

Because of this ease of migration and quick access to the vote, scholars of immigration and immigrant adaptation have paid relatively little attention to the process of Puerto Rican adaptation to civic and political life in the United States (Duany 2002, chapters 7 and 8, as examples). For many of the same reasons, as international migration scholars have increasingly focused their attentions on transnational engagement among immigrants, they have overlooked the potential for Puerto Ricans in the United States to maintain civic and political ties in Puerto Rico. In this essay, we analyze this aspect of the Puerto Rican migrant experience to assess whether Puerto Rican migrants engage the civic and political life of Puerto Rico in a manner demonstrably different than do other large Latino migrant populations in the politics of their nations of origin.

The Rediscovery and Expansion of Immigrant
Transnational Engagement

There has long been an assumption that over time immigrants begin severing ties with their countries of origin and develop closer ties and allegiances with the host country (Schlesinger 1998; Handlin 1973 [1951]; Gordon 1964). This perspective has been tempered by research noting the greater prevalence of transnational ties among contemporary immigrants than in previous eras (Portes 1999; Shain 1999; Basch et al. 1994; Glick Schiller 1999; Glick Schiller et al. 1995, 1992). The core idea advanced by these studies is that advances in technology facilitating communication and travel, an increase in economic and political ties between the United States and immigrant-sending countries, a greater tolerance in the United States for ethnic pluralism, and encouragement of immigrant-sending countries to develop and maintain connections with their emigrés have enabled immigrants to forge and sustain transnational links to a greater degree than immigrants from previous waves (Foner 2001; Guarnizo 2001). While the ability of immigrants to maintain a foothold in two countries is not a new phenomenon (Morawska 2001; Foner 2000), the scale, density, and duration of contemporary transnational ties surpass those of previous immigrations. Analysis of the meaning and significance of these ties has become an emerging field, traversing many social science and humanities disciplines, with different scholars emphasizing different aspects of the transnational experience (Itzigsohn 2000; Vertovec 1999; Smith and Guarnizo 1998; Glick Schiller et al. 1995; Basch et al. 1994).

Although a burgeoning field, much of the present scholarship on transnational ties remains informed by qualitative or case study analyses (Vélez-Ibáñez and Sampaio 2002; Hamilton and Stoltz Chinchilla 2001; Levitt 2001; Jones-Correa 1998; Duany 1994; de la Garza and Hazan 2003). Despite the rich insights generated by these studies, their small samples and specific geographic focus prevent us from making firm generalizations about the migrant group studied or migrant groups generally. Few works examine transnational processes empirically or comparatively (Barreto and Muñoz 2003; DeSipio 2003; Jones-Correa 2001b; Pachón et al. 2000). As important, few studies analyze how transnational engagements change over the life course of the migrant (DeSipio 2002b). This project partially fills these omissions by empirically analyzing two types of transnational activities as a tool to assess whether the Puerto Rican experience can be understood as similar to or distinct from those of other Latino migrants. These are: involvement in home-country associations/activities and participation in home-country politics. More specifically, we seek to address the following questions: (1) Do transnational civic and political ties vary among Puerto Rican migrants? (2) Do these patterns differ between Puerto Rican migrants and immigrants from other Latin American nations that send large numbers of the émigrés to the United States?

We analyze these questions using survey data from a Tomás Rivera Policy Institute (TRPI) survey of transnational civic and political ties among Latino immigrants.[1] The survey, which is discussed in greater depth later, offers comparative data on four of the five largest Latino immigrant/migrant populations — Mexican, Dominican, and Salvadoran immigrants, in addition to Puerto Rican migrants. Because their opportunities for ongoing relations in Cuba's civic and political life are restricted, TRPI did not include Cuban immigrants, who would make up the final of the top five Latino immigrant/migrant populations.

Transnational Ties and Puerto Rican Exceptionalism

An ambiguous concept, transnationalism as applied to immigration is typically defined as "the process by which immigrants forge and sustain simultaneous multistranded social relations that link together their societies of origin and settlement" (Basch et al. 1994, 7). A plethora of individual, household, and structural factors are argued to influence transnational ties (Foner 2001; Guarnizo 2001; Basch et al. 1994). However, the intensity of contemporary transborder ties is largely facilitated by three factors: advances in transportation and communication technology, the globalization of capital, and a greater tolerance in the United States for ethnic pluralism (Pessar 1996; Basch et al. 1994). This emerging scholarship challenges the traditional view of migration that treats it as a unidirectional process whereby "uprooted" migrants travel to a new country and begin a process of severing ties with the old country while developing closer ties with the new homeland (Handlin 1973 [1951]; Gordon 1964).

Transmigration research often situates the migration process into a world systems theoretical framework (Basch et al. 1994). The core idea is that the growing economic and political ties between industrialized nations and underdeveloped nations facilitate migration and transnational processes. Arguably, this asymmetric relationship greatly benefits elites in both the core and periphery countries, but, if so, it comes at the expense of workers generally and in particular those in the periphery. In an effort to improve their economic and social fortunes, individuals in the periphery migrate to the core/industrialized countries to assist families and communities in the home countries by sending remittances. Should the émigrés' fortunes flounder in the host country, returning to the home country remains an option for those who have maintained ties. Thus, migration and transnational ties are a reaction to present-day global realities and are a novel strategy for diversifying risk (Levitt 2001; Glick Schiller et al. 1995, 1992; Basch et al. 1994; Grasmuck and Pessar 1991).

Since transmigrants were viewed as seeking to diversify risk, much of the initial scholarship argued that ties between migrants and communities in the homeland were being initiated and sustained from "below" at the grassroots level (Smith and Guarnizo 1998; Smith 1994). The inability of nation states to regulate immigrant-initiated transnational activities (Smith and Guarnizo 1998; Kearney 1991) has caused concern among some who view these ties as a threat to national cohesion (Huntington 2004, 1997; Glazer and Moynihan 1975). Others view these ties as an impediment to the socioeconomic and political incorporation of immigrants in the United States through the development of a "transient mentality" or an "ideology of return" among them (Torres-Saillant 1989). Many more take an optimistic position by arguing that transnational processes are necessary for enhancing the social, economic, or political well-being of migrants, their households, and communities in the home and host countries (Levitt 2001; Shain 1999; Jones-Correa 1998; Pessar 1996; Glick Shiller et al. 1995).

This initial view of "transnationalism from below" was quickly challenged by studies observing that nation-states were increasingly co-opting and advancing these practices by offering dual citizenship, advocating on behalf of their émigrés, and sponsoring a variety of programs designed to forge ties with migrant communities abroad (Itzigsohn 2000). At the same time, immigrant-sending countries were encouraging émigrés to pursue U.S. citizenship and become active in American politics (Guarnizo 2001). These efforts were not driven by benevolence, but by a desire to secure, increase, and sustain remittance and tourist dollars from abroad, which has become the largest source of foreign revenue for many third world countries (Itzigsohn 2000). Among Latin American countries, involvement in facilitating ties with their diasporas has intensified in the last decade (Jones-Correa 2001b, 1995; Guarnizo 2001; de la Garza and Pachón 2000). A critical indicator of this is the recognition of dual nationality. Immigrant-sending countries have extended many, but not all of the rights of citizenship to émigrés who naturalize abroad and, in some cases, to their émigrés' children. Before 1991 only four Latin American countries recognized dual nationality. Since then an additional six have. Specifically for the Latinos in our study, El Salvador recognized dual nationality in 1983, the Dominican Republic in 1994, and Mexico in 1998.

Puerto Rico's commonwealth status makes it unique among Latin American and Caribbean countries. Since 1917, Puerto Ricans, whether born in the U.S. mainland or Puerto Rico, have been U.S. citizens. As American citizens, Puerto Ricans have been more likely than other migrant groups to engage in revolving migration, a phenomenon long celebrated in Puerto Rican literature. Estimates on circular migration flows range from 10 to 45 percent of the total flow (Duany 2002). Citizenship arguably enables Puerto Ricans to simultaneously participate in U.S. and Puerto Rican politics to a degree unavailable to other Latin Americans (Duany 2002; Rodriguez 1993). Puerto Rican exceptionalism is also facilitated by another factor—the relative size of the Puerto Rican population in the U.S. mainland compared to the population in Puerto Rico. In 2004 approximately 3.8 million Puerto Ricans lived in the United States mainland and 3.9 million people lived in Puerto Rico.

According to Yossi Shain (1999) the presence of significant numbers of populations outside their territorially defined nation-states will cause the homeland to take an interest in their diasporas, which in turn creates transnational networks. Large numbers of fellow "countrymen" abroad may not only provide significant amount of remittances but also have the ability to act as a potential ethnic lobby, shaping economic and political ties between the United States and the homeland (DeConde 1992). This was evident during the North American Free Trade Agreement (NAFTA) debates when Mexico actively courted Mexican American–appointed and elected officials to promote this agreement (Shain 1999; de la Garza and Pachón 2000).

Although each of the four homelands has significant numbers of émigrés in the United States, all pale in comparison to Puerto Rico in terms of share of the "national" population. While Mexicans in the United States make up 60 percent of the U.S. Latino population, they only constitute 25 percent of Mexico's population. The number of Puerto Ricans on the mainland, however, nearly equals the population of Puerto Rico. (See table 6.1.) Perhaps this is one of the reasons why since 1948 Puerto Rico has created government institutions concerned with the well-being of the Puerto Rican diaspora, while most other Latin American countries have yet to develop these institutions. Mexico, for example, only began to develop such institutions in 1990. According to Jorge Duany, Puerto Rico's efforts "constitute one of the earliest examples of a transnational migrant policy by any state, whether colonial or sovereign" (2002, 183).

This discussion should not belie the fact that some transnational links have been initiated from the diaspora. Among our cases, the extension of dual nationality and the right to vote in elections in the Dominican Republic was largely the result of "bottom-up" pressure from Dominicans in New York City (Jones-Correa 2001b). Since the 1980s, Salvadorans in the United States have played prominent roles in supporting progressive groups in the homeland, many of which remain active today (Hamilton and Stoltz-Chinchilla 2001). Yet, the Puerto Rican diaspora has a longer and perhaps more intense pattern of initiating transnational political ties with the homeland. For example, while Chicano activists in the 1960s strongly

TABLE 6.1

Ratio of immigrant and ancestry populations to home-country populations

Country	Home-country pop.	Immigrant pop.	Ratio
Mexico	105,000,000 (2004)	26,630,000 (2004)	3.9:1
Puerto Rico	3,895,107 (2004)	3,840,000 (2004)	1.01:1
Dominican Republic	8,715,602 (2003)	764,945 (2000)	11.4:1
El Salvador	6,470,379 (2003)	655,165 (2000)	9.9:1

Sources: U.S. Bureau of the Census 2001; 2003; 2005a; 2005b. U.S. Department of State 2005; *Central Intelligence Agency World Factbook,* http://www.cia.gov/cia/publications/factbook/, accessed April 15, 2004.

Note: The 2000 Census data for Dominican- and Salvadoran-origin and ancestry populations in the United States likely underestimate the populations. Rubén Rumbaut estimates that there were 1,115,481 1st- and 2nd-generation Dominicans and 1,535,850 1st- and 2nd-generation Salvadorans in the United States and counted in the Current Population Survey in the 1998–2002 period. Using these figures, the Dominican ratio drops to 7.8:1 and the Salvadoran to 4.2:1.

identified with many third world national liberation struggles, only mainland leftist Boricua organizations organized in Puerto Rico on behalf of independence (Melendez 2003; Torres 1998). Such organizing on both the mainland and island extends back to the 1880s and continues to the present. Since 1978 grassroots activism on the part of the Puerto Rican diaspora has been stimulated by events in Vieques. Among those arrested in recent protests in Puerto Rico and the mainland were the three Puerto Rican representatives in the U.S. House of Representatives, Luis Gutierrez (D-IL), Nydia Velasquez (D-NY), and Jose Serrano (D-NY).

We then have reason to believe that Puerto Rico's commonwealth status affords Puerto Ricans a unique opportunity to establish and maintain transnational ties to a greater degree than other Latino migrants. Is this in fact the case? To answer this, we turn to examine the results of the TRPI's 2002 immigrant survey.

Comparing Latino Civic and Political Transnational Ties

The 2002 TRPI Immigrant Participation Survey included a variety of questions measuring transnational ties among Puerto Ricans, Mexicans, Salvadorans, and Dominicans in the United States. TRPI conducted this survey in July and August 2002. The sample includes at least four hundred respondents from each of these immigrant nationality groups, with a total respondent pool of 1,602. Respondents were randomly selected from within households. All interviewers were fully bilingual, and approximately 94 percent of respondents answered the questionnaire in

TABLE 6.2
Residential and political focus, by national origin

	Mexico %	Puerto Rico %	El Salvador %	Dominican Republic %
Residential intentions				
Plan to make a permanent home of the United States	62.3	61.2	71.1	49.7
Plan to return to nation of origin	37.7	38.8	28.9	39.0
Visits to nation of origin (2000–2001)				
None	45.0	54.0	41.3	65.3
One or more	55.0	46.0	58.8	34.8
Average number of visits among those who did visit home nation	2.69	2.24	2.29	2.31
Locus of political concerns				
Country of origin	14.5	8.2	11.0	9.3
United States	27.2	20.7	23.5	28.4
Both equally	52.4	65.5	62.1	61.6
Doesn't follow politics	5.9	5.6	3.4	0.8

Source: Tomás Rivera Policy Institute Immigrant Political Participation Survey.

Spanish. (For a detailed description of the survey and sample demographics, see Louis DeSipio and colleagues 2003.)

A quick review of questions measuring some of the most common forms of transnational ties offers little evidence that Puerto Ricans in the United States have a different relationship to Puerto Rico than do Latino immigrants to their home countries. Differences, where they exist, are relatively slight. (See table 6.2.) Puerto Ricans, for example, were somewhat less likely than Salvadorans and considerably more likely than Dominicans to plan to make a permanent home of the United States. Slightly more than 60 percent of Puerto Ricans (and roughly the same share of Mexican immigrants) took this position. The majority of Puerto Rican migrants had not visited Puerto Rico in the two years prior to the survey. This share of non-home nation visitors was approximately 10 percent higher than the rate of nonvisitors among Mexican and Salvadoran immigrants and 10 percent lower than the share of nonvisitors among Dominicans. Those Puerto Ricans who did visit Puerto Rico over that two-year period averaged 2.24 visits. This number of visits was the lowest of the four countries under study, but not by a wide margin. Finally, Puerto Ricans were somewhat less interested in the politics of Puerto than are Latino immigrants in the politics of their home nations. This gap, however, was more than compensated for by the fact that Puerto Rican migrant respondents were the most likely to report that they were interested in the politics of both the United States and Puerto Rico.

These measures may not offer much insight into the transnational civic and political engagement of Latino migrants/immigrants. To gage transnational civic and political engagement with greater precision, we next consider the questions designed to measure involvement in home-country associations/activities and participation in home-country politics. Four questions in the TRPI survey measured involvement in home country associations/activities:

- "Over the last year, have you gone to a meeting to discuss the politics of [Home Country]?"
- "Over the last year have you attended a cultural or educational event related to [HC]?"
- "Over the last year have you been a member of an organization that seeks to promote cultural ties between the United States and [HC]?"
- "Over the last year have you been a member of an organization of people from your hometown or state in [HC]?"

Participation in home country politics is measured by three questions:

- "Some migrants continue to participate in the politics of their home nations while others do not. Have you voted in an election in [HC] since you migrated to the United States?"
- "Have you contributed money to a candidate running for office or political party in [HC] since you migrated to the United States?"
- "Have you gone to a rally in the United States in which a candidate for office in [HC] or a representative of a political party in [HC] spoke?"

A review of bivariate data on respondents' answers to these questions indicates somewhat more variation than in terms of transnational civic and political engagement. (See table 6.3.) Puerto Rican and Dominican migrants generally show higher levels of involvement in home-nation associations and activities and home-nation politics than Mexican and Salvadoran migrants do. The activity most engaged in was attending a cultural or educational event related to the home country. Fully 43 percent of Puerto Rican migrants and 44 percent of Dominican migrants, for example, had attended a cultural or educational event related to Puerto Rico or the Dominican Republic in the past year. The comparable figures for Mexico and El Salvador were 27 percent and 23 percent, respectively. The transnational activity least engaged in was contributing money to home-country candidates and parties.

Here again, Puerto Rican and Dominican migrants displayed a higher level of involvement vis-à-vis Mexican and Salvadoran migrants. Yet, for the following three activities, (1) gone to a meeting to discuss the politics of the home country,

TABLE 6.3

Mexican, Puerto Rican, Salvadoran, and Dominican migrant transnational engagement

	Mexico %	Puerto Rico %	El Salvador %	Dominican Republic %
Latin American migrant involvement in home country associations/activities				
Over the past year, have you . . .				
Gone to a meeting to discuss the politics of [HC]	6.2	14.6	5.8	21.8
Attended cultural or educational event related to [HC]	26.6	42.7	23.1	43.9
Been a member of an organization that seeks to promote cultural ties between the United States and [HC]	6.7	15.2	5.6	12.8
Been a member of an organization of people from your hometown or state in [HC]	8.5	12.1	7.8	22.8
Latin American migrant participation in home country politics				
Voted	9.5	14.6	8.5	15.0
Contributed money to candidates or parties	2.0	5.3	2.8	6.3
Gone to a rally in the U.S for an [HC] candidate or party	2.7	11.6	2.3	17.3

Source: Tomás Rivera Policy Institute Immigrant Political Participation Survey.
Note: [HC] refers to name of respondent's home country.

(2) become a member of an organization of people from your hometown or state in the home country, and (3) gone to a rally in the United States for a home-country candidate, Dominican migrants display much higher levels of involvement than the other groups do. Overall, the results show that migrants, regardless of nation of origin, were more likely to report having been involved in home-country associations or activities within the United States than they were to report involvement in home-country politics. This difference may be the result of greater costs associated with involvement in home-country politics or simply that these types of activities are tied to home-country election cycles, thus occurring with less frequency.

Modeling Puerto Rican and Other Latino Transnational Engagement

These bivariate results, of course, could obscure significant differences in the composition, experiences, and attitudes of these Latino national-origin groups. Puerto Rican and Mexican migrants, for example, have, on average, resided in the United

States for somewhat longer. Salvadoran migrants are the youngest Latino immigrant population and have the lowest incomes. Although not directly relevant to this study (because we are somewhat limited in the immigrant characteristics that we can examine to compare the non–Puerto Rican and Puerto Rican migrants in the study), Mexican immigrants are the most likely to be in the United States in an undocumented status.

To evaluate what predicts Puerto Rican engagement in transnational politics and to compare that experience to those of the other three Latin American émigré populations in the study, we employ logistic regression analyses to predict both forms of transnational civic and political engagement: (1) involvement in home-country associations/activities and (2) involvement in home-country politics.[2] The model includes three components that previous scholarship in this area suggests would predict political engagement and transnational engagement: individual demographic characteristics, immigrant characteristics, and measures of incorporation and efficacy. We have no expectations that these variables will have a differential effect across the two types of transnational activities studied here. Thus, our description of the variables and their theoretical effects apply to both activities.

We include three demographic characteristics: age, education, and income.[3] The influence of each of these characteristics is widely understood for U.S. political engagement, though their effect on immigrant adaptation and transnational politics is less clear (DeSipio 1996, 2002b; DeSipio et al. 2003). Older immigrants are more likely to have been socialized in the home country and have stronger familial and social ties to the home country. As a result, we expect older migrants will be more engaged in transnational politics. We disagree about the expected influence of high levels of education. On the one hand, higher levels of education could give migrants the resources to acculturate and engage U.S. politics. On the other hand, higher levels of education would give migrants greater resources to participate in home-nation politics. We have no expectations for the expected influence of income, though some find that individuals with greater socioeconomic resources have an easier time traveling back to the home country and/or engaging in transnational entrepreneurial activities (Levitt 2001; Guarnizo 1997). The degree to which income promotes participation in home-country associations and politics is an open question.

We also look at three immigration characteristics: plans for long-term residence, location of family, and ratio of life spent in the United States. We see the *plans* for long-term residence as a measure not necessarily of where the respondent will actually live in the future, but instead of where the respondent sees himself/herself in the long term. We anticipate that immigrants who see themselves returning to their home nations as being more likely to be engaged in transnational political activities (DeSipio 1996). Since return has fewer consequences for Puerto Ricans, we would expect this variable to have particularly strong predictive value for Puerto Rican respondents. Second, we include the location of most of the respondent's family. We would anticipate that those who reported having transnational families would be more likely to be engaged in home-nation focused civic and political life (DeSipio 2002b). Finally, we look at ratio of life spent in the United States (calculated as length of residence in the United States divided by age). We expect that respondents with higher U.S.-residence ratios will have lower engagement in their home-nation politics.

Our immigration predictors are somewhat atypical. By including Puerto Ricans, however, we are somewhat limited in what we can include while maintaining comparability. (This is the asterisk that we refer to in the first paragraph of the essay.) We cannot include either citizenship status or visa status that would be routinely included in an analysis of political attitudes, values, or behaviors of immigrant-ethnic populations. We expect that the U.S.-residence ratio variable captures some of these other immigrant-related characteristics for the non–Puerto Rican respondents. Those with lower ratios will probably include a higher share who are not in legal resident statuses and those with a higher U.S. share will include a higher share of naturalized U.S. citizens.

Finally, we include three measures of incorporation and efficacy. We include: level of attention paid to coethnics in the United States, the experience of discrimination in the United States, and migrant perception of their influence on the politics of their home nation. The degree to which migrants follow events pertaining to their fellow nationals can be taken as a measure of ethnic cohesion. Since political events in the home country are likely to affect the émigré population as a whole, we believe that higher levels of attention to coethnics are associated with higher levels of interest and engagement in the politics and civic life of home nation. The experience of discrimination variable assesses perception of discrimination by one or more of following: the police, at the workplace, when buying or renting a home, or by school officials. Perception of discrimination has been shown to be a positive predictor of political engagement in domestic politics (DeSipio 2002a; Pantoja and Segura 2003; Pantoja, Ramirez, and Segura 2001), and, it is argued, to foster attachment to the home country (Basch et al. 1994). We anticipate that discrimination will be associated with higher levels of transnational politics and civic engagement. Finally, we include an efficacy measure, though not the traditional one. In this case, it is a measure of how much influence individuals believe they have on home-country politics. We expect that increased political efficacy toward the home country would lead to greater transnational engagement.

Results

Puerto Rican migrants who are engaged with associations and activities concerned with Puerto Rico are migrants who have spent a lower share of their lives in the United States, who pay relatively more attention to other Puerto Ricans, and who believe that they have influence on Puerto Rican politics. (See table 6.4.) Demographic characteristics of Puerto Rican migrants play no statistically significant role in these activities.

For other Latino immigrants, however, increasingly high levels of education predict transnational associational membership and transnational activities as does the experience of discrimination in the United States. Latin American migrants with long-term plans to reside in the United States are less likely to be transnationally engaged. As with Puerto Rican migrants, spending a higher share of one's life in the United States reduces the likelihood of transnational engagement.[4]

Turning to the predictors of transnational electoral engagement among Puerto Rican migrants and other Latino immigrants, the results show a somewhat similar pattern. (See table 6.5.) Increasing age predicts home-nation electoral engagement for both respondent groups. Higher levels of efficacy in the sending nation also positively predict the likelihood of electoral participation for both groups, though the effect is more consistent and stronger for Puerto Ricans.

As was the case with the model predicting participation in transnational associations and activities, more characteristics proved significant in predicting electoral behaviors among the non–Puerto Rican Latino immigrants. Post–high school education (relative to respondents with grade school education or less) and the experience of discrimination in the United States increase the likelihood of involvement in home-country electoral activity. Plans for long-term residence in the United States decrease this likelihood.[5]

Conclusions

Overall, the evidence is mixed on the questions we ask in this piece. Contrary to expectations that Puerto Rican migrants would display higher levels of transnational civic and political ties than the other Latino migrant groups, we find little evidence in support of Puerto Rican exceptionalism. Although Puerto Ricans did appear to have stronger home-country ties than Mexican or Salvadoran migrants, they rarely surpassed those established by Dominicans. In some cases Dominican transna-

TABLE 6.4
Predictors of home-country associations and activities

Independent variable	Puerto Ricans		Other Latino Immigrants	
	Odds Ratio	SE	Odds Ratio	SE
Demographics				
Age	−0.004	0.010	0.002	0.006
Education (grade school or less)				
Some high school	−0.183	0.388	0.762***	0.208
HS graduate	0.537	0.442	0.897***	0.224
Post–high school	0.536	0.431	1.551***	0.227
Household income ($15,000 or less)				
$15,000–$24,999	0.255	0.409	0.121	0.212
$25,000–$34,999	−0.517	0.541	0.176	0.260
$35,000–$49,999	0.956	0.599	0.421	0.313
$50,000+	0.315	0.534	−0.351	0.373
Don't know/refused	−0.895	0.416	−0.150	0.224
Immigration characteristics				
Plans for long-term residence (home country)				
Not sure	−0.103	0.409	−0.318	0.231
U.S.	−0.295	0.336	−0.375**	0.178
Location of family (most in home country)				
Equally divided	0.079	0.355	0.024	0.195
Most in United States	0.024	0.397	0.175	0.219
Ratio of life spent in the United States	−1.269**	0.636	−0.865**	0.419
Incorporation/efficacy				
Level of attention paid to coethnics (hardly at all)				
Now and then	0.226	0.550	0.383	0.310
Some of the time	1.051*	0.562	0.485	0.311
Most of the time	1.193**	0.532	0.773*	0.298
Experience of discrimination in U.S. (none)				
One agency	0.061	0.420	0.396**	0.193
Two or more agencies	0.301	0.368	0.452*	0.257
Migrant influence on HC politics in last year (none)				
Not much	1.505***	0.542	−0.173	0.314
Not sure	0.312	0.547	−0.302	0.331
Some	2.022***	0.569	0.208	0.310
A great deal	1.372***	0.548	0.100	0.296
Constant	−0.925	0.892	−1.344***	0.517
Total cases	282		837	
Predicted correctly	70.6%		66.5%	
	R²=.320		R²=.159	

*** p < 0.01   ** p < 0.05   * p < 0.10
Source: The TRPI Immigrant Political Participation Survey, 2002.
Note: "Other Latino immigrants" includes Mexican, Salvadoran, and Dominican immigrants.

TABLE 6.5
Predictors of home-country electoral activity

Independent variable	Puerto Ricans Odds Ratio	SE	Other Latino Immigrants Odds Ratio	SE
Demographics				
Age	0.021**	0.010	0.030***	0.008
Education (grade school or less)				
Some high school	−0.002	0.403	0.379	0.265
HS graduate	−0.768	0.492	0.201	0.289
Post–high school	−0.133	0.445	0.886***	0.270
Household income ($15,000 or less)				
$15,000–$24,999	−0.667	0.427	0.136	0.262
$25,000–$34,999	−0.804	0.576	0.013	0.317
$35,000–$49,999	−0.993	0.618	−0.701	0.444
$50,000+	−0.309	0.543	0.236	0.436
Don't know/refused	−0.904***	0.442	−0.084	0.275
Immigration characteristics				
Plans for long-term residence (home country)				
Not sure	0.062	0.435	−0.943***	0.293
U.S.	0.248	0.344	−1.005***	0.215
Location of family (most in home country)				
Equally divided	0.178	0.364	0.102	0.240
Most in United States	−0.557	0.419	0.079	0.268
Ratio of Life Spent in the United States	−0.384	0.649	−0.379	0.526
Incorporation/efficacy				
Level of attention paid to coethnics (hardly at all)				
Now and then	0.969	0.640	0.354	0.410
Some of the time	0.887*	0.664	0.363	0.410
Most of the time	1.460**	0.624	0.687*	0.385
Experience of discrimination in U.S. (none)				
One agency	0.186	0.441	0.441*	0.234
Two or more agencies	−0.166	0.387	0.892***	0.283
Migrant influence on HC politics in last year (none)				
Not much	0.318	0.565	0.158	0.394
Not sure	−0.254	0.586	−0.062	0.420
Some	0.371	0.568	−0.088	0.401
A great deal	−0.364	0.580	0.265	0.371
Constant	−2.353***	0.971	−3.063***	0.643
Total cases	285		845	
Predicted correctly	74.7%		82.1%	
	R^2=.141		R^2=.142	

*** $p < 0.01$ ** $p < 0.05$ * $p < 0.10$
Source: The TRPI Immigrant Political Participation Survey, 2002.
Note: "Other Latino immigrants" includes Mexican, Salvadoran, and Dominican immigrants.

tional ties far exceeded those created by the other Latino groups. Yet, in terms of the reasons why different Latino migrants engage in transnational civic and political participation, Puerto Ricans do appear to become engaged for different reasons. For Puerto Ricans, the immigration/incorporation variables (and ratio of life spent in the United States) prove to be the major predictors of transnational engagement. Among the immigrant incorporation variables, the two that proved significant were home country-focused ones: ethnic cohesion and efficacy. For the other Latino immigrants, demographic and immigration variables (again, along with ratio of life spent in the United States) proved more important to predicting the outcome.

Home-country electoral activity, conversely, saw less difference between Puerto Rican and non–Puerto Rican migrants. The model for the non–Puerto Rican migrants did see some additional variables prove to be significant, however. Again, the immigration variables — particularly the long-term residential intentions — play a more important role for non–Puerto Rican–Latin American immigrants. Interestingly, perception of discrimination in the United States also proves to be a statistically significant positive predictor of home-country electoral activity for the non–Puerto Rican–Latin American immigrants. Discrimination was unimportant as a predictor for Puerto Ricans.

Although small sample sizes should offer some caution in interpreting these results, they suggest one important difference in the experience of Puerto Rican migrants and Latin American immigrants. Specifically, except for share of life spent in the United States, immigration characteristics do not drive Puerto Rican connections with Puerto Rico. These immigration characteristics do play a role for Latin American immigrants. In their place for Puerto Rican migrants are attitudes, both toward their coethnics and toward their sense of influence/efficacy on the government of Puerto Rico.

This explanation for these differences cannot be determined from the survey data reported here. In part, the different experience of the Puerto Rican migrants must derive from the long-term efforts of the Puerto Rican government to serve as a resource for and sometimes to organize Puerto Ricans in the United States. These efforts date back to the late 1940s, with the creation of the Migration Division, and have been a continuing objective of the Puerto Rican government, now under the auspices of the Puerto Rico Federal Affairs Administration. To the extent that the difference, however, is a function of the long-term nature of the Puerto Rican commitment to organizing its émigrés, the gap with (some) other Latin American émigré populations will decrease. Of the three countries under study here, both the Dominican and Mexican governments have begun these outreach efforts over the last decade and seem to be committed to continuing these efforts. El Salvador has been less involved, in part as a result of the divisions that are a legacy of the civil war, but it has begun to initiate some targeted outreach from some of its consulates in the United States.

It is quite likely, however, that not all of the differences between Puerto Rican and other Latin American immigrant populations are the result of the legacy of Puerto Rican government outreach to Puerto Ricans in the United States. The relative unimportance of the immigration characteristics in the experience of transnationalism among Puerto Rican migrants indicates that the unique relationship between the United States and Puerto Rico has created an opportunity for Puerto Rican transnationalism to emerge that is different from that of other Latin American émigré populations. This suggests that the failure of previous immigration scholarship to theorize about and analyze Puerto Rican migrant adaptation represents a substantial gap in our understanding of the dynamics of immigrant transnational engagement in general. More important, it misses a natural experiment in the study of transnationalism whereby the immigration experience—controlled more by the receiving country than the sending country—is removed from the picture. To the extent that transnational politics becomes a more central element in the study of ethnic politics in the United States, the experience of the Puerto Rican migration needs to be moved to a more central position (and the asterisk needs to be removed from much of our analysis).

Notes

1. We would like to express our appreciation to the Tomás Rivera Policy Institute for making these data available for our analysis. The survey was designed by Louis DeSipio, Rodolfo O. de la Garza, Harry Pachón, and Jongho Lee. A more detailed discussion of the design of the survey and the findings related to the relationships between home-country political activities and U.S. political engagement among Latino immigrants appears in DeSipio et al. 2003.

2. We have structured the dependent variable to distinguish transnationally engaged immigrants from the nontransnationally engaged. Since most respondents were not engaged in transnational activities, respondents who engaged in at least one activity were coded 1 and all others were coded 0. Our purpose here is not to measure the depth of transnational engagement in which we would distinguish by number of transnational involvements. The underlying survey asks only about involvement/noninvolvement in the activity, not the number of times the respondent had been involved in each activity.

3. A large share of the missing data are the result of respondents not providing their age. Approximately 15 percent of respondents did not provide their age. Year of migration was also problematic for many respondents; approximately 13 percent of respondents did not answer this question. (Many who didn't answer one didn't answer the other.) Clearly, these are very important variables for our analysis, so we tolerate higher rates of missing data than we would otherwise like.

4. Our goal here is to distinguish Puerto Rican from other Latino migrants, but it would

be disingenuous to homogenize the other Latino immigrant populations. We ran a separate specification of the model that included country of origin. Dominican migrants were approximately 2.3 times as likely to engage in the transnational associational activities than were Mexican immigrants controlling for other variables in the model. Salvadoran migrants were not statistically different from Mexican migrants.

5. We again tested this the non–Puerto Rican model with national origin added. Again, Dominican immigrants were considerably more likely than Mexican immigrants to report having been involved in home country electoral activities controlling for other factors in the model. Salvadoran immigrants were not statistically different from Mexican immigrants.

PART 3

Latino Coalitional Politics

Bonding and Bridging

Latinos and Social Capital

Sylvia Manzano

R OBERT PUTNAM'S *Making Democracy Work* (1993) and the subsequent *Bowling Alone* (2000) were met with both dramatic praise and criticism from members of the academic community (Tarrow 1996; Brehm and Rahn 1997; Edwards and Foley 1998; McLean et al. 2002). His research on declining levels of social capital and civic engagement and the public consequences of these phenomena became a lightning rod for those who study political behavior. Why the controversy? Putnam was lauded for his unique social capital approach as he attempted to explain apathetic America (Rahn, Brehm, and Carlson 1999; Uslaner 1999). Others were more critical of his conceptualization of social capital in his research (Levi 1996; Greeley 1997; Alex-Assenoh 2002). Though not unique to Putnam's work, the lack of attention to diversity-related issues and how social capital may operate differentially according to ethnic or racial context is a legitimate criticism (Segura, Garcia, and De la Garza 1999; Edwards and Foley 2000; Segura, Pachón, and Woods 2001; Hero 2003). While it is true that Putnam does not fully address social capital and its relationship with minority groups, he does provide an interesting, if not compelling, theoretical argument that is ripe for testing in the context of ethnic political behavior.

This essay considers how Latino political behavior may be shaped and influenced by social capital. Latinos now compose the largest minority group in the United States and approximately 13 percent of the national population. Despite these numbers, it is also true that sizeable proportions of the Latino population are ineligible to vote because of age or citizenship status (Hero 1992; DeSipio 1996; Gonzalez-Baker 1996). Such being the case, it is useful to conceptualize Latino political behavior in activities that extend beyond the voting booth — such as participating in demonstrations, signing petitions, or volunteering for a campaign. There is evidence that Latinos participate in nonelectoral political activities at higher rates than others, thus overcoming some of the legal limitations placed on their participatory options (Leal 2002; Wrinkle et al. 1996; Garcia 1988). Protests that took place in the spring of 2006 illustrate this point. Approximately 3 million Latinos of all ages and citizenship statuses marched in cities across America to voice their opposition to new, highly restrictive immigration laws that were pending in the House of Representatives. Socioeconomic factors offer only limited explanation of Latino political behavior (Hritzuk and Park 2000); it behooves us to employ theoretical models that move beyond SES to better understand how and why Latinos participate in the American political system. This is the point where social capital and Latino politics meet. Social capital, as conceptualized and popularized by Robert Putnam, allows for exploration of the social, personal, public, and institutional resources that Latinos possess. This theoretical framework makes it possible to examine how those resources function in Latino political participatory behaviors.

To test whether Putnam's version of social capital is applicable to Latinos (or any other population for that matter), a research design must be created that is inclusive of the many social capital components Putnam discusses. Contrary to what critics have suggested, social capital is not defined merely by organizational membership (Alex-Assenoh 2002; Fischer 2001; Ladd 1996). Though Putnam extensively studies organizations, he clearly states that social capital is composed of a combination of resources: community and organizational life, engagement in public affairs, community volunteerism, informal sociability, and social trust (Putnam 2000, 291). Across disciplines, research supports the merits of social capital in explaining a variety of political, social, and economic phenomena (Newton 1997; Edwards and Foley 1997). In the political world, social capital connects people in ways that influences political participation. Does social capital have the same explanatory power within the Latino population as it has demonstrated among the Anglo population?[1]

For the most part, research on the relationship between political behavior and social capital has been explored in the context of the majority population and electoral politics (Putnam 2000; Rahn, Brehm, and Carlson 1999). Less attention has been directed toward a fuller array of participatory modes, much less exploring their explanatory potential for minority populations (Garcia and Manzano 2001). This essay considers how social capital itself may be mitigated by ethnicity and then evaluates how these resources influence Latino political behavior.

What Is Social Capital?

There is evidence that greater numbers of Americans are less connected to social groups and networks than ever before (Skocpol 1999; Putnam 2000). Arguably, political participation has declined as a consequence. Social capitalists agree that the by-products of social networks are skills and resources that, for the most part, positively manifest themselves in a variety of personal and public venues that benefit both the individual and society. Specific to political science, social capital attempts to identify and establish linkages among individuals whereby they become coupled to others and to a larger political community. As a result, greater accumulation of social capital provides resources for political involvement and expression. Social capital as defined and popularized by sociologist Robert Coleman (1988) is a resource for action within an individual's social structure. He identified three primary components: obligations and expectations, information channels, and social norms. The essential characteristic of social capital is its convertibility: it may be transformed into numerous forms of capital (Massey 1999).

Social capital creates and maintains community. Broadening the application of social capital to the political world recognizes how social networks can transform skills, resources, and connections into an active political life. Political participation levels are affected by the extent of social capital accumulated whereby higher levels of social capital are associated with higher levels of participation and a wider range of political activities. Information channels created through social capital depress information costs for all community members. The social norms within these networks also constitute a powerful form of social capital that may encourage or discourage development of social networks beyond the individual's core community (Coleman 1988).

An idea central to the social capital literature is the differentiation of two types of social capital—bridging and bonding. Bridging activities extend an individual outside of his environment and broaden social networks and experiences. Bridging activities are defined by inclusive social connectedness across lines of class, ethnicity, gender, race, and broader lines of community building. Bonding capital is developed via associations within one's core community that may include voluntary organizations, religious institutions and residential enclaves. Bonding social capital reinforces exclusive identities (i.e., race, ethnicity, gender, class) and defines the scope of societal interactions. Social capital may be developed in both bonding and bridging activities, but there is not much research on the relationship between these different kinds of capital and political behavior. Does one kind of social capital influence political participation more than the other?

The Latino population possesses unique characteristics that make the bridge versus bond discussion particularly relevant. Bilingualism, Spanish-language usage, multilingual media consumption, national-origin group, nativity, and citizenship status are all factors that can have a strong influence on the kind of social capital available. Latinos may be more connected to coethnics (or non-Latinos, for that matter) via these variables. For Latinos, bridge and bond social capital resources are shaped by ethnic-related factors that may work in concert to funnel Latino political participation into Latino-specific or a more ethnically mixed political environment. For example, Latinos who accumulate more bond social capital may be more inclined to vote in an election when a Latino candidate is on the ballot.

The bonding strand of social capital arguably can be damaging to the economic, social, and political well-being of an individual. A strongly bonded community's social norms, obligations, and expectations may work to the detriment of the entire community. A social network that discourages and hinders bridging with out-group members limits available opportunities and benefits (Portes and Landolt 1996). Additionally, high levels of internal trust and dense social networks may also generate distrust toward those who are not a part of the core community (for example, those of dissimilar race or ethnicity). People within an exceedingly bonded social structure may be less prone to participate in some forms of political action discouraged by their community. There is some concern that a bond-based social capital (particularly centered on race or ethnicity) may insulate persons from involvement in broader, significant political activities.[2] Conversely, race and ethnicity can be powerful forces for social capital development to advance group interests and goals.

Research in the immigration literature finds that the combination of social capital and unique Latino characteristics produce specific outcomes. An immigrant's social capital resources become valuable commodities in the complex effort to migrate to the United States. Information that comes via social and familial ties may be used not only to assist in crossing the border but also to gain employment, secure housing, navigate legal complexities, and settle in the United States (Massey and Espinoza 1997; Zanhiser 1999). Over time migration becomes self-perpetuating, because each act of migration creates additional social capital that promotes and sustains more migration.

Social Capital Resource Development

Putnam specifies five dimensions of social capital. They include: (1) organizational involvement, (2) engagement in public affairs, (3) community volunteerism, (4) informal sociability, and (5) social trust. All five of Putnam's broad social capital categories correspond to concepts and components in the civic engagement and mobilization literatures. There is abundant evidence that different forms of mobilization yield specific acts of participation. Resources, attitudes, and social involvement levels are traits that individually or in combination yield specific participatory responses. Steven Rosenstone and John Hansen (1993) identify education, gender, race, language, and political efficacy as critical precursors to political participation. Norman Nie, Jane June, and Keneth Stehlik-Barry (1996) and Sidney Verba, Kay Lehman Scholzman, and Henry E. Brady (1995) agree that education is a central component to mobilization and civic engagement. Education primes individuals for mobilization and increases resources by creating and extending social networks. Moreover, education decreases information and participation costs, making mobilization and participation easier for highly educated populations (Putnam 2000; Nie, Junn, and Stehlik-Barry 1996; Verba, Scholzman, and Brady 1995). Educated individuals benefit from organizational exposure, institutional rules, and comprehending the benefits of working through a bureaucracy—which are experiences that can be directly applied to many forms of political participation.

Again, there is much scholarly concurrence regarding the importance of social connectedness in preparing and motivating individuals to participate in politics. Even in the least formal of settings, individuals use their casual acquaintances and relationships to transmit and discuss political preferences (Leighley 1990; Mc-Clurg 2003). The informal social flow of political information depresses information costs and mobilizes others to participate in politics (Giles and Dantico 1982; Huckfelt et al. 1999). In more formal contexts, there is evidence showing the importance of networks that are created in society's other institutions. The workplace, churches, and formalized voluntary organizations are sources of political skill and network building that prepare one for political participation (Ayala 2000; Greeley 1997; Nie, Junn, and Stehlik-Barry 1996; Verba, Scholzman, and Barry 1995; Sobel 1993). Additionally, the resources acquired in these venues have the effect of maintaining civic and political interest at a level that will encourage long-term participation over one's lifetime (Putnam 2000; Skocpol 1999; Berry 1999). Participation in these institutions places individuals in a setting with opportunities to become mobilized, to mobilize others, and to develop skill-building experiences (Brady et al. 1999).

Social capital developed in these different venues influence political participation. However, we still know very little regarding the ethnic context of social capital development. There is a need to examine bridge and bond social capital resources, where bridge social capital corresponds to a multiethnic context and bond to the coethnic setting. Additionally, individuals can participate in politics in a bridge or bond context as well. Specifically, Latinos (when given the opportunity) may choose to participate in Latino-specific political activities or non-Latino-specific activities. Using data from the Latino National Political Survey (LNPS), I examine whether the type of social capital resources (bridge or bond) corresponds to Latino or non-Latino-specific political participation.

Hypotheses

Because there is little known about the relationship between social capital and Latino political participation, this study embarks on exploratory testing to field some initial outcomes. The social capital literature has not fully addressed variations in bridged and bonded capital among and between ethnic and racial groups. Do bond social capital resources encourage Latinos to politically bond with coethnics? Are Latinos less likely to participate in non-Latino specific politics because of their excessively bonded social capital resources? What effect does Latino-oriented social capital have on political participation?

Given the findings in the political behavior, social capital, and Latino politics research, I develop three hypotheses regarding Latinos and social capital. (1) Among Latinos, bond social capital has a positive and significant influence on participation in Latino (bond) political activities, (2) Bond social capital will decrease participation in non-Latino (bridge) political activity, and (3) Bridge social capital resources will have differing outcomes for Latino and Anglo participation in general (bridge) political activity.

Data and Measures

The Latino National Political Survey is the data source used in this study. The LNPS includes 2,817 Latino respondents, half of whom are women. The three largest Latino national origin groups in the survey number 1,546 Mexicans, 589 Puerto Ricans, and 682 Cubans; 470 non-Hispanic whites (Anglos) are also included. The data set includes a wide array of variables related to demographics, socioeconomic status, political attitudes, and civic participation (de la Garza et al. 1992). A noteworthy benefit of the LNPS for the study of Latinos and social capital is that several survey items are presented in the very context of bridging and bonding.[3] This format allows me to assess the two types of social capital among Latinos in several aspects of civic and political life. Unfortunately, questions regarding Latino-specific activities and attitudes were not included in the Anglo questionnaire, limiting some of the inferential possibilities. Nonetheless, the data provide considerable amounts of information to proceed with the study of social capital and the finer points of bridging and bonding.

Independent Variables

Two sets of independent variables are selected to measure bond and bridge social capital. Both kinds of social capital are evaluated using five social capital categories: organizational involvement, engagement in public affairs, community volunteerism, informal sociability, and social trust.

Organizational Involvement captures the individual's participation within several social contexts, including workplace, educational, and religious institutions. Consistent with the literature, the following variables are used to measure bridge organizational involvement: frequency of church service attendance, supervising others at work, and attending a PTA meeting.[4] The bonding measures for organizational involvement are: ethnicity of organization members, membership in a Latino organization, and a belief that Latino organizations advocate Latino interests.[5]

Engagement in Public Affairs accounts for attention and interactions with others regarding civic issues. The following dichotomous variables account for bridge engagement in public affairs: following politics, discussing civic problems with others, and discussing voter registration. The following variables are used to assess bond engagement in public affairs: attention to Latino politics, discussing Latino problems with others, and awareness of an opportunity to vote for a Latino candidate.

Community Volunteerism is measured with only one variable for each category because of data limitations. The bridge volunteerism variable is measured using a survey item that asks if the respondent has worked to solve community problems. The bond community volunteerism measure tells us if the individual has worked to resolve Latino-specific problems in the community.[6]

Informal Sociability accounts for the respondent's social and daily contacts. It gives a sense of the person's exposure to and experience with coethnics and others. Ethnic residential density captures this dimension inasmuch as it tells us the ethnic context in which the respondent lives. It is possible to make some inferences regarding the amount of informal bridging taking place, given the diversity of the immediate community. The LNPS provides three bridge variables that measure the ethnic density of the respondent's residence. Measures of Latino informal sociability include survey items that measure discrimination experience, ethnicity of friends, and perception of a common Latino culture.[7] These variables measure a sense of common experience and community with other Latinos that is exclusive to the group.

Social Trust measures account for trust in government, other people, and society at large. The variables included for bridge trust are perceptions of people's helpfulness and trustworthiness and perceptions of government. Bond trust variables measure Latino-specific attitudes; respondents are asked whether Latinos are more helpful and whether they make better public servants. Latinos are also asked whether they feel an obligation to work toward the election of more Latino public officials.

Dependent Variables: Political Participation

The dependent variables for participatory activities are divided into the two categories of social capital: bridging and bonding. The dependent variable used to assess bridging political activities is a measure of general political involvement.[8] This variable was created by summing participation in seven dichotomous political activities, which include: (1) wore a campaign button, (2) signed a petition, (3) volunteered for a campaign, (4) wrote a letter to the editor, (5) made a donation to a campaign, (6) participated in political rallies, and (7) attended a public meeting.[9] A scale reliability test confirmed that this method was suitable for the data.[10]

The dependent variable used to assess bonding political activities is also a measure of seven political activities specific to Latinos. Again, participation in these dichotomous variables was summed. The activities considered in this variable are: (1) mobilized other Latinos to vote as a group, (2) signed a petition regarding Latino matters, (3) volunteered for a Latino campaign, (4) wrote a letter to an editor regarding Latino concerns, (5) donated money to Latino candidate(s) or campaign(s), (6) participated in a boycott regarding a Latino concern, and (7) participated in a demonstration regarding a Latino issue. Again, the scale reliability test confirmed that this was suitable for these data.[11]

Large portions of the Latino population are faced with two major barriers to electoral participation: language and citizenship status. This being the case, it is best to evaluate political participation using measures that do not require citizenship or strong English ability to participate. Thus, voting specific activities were omitted from these two dependent variables.[12]

Model 1: General Political Activity and Bridge Social Capital

The first model measures the effect of bridge social capital indicators (in five categories) on general political involvement.[13] In this model Latinos and their Anglo counterparts are included in the data.[14] This evaluation is critical, because we are able to observe differences in how social capital may vary between these two groups. Variables used in the general political activity models include responses from both Latinos and Anglos. All of the items used in the general political model are categorized as bridging variables. This regression shows how bridge social capital resources influence Latino participation (positively or negatively) in non-Latino specific political activities.

Model 2: Latino Political Activity and Bond Social Capital

The second model tests the influence of bonded social capital variables on Latino political participation. The survey items employed in this Latino-specific model are closely related to the survey items in the previous models when it is appropriate.[15] At the same time, there are also variables included in this model that are specific to Latino respondents and are meant to distinguish the political and social uniqueness of the population in relation to social capital. This model demonstrates whether bond social capital resources encourage or discourage Latino participation in Latino-specific political acts.

Models 3 and 4: General/Latino Political Activity and Bond/Bridge Social Capital

Two additional regression models are produced. One model uses general political activity as the dependent variable and bond social capital indicators as the independent variables. The final OLS model has Latino political activities as the dependent variable and bridge social capital indicators as the independent variables. These tests are conducted to evaluate how bond social capital may help or hinder political participation in a non-Latino context. These regressions also test whether bridge social capital resources actually enhance Latino political participation. Both of these models examine the functionality of bridge and bond social capital in different ethnic political contexts.

Findings: Social Capital and Participation Multivariate Analysis

Four OLS models were estimated to evaluate the relationships between bridge and bond social capital and general and Latino political participation. The model significance tests illustrate that social capital influences Latino political participation in different ethnic contexts. These first indicators show bridge social capital resources have a more positive influence on political participation in both general and Latino specific political settings.

Results: Bridge Social Capital

Tables 7.1 and 7.2 deal with bridge social capital resources. Those with high levels of bridge capital should be well poised to participate in both their own ethnic communities and beyond. In table 7.1, general political activity that is *not* Latino specific (or bridging activity) is the dependent variable. Table 7.2 has bond (Latino specific) political activity as the dependent variable.

ORGANIZATIONAL INVOLVEMENT variables are all positively and significantly related to bridge participation in the first regression analysis. Attending a PTA meeting, supervising others at work, and attending religious services all have positive influences on participation in general political activities. When Latino political activity is the dependent variable (see table 7.2), the coefficients for church attendance and PTA attendance are again positive and significant. Supervising others at work did not have a significant relationship with Latino-specific political participation. Regardless of the ethnic political context, organizational involvement of the bridge variety is positively associated with political participation.

ENGAGEMENT IN PUBLIC AFFAIRS produced positive and significant coefficients for all three variables in both of the political activity models. Of the three indicators, discussing community problems with others had the strongest influence in both equations (table 7.1 b=.385, table 7.2 b=.303). Following current affairs and discussing voter registration also had a positive influence on both coethnic and general political activity. Interestingly, the engagement in public affairs coefficient values are at similar levels in both regressions.

COMMUNITY VOLUNTEERISM measures show that those who have worked to resolve community problems are more likely to participate in both Latino and general political activities. It is worth noting that community volunteerism produces the

TABLE 7.1
Bridge activity and bridge social capital

Independent variable	B	SE
Organizational involvement		
Religious service attendance	**0.194	0.066
Attend PTA meeting	**0.271	0.081
Supervise others at work	**0.271	0.080
Engagement in public affairs		
Follow current affairs	**0.231	0.060
Discuss voter registration	*0.185	0.081
Discuss community problem	**0.385	0.083
Community volunteerism		
Work to resolve problem	**1.558	0.098
Informal sociability		
Residential ethnic density-Mexican	−0.009	0.016
Residential ethnic density-P.R.	0.041	0.029
Residential ethnic density-Cuban	−0.029	0.022
Social trust		
Government trust	−0.029	0.061
Trust people	*0.229	0.111
Helpfulness of people	0.151	0.087
Controls		
Ethnicity	−0.024	0.113
Gender	−0.056	0.079
Education	**0.159	0.047
Constant	**−1.550	0.356

R .584   R Square .341   Adj R Sq .331   SE 1.291   F 36.474   Sig F 0.00
* p < 0.05   ** p < 0.01

highest coefficient values in both models (table 7.1 b=1.558, table 7.2 b=.986). Of the two types of participation, working to resolve problems has a larger influence on bridge political activity than Latino political activity.

INFORMAL SOCIABILITY: Proximity to Mexican, Puerto Rican, and/or Cuban origin communities was not significantly influential on either general or Latino political participation. Additionally, the substantive values for these three variables were the three lowest values in both regression models.[16] An additional consistency (though statistically insignificant) in the models is the negative relationships between Cuban residential ethnic density and political participation (b= −.029 and b= −.024). There is therefore no strong evidence here of a relationship between ethnic residential enclave and political participation in any ethnic political context.

TABLE 7.2
Bond activity and bridge social capital

Independent variable	B	SE
Organizational involvement		
Religious service attendance	**0.189	0.062
Attend PTA meeting	**0.203	0.077
Supervise others at work	0.063	0.076
Engagement in public affairs		
Follow current affairs	**0.236	0.055
Discuss voter registration	*0.147	0.077
Discuss community problem	**0.303	0.079
Community volunteerism		
Work to resolve problem	**0.986	0.097
Informal sociability		
Residential ethnic density-Mexican	0.004	0.015
Residential ethnic density-P.R.	0.030	0.026
Residential ethnic density-Cuban	−0.024	0.019
Social trust		
Government trust	−0.065	0.057
Trust people	0.189	0.112
Helpfulness of people	−0.102	0.082
Controls		
Gender	*−0.145	0.074
Education	0.043	0.042
Constant	**−1.064	0.313

R .478   R Square .228   Adj R Sq .216   SE 1.108   F 18.214   Sig F 0.00
* p < 0.05   ** p < 0.01

Social Trust examines a respondent's attitudes toward government and people. Only one measure, trust in others, produced positive and significant results in the general participation model (b=.229). The same measure in the Latino participation model was nearly significant (p=.09), and the coefficient was substantively a bit weak. Trust in government was negatively related to either type of participation, though the coefficients produced were not significant. Perceptions of people's helpfulness had opposite effects; higher levels of trust are associated with decreased Latino participation and increased levels of general activities, but these relationships were also statistically insignificant. This rubric of social capital has some merit, but the data do not support social trust as much as some of the other categories.

The Control Variables included in the two models varied slightly. Ethnicity is included in the first model that measures bridged/general political activity.[17] It is excluded from table 7.2, which accounts for Latino political activity, because the dependent variable here includes only Latino responses. Gender and education are also employed as control variables. The regressions produced varied results for these control variables. As would be expected, education had a positive and significant effect on general/bridge participation (b=.159). While gender and ethnicity were negatively related to bridge political activities, both were statistically insignificant in this regression. This statistically insignificant outcome is interesting, because it points out that social capital, as measured here, functions similarly for Latinos and their Anglo counterparts. The last model produced no significant relationship between Latino political activity and education levels, although there was a significant gender gap, whereby Latinas were significantly less inclined to participate in Latino political activities (b= −.145). This may be indicative of gender gaps in social capital accumulation.[18]

Bridge capital has a significant influence on Latino political participation. The data show that social capital that is accumulated in activities characterized by direct contact and conversation with others has the strongest influence on political participation. Three of Putnam's rubrics (organizational activities, engagement in public affairs, and community volunteerism) have the strongest overall influence on Latino participation in any ethnic political context. Also note that organizational involvement, engagement in public affairs, and community volunteerism are all stronger predictors than education.

Results: Bonding Social Capital Indicators

Tables 7.3 and 7.4 incorporate bonding social capital indicators as the independent variables. In table 7.3, Latino political activity (or bonding activity) is the dependent variable. Table 7.4 has general (bridge, non-Latino) political activity as the dependent variable. Only Latino respondents are included in these analyses.

ORGANIZATIONAL INVOLVEMENT variables are largely unrelated to political participation in both analyses. Only one measure, the perception that Latino organizations advocate Latino interest, has a significant and positive influence on either type of political participation. Those who perceived Latino groups to represent their interests were more inclined to participate in Latino politics (b=.645). Membership in Latino organizations also has a positive effect on participation in Latino politics, but is only marginally significant (p=.09). The findings in table 7.3 also indicates that the ethnic composition of the organization to which one belongs does not have a significant relationship with participating in Latino-oriented political events. When general participation is the dependent variable, the data show all three organizational involvement variables produce positive coefficients, but none

TABLE 7.3
Bond activity and bond social capital

Independent variable	B	SE
Organizational involvement		
Ethnicity of organization members	0.007	0.261
Membership in Latino organization	0.998	0.585
Latino organizations advocate interests	*0.645	0.284
Engagement in public affairs		
Attention to Latino issues	**0.588	0.171
Discuss Latino community problems	0.497	0.268
Opportunity to vote for a Latino	**0.667	0.267
Community volunteerism		
Work to resolve Latino issue	−0.116	0.276
Informal sociability		
Experience discrimination	0.364	0.270
Ethnic group of friends	−0.051	0.166
Latino shared culture	0.382	0.305
Social trust		
Helpfulness of Latinos	*0.601	0.261
Latinos should help elect Latinos	0.129	0.141
Latino officials help Latinos	−0.081	0.132
Controls		
Gender	−0.304	0.268
Nativity	0.171	0.339
Language	−0.128	0.189
Education	−0.109	0.154
Constant	−1.945	1.157

R .593   R Square .351   Adj R Sq .277   SE 1.558   F 4.746   Sig F 0.00
* $p < 0.05$ ** $p < 0.01$

are significant. Involvement with Latino organizations has a varied influence on political participation. Most of the measures tested here do not enhance Latino participation. Even so, it is important to note that bond social capital that is heavily entrenched in the Latino community does not discourage participation either. Rather, most Latino organizational involvement did not have an effect on Latino participation one way or the other.

The Engagement in Public Affairs variables produced a mixed bag of results. In terms of the coethnic political participation dependent model, attention to Latino issues and awareness of a Latino candidate were both positively and significantly correlated to participation in Latino politics (b =.588; b=.667). Discussing Latino problems with others also had a positive effect, b=.497, and is mar-

TABLE 7.4
Bridge activity and bond social capital

Independent variable	B	SE
Organizational involvement		
Ethnicity of organization members	0.381	0.305
Membership in Latino organization	0.274	0.687
Latino organizations advocate interests	0.195	0.332
Engagement in public affairs		
Attention to Latino issues	0.178	0.200
Discuss Latino community problems	*0.606	0.313
Opportunity to vote for a Latino	0.040	0.313
Community volunteerism		
Work to resolve Latino issue	0.030	0.322
Informal sociability		
Experience discrimination	0.492	0.316
Ethnic group of friends	0.077	0.194
Latino shared culture	0.090	0.357
Social trust		
Helpfulness of Latinos	0.410	0.306
Latinos should help elect Latinos	0.287	0.164
Latino officials help Latinos	−0.240	0.154
Controls		
Gender	−0.341	0.313
Nativity	−0.519	0.397
Language	−0.218	0.221
Education	0.104	0.181
Constant	0.480	1.351

R .487   R Square .238   Adj R Sq .151   SE 1.824   F 2.731   Sig F 0.00
* p < 0.05

ginally significant at p=.06. All of these coefficients are strong relative to the rest of the Latino participation model. Generally speaking, these variables appear to be good measures of the relationship between Latino engagement in public affairs and Latino political participation. Conversely, general participation is significantly correlated with only one of the engagement in public affairs variables: discussion of Latino community problems (b=.606). Attention to Latino issues and awareness of a Latino candidate are positively related to general participation but are not statistically significant. Having the opportunity to vote for a Latino candidate is the strongest predictor of Latino participation in either of the two models. This is an interesting finding given the rise in the number of Latino candidates, particularly at the local levels of government.

THE COMMUNITY VOLUNTEERISM indicator has a negative relationship with Latino participation, but a positive relationship with general participation. Those who report working to resolve Latino community problems are not significantly more or less likely to participate in politics. As more data on Latino participation become available, it will be possible to improve on this measure for further testing.

THE MEASURES FOR INFORMAL SOCIABILITY in the bonded context are meant to capture some of the uniqueness of the Latino social experience. None of these variables were significantly correlated with participating in Latino or non-Latino political activities. Having a diverse group of friends was negatively related to Latino participation. The five other relationships, though insignificant, were in the positive direction. Ethnicity of friends, perceptions of a shared Latino culture, and experience with discrimination, as measured here, do not influence political participation.

SOCIAL TRUST variables are directionally mixed and mostly insignificant. The one exception is that perceptions of Latinos as helpful to each other, which is positively and significantly related to Latino political activity ($b = .601$). And though in the positive direction, Latino helpfulness was not significantly correlated with general participation. Opinions about Latino public officials were negatively correlated with both Latino and non-Latino political activity, but again, insignificant. Feeling that Latinos should help elect other Latinos to public office was positively associated with Latino participation but was also statistically insignificant. This same variable was near significant ($p = .08$) in the model where general political activity was the dependent variable. That is to say, the belief that Latinos should work to elect coethnics had a positive influence on bridge participation. Overall, bond measures of social trust employed here are not strongly associated with political participation.

THE CONTROL VARIABLES included gender, nativity, language, and education.[19] Not a single one of the control variables was statistically significant when using bonding measures of social capital. Though it should be noted that there were consistent negative relationships found in the case of women and Spanish speakers, where both are less inclined to participate in either Latino or non-Latino political activities. Foreign-born respondents seem more inclined to participate in Latino activities, but the opposite is true for general political activities. Higher levels of education are positively associated with general political activity, but negatively correlated with Latino activity. Again, none of the aforementioned relationships meet significance test requirements. True as that may be, these outcomes are still of interest, as the standard control variables did not withstand testing. Again, it is important to recall that even though bond social capital did not increase Latino participation, it did not depress participation either.

Conclusions and Implications

The outcomes of the analysis yield several useful findings. First, it is clear that social capital does indeed have two distinct dimensions. The bifurcated analysis made the pronounced differences evident. The varied influence of bridge versus bond social capital resources on a range of political activities is clear. Contrary to the first and second hypothesis, bridging variables provided stronger explanatory power and relationships with both Latino and general political participation. Bond capital resources had consistently insignificant, and often substantively negative, influences on either form of political activity.

Specific to Latinos, it appears that social capital does highlight a pattern of participatory outcomes. Organizational involvement, engagement in public affairs, and community volunteerism, of the bridge variety, had the most pronounced effects on political participation in both ethnic contexts. This means that higher levels of bridged capital yield higher levels of political participation. The social capitalists who posit that increased bridged social capital yields increased political activity, regardless of its ethnic orientation, are supported with these findings. Bond social capital does not have much of a positive effect upon Latino political activity (certainly not in comparison to the bridge capital measures) and even less influence on general political activities. A more insular orientation, arguably, can depress any form of political involvement. Those hypotheses are not quite supported with the findings here. Rather, Latino insularity had no real significant influence on participation.

While a number of questions have been addressed in this essay, many steps can be taken to further this line of inquiry. It would be worthwhile to seek out new and complementary data sets that can broaden the measurement of several social capital categories. In light of the spring 2006 Latino protests, it is likely that much has changed in the minds and political experiences of Latinos. A newer data collection effort that can tap into contemporary Latino social capital resources might produce very different results than those found here — especially in terms of bond social capital.

Recall that the most significant predictor of Latino political participation in Latino politics was awareness of a coethnic candidate. Many cities and state governments have experienced a surge in Latino candidates and office holders since the

LNPS (1989). The effect of Latino candidates and elected officials on social capital is another dimension that merits further investigation. Venues for Latino social capital accumulation have also changed since the LNPS. The number of Latinos in the United States is larger as is the number of Latino office holders, Latino labor union members, Spanish-language media outlets, and use of protest politics. It would be useful to examine more contemporary Latino social capital and its effect on political participation in both Latino and general politics.

One issue that remains unresolved in this study is the role of bonding and bridging among Anglos. Indeed, Putnam has cited problems with assessments of bridging and bonding: "I have found no reliable, comprehensive, nationwide measures of social capital that neatly distinguish bridge and bond. . . . We must recognize that that these two kinds of capital are not interchangeable" (2000, 24). To make comparisons between Latinos and Anglos, we need to assess how bonded and bridged white respondents are within their own context. This data set did not make such analysis possible. It would be useful to explore how these two ethnic populations acquire and express bridge and bond social capital differently and the implications of those variations. To what extent are Anglo social capital resources of the bond and bridge variety? Furthermore, it would be useful to analyze how Anglos employ their social capital resources in both coethnic and non-Anglos political participation.

To determine how social capital influences American politics and participation, more empirical testing must be conducted that reflects the diverse population. Taking the bridge and bond dimensions into account will bolster our understanding of social capital, Latino politics and American politics altogether.

Notes

1. Robert Putnam, 2000, illustrates that high levels of social capital among whites is correlated with high levels of political participation.

2. Mexican immigrants, for example, are frequently relegated to specific occupations and geographic regions because they are so reliant on their limited social network in the United States (Massey 1999; Massey and Espinoza 1997).

3. For example, a respondent will be asked if he thinks people are helpful (bridge). Later in the survey, the respondent will be asked if he thinks people of his national-origin group are helpful (bond).

4. Attending PTA meeting and supervising others at work are coded 0=no, 1=yes. Religious service attendance is coded on a three-point scale: never, seldom, and frequently.

5. Membership in organization and advocacy of Latino organizations are coded as 0=no,

1=yes. Ethnicity of membership is coded 1=mostly coethnics, 2=mix of coethnics and others, 3= mostly not coethnics.

6. Coded as 0=no, 1=yes.

7. Perceptions of discrimination and a common Latino culture are coded as 0=no, 1=yes. Ethnicity of friends is a five-point scale that ranges from all coethnics to all of a different ethnic background.

8. Political activities that are not directly related to a campaign or cause that is Latino specific.

9. Two thirds of Mexican and Puerto Rican–origin respondents, as well as half of Cuban origin respondents in the survey, reside in areas where at least half of the population is non-Latino. Thus we can assume the respondents have had ample opportunity to participate in non-Latino specific political activities.

10. Chronbach Alpha =.72.

11. Chronbach Alpha =.65.

12. However, since voting is the standard political expression, it is useful to include an analysis of electoral activities associated with social capital variables. In a separate research paper, I employ logistic regression to conduct a more thorough analysis of these relationships.

13. That is to say that the political involvement included in this model is not limited to activities within the respondent's ethnic group.

14. Limitations in the data made it impossible to further disaggregate the Latino population in this model.

15. For example, the question on community volunteerism in the bridged model asks whether the respondent has worked to solve community problems. The question in the bonded model asks whether the respondent has worked to solve Latino community problems.

16. The coefficients range from a high of b=.004 (Mexican residential density and Latino/bond participation) to a low of −.029 (Cuban residential density and general/bridge participation).

17. Ethnicity is measured as 0=Anglo; 1=Latino.

18. I examine levels of social capital accumulation among Latino subgroups in a related research project.

19. Nativity: Dummy variable: 0=foreign born, 1=U.S. born. Language: Measured as mostly English, fully bilingual, or mostly Spanish.

A Place at the Lunch Counter

Latinos, African Americans, and the
Dynamics of American Race Politics

Helena Alves Rodrigues and Gary M. Segura

THIS SOCIETY, AND SCHOLARS who study it and its politics, arguably have an historical construction of a racial dynamic that is binary and largely African American–white. That is, when we approach questions of race, it has been through the analytic lens of an African American–white dynamic. And when our discussions moved beyond these issues, we generally viewed the emerging issues as analogues of the first, that is, a Latino/white dynamic, a Native American/white dynamic, and an Asian/white dynamic, each of which we assumed would mimic — to one degree or another — the African American experience.

The rapid growth of the Latino population has upset these approaches in two important and distinct ways. First, Latino population growth can be seen by African American political and intellectual elites as a serious threat to the place African Americans hold in the conscience of the nation and our national self-conception. If the race problem has always been an "African American" problem, the presence of a new player (or at least newly powerful and sizable) is sure to change those dynamics — and in unpredictable ways.

Second, the presence of two sizable and politically important minority groups raises questions about their relationships with one another. That is, whether we are more interested in the relations of African Americans with white America, or the relations of Latinos with white America, we can no longer ignore the importance and implications of the relations of Latinos and African Americans with one another.

It is to that relationship that we turn in this essay. What is the nature of black-brown relations in America? What is the future? Are Latinos and African Americans likely to emerge as two players on the same political team, or will their relationship prove more complex?

That Latinos and African Americans are likely, even inevitably, coalition partners in American politics is broadly and commonly accepted. Observers across the political spectrum speak of black-brown coalitions as the natural and expected course of evolution in minority group politics. This may, in fact, turn out to be the case. Latinos and African Americans share a number of politically relevant common characteristics. These include education and income levels significantly below the national averages, with all of the attendant correlates, such as lower homeownership rates, higher-than-average unemployment rates, higher likelihood of being victimized by both violent and nonviolent crime, and often significant residential segregation in inner cities or inner-ring suburbs. Occasionally, this residential concentration is collocated, that is, where African Americans and Latinos are living in shared or adjacent neighborhoods. In addition, both groups face historically high obstacles to election to public office, not the least of which is racial hostility among non-Latino whites (Anglos).

Beyond shared objective conditions, Latinos and African Americans are more Democratic in partisanship than nonminority Americans.[1] Non-Cuban Latino voters are stable Democrats at rates exceeding 60 percent (DeSipio and de la Garza 2002), and Democratic identification seems to be positively associated with length of time in the United States, as well as age-related increases in partisan strength (Cain, Kiewiet, and Uhlaner 1991). Latino Democratic partisanship favors the formation of biracial coalitions with African Americans, because, of all the partisan social groups in the United States, African Americans are the most loyal to the Democratic Party (Rosenstone, Behr, and Lazarus 1984, 169–70), a result that is consistent across gender, region, and a variety of demographic categories (Tate 1993).

But a contrary view would suggest there are any number of factors — political, social, and economic — that may well serve to undermine this commonality. Recent political events provide anecdotal evidence for both viewpoints. Mayoral races in America's two largest cities in 2001 and 2005 offer excellent examples of both Latino–African American cooperation *and* rivalry. And competition for economic resources and the attention of political parties and actors may well pit the interests of each group against the other.

Unfortunately, the amount of scholarship devoted to these issues has been modest. We'll survey the extant work further on. Fortuitously, however, the relative absence of an extensive literature allows us to think more broadly about how a comprehensive research program on this topic might proceed. That is, we can offer a systematic appraisal of what questions should emerge and how we might address them.

In this essay we will offer a conceptual framework to shape this new research program. We will argue that the important and interesting questions on black-brown relationships can be asked across multiple dimensions and at multiple levels of analysis. In so doing, we will review the existing literature to outline what progress has been made on any of those dimensions and where future work is most needed. Finally, we will offer some evidence of our own with regard to which direction this intergroup relationship might evolve.

We are governed here by our own perceptions of human decision making and our take on the nature of Latino and African American interaction. Loosely stated, our perception is rationalist in nature. That is, Latinos and African Americans will cooperate when, at the mass or elite level, they perceive that it is in their interest to cooperate—and not otherwise. We see significant evidence of sufficient points of commonality between the groups and their political positions so that a coalition, if carefully orchestrated, is clearly possible. We also see, however, sufficient evidence of affective indifference or distance, a general lack of affinity—particularly on the part of Latinos toward African Americans—so that this coalition is neither inevitable nor, in some cases, even likely. These outcomes, of course, are endogenous to more than individual attitudes and elite strategies but will be the product of the interaction of both within each group and between these groups and are clearly going to be affected by the policy actions and political strategies of Anglos in the system, who have interests of their own.

A Framework for Considering Issues of Black-Brown Relations

Interactions between African Americans and Latinos, we have suggested, will evolve as a consequence of the preferences, interests, and attitudes of each group. The outcomes may also vary across social strata and issues, however. We have identified three particularly salient dimensions in figure 8.1.

Figure 8.1 arrays the conflict and cooperation points between the two groups across three dimensions: elite vs. mass behavior, attitudinal factors versus political actions, and distinctly electoral or political concerns versus more generally socioeconomic issues. The resulting eight cells each represent potential areas of inquiry.

Political, Social, and Economic Elites and Mass Publics

The role of political elites in shaping the preferences and attitudes of the mass public is, by now, well known if not well understood (Page and Shapiro 1992, Stimson 1990, Ginsberg 1986, Kuklinski and Segura 1995). The information asymmetries

FIGURE 8.1
A conceptual framework for understanding the dimensions of black-brown relations

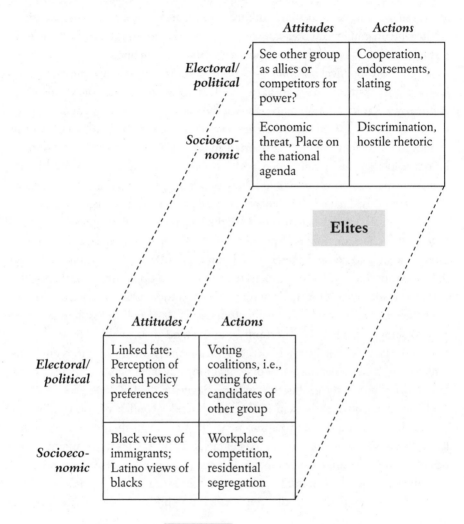

that favor elected officials, interest group entrepreneurs, party leaders, and community activists can, under reasonable circumstances, allow elites to mobilize opinion behind strategies that they, the leadership, have agreed to pursue. The effort is not always successful (Carmines and Kuklinski 1991), and there are certainly occasions where elite unanimity can break down (Page and Shapiro 1992), but political leadership often has the capacity to shape mass opinion and action.

Conversely, political coalitions—of necessity—will need to operate at the mass level, at least instrumentally, to have an effect on electoral and policy outcomes. Antipathy, or at least indifference, among the people can severely undermine coordination efforts agreed to at the elite level. For example, if Latino and African American office holders jointly supported an African American candidate for public office, perhaps as a consequence of a political exchange, there would be no guarantee that Latino voters would follow such a suggestion if the local communities were at odds. That is, it will not always be clear that elites can deliver the policy support—much less the actual votes—of the communities they represent.

Similarly, as economic and political conditions have improved for these two groups, some middle- and upper-class Latinos and African Americans have used their newfound resources to augment both power and opportunity for themselves and their respective group (Landry 1987, Jennings 1992, Dawson 1994), a pattern documented among white ethnics incorporated into the political system in earlier eras (Wolfinger 1965). This opportunity, however, need not facilitate biracial cooperation. In fact, the coalitional efforts of African Americans and Latinos are likely undermined if an influential leader of either group advances only the interests of his or her own group to the exclusion of others (Betancur and Gills 2000).

Political scientists interested in the emergence of conflict or cooperation between African Americans and Latinos may choose to focus their inquiry on either level of analysis. They may, in fact, be better served by looking at the internal politics of coalition within each group, an approach that would cause them to look at both the elite and mass strata. In either event, we are cautioned to understand the possibilities of similarity *and* difference when we shift our attention from one to another.

Attitude ≠ Action

We have just suggested that elite leadership in coalition formation will be more successful in the fertile ground of mass support and severely constrained when popular attitudes do not favor such an alliance. Attitudinal support for coalitions is an area of focus in extant research on black-brown relations, specifically the individual orientations of Latinos and African Americans toward coalition behavior.

Dissatisfaction with economic realities has been found to contribute to the likelihood of support for such cooperation. Kent Tedin and Richard Murray (1994), for example, have found that individual-level concern over economic conditions, such as poverty and unemployment, is associated with support for biracial coalition activities among both African Americans and Latinos, though to different degrees.

There is evidence, however, that these expectations have their limits. While the most vulnerable in each group, for instance those with less material wealth and political resources, may, by virtue of greater shared circumstances, be more supportive of biracial cooperation, this may not be the case if competition over scarce jobs and resources comes to characterize a particular environment. In that instance, poorer and less-educated respondents are *less* likely to favor coalitional strategies (Jackson, Gerber, and Cain 1994). Attitudinal support for coalitions is therefore not a given, and potentially is problematic.

Attitudes and political actions are, however, quite distinct, and the mere presence of supportive attitudes—which we have suggested may not be in place—is not alone sufficient to ensure cooperative action. There is often a significant disjuncture between individual preferences and the actions they take. We may find, for example, instances where African Americans and Latinos pursue the same policy option or support the same candidate for very different reasons, or because circumstances structure choices, not as a consequence of widespread policy agreement. For example, African American political leaders may choose to support a more permissive immigration policy—perhaps an amnesty plan—not because they share the same attitudes and incentives on immigration that Latino elected officials do, but because they might believe that African American wages would increase if undocumented labor became legal, or because the value of that intergroup cooperation is important for securing reciprocity on an issue of importance to African Americans at a later date. That is, the commonality of behavior reflects strategic or individual calculations of utility and is not a reflection of shared preferences.

Similarly, we may find circumstances where general attitudinal agreement between the two groups does not result in similar actions. For example, Latino and African American voters might agree on a wide variety of issues yet still choose to support different candidates at any level of government.

The aforementioned 2001 and 2005 New York and Los Angeles mayoral elections are a good example of how attitudes and actions are occasionally disconnected and whether or not black-brown coalitions can or will emerge. In New York in 2001, Latino and African American voters united to support Bronx Borough president Fernando Ferrer in the Democratic primary. His loss to Mark Green, in what was perceived to be a racially polarized campaign, prompted majorities of both groups to abandon the Democratic nominee and ensure the election of

Michael Bloomberg in the general election. In the 2005 mayoral run, Fernando
Ferrer faced a number of primary opponents, including an African American candidate, but he narrowly won the Democratic nomination over chief rival Anthony
Weiner. Ferrer was ultimately defeated in the general election by the billionaire
incumbent Republican mayor Michael Bloomberg. Despite his loss to Bloomberg, Ferrer won the majority of votes (59 percent) in the Bronx, a borough with
a large African American population. Much of his success among African American voters is attributed to his advocacy of lower-cost housing, as well as endorsements by unions, city organizations, and prominent Democrats like the Reverend
Jesse L. Jackson.

Unlike the 2001 and 2005 mayoral elections in New York, in the Los Angeles 2001 mayoral election, African American and Latino voters backed rival candidates, each of whom made it to the general election in the nonpartisan system. In
the end, an Anglo Democrat, James Hahn, was elected on the strength of African
American and Republican support, over a Latino candidate with a primarily Latino and liberal base, Antonio Villaraigosa. By contrast, in the 2005 Los Angeles
mayoral runoff election, which was a rematch of the 2001 contest, Villaraigosa defeated Hahn. Hahn had lost a big share of his support among African American
voters who were dismayed with his performance and failure to meet 2001 campaign
promises, and in particular, his decision to replace police chief Bernard Parks, an
African American. Parks, in fact, was a candidate in the primary election and subsequently endorsed Villaraigosa in the runoff. Villaraigosa garnered 59 percent of
the votes, becoming the first Latino mayor of Los Angeles since the nineteenth
century. Since his mayoral victory, Villaraigosa has been forthright in expressing
that his agenda extends beyond the interests of Latinos and that he is interested in
building a coalition.

We have no reason to believe that policy preferences or attitudes varied widely
across the settings. Presumably, in both locations, both African American and Latino voters prefer candidates of their own ethnicity rather than those from the other
group, or at the very least, candidates with significant loyalty to their own community. Rather, the manner in which choices were structured—available candidates
and the nature of the local electoral system—resulted in different actions in the two
cities, at least in 2001. Conversely, it is likely that voters from both groups in Los
Angeles shared many policy preferences but in 2001 could not agree on who best
could actualize those preferences, while in 2005 they came closer to agreeing on
who could best build bridges and represent preferences across the communities in
Los Angeles.

A second distinction between the cases is the strategic conditions faced by minority voters. African Americans and Latinos both represent sizable communi-

ties in New York, whereas in Los Angeles, Latinos are on the verge of becoming an outright majority in a city whose African American population and political influence is perceived to be shrinking. While both minority groups in New York in 2001 and 2005 felt their interests would jointly be served with a Ferrer mayoralty, the outcome of the 2001 election in Los Angeles was perceived as zero sum. In short, the prospects for political coalition will be inexorably tied to the relative size of the two groups, their joint local political history, the perception of rivalry or cooperation with respect to resources, and the available candidates. We will return to this issue shortly.

Political circumstances will vary widely across the United States and over time. The cases of New York and Los Angeles illustrate how context matters in shaping the individual and collective political decisions of minority voters and their elites. The specificity of circumstances necessary for one outcome or the other should not be underestimated. For example, absent James Hahn's historic familial ties to the African American community in Los Angeles, it is unlikely that African Americans and Latinos would have been separated in 2001 by a political divide. The mayoral election in Los Angeles in 2005 may well have witnessed the emergence of a black-brown coalition reflective of changing political circumstances.

Scholars seeking to explore the mechanics of black-brown coalitions will therefore have to address whether emerging cooperation is the product of genuinely shared values and preferences or rather the result of circumstances and structured choices. Similarly, when points of conflict emerge, we will need to differentiate whether the source of that conflict is really in divergent values and preferences or is the product of more tactical or strategic considerations by community leaders.

Socioeconomic Circumstances and Political Implications

The final dimension is perhaps the most familiar. As scholars, we need to distinguish between the purely political aspect of black-brown relations and the more socioeconomic aspects. As political scientists, we naturally focus most of our attention on electoral behavior and policy preferences and outputs. To be sure, the degree of cooperation or conflict between Latino and African American voters and elected officials is of critical importance to determining the effect either group has on the political system.

But the economic and social condition of Latinos and African Americans alike, some of which were described above, create two realities. The first is that shared circumstances work to define common interests. That both groups find themselves near the bottom of most social hierarchies suggests at least the possibility of shared economic and social interests with regard to income distribution, educational equity, and job opportunities, and the entire array of civil and voting rights protections.

Shared socioeconomic circumstances, however, lead to shared positions only when the similarity of circumstances and their root causes are accurately perceived. And, of course, not all Latinos and African Americans share socioeconomic circumstances emblematic of the average experience of the other group. Specifically, middle-class Latinos or higher-educated African Americans might not necessarily perceive their own coethnics, let alone the other group, as sharing needs and, hence, political interests. To the extent that social location varies at the individual level, so too should the sense of shared political goals, *ceteris paribus*.

Another complication is that the recognition of common interests between African Americans and Latinos is also influenced by the level of immigrant incorporation or assimilation into the U.S. polity or society. The shared economic and material circumstances, the history of African American political exclusion, and even the contemporary circumstances of African Americans in the United States are not necessarily familiar to the newly arriving immigrant. The realities and origins of social relations in this society are learned, just as the laws, business practices, and language are learned. Those most familiar with the U.S. political system, and more completely incorporated into U.S. society, should have a clearer perception of how their interests and those of African Americans might be consonant.

While common circumstances may lead to the perception of shared interests, a second likely effect simultaneously exists—the very high likelihood that these groups will be forced to engage in competition over jobs, over control of labor unions and sectors of the economy, and even over demographic hegemony at the neighborhood level. At least one characteristic of being near the bottom of the socioeconomic hierarchy is the increased salience afforded to matters of economic survival. This competition in society and in the economy, we believe, is very likely to foster some degree of resentment between the groups at the mass level. Issues such as competition for resources and status, stereotypes, and cultural differences have already been found to influence the perceptions and behaviors of these two groups (Robinson 2002). These same forces may even trigger hostile rhetoric and outright economic discrimination at the elite level.

Racial resentment between African Americans and Latinos would obviously not bode well for effective political coalition. Moreover, such resentment is sure to foster competition. The belief that members of one's particular group are collectively oppressed and unfairly treated by society has been found to be associated with the propensity to see other groups as competitive threats (Bobo and Hutchings 1996). These perceptions may develop from simple self-interest, orthodox prejudice (i.e., negative stereotyping), and beliefs about social stratification and inequality (Bobo and Hutchings 1996). On the question of whether Latinos have suffered less discrimination in the United States than African Americans have, the notions of the "invisibility" of the Hispanic community and the long practice of not counting "Hispanics" as a separate group on the U.S. Census must be considered. Among the arguments is that discrimination against Latinos is not as well-documented as that suffered by African Americans, and further, that sometimes this discrimination took the form of local practice rather than state-enforced laws, for example, "No Mexicans or Dogs Allowed" (Kamasaki and Yzaguirre 1995; see also San Miguel 1987).

The emergence of political coalitions between African Americans and Latinos thus depends on both the presence *and* the perception of shared circumstances. Political coalition and collective action requires individuals to perceive that their fate is linked, first, to others in their own social group and, second, between their group and another (Dawson 1994, 77). That is, for Latinos and African Americans to coalesce politically, Latinos must perceive a sense of "linked fate" or common interests with other Latinos, and they must perceive a similar, albeit weaker, link to the interests and fates of African Americans. Absent this sense of group solidarity and sentiment of intergroup shared interests, and even in the presence of shared socioeconomic circumstances, coalition is far less likely.

Evidence of Extant Cooperation?

There are a variety of anecdotal accounts of cooperation between Latinos and African Americans. For example, a recent news story documented the formation of an alliance between local League of United Latin American Citizens (LULAC) and National Association for the Advancement of Colored People (NAACP) chapters in, of all places, Spokane, Washington (Graman 2004). There clearly are occasions when leaders or members of the two groups cooperate. It is less clear how pervasive this is.

There is a modicum of literature examining whether and when black-brown coalitions have emerged. In what is perhaps the first scholarly attempt to discuss the formation of these coalitions, Charles Henry (1980) describes how both groups "suffer" similar social inequalities, such as median household incomes, unemployment, and college completion rates. These similar inequalities should naturally lead to the formation of political alliances, Henry argues, but he finds that Latinos have little interest in forming an alliance with African Americans (Ambrecht and Pachón 1974).

Studies of political context and the creation of interethnic coalitions have generally focused on whether the demographic or institutional circumstances were most likely to result in cooperative or competitive behavior. For example, some municipal-level case studies have focused on elections and candidates and detailed the success or failure of biracial coalitions (Henry 1980, Falcon 1988, Sonenshein 1989). Others have identified the factors predicting the formation of black-brown coalitions (Browning, Marshall, and Tabb 1984, Meier and Stewart 1991a).

According to Raphael Sonenshein (1989), visionary group leaders, especially those who supervise strong community organizations, are essential for developing and sustaining multiracial political coalitions between African Americans and Latinos. Further, the most effective coalitions are those that begin building in communities with strong political organizations already in place. Karen Kaufmann, like Sonenshein, also argues that the prospects for future coalitions between African Americans and Latinos rests in part on the role that Latino leadership and political organizations play, in this case by promoting strong panethnic identities (Kaufmann 2003).

In a more recent discussion of the coalition prospects between African Americans and Latinos, Nicholas Vaca (2004) argues few formal or even informal coalitions exist between Latinos and African Americans, because these two disenfranchised groups should not be presumed political allies. Using case studies from New York; Los Angeles; Miami; Washington, D.C.; Compton; and Houston, Vaca describes how language barriers, competition over affirmative action, and the overlooked contributions of Latinos during the American civil rights movement have prevented the formation of coalitions. African Americans, Vaca defends, view Latinos and their growing numbers as a threat to their social, economic, and political benefits. Further, Latinos do not view African Americans as an oppressed group in the same way other Americans may view them and their experiences. Such contrasting perceptions of each other inevitably lead to strained relations.

Other work offers a similar perspective. Despite similar histories of inequality, African Americans and Latinos have forged only tenuous partnerships. If the comparison of histories is contentious, focusing political activity specifically on racial and ethnic issues raises their salience and potentially further undermines the strength of the coalition. For example, Jennifer Hochschild and Reuel Rogers (2000, 6–7) argue that when a multiracial coalition focuses on issues of racial and ethnic equality, it is likely to fragment into competitive factions. Further, the benefits of biracial coalitions are sometimes unattainable as a consequence of past political disagreement, individual attitudes about the other group, and fear that the other minority group might gain the upper political hand (Tedin and Murray 1994).

Leni Guinier and Gerald Torres (1999) disagree and reason that the most effective way to involve minorities in racially inclusive coalitions is to organize them around political issues that are explicitly race specific. Racial minorities are less likely to respond to calls for coalition building, Guinier and Torres maintain, if their leaders do not speak first to them about matters that relate to their racial experiences. Only then would it be possible to get racial minorities to expand their concerns and embrace issues that interest all groups.

Cooperation and biracial coalitions are most likely to emerge when the two groups face equal circumstances in terms of status and class. This strategy is less likely to be successful if the relative positions of the two groups are different (Giles and Evans 1985). If the two groups are unbalanced in size or political power, the racial or ethnic group with the most representation in city and county government may fare better than the other racial or ethnic groups in terms of public service jobs and other government benefits. Thus, the better-positioned group might reasonably be less than eager about forming a coalition (Deutsch 1985; see also Browning, Marshall, and Tabb 1984, Sonenshein 1986, Warren, Stack, and Corbett 1986, Butler and Murray 1991, Meier and Stewart 1991a). In fact, they might choose to attempt a coalition with Anglos and may themselves be attractive to Anglos as a coalition partner. Such an environment will produce far more interminority competition than cooperation.

Evidence of competition, not surprisingly, is significant. For instance, Latinos have been found to make less progress in terms of socioeconomic well-being and political power in cities with African American majorities or pluralities (McClain and Karnig 1990). Further, African American and Latino municipal employment outcomes covary negatively with Anglo municipal employment, suggesting even more competition for these jobs (McClain 1993).

Competition extends to other segments of the environment as well, including political representation and the drawing of electoral districts. For example, while election results from 118 large, multiracial school districts indicate that as the African American population increases, political representation of Latinos increases, the reverse is not true. When the population of Latinos grows, African Americans do not gain but, in fact, lose political representation (Meier and Stewart 1991b). With respect to the drawing of district lines, the lack of cooperation might intensify because of redistricting, particularly in states such as New York and Texas, where African American and Latino leaders have debated the vote dilution of Latinos and the drawing of new majority African American districts (Tate 1993).

Exploratory Data Analysis

What do Latinos think of African Americans? Do they perceive themselves as having more in common with African Americans or with Anglos? To what degree do these two groups share positions on issues of importance? To answer these questions, we turn our attention to the analysis of opinion data that may provide some insight into these issues.

In the summer of 1999, the *Washington Post,* in cooperation with the Kaiser Family Foundation and Harvard University School of Public Health, conducted a national survey of Latinos. In addition to more than 2,400 Latino respondents, the survey also included companion samples of approximately 1,800 Anglos and 285 African Americans. The presence of companion samples allows us to make comparisons across groups on attitudes about commonality with others.

A. Cross-Minority Sense of Commonality

All respondents were asked a battery of questions regarding their perception of commonality with other groups. Specifically, respondents were twice asked "How much do ‹‹respondent's group›› have in common with ‹‹one of the other two groups››?" Respondents could offer a response from "a lot in common" to "nothing at all in common." Each of these variables range from zero (0) to three (3), with the higher values serving as an indication of a perception of greater commonality. Group means for perceptions of other groups, as well as between groups analysis-of-variance and t-tests, are reported in table 8.1.

Neither Anglos nor Latinos distinguish between other groups in their self-reported perceptions of commonality. The Latino average toward both African Americans and Anglos hovers just above 1 ("only a little in common") and the between variable difference of means is insignificant in both instances. For Anglos, their perceptions of both African Americans and Latinos are both slightly above 2 ("a fair amount in common"), again with between variable differences highly insignificant. By contrast, African Americans make clear and significant distinctions between Anglos and Latinos. The average self-reported commonality toward Anglos was approximately 1.7, while the average toward Latinos was 2.1. That is, African American respondents were significantly more likely to perceive commonality with Latinos than with Anglos.

Looking at table 8.1 for cross-group comparisons is also informative. While African Americans and Anglos hold similar attitudes about Latinos, each group holds a higher view of commonality with the other than do Latino respondents, who are significantly less likely to see commonality with each of the other groups.

The results from table 8.1 have important potential implications for the likelihood of black-brown coalitions. Latinos systematically see less in common with *both* African Americans and Anglos than those groups see in Latinos. They are the reluctant parties in these potential coalitions. Importantly, there appears to be no

TABLE 8.1
**Mean perceptions of commonality perceptions between
groups by race/ethnicity**

Respondent ethnicity	Target Group			Between target difference of means
	Latino	Black	White	
Latino		1.186	1.205	
		(0.988)	(0.975)	t = −0.796
		n = 1943	n = 1943	t-prob. = 0.426
Black	2.108		1.714	
	(0.864)		(0.844)	t = −6.715
	n = 269		n = 269	t-prob. = 0.000
White	2.096	2.094		
	(0.752)	(0.756)		t = 0.12
	n = 1690	n = 1690		t-prob. = 0.905
Between group ANOVAs F-test	F = 0.03 F-Sign. = 0.860	F = 963.39 F-Sign. = 0.000	F = 70.68 F-Sign. = 0.000	

Source: Washington Post/Kaiser/Harvard 1999 National Survey on Latinos in America (NSLA).
Note: Commonality ranges from zero (0) to three (3), with three indicating "a lot in common."

difference in Latino perceptions of commonality with the two other groups. That is, Latinos as a group appear indifferent between their potential suitors, a result that should suggest considerable caution when evaluating the attitudinal support for black-brown coalitions among Latinos. Conversely, this indifference among the Latino public does offer elites and political leadership considerable latitude in crafting strategies for group advancement.

Curiously, Anglos assessments appear to be similarly undifferentiated by group. It is occasionally suggested (Meier and Stewart 1991b) that Anglos would generally prefer to coalesce with Latinos but, at least in terms of self-reported perceptions of shared circumstances, that does not appear to be the case. Anglos claim to perceive very similar levels of commonality with African Americans and Latinos.

Finally, there does appear to be some distinction drawn among African Americans on average. African American respondents report a higher sense of commonality with Latinos than Anglos, though the difference was modest (albeit significant). That is, while African American responses, on average, appear to be more akin to Anglo attitudes than Latinos, these respondents do draw distinctions between their perceptions of Latinos and Anglos. This suggests at least some modest support among African Americans for black-brown coalition building.

Race/Ethnicity and Shared-Issue Positions

The perception of how much one group has "in common" with another is an important element in the building of political coalitions. But it is not necessarily the case that this perception translates into a shared political orientation. In table 8.1, we saw that Latinos perceived Anglos and African Americans more or less the same in terms of how much they have in common, but this perception may not reflect the underlying political reality with respect to shared positions on important political issues. If policy, rather than sentiment, was the essential building block of coalitions, then in principle we would expect that the likelihood of black-brown coalitions would be higher should African Americans and Latinos share numerous issue preferences — or at least more numerous than either share with Anglos.

We tested this by looking at a variety of issue preferences about which respondents were queried in the 1999 survey. Specifically, we looked at eleven different issues, including eight issues of national concern and three specifically of interest to various Latino populations. The mean opinion on these issues by group is reported in table 8.2, along with between-groups analysis of variance (ANOVA) results.[2]

Focusing first on the eight issues of national concern, differences between average opinion among Latinos and Anglos are significant in seven of eight instances. Similarly, black-white differences were significant on seven of eight issues.

By contrast, differences between African American and Latino mean opinion were significant only three times and marginally so a fourth. In one instance — *Abortion* — Latinos hold the most conservative opinion of the three groups and African Americans the most liberal. In the cases of *Assisted Suicide* and *Gun Control,* Latinos hold opinions between those of non-Hispanic whites and African Americans, closer to Anglos on *Gun Control* and closer to African Americans on *Assisted Suicide.* And on *School Vouchers,* both Latinos and African Americans appear to be more supportive than Anglos, though the difference between the two groups is also significant. On the remaining four issues — *Military Spending, Affirmative Action, Death Penalty,* and *Government Health Plan* — Latino mean opinion is statistically indistinguishable from African American mean opinion.

What can we conclude from the distribution of group opinion on each of these eight national issues? It is relatively clear that both Latinos and African Americans, choosing strictly on the basis of issue positions, would be better suited to black-brown coalitions than the alternative. On six of eight issue positions, Latino and African American opinion was closer than either group was to non-Hispanic whites. This similarity of issue preference should enhance prospects for interethnic coalition politics. Again, we need to caution that the degree to which a respondent holds these "common" opinions will vary greatly, as will the relative salience

TABLE 8.2
Mean issue preferences by race/ethnicity and interethnic differences

	Group means (Std. deviations)			Between group analyses of variance		
				Latino-black	Latino-white	Black-white
Issue	Latino	Black	White	difference	difference	difference
Military spending	0.016	0.083	0.265	F = 2.24	F = 136.08	F = 15.14
(−1 = decrease)	(0.681)	(0.735)	(0.669)	F prob.= 0.135	F prob.= 0.000	F prob.= 0.000
(1 = increase)	n = 2312	n = 277	n = 1753			
Affirmative action	0.220	0.260	0.182	F = 2.67	F = 7.88	F = 10.00
(1 = support)	(0.414)	(0.439)	(0.386)	F prob.= 0.102	F prob.= 0.005	F prob.= 0.002
(0 = oppose)	n = 2361	n = 277	n = 1755			
Abortion	0.481	0.604	0.594	F = 13.33	F = 46.53	F = 0.05
(1 = pro-choice)	(0.500)	(0.490)	(0.491)	F prob.= 0.000	F prob.= 0.000	F prob.= 0.818
(0 = anti-choice)	n = 2354	n = 273	n = 1747			
Assisted suicide	0.440	0.392	0.633	F = 3.44	F = 137.38	F = 60.22
(1 = support)	(0.497)	(0.489)	(0.482)	F prob.= 0.064	F prob.= 0.000	F prob.= 0.000
(0 = oppose)	n = 2319	n = 268	n = 1699			
Death penalty	0.580	0.537	0.779	F = 2.27	F = 175.95	F = 71.11
(1 = support)	(0.494)	(0.500)	(0.415)	F prob.= 0.132	F prob.= 0.000	F prob.= 0.000
(0 = oppose)	n = 2277	n = 270	n = 1714			
School vouchers	0.693	0.526	0.448	F = 19.25	F = 176.17	F = 4.08
(1 = support)	(0.462)	(0.500)	(0.497)	F prob.= 0.000	F prob.= 0.000	F prob.= 0.044
(0 = oppose)	n = 1558	n = 196	n = 1381			
Government health	0.853	0.877	0.642	F = 1.73	F = 246.89	F = 59.71
(1 = support)	(0.355)	(0.329)	(0.480)	F prob.= 0.189	F prob.= 0.000	F prob.= 0.000
(0 = oppose)	n = 2340	n = 276	n = 1685			
Gun control	0.653	0.77	0.642	F = 9.42	F = 0.20	F = 13.77
(−1 = weaker)	(0.629)	(0.506)	(0.553)	F prob.= 0.002	F prob.= 0.653	F prob.= 0.000
(1 = stronger)	n = 2345	n = 282	n = 1777			
NAFTA	0.517	0.322	0.212	F = 4.10	F = 46.43	F = 1.05
(−1 = bad)	(0.840)	(0.934)	(0.963)	F prob.= 0.043	F prob.= 0.000	F prob.= 0.306
(1 = good)	n = 735	n = 87	n = 945			
Puerto Rican statehood	0.112	0.300	0.189	F = 9.73	F = 6.34	F = 3.71
(−1 = independent)	(0.869)	(0.828)	(0.814)	F prob.= 0.002	F prob.= 0.002	F prob.= 0.054
(1 = state of the U.S.)	n = 1727	n = 233	n = 1380			
Relations with Cuba	0.675	0.623	0.604	F = 2.62	F = 18.94	F = .33
(1 = support)	(0.469)	(0.486)	(0.489)	F prob.= 0.106	F prob.= 0.000	F prob.= 0.562
(0 = oppose)	n = 1842	n = 244	n = 1605			

Source: Washington Post/Kaiser/Kennedy School 1999 National Survey on Latinos in America (NSLA).
Note: For military spending, gun control, and Puerto Rican statehood respondents preferring no change are coded zero (0).

attached to each issue. Nevertheless, the similarity of mean responses suggests co-alitional possibilities.

National Origin Groups—Does Within-Latino Variation Shape Coalitional Opportunities?

The last three issues reported in table 8.2 are different than the others on two di-mensions. First, these are issues in which the Latino population is likely to have much more interest. Second, and important, there may be considerable variation in this opinion across the national-origin groups among Latinos.

Results in table 8.2 include only those Latinos *not* from the subgroup most directly affected by the policy at hand. That is, Mexican Americans are not in-cluded in our mean opinion regarding the North American Free Trade Agreement (NAFTA), Puerto Ricans are not included in Latino opinion about the island's fu-ture status, and Cuban Americans are part of the mean Latino response to reestab-lishing diplomatic relations with the island. As we can see, Latinos excluding the most affected groups are closer to African Americans than Anglos on both NAFTA and Cuba. Non-Mexican Latinos appear significantly more supportive of NAFTA than are African Americans, and non-Cuban Latinos are marginally more support-ive of relations with Cuba than are African Americans, though in both instances Latino opinion is closer to that of African Americans than Anglos. The status of Puerto Rico, however, appears to be different. In that instance, non–Puerto Rican Latinos hold opinions very different from blacks, while insignificantly different from Anglos.

If, however, we look again at the national-origin groups most affected, a some-what different picture emerges. The mean response on the NAFTA question was .483 among Mexican Americans, so Mexican Americans are indicated to be less supportive of NAFTA than other Latinos.[3] This mean is insignificantly different from African American opinion. Similarly, and as expected, Cubans are indicated as far less supportive of reestablishing ties with the island nation, with a mean re-sponse of .487, a number significantly lower than both Anglos and African Ameri-can support and now closer to the opinion of Anglos than African Americans. By contrast, Puerto Rican support for statehood indicates as much higher than among other Latinos,[4] with a mean score of .276, a value significantly higher than Anglos and much closer to African American opinion on the issue.

Disaggregation of Latino opinion into nationality groups is important for two reasons. First, ethnicity and black-brown relations are largely "lived" on a local level, and local Latino communities are often dominated by a single nationality group, for example, Mexican Americans in Southern California and South Texas,

Cubans in Miami, Salvadorans in D.C., and Puerto Ricans and Dominicans in New York. In such instances, coalition with African Americans will not depend on the similarity of African American opinion to *all* of Latino opinion but to the sentiments of those *Latinos most proximate.* Second, on these nationality-specific issues, a change of focus from all Latinos to just the relevant nationality group actually changes our conclusions about the effect of the issue in fostering cooperation or stirring conflict. Looking at just the relevant groups, African American and Latino opinion are closer on NAFTA and Puerto Rican status, increasing the possibility of cooperation in those instances, and further apart on Cuba, where we would anticipate more conflict than cooperation on this issue, an expectation consistent with the recent history of metropolitan Miami where black-brown relations are best described as tense.

Summary and Conclusion

What can we therefore say about the prospects for Latino and African American political cooperation? We have suggested that answering this question requires us to look at both the attitudes and actions of elites and members of the mass public, across both socioeconomic issues and expressly political concerns. While most research will, of necessity, focus on a specific aspect of this relationship, we have cautioned the reader not to draw grand conclusions about the future of black-brown relations without surveying the effects across each of these dimensions.

We may find different answers in different places. In fact, we would expect as much, an expectation supported by the very conflicted and inconsistent findings within the existing work. There is only mixed evidence of successful coalition building, and when this does happen, it does so because the perceived interests of each group are facilitated in the arrangement—not merely on principle alone. The substantial evidence of competition at all levels and across social, economic, and political facets of American life, are clearly suggestive that interests of the two groups are not always consonant, and with predictable effects.

Our own exploratory analysis was most revealing as well. Latinos show little collective perception that they have much in common with any other group in society. By contrast, African Americans clearly see the Latino experience as closer to their own. What this suggests about the likelihood of coalition building is not entirely clear, though clearly *not* encouraging.

Despite their reluctance to identify with other groups, Latinos do share considerable policy agreement with African Americans, a more positive sign and one clearly at the center of the partisan cooperation that already exists. We did, however, raise the importance of subgroup differences as a crucial contextual element, since black-brown relations will evolve across a variety of local environments.

One could argue that the future of African American and Latino political fates is inexorably tied, one to the other. The struggle for racial and ethnic equality is changing as a consequence of the country's changing demography. How exactly this will evolve is a large and fertile field of inquiry that deserves considerable attention.

Notes

1. With the exception of Florida, regarding Latinos, where Cubans are equally loyal Republicans.

2. A highly technical question on HMOs was not included.

3. This is an interesting finding in itself, and worthy of further inquiry.

4. Another interesting finding, and contrary to the prevailing wisdom in certain sectors of the academy.

Cooperation and Conflict in Multiracial School Districts

René R. Rocha

T HE PROBLEM OF intergroup or interracial conflict has grown more complex as the landscape of America itself has become more diverse. The number of minorities (non-Anglos) has grown considerably in recent years. Likewise, the composition of minorities has grown increasingly more diverse. Several recent studies have been quick to point out that the rapidly growing Latino population has complicated the situation, as Latinos now compose the largest minority group in the nation (12.5 percent compared to 12.3 percent African American). Moreover, the geographic isolation of minorities is becoming less prevalent. It is becoming increasingly evident that the majority of Latino political activity does not occur on the ranchland of South Texas, as V. O. Key (1949) believed, but rather in urban centers such as Houston, Chicago, and Los Angeles—locations that, of course, also have reasonably-sized African American populations.

These trends have renewed scholarly interest in the manner in which minority groups relate to one another and whether or not those relations are characterized by interracial conflict or cooperation (McClain et al. 2003, Rodrigues and Segura 2003, Meier, McClain, Wrinkle, and Polinard 2004). The extent to which interminority relations are dominated by collaboration or discord holds considerable implications for the formation of rainbow coalitions and the general political process in a variety of urban settings. This essay is an attempt to understand what conditions result in interminority competition or cooperation.

The setting for this study is a sample of over three hundred multiracial school districts in Texas over eight years. School districts provide an excellent forum for examining multiracial coalitions because of the number of representational and policy indicators they provide. Moreover, school districts also vary greatly in terms of racial contexts and allow a large degree of discretion in terms of faculty hiring and policy implementation. This essay extends the literature on minority coalition building by examining hiring within these school districts, as well as how the demographic composition of school district teachers influences outputs. This approach is somewhat analogous to Paula McClain and Albert Karnig (1990) and McClain (1993), who examined interminority competition with respect to municipal employment. This project also borrows from an approach taken by Kenneth Meier, Paula McClain, Robert Wrinkle, and Jerry Polinard (2004), who examined the issue of interminority competition at the school district level. However, this project uses a considerably larger data set and also corrects for some of the methodological shortcomings Meier and colleagues (2004) faced.

How Are Interminority Relations Best Characterized?

Numerous scholars have examined the way racial/ethnic groups interact with one another. Recent work has focused on how these interactions differ under various circumstances. For example, when a political scenario is viewed within a zero-sum context (that is, the political benefits under question are limited), we would anticipate a higher level of interethnic discord. When removed from a zero-sum context, however, this relationship should be characterized by increased degrees of cooperation (Meier et al. 2004).

Despite this, interminority relations remain heavily influenced by a variety of other factors. Rodolfo de la Garza (1997) suggests that several points are likely responsible for the inability of Latinos and African Americans to form numerous and long-lasting rainbow coalitions. These include:

1. Resentment among many blacks over Latino access to affirmative action programs that blacks believe were designed for them.
2. Tensions because of the perception that immigration results in job displacement and the reallocation of public resources to Latinos rather than to blacks.
3. Battles over reapportionment and redistricting. Population is the foundation for allocating legislative seats. The numbers of state legislative seats is fixed, while the number of congressional seats allocated to each state may vary as a

result of the census. In cities with substantial Latino and black populations, these groups often live in juxtaposition. Where Latino population growth greatly exceeds black population growth, any increase in legislative seats designed to accommodate the growth of the Latino population could come at the expense of blacks. (453)

Relying primarily on survey data, the literature thus far has found that support for different coalitional strategies varies with economic conditions, perceived social distance, experiences with discrimination, income, education, group size, age, political integration, and the amount of resources available to each group (Dyer, Vedlitz, and Worchel 1989; Jackson, Gerber, and Cain 1994; McClain 1993; Meier and Stewart 1991a; Garcia 2000). John Garcia (2000) finds that Latino support for programs geared toward helping African Americans increases with education, perception of African American discrimination, and levels of political attentiveness. Brian Jackson, Elizabeth Gerber, and Bruce Cain (1994) note that African Americans in Los Angles felt close to Latinos when compared to national figures. Age is also a positive influence on support for political strategies that would foster interracial cooperation. As with most previous research, socioeconomic status positively affects support for Latino–African American coalitions.

Aside from the demographic characteristics that facilitate or hamper efforts to form multiracial coalitions, a number of social and structural variables influence the process. Perceived social distance is perhaps the most often studied of these influences (Dyer, Vedlitz, and Worchel 1989; Meier and Stewart 1991a; McClain et al. 2003). Kenneth Meier and Joseph Stewart (1991a) point out that while ideological similarity might aid in the creation of rainbow coalitions, elevated levels of social distance make such an outcome unlikely.

Based on a survey of 1,200 Texas residents, James Dyer, Arnold Vedlitz, and Stephen Worchel (1989) noted that for most types of social interaction, especially interactions that require the formation of a substantial permanent relationship (i.e., intermarriage), both African Americans and Latinos preferred to associate with Anglos. Similarly, Jackson, Gerber, and Cain (1994) found that African Americans nationally were much more likely to identify with Anglos than with Latinos. A sample they drew from the Los Angeles area generated comparable results.

The presence of social distance is compounded by the unique ethnic situation in which Latinos find themselves. As the U.S. Census form indicates, Latinos (or Hispanics, to use census terminology) can be "white" and constitute a unique subgroup within that categorization. Carlos Munoz and Charles Henry (1986, 607) observe that, "most Latino political leaders have historically promoted a white identity for Latinos and this has contributed to a lack of interest in building rainbow coalitions." This approach also does not consider the difficulties that may arise when Latinos are considered in nonpanethnic terms. Thus, while political ideology would seem to lead minorities to form rainbow coalitions, social distance lends support to the "Power Thesis," which concludes that Anglo-Latino coalitions are more likely than interminority ones.

In their examination of this topic, Meier and Stewart (1991a) find that there is a trade-off between African Americans and Latinos in terms of beneficial education policies. Yet, other studies have found that interminority coalitions have formed to contend with problems shared by the African American and Latino communities, such as poor socioeconomic conditions. Moreover, coalitions have also been observed for potential "wedge issues," such as immigration (Estrada, Garcia, Marcias, and Maldonado 1981; Browning, Marshall, and Tabb 1984; Espiritu 1992).

Taking this previous literature into account, we might expect interminority relations in the bureaucracy to be characterized in several different ways. McClain (1993) offers what is arguably the best articulation of these hypotheses:

Interminority Cooperation: Gains by African Americans in terms of policy and representation will increase along with gains made by the Latino community, and vice versa.

Interminority Conflict: Alternatively, gains by African Americans in terms of policy and representation may come at the expense of gains made by the Latino community, and vice versa.

Interminority Independence: Gains made by one group will be unrelated to gains made by the other.

McClain (1993) found evidence that representational gains on the part of African Americans are likely to negatively affect Latinos, while gains made by Latinos do not necessarily limit African American opportunities. Thus, while we might expect interminority relations to be generally characterized by competition or cooperation, it is conceivable that the true relationship is mixed. Moreover, the degree of competition or cooperation may vary. That is, even if African American–Latino relations are found to be competitive or cooperative, African American representation might negatively or positively influence Latino representation to a greater or lesser degree than Latino representation influences African American representation.

Minority Experiences in the Education Policymaking Process

The history of minorities within the education system is filled with accounts of inequality and disparate treatment for both African Americans and Latinos (Barr 1995; San Miguel 1986, 2001; Woodson 1933). This, combined with the importance of education for improving the quality of life and creating opportunities for upward social mobility, has led minority activists to make equality within the educational system a high priority (Barr 1995). Recent attempts to ameliorate the condition of minorities within the education system have been aided by the election of minorities to school boards as well as by the hiring of minority administrators and teachers. The election of minorities to school boards increased substantially in the 1980s, largely as a result of the adoption of single-member district systems and the resulting elimination of a number of at-large electoral arrangements (Meier, Stewart, and England 1989; Welch 1990; Barr 1995).

While such progress might offer encouragement to proponents of racial equity within the educational system, serious obstacles continue to exist. In Texas, for example, only 37 percent of African Americans attended desegregated school as of 1989. Likewise, as late as twenty years ago, only three African Americans held the position of superintendent in the over one thousand school districts in Texas (Barr 1995). By 1995 that number had only climbed to eight. Similar inequities exist at the level of school administration and teachers. These factors have combined to ensure a relatively high degree of salience for race within the educational system. This concern has not ignored the potentially conflicting goals that minority groups may advocate. Along with the three points mentioned earlier, de la Garza (1997, 453) also notes that African American–Latino relations have suffered from

> tensions resulting from Latino population growth that produces Latino majorities in schools that previously had black majorities, administrators and staff. Latino demands for curricular reform and staffing changes thus become Latino-black competitions.

Using the education system as a setting for this study, I develop the following operational hypotheses.

Operational Competition Hypotheses:
As the number of African American administrators within a school district increases, the number of Latino administrators will decrease, and vice versa.

As the number of African American teachers within a school district increases, the number of Latino teachers will decrease, and vice versa.

As the African American TAAS (standardized test) pass rates increase, the Latino pass rate will decrease.

Operational Cooperation Hypotheses:

As the number of African American administrators within a school district increases, the number of Latino administrators will likewise increase, and vice versa.

As the number of African American teachers within a school district increases, the number of Latino teachers will likewise increase, and vice versa.

As the African American Texas Assessment of Academic Skills (TAAS) pass rates increase, the Latino pass rate will likewise increase.

Data and Methodology

The data for this study are taken from a sample of multiracial school districts in Texas. Data sources include the Texas Education Agency, the National Association of Latino Elected Officials (NALEO), the Joint Center for Political and Economic Studies, and the 1990 Census. To be considered multiracial, districts were required to have a student enrollment that was over 5 percent African American *and* over 5 percent Latino. Texas is rivaled only by California in terms of multiracial districts. However, the Texas Education Agency requires districts to report a number of performance indicators by race, making it a superior population from which to draw a sample. The data for the analysis pool performance indicators and representational variables for the years 1994 through 2001. This yields approximately 1,980 cases.

Dependent Variables

Three dependent variables are considered in this study. The first two variables consist of the percentage of African American/Latino administrators and the percentage of African American/Latino teachers. These variables should be adequate for testing hypotheses regarding representation and have the added benefit of being placed within a zero-sum context.

A third variable measures the pass rate on the TAAS exam for African Americans and Latinos. The TAAS exam was a standardized exam, the passage of which was required for high school graduation. TAAS pass rates are highly salient within the educational bureaucracy as well as among the general public. Although the TAAS exam is not necessarily an encompassing measure of all the educational objectives school districts strive to meet, it is critical to the state's educational accountability system and is consistently ranked as the top priority of superintendents within the state.

Independent Variables of Interest

Benefits in terms of policy are likely to be the result of racial/ethnic representation. The causal process of representation in the education policymaking process is relatively well established (Fraga, Meier, and England 1986; Meier, Stewart, and England 1989; Polinard, Wrinkle, and Longoria 1990; Polinard et al. 1994; Leal and Hess 2000).

School board members directly influence the hiring of upper-level officials within the educational bureaucracy, namely superintendents and school administrators. Administrators, in turn, influence the hiring of teachers, education's version of street-level bureaucrats (Meier and Stewart 1991b). Teachers, who possess relatively substantial amounts of discretion, can then influence outputs such as student performance.[1] This influence can occur through a variety of direct as well as indirect means, such as serving as role models and providing more effective instruction. (Aaron and Powell 1982; Cole 1986; Meier and Stewart 1991b; Hess and Leal 1997; Meier, Wrinkle, and Polinard 1999).[2]

Accordingly, when modeling the racial/ethnic composition of administrators, representation on the school board is the independent variable of primary interest. Data on the percentage of Latino school board members were coded from the roster of elected Latino officials produced annually by NALEO. An analogous roster for African Americans is gathered by the Joint Center.

When modeling composition at the teacher (street) level, administrative representation becomes the key independent variable. Lastly, when modeling bureaucratic outputs (student performance), the racial/ethnic composition of the teaching staff is an independent variable of concern.

Control Variables

To accurately estimate the effects of our key independent variables, several other rival explanations must be taken into account. For the most part, these explanations can be linked to district resources and constraints, all of which should influence the performance of school districts to some degree.

The percentage of low-income students in a district is among the most profound

of these constraints. Lower levels of socioeconomic status limit the educational resources available to children and make the process of education more difficult. To
account for poverty, I control for the percentage of students within a district who
qualify for the state's free lunch program. This should provide an appropriate gauge
of the percentage of low-income students in a district.

The relationship between expenditures and educational performance remains
unsettled (Hanushek 1996; Hedges and Greenwald 1996; Evans, Murray, and
Schwab 1997). Despite this, increased expenditures remains a potentially positive
influence on outputs. For this reason, I control for several measures of district expenditures. The first among these is per-pupil expenditures on instruction. Per-
pupil expenditures for noninstruction purposes (such as athletics) are not considered, as they should not directly influence student performance. A second measure
of expenditures consists of average teacher salaries. Higher teacher salaries should
increase performance by attracting more talented teachers (Hanushek 1996). Lastly,
state aid is used as a control. Such aid is a method of supplementing districts whose
tax bases provide them with comparatively low revenue. Increases in levels of state
aid should also have a positive affect on performance indicators.

The final control variable introduced into my models is a rough measure of the
quality of the school. This variable is crucial, as it ensures that differences in student performance are not the result of minorities systematically attending schools of
lesser quality. Meier, McClain, Wrinkle, and Polinard (2004) relied on a measure
of Anglo student performance to control for school quality. As high-quality schools
are likely to raise the performance of all students, Anglo performance should at
least provide a baseline for district quality (Weiher 2000). The use of this measure
is further bolstered by the Christopher Jencks and Meredith Phillips (1998) observation that minority student performance should increase when minority students
are placed within a high achieving atmosphere.

Endogenous Variables

In a similar study, which also employed a school district data set, Meier and colleagues (2004) note that questions regarding minority cooperation and conflict
involve analyzing trade-offs between minority groups. These trade-offs complicate the estimation of statistical models, as an endogenous relationship emerges
wherein, for example, representational gains by Latinos in terms of teaching or
administrators might influence the representation of African Americans, since the
number of administrators and teachers is limited. The endogenous relationship
presented here means that ordinary least squares (OLS) is an unsuitable method
of estimation. As a result this study relies on three-stage least squares (3SLS). The

3SLS approach tackles the problem of reciprocal causation by relying on the use of exogenous instruments (Greene 2003; Kennedy 2003). The 3SLS approach obtains estimators by first regressing the theoretically endogenous independent variables against a list of instruments. These fitted values are then retained and used in the regression in place of the theoretically endogenous independent variables. Unlike 2SLS, 3SLS uses *all* the exogenous instruments for each of the endogenous variables and is preferred because it accounts for correlations between the disturbances in the different structural equations (Greene 2003).

The instruments used here include the percentage of low-income students, average teacher salary, the amount of state aid received by a district, instructional expenditures, the percentage of Latinos living in poverty, the percentage of African Americans living in poverty, the percentage of Latinos who possess a college degree, and the percentage of African Americans who possess a college degree. Additionally, African American and Latino representation on the school board are included as instruments for the models in table 9.1. The instruments for the models presented in table 9.2 are similar to those offered in table 9.1, except here the percentage of African American and Latino administrators are included as representational instruments. Each group's representation in terms of teachers is added to the instruments used for table 9.4.

The use of this time-series data set raises concerns with the possible presence of serial correlation and heteroscedasticity. To control for serial correlation, I insert a set of dummy variables representing individual years in all the models presented here. Examining the residuals for each year indicated that heteroscedasticity was not an issue in these models, thus no such corrections were used. Levels of multicollinearity were also within acceptable levels in all these models.

Findings

As mentioned earlier, the findings produced by these models are largely in line with the expectations suggested by the previous literature. Table 9.1 presents the 3SLS estimates with the percentage of African American and Latino administrators as the dependent variables. In support of the competition hypothesis, we find that interminority relations are *not* characterized by simultaneous gains. Also, in accordance with theoretical expectations, representation on the school board has a significantly positive effect on administrative personnel. Interestingly, the coefficient for African American school board members on African American administrators is over twice as large as the analogous coefficient for Latinos (.62 and .27, respectively). This indicates that African Americans may be more effective than Latinos at translating

TABLE 9.1

Impact on the percentage of administrators who are African American and Latino

	African American	Latino
% African American administrators	—	$-.067^{**}$
		$(.023)$
% Latino administrators	$-.210^{*}$	—
	$(.083)$	
% African American school board	$.617^{**}$	—
	$(.020)$	
% Latino school board	—	$.274^{**}$
		$(.018)$
% low-income students	$.302^{**}$	$.222^{**}$
	$(.027)$	$(.017)$
Average teacher salary (000s)	$.002^{**}$	$.001^{**}$
	$(.0001)$	$(.0001)$
Teacher experience	$-.699^{**}$	$-.579^{**}$
	$(.157)$	$(.119)$
State aid	$-.001^{**}$	$.233E-03$
	$(.0001)$	$(.002)$
Intuitional expenditures (per pupil)	$-.006^{**}$	$-.003^{**}$
	$(.001)$	$(.001)$
Latino poverty	—	$-.027\pm$
		$(.014)$
% Latino with college degree	—	$.130^{**}$
		$(.031)$
African American poverty	$-.077^{**}$	—
	$(.015)$	
% African American with college degree	$.059^{**}$	—
	$(.023)$	
Constant	-28.991^{**}	-32.981^{**}
	(4.838)	(3.128)
N	1981	1981
R^2	.49	.27
χ^2	726.89	1941.32

$\pm$ p<0.10 * p<0.05 ** p<0.01
Note: Coefficients for individual years not shown. Standard errors in parentheses.

their political offices into descriptive representation in the bureaucracy. The co-efficients for the other independent variables of interest, the percentage of administrators from the competing minority group, show that increasing the percentage of Latino administrators negatively influences the percentage of African American administrators and vice versa. This finding complements the work of Selden (1997), who similarly found that the hiring of African Americans by the Farm Home Administration negatively affected the number of Latinos employed.

In contrast to McClain's findings (1993), table 9.1 also indicates that gains made by the Latino community are likely to be far more detrimental to African Americans (coefficient = −.21) than gains made by African Americans are to Latinos (coefficient = −.07). Meier and Stewart (1991a) suggest that in a multiracial setting Anglos are much more likely to form coalitions with Latinos than with African Americans (for the reasons discussed earlier, including lower levels of social distance and more compatible political ideologies).[3] Viewed in this light, it seems plausible that Latino gains disproportionately hurt African Americans because of Anglo support in these multiracial settings. This level of support cannot be replicated by African Americans, minimizing the extent to which African American gains impair Latinos in this regard.

In addition to trade-off effects, I examine whether school board members influence this process directly. Latino school board members influence the number of African American administrators because they advocate hiring Latinos and thus limit the slots available to African Americans. However, it is conceivable that a direct relationship exists. Table 9.2 shows this to be the case. An increase in the percentage of African American school board members lowers the proportion of Latino administrators even when controlling for African American administrators. Yet, the reverse is not true. The coefficient for Latino school board members is insignificant in this case. This finding contrasts with those of Meier and colleagues (2004) who found a direct relationship for *both* Latinos and African Americans. If, as suggested earlier, African American school board members are more effective than Latinos at translating their political power into descriptive representation, this may explain the results in table 9.2.

In table 9.3 we see that the relationship in terms of teachers is similar to that of administrators. Once again, we see that interminority competition appears to be the norm. Increases in the proportion of the teaching staff that is African American and Latino is associated with lower levels of Latino and African American teachers. As with administrators, the coefficient for the effect of Latinos on African Americans (−.13) is substantially larger than the coefficient for African Americans on Latinos (−.08). However, the difference is not as large as it was with administrators. This implies that the phenomena predicted by the Power Thesis are more likely to occur

TABLE 9.2
**Impact on the percentage of administrators who are
African American and Latino**

	African American	Latino
% African American administrators	—	−.067**
		(.023)
% Latino administrators	−.210*	—
	(.083)	
% African American school board members	.605**	−.322**
	(.031)	(.105)
% Latino school board members	.045	.298**
	(.119)	(.022)
N	1981	1981
R^2	.47	.26
χ^2	1880.77	542.6

± p<0.10   * p<0.05   ** p<0.01

Note: Controls not shown. Coefficients for individual years not shown. Standard errors in parentheses.

at higher levels of the bureaucracy or at levels that can be more directly influenced by political forces. Levels of the bureaucracy that are more insulated from overtly political forces are slightly less likely to experience the same outcome predicted by the Power Thesis. Alternatively, scarcity may be the driving factor behind this relationship. As resources become scarcer, one minority's gain is more likely to become another's loss. Administrative positions are fewer in number than teaching slots, and therefore exaggerate the level of interminority competition.

Upper-level bureaucratic representation also appears to be significant, as increased levels of same-race administrators positively influence representation at lower levels of the bureaucracy. Although the coefficient for same-race administrators is slightly larger for African Americans than for Latinos, the difference is not as great as it was when considering the relationship between school board representation and administrators. Thus, while African Americans still appear to be more effective at translating their representation at higher levels of the bureaucracy to lower levels, their effectiveness appears to be stronger at the school board level. Attempts to uncover a direct relationship, as we saw in table 9.2, were made. However, the coefficients for the influence of administrators on teachers were insignificant, indicating that no direct relationships exist (results not shown).

Lastly, I examine the influence of interminority competition on a policy output measure, student performance on the TAAS exam. Unlike the composition of

TABLE 9.3

Impact on the percentage of teachers who are African American and Latino

	African American	Latino
% African American teachers	—	−.078**
		(.012)
% Latino teachers	−.125**	—
	(.028)	
% African American administrators	.587**	—
	(.020)	
% Latino administrators	—	.499**
		(.011)
% low-income students	.096**	.100**
	(.012)	(.008)
Average teacher salary (000s)	.162 E-03±	.001**
	(.001)	(.0001)
Teacher experience	.311**	−.197**
	(.157)	(.058)
State aid	.156 E-03	−.207 E-04**
	(.001)	(.000)
Intuitional expenditures (per pupil)	.116 E-03	−.001**
	(.002)	(.0001)
Latino poverty	—	−.005
		(.007)
% Latino with college degree	—	.061**
		(.015)
African American poverty	−.007	—
	(.008)	
% African American with college degree	.003	—
	(.011)	
Constant	−10.024**	−13.573**
	(2.228)	(1.578)
N	1981	1981
R^2	.73	.66
χ^2	3804.59	5419.36

± p<0.10   * p<0.05   ** p<0.01

Note: Coefficients for individual years not shown. Standard errors in parentheses.

TABLE 9.4
TAAS pass rates for African Americans and Latinos

	African Americans	Latinos
African American pass rate	—	.308**
		(.072)
Latino pass rate	.985**	—
	(.095)	
% African American teachers	.146**	—
	(.036)	
% Latino teachers	—	.089**
		(.036)
Anglo pass rate	.009	.562**
	(.074)	(.062)
% Black students	−.138**	—
	(.026)	
% Latino students	—	−.130**
		(.024)
% low-income students	.104**	.222**
	(.025)	(.017)
Average teacher salary (000s)	.143 E-03	.232 E-03
	(.002)	(.000)
Teacher experience	−.228	−.579**
	(.165)	(.119)
State aid	−.002	.233E-03±
	(.002)	(.000)
Intuitional expenditures (per pupil)	−.006	.008*
	(.004)	(.003)
Latino poverty	—	−.053**
		(.016)
% Latino with college degree	—	−.024
		(.029)
African American poverty	−.038**	—
	(.013)	
% African American with college degree	.155**	—
	(.020)	
Constant	−13.602**	−9.634*
	(4.663)	(4.597)
N	1903	1903
R²	.60	.71
Chi²	3514.92	4339.28

± p<0.10 * p<0.05 ** p<0.01
Note: Coefficients for individual years not shown. Standard errors in parentheses.

administrative staff and faculty, student performance does not occur within a zero-sum context. That is, the success of an African American student on the TAAS exam does not necessitate a corresponding failure for a Latino student. Rather, both groups can make gains independently of one another. Meier and colleagues (2004) found that removing interminority success from a zero-sum game also removes the inevitability of competition, facilitating the development of a cooperative relationship.

The results presented in table 9.4 speak to this conclusion. Here, African American success is characterized by a complementary increase in student achievement on the part of Latinos and vice versa. Latinos appear to benefit also from increases in the Anglo pass rate, a proxy measure for overall school district quality. The coefficient for the effect of Latino test scores on African Americans is slightly larger than the coefficient for the reverse relationship, .99 and .31 respectively. As was the case for administrators and teachers, representation appears to have a slightly more positive effect on African Americans than it does for Latinos. Combined, these three findings show a consist relationship with regard to the effectiveness of African American representatives compared to Latinos.

Discussion and Conclusions

These results can be interpreted in a variety of ways. Most obviously, it appears that scarcity of resources fosters competition between groups that might otherwise be expected to form cooperative relationships. This supports the initial work on relations done by McClain (1993), who found that economic conditions engender competition. Another reading of these results might indicate that interminority hostility increases as the process becomes more politicized. The more insulated a set of actors are from political forces, the less emphasis they place on racial heuristics for determining of "who gets what when." While it is easy to see how electoral politics might be aided by the use of racial heuristics, street-level bureaucrats may interpret their mission in less competitive and cynical terms.

James Jennings (1997) remarks that "it is clear that the bigger American cities and key electoral states are becoming increasingly populated by blacks *and* Latinos." A proper understanding of how African American–Latino relations operate is becoming increasingly necessary for scholars who desire to fully understand the dynamics of influential political bodies. The last pages of *Pursuing Power* (Garcia 1997), the last major work collected on the subject of Latino Politics, lists several questions that the literature has thus far not fully addressed. The first two of these questions read, "What is the history of black and Latino political relationships in different cities regarding various policy issues?" and "What conditions or factors lead to political cooperation or competition between black and Latino activists?" While several scholars have used survey data to understand the attitudinal foundation of interminority coalitions, (Jackson, Gerber, and Cain 1994; Garcia 2000; Rodrigues and Segura 2003), we know far less about how competition plays out in the bureaucracy and policymaking process (see McClain and Karnig 1990; McClain 1933; Meier and Stewart 1991b). Further research should continue to use measures of different representational and policy outputs to fully understand the dynamics of rainbow coalitions.

Notes

1. For a more thorough discussion of the representation and casual linkages in the education political making process, see Meier, Stewart, and England (1989, 9–39).

2. This is a very top-down conceptualization of the education system. Although we know from previous literature (Meier and Smith 1994) that the educational system possesses some bottom-up characteristics, this straightforward view of the process is used for this analysis.

3. This is referred to as the Power Thesis.

Latinas in Latino Politics

Luis Ricardo Fraga and Sharon A. Navarro

IN THIS ESSAY, we classify the literature on Latinas in Latino politics into two major analytical categories. The first category identifies largely *descriptive differences* between Latino men and Latinas. The differences focus on the traditional dimensions of political analysis, including public opinion and political participation, with a special emphasis on organizational leadership and electoral representation. The second category we term *prescriptive possibilities*. This literature focuses on Latina feminist writings and emerging models of Latina legislative representation. Unlike the first category, these literatures explicitly develop understandings of the transformative, that is, institution changing, potential of new ways of conceptualizing the interests of Latino communities and developing related strategies of policy advocacy built on the intersectionality of Latinas in the American polity. It is this later category that we find the most intellectually rich and also most likely to affect the future practice(s) of Latino politics, especially the role of Latinas in Latino politics.

Descriptive Differences

Public Opinion

The earliest study to note gender differences in Latino public opinion was conducted by Robert Brischetto and Rodolfo de la Garza (1983). They found that Mexican origin women were more favorably predisposed to the Democratic Party than were Mexican-origin men. Mexican-origin men were more predisposed to the Republican Party. This study was based on respondents from selected cities. Similarly, based on a survey in one California congressional district taken in the 1980s, Bruce Cain and Roderick Kiewiet (1985) found that Latinas were more likely to self-identify as Democrats than Latino men, but they were not any less likely to identify with the Republican Party. Susan Welch and Lee Sigelman (1992) were the first to explicitly examine gender differences between Latinas and Latino men with national data. They found a small difference in political ideology, modest differences in party identification, and the largest difference in presidential vote choice. Using presidential election exit poll data in the 1980s, they noted that Latinas tended to identify as slightly more liberal, significantly less likely to identify with the Republican Party, and slightly more likely to vote for Democratic presidential candidates. Because their data were aggregated to the national level, the authors were not able to examine possible differences by region or by national-origin group.

Several studies find no gendered differences in attitudes toward immigration (Wrinkle 1991; Binder, Polinard, and Wrinkle 1997; Hood, Morris, and Shirkey 1997). Using 1996 exit poll data, however, Carol Hardy-Fanta reports that Latinas favor decreasing immigration more than do Latino men (Hardy-Fanta 2000).

The most thorough analysis of gender differences in public opinion is provided by Lisa Montoya (1996). Using the 1989 Latino National Political Survey (LNPS), she found that some differences existed between Latino men and Latinas, but there were also variations by national-origin group. Additionally, the differences were not always in the same direction as predicted by studies of the gender gap among Anglos. Controlling for age, income, nativity, and "born-again" experience, she found that Mexican-origin men supported higher spending on defense than did Mexican-origin women. Gender differences were not statistically significant for Puerto Ricans or Cubans. In the area of spending on social welfare programs, she found statistically significant differences by gender across the three national-origin groups examined. Finally, Montoya found that the most consistent gender differences in public opinion were in the area of "women's roles" (Montoya 1996, 261–62).[1] She stated that, "Latinas [across all national-origin groups] are more likely than Latinos to favor modern or very modern roles for women," although the differences were not dramatic (270).

Political Participation

Few studies have specifically examined gendered differences in the political participation of Latinas and Latino men. One consistent finding is that there are no major differences in either propensity to vote or in presidential preferences (MacManus, Bullock, and Grothe 1986; Lien 1994, 1998; Montoya 1997). However, the predictors of turnout do seem to have some gender-based variation. Latina heads of households are less likely to vote than are males (Uhlaner, Cain, and Kiewiet 1989). Montoya (1997) found that the most consistent predictors of Latina turnout were related to organizational participation, including church attendance and school involvement.

Similarly, most survey-based studies have found little difference between Latinas and Latino men regarding rates of nonelectoral participation.[2] No major differences in the likelihood of making a financial contribution to or volunteering for a campaign, attending a rally, contacting elected officials, or working to solve a community-related issue have been found (Montoya 1997; 2000). However, Montoya, Hardy-Fanta, and Sonia Garcia (2000) reported that predictors of likelihood to participate in such activities do seem to display patterns of "gendered affluence," that is, Latinas who are more wealthy, report civic skills, and participate in groups generally do seem to participate more in nonelectoral activities. No consistent predictors of the participation of Latino men in such activities have been found (Montoya 2000).

Electoral Representation

Five studies report findings regarding Latinas in elective office. Harry Pachón and Louis DeSipio (1992) found that Latinas composed 30.1 percent of all Latina/o elected officials in 1992, when women as a whole were only 17.2 percent of all elected officials in the country (as reported in Montoya, Hardy-Fanta, and Garcia 2000, 558). Takash's study was specific to Latina elected officials in California (1993). Her survey of 50.6 percent of the 150 Chicana/Latina elected officials in the early 1990s revealed that "proportionally, more Latinas serve as elected officials than women in general" (341) and that 64 percent had never experienced prior elective or appointive office, although "68% participated in campaign work, 61% claimed community activism . . . and 70% served as board members of local organizations" (344). She also found that 67 percent won in at-large elections for local office, that

TABLE 10.1
Hispanic elected officials by level of government, 1990–2002

| | *Year* | | | | | | | | | | | | |
	1990	*1991*	*1992*	*1993*	*1994*	*1995*	*1996*	*1997*	*1998*	*1999*	*2000*	*2001*	*2002*
U.S. representative	10	11	11	17	17	—	17	18	18	18	19	19	19
State	134	140	139	163	184	—	163	183	181	194	198	197	208
County	351	378	386	406	401	—	357	376	392	375	398	403	444
Municipal	1290	1314	1362	1474	1647	—	1295	1223	1351	1346	1464	1443	1516
Judicial/law enforcement	583	596	628	633	651	—	546	517	530	494	465	454	532
School board	1458	1489	1554	1582	1578	—	1278	1251	1299	1289	1392	1412	1603
Special district	178	175	160	145	147	—	125	128	134	128	120	125	142
Total	4004	4103	4240	4420	4625	—	3781	3696	3905	3844	4056	4053	4464

Source: National Association of Latino Elected and Appointed Officials (NALEO).

68.2 percent were the first Latinas to serve in their positions (344), and that while over 80 percent of Latina officials supported feminist goals, just over 50 percent actually labeled themselves as feminists. Finally, and perhaps most significant, she found that these officials seemed more concerned with issues affecting Latinos generally that those that might be considered women specific (353).

Christine Marie Sierra and Adaljiza Sosa-Riddell (1994) reported that in 1987 there were a total of 592 Chicana/Latina elected officials, and in 1989 there were 744. They also noted that Latinas were recently elected to important positions at national, state, and local levels (1994, 309–11). Hardy-Fanta found that "[b]etween 1968 and 1994, Latinas [in Massachusetts] won 56% of their election campaigns while Latino men won only 15%" (as reported in Montoya, Hardy-Fanta, and Garcia 2000, 559).

Table 10.1 presents the patterns of representation for all Latino and Latina elected officials for the period 1990–2002. These data demonstrate that there has been a 90 percent increase in representation in the U.S. Congress, a 55 percent increase at the state level, a 26 percent increase at the county level, a 17 percent increase in municipal office, and only a 1 percent increase at the school board level.[3] Table 10.2 presents these data for Latinas. Latinas had 27.4 percent of all elected positions held by Latinas and Latinos. Latinas had the highest representation within the Latino ethnic delegation in state senates at 40 percent, followed by 33 percent in county offices, 32 percent in Congress, 32 percent in school boards, 26 percent in state lower houses, 24 percent at the municipal level, 23 percent in judicial/law enforcement, and 17 percent in special districts. What is most interesting, however, is the magnitude of the increase in Latina representation over the course of the

TABLE 10.2

Female Hispanic elected officials by level of government, 1990–2002

	1990	1991	1992	1993	1994	1995	Year 1996	1997	1998	1999	2000	2001	2002
U.S. representative	1	1	1	3	3	—	3	4	4	5	5	6	6
State	16	17	16	32	38	—	38	48	50	53	54	58	61
County	106	118	123	127	125	—	121	134	135	139	139	131	146
Municipal	223	256	277	319	371	—	277	267	304	312	344	335	361
Judicial/law enforcement	59	68	84	90	95	—	87	88	90	96	93	104	120
School board	358	405	454	459	454	—	117	90	125	129	440	445	506
Special district	19	21	18	19	18	—	14	17	19	23	20	25	24
Total	792	886	973	1049	1104	—	657	648	727	757	1095	1204	1224

Source: National Association of Latino Elected and Appointed Officials (NALEO).

1990s. There was a 500 percent increase in the number of Latina members of Congress (one to six) and a 280 percent increase in state offices (sixteen to sixty-one). More modestly, Latina increases of 37 percent also occurred at the county level, 55 percent at the municipal level, and 41 percent in school boards. At each level of government, Latina increases far outpaced increases in Latina/o ethnic representation overall.

Luis Fraga, Valerie Martinez-Ebers, Ricardo Ramírez, and Linda Lopez (2001) provide the first and still only state-specific analysis of gendered patterns of Latina/o representation in state legislatures. The states they examined were Arizona, California, New Mexico, and Texas. Together, the Latina and Latino state legislators in these states compose 56 percent of all Latina and Latino state legislators in the country.

Their study makes two important discoveries. First, patterns of both gender and ethnic representation vary considerably by state (Fraga et al. 2001, 5–7). Not only is there variation in the overall magnitude of both gender and ethnic representation, but there is also considerable variation in the gendered representation within the Latina/o delegation, given overall patterns of gendered representation in state legislatures. We updated their data in these four states to 2004 and find, for example, that although New Mexico had the highest proportion of Latina/o legislators as a percentage of all legislators (35–40 percent) from 1990 to 2004, it also had the lowest Latina representation within the Latina/o total delegation until 2000 (7–23 percent) and now equals Arizona at about 27 percent Latina representation. Texas was second to New Mexico in the size of its Latina/o state delegation, growing from 13 percent in 1990 to 19 percent in 1998—when it shared the second highest representation percentage with California. However, Texas in 2004 had the lowest level of Latina representation within the Latina/o delegation at 21 percent, a decline that first began in 1998. Of these four states, the only one to experience a substantial increase in its Latina/o state delegation is California, where it increased from 6 percent in 1990 to 23 percent in 2004. More dramatically, California has also had the greatest increase in Latina representation over this period. Latinas represented only 14 percent of the Latina/o delegation in 1990, but in 2004 they composed 41 percent. An exclusive focus on national trends can therefore mask considerable state specific differences.

The second major finding of these authors is that "[trends] in Latina state legislative representation may be more tied to increasing gender representation than to increasing ethnic representation. Latina representation increases even when Latino representation remains constant" (Fraga et al. 2001, 7). This finding suggests that states may experience increases in Latina representation that are less tied to demographic trends than is the case for male Latino representatives. It also suggests that state-specific traditions of partisanship, campaign finance, district size, term limits, and other elements of institutional design can greatly affect current patterns and future trends in the electoral success of Latinas and Latino men, but perhaps most especially for Latinas.

Organizational Activism

The role of Latinas in national and especially local organizations is one area where research using a case-study methodology has presented consistent findings. Latinas have always been involved in this type of activity and have very often had significant leadership roles. This literature rarely compares Latinas to Latino men, however. Latina participation has been most studied in three distinct types of organizations: labor unions, community-based organizations, and electoral organizations.

LABOR

The workplace has always been an arena where Latinas have had central roles in organizational leadership. One of the first national labor figures of Mexican descent was Lucy Eldine Gonzales, who was born in Johnson County, Texas. Most historians list her as Mexican Indian. In the 1870s she was a charter member of the Chicago Working Women's Union, and in 1905 she was a founding member of the Industrial Workers of the World (IWW) (Asbaugh 1976, 267–68; Boyer and Morais 1974).

In Puerto Rico, one of the most extraordinary women labor leaders of the first decade of the twentieth century was Luisa Capetillo (1880–1922), a socialist labor organizer and a writer who worked to raise the consciousness of workers and who argued on behalf of equal rights for women (Acosta-Belen 1986). Other women leaders in the Puerto Rican labor movement included Concepcion Torres, who in 1902 became the first Latina woman in the Puerto Rican labor movement to deliver a speech at a public rally, and Juana Colon, who was known as the "Joan of Arc of Comerio," a leader and an active organizer of the tobacco strippers. Other leaders were Genara Pagan and Emilia Hernandez, who presided over the Women's Organizing Committee of the Federación Libre de Trabajadores (FLT), and Franca de Armino, who led the Popular Feminist Association, founded in 1920 (Azize 1987).

By the 1930s, in the canneries, garment factories, and pecan-shelling industry, Latinas were in the vanguard of the rank and file. The Formation of the Congress of Industrial Organizations (CIO), the United Cannery, Agricultural, Packing, and Allied Workers of America (UCAPAWA), and the International Ladies Garment Workers Union (ILGWU) gave Latinas other organizations in which to play leadership roles.

The pecan industry of San Antonio, for instance, employed between five thousand and twelve thousand Mexicans in the early 1930s (Walker 1965a). Working conditions in factories led to workers organizing a major strike in 1931; Emma Tenayuca, in her early twenties, rose as a leader of this effort. Later, Tenayuca served as an organizer for the Workers Alliance, an attempt to organize the unemployed. Tenayucca led demonstrations attracting as many as ten thousand participants (Walker 1965a, 30–41).

In 1933 the ILGWU began to recruit heavily among Mexican-origin women. Rosa Pesotta became a highly successful organizer for that organization. From 1933 to 1937, Pesotta organized two strikes on behalf of Mexican American women workers. According to Julia Kirk Blackwelder (1984), Latina workers went out on strike against low wages and poor working conditions much more often than did Latino men.

In California, Dolores Huerta became vice president of the United Farm Workers (UFW) in the late 1960s. She is still a major figure in the agricultural workers labor movement. In *Women's Work and Chicano Families*, Patricia Zavella provided the first extensive critical examination of power dynamics (that included the intersection of race, class and gender) by Latinas on the factory floor and in their living rooms. She revealed the intricate negotiations of family, networks, and decisions made by Mexican cannery workers in the Santa Clara Valley of California in the 1970s (1987).

Nora Hamilton and Norma Chinchilla (2001) conducted a twenty-year study of the Salvadoran and Guatemalan Latina experience in Los Angeles. Apart from their individual efforts, many women immigrant workers have worked in collaboration to collectively improve their situation. Unions such as the ILGW (now UNITE) and Service Employees International Union (SEIU) reversed their longstanding practice of ignoring immigrants and hired Mexican, Guatemalan, and Salvadoran immigrants, many of them women, as organizers.

La Mujer Obrera, a grassroots Latina organization, has gained attention because of the consequences of the North American Free Trade Agreement (NAFTA). Navarro analyzes how this organization's geographic location along the U.S.-Mexico border affects the structure and content of the sociopolitical identities of Latina workers (Navarro 2002). Gender, class, race, language, and geographic location intersect to form both the individual and collective sociopolitical identities of these women workers. Moreover, these identities shape political grassroots organizing and the potential for forging cross-border coalitions.

COMMUNITY-BASED ORGANIZING

The development of neighborhood-based organizations has been another area where Latina organizational activism and leadership is well documented in another series of case studies. Activists like Julia Luna Mount and her sister, Celia Luna de Rodriguez, were central leaders in neighborhood organizing in Los Angeles since the 1930s. In the 1960s, Luna de Rodriguez organized the Barrio Defense Committee to speak out against police abuse. Luna Mount was one of the leading voices against the Vietnam War in East Los Angeles (Ignacio Garcia 1997).

In 1967, Vicky Castro, an East Los Angeles student, was president of the Young Citizens for Community Action (YCCA), the precursor of the Brown Berets. She was also a leader in the 1968 school walkouts in Los Angeles. In 1967, Alicia Escalante founded the East Los Angeles Welfare Rights Organization (which later became the Chicano National Welfare Rights Organization) and was also a leader of *Católicos por la Raza* (Acuña 1984, 145).

The critical role of Latinas in neighborhood organizing is clearly demonstrated in Mary Pardo's analysis of the Mothers of East Los Angeles organization (1990, 1998). These Latinas mobilized for lights and recreational leaders at local parks. Later they became critical in preventing the placement of a prison in East Los Angeles. In her study of Latina and Latino leadership in Boston, Massachusetts, Hardy-Fanta (1993) found that, unlike many Latino male community leaders, Latinas clearly conceived of community organizing as interpersonal. The connectedness of individuals and groups to one another was emphasized. Grassroots, individual, family, and friendship networks were key to the organizing efforts of Latinas to build lasting community relationships. The role of interpersonal networks in community organizing also appears in Gabriele Kohpahl's (1998) *Voices of Guatemalan Women in Los Angeles.* This author studied two organizations, one consisting of non-Mayan refugee women and the other of Mayan refugee women. They found that many members built on experiences organizing themselves in their home countries.

Milagros Ricourt and Ruby Danta (2003), in their ethnographic study of pan-ethnicity in the New York City neighborhoods of Queens and Corona, revealed that Latinas' interpersonal relationships and networks were central to the establishment and maintenance of a strong pan-Latino organization. These Latinas had diverse origins, including Colombian, Cuban, Dominican, Ecuadorian, Peruvian, Puerto Rican, Uruguayan, and others. These women realized that there was strength in numbers and established the pan-Latin American organization to demand that specific issues and concerns be addressed by elected officials.

ELECTORAL ACTIVISM

Although much less extensively, there is evidence that Latinas have also been consistently involved in leadership roles in organizations with a specific focus on traditional means of political participation, especially voting and elections. For example, Virginia Musquiz was a central leader in the original 1963 Crystal City, Texas, takeover by Mexican Americans. In 1964, she ran unsuccessfully for state representative, and in 1965 she campaigned for the Crystal City Council. In 1969, Musquiz helped organize what became know as the Crystal City walkouts that led to the takeover of city government (Navarro 1998). Maria Hernandez, originally of Lytle, Texas, helped form the La Raza Unida Party in Crystal City in the late 1960s. This was a Chicano nationalist political party that won several local elections in areas of South Texas (*Jose Angel Gutierrez Papers* 1959–1990).

In the mid-1960s, Linda Benitez became a member of the executive board of the Los Angeles Central Committee of the Democratic Party (Chavez 1997). Julia Luna Mount ran for the Los Angeles School Board in 1967 when many Latinos were first expressing great concern with educational inequity in the public schools. Although she lost, she later became a founding member of the Peace and Freedom Party (Ignacio Garcia 1997).

The political fervor of the 1960s was not exclusive to Chicanas. Although their political goals were distinct, Cuban-origin Latinas established their own organizations to assist the independence movement, among them Hijas del Pueblo in New Orleans and the Junta Patriotica de Dama de Nueva York (Estrade 1987, 176). Estade goes on to document the role women played in the Partido Revolucionario Cubano (PRC), which had the sole purpose of working for the liberation of Cuba. As each year decreased their chances of returning to Cuba, women increasingly began to work toward improving the quality of their lives in the United Sates. A handful of political organizations emerged that were exclusively for women, among them the Union de Mujeres, the Curzada Femenina Cubana, the Movimiento Femenino Anticomunista de Cuba, and the Organización de Damas Anticomunistas Cubanas (Pérez 1986, 126–37).

Prescriptive Possibilities

In this section we characterize the literature on Latinas in Latino politics that has a clear prescriptive component. This literature goes beyond simply noting differences between Latinas and Latino men or the cataloguing of the roles that Latinas have had in a variety of political arenas. It is prescriptive in that it builds frameworks of analysis from which normative goals and strategies of influence, with a special emphasis on coalition building, can be derived. The primary source of this analysis comes from a richer interpretation of the unique position—at the intersection of feminism, ethnicity, and class—that Latinas occupy in the American polity.

Latina Feminism and Authentic Voice

Latina writings discuss resistance, reaffirmation, and self-representation—a break from the cycle of perpetrator/victims. The publication of Latina feminist newspapers, newsletters, and pamphlets in the 1960s provided a basis for the development of a feminist communication network for Latinas. As in other feminist movements, activity within the Latina community was facilitated by the rise of a feminist press. In 1971, the first issue of the Latina newspaper *Hijas de Cuauhtemoc (Daughters of Cuauhtemoc)* called for the elimination of sexism in every aspect of Latinas' lives. Similarly, another newspaper, *Regeneración*, called for the end of subservient status for Latinas. *El Grito*, one of the first Chicano journals with an intellectual focus, called on Chicanas to challenge sexism and discrimination and to develop survival strategies. Other publications that raised consciousness among Latinas included *Encuentro Femenil, La Comadre,* and *Hembra.*

Latina feminists have organized numerous regional and national conferences to address their concerns. These meetings were designed to draw attention to the most pressing needs of Latinas. One of these organizations was Mujere Activias en Letras y Cambio Social (MALCS), founded in 1983 by women in higher education at the University of California, Berkeley. In 1988, Beatriz Pesquera and Denise Segura administered a questionnaire to women on the MALCS mailing list. They sent the questionnaire to 178 women, and 101 were completed and returned. From the responses, Pesquera and Segura developed a three-part Chicana feminist typology: Chicana cultural nationalists, Chicana liberal feminists, and Chicana insurgent feminists. According to Pesquera and Segura, Chicana cultural nationalists write as a result of increased political awareness with a commitment to the cultural ideals of the Chicano movement. For these feminists, their vision is anchored in the ideology of *la familia*. Chicana liberal feminists focus on improving the well-being of the Chicano community as a whole, with a specific emphasis on improving the status of Chicanas. Chicana insurgent feminists, by contrast, call for a radical restructuring of society, where disadvantages based on gender, class, and sexuality no longer exist (1993, 95–116).

Naomi Quiñónez (2002) suggests that there are two waves of Chicana feminism. The "first wave" feminists incorporated issues of race, class, and gender by addressing the experiences of poor and working-class Mexican and Mexican American women (129–51). It was a bold move for Latinas to reject the role restriction placed on them and an even stronger step to suggest that the "triple oppression" of Latinas should be an issue within the movement (Hancock 1971, 1–6). Most of the writing during the late 1960s and early 1970s was replete with responses to Chicanas and "loyalist" Chicanas who claimed that the feministas were being divisive to the movement and products of "Anglo bourgeois feminism" (Nieto-Gomez 1973; 1974, 34). Chicana feminists articulated a support for political unity (Vidal 1971, 31–32), which called for a fuller participation of Chicanas in all aspects of the Chicano movement. Chicana feminists understood that one of their first needs as activists was to become an integral part of the movement as leaders (Nieto 1974, 41). Quiñónez's "second wave" writers (after the period of the Chicano movement) are said to possess other motives for writing that are not central to the ideas of the Chicana/o movement. These feminists, according to Quiñónez, have no close connection to the Chicano movement.

More elaborate analyses and research—as well as the emergence of poetry, fiction, and autobiographical testimony—distinguish Latina writings in the second half of the 1970s. The starting point was the rejection of traditional images and the debunking of social science myths about the Chicana. The result was the redefinition of the Chicana—by the Chicana. Chicana writers took on mainstream social science to dispel the belief that Chicanas were inherently passive. In the mid-1970s, Maxine Baca Zinn wrote articles in which she stated that "the passive, submissive, Mexican woman is a creation of social scientists and journalists who have taken for granted the idea that women are dependent and unproductive creatures" (Baca Zinn 1975, 19). In her article "Chicanas: Power and Control in the Domestic Sphere," Baca Zinn reexamines Chicanas within the family to show that "they have had great influence on Chicana survival in an Anglo-dominated society" (19). It is the mother's role within the family that helps preserve its stability and its source as a "refuge and protection from an oppressed society," she writes (29).

In *Borderlands/La Frontera* (1987), Gloria Anzaldua delineates the importance of spirituality as part of the mestiza consciousness, further enriching the understanding of Chicana feminism. The manifestation of mestiza consciousness is a personal psychological process of rebirth, according to Anzaldua—it is a consciousness that transforms race and opposition into activism and agency. In *Making Face/Making Soul: Haciendo Caras* (1990), Anzaldua explicates the complex and competing social, political, and cultural forces that shape—sometimes quite brutally—the experiences of women of color in the United States. It is only through the full understanding of these forces that efforts can be mobilized for creative and necessary social change.

Latina Intersectionality

The multiple social spaces that Latinas occupy simultaneously as women, mothers, workers, partners, ethnics, and potential agents of social change has become a growing area of writing known as Latina intersectionality. It builds on the previously described understandings of feminism. Interestingly, it initially served to focus on the ways in which simultaneity served to compound disadvantage in family, work, and politics for many Latinas. Later, however, this simultaneity also led to explicit calls for using this intersectionality as a basis for forming cross-group coalitions of understanding and action to pursue changes in cultural practice and worker treatment to better serve the needs and interests of Latinas.

Labor segmentation has served as a central focus for those writing about Latina intersectionality. For some scholars, the family was the initial focus for understanding the potential disadvantages of intersectionality. Latinas noted that the division of labor was unequal in both working class and professional households (Pesquera and Segura 1993) and that gender inequality in the household was connected to gender inequality in the work place (Zavella 1987). Together, Latinas' experiences in family and work reinforced their subordination.

Denise Segura studied the participation of Latinas in the workplace and concluded that there is systematic concentration of Latinas in the "secondary labor market" and gender-specific jobs in the "primary labor market" (1988). At all job categories, Latina workers made less then their Latino male counterparts or white workers. The labor segmentation of Latinas creates a "triple oppression" that is reinforced by gender role socialization, racial discrimination by employers, the education process, and the institutional constraints of labor marketing structuring. Another sociologist, Marta Lopez-Garza, examined Mexican and Central American women in Los Angeles and assessed the major variables affecting labor force participation. She has also initiated a study of the activities of Mexican and Central American women in the informal economy sector (1986).

In addition to work that assesses Latina labor force participation in the United States, Latina social scientists are studying the work experience of Mexicanas on the U.S.-Mexico border, thereby presenting a further dimension of Latina intersectionality. Rosalia Solorzano-Torres, for example, notes that most studies on the immigration experience not only leave out the experience of women but also make assumptions about the immigration experience that ignore their existence. In her own study of "Female Mexican Immigrants in San Diego County," she observes that nearly two thirds of the women she studied worked in the maquila sector before they immigrated to San Diego (1987). Vicki Ruiz (1987) writes in more detail about the Mexican domestic workers in El Paso. She concludes, "through frequently victimized, Mexicana domestics are not victims, but women who meet each day with integrity and endurance" (74).

In the foreword to the second edition of *This Bridge Called My Back: Writings by Radical Women*, Cherrie Moraga and Gloria Anzaldua (1984, xxiii) write that Chicanas "are beginning to realize that we are not wholly at the mercy of circumstance, nor are our lives completely out of our hands . . ." Anzaldua and Moraga see that Chicanas are not alone, and thus they must reach out for connections to other women, especially other women of color. *The Bridge Called My Back* represents an important coming out for lesbian women of color, an escape from the silence. Moreover, Anzaldua and Moraga explore how issues of race, gender, and community have changed over the past twenty years with the greater recognition of diversity and the multicultural nature of contemporary society. Many essays examine the increasing flexibility and permeability of racial, sexual, and gender identities and their effect on feminism and the fight for social justice. Moraga and Anzaldua redefine queer, female, and Latino/a identities and propose developing inclusionary movements for social justice.

Latina Legislative Representation

No known study has systematically examined the representational consequences of the increasing presence of Latinas at all levels of government. One study does present an exploratory analysis of the differences in representational roles, styles, and strategies of advocacy between Latina and Latino state legislators. Fraga, Martinez-Ebers, Ramírez, and Lopez (2001) examined differences between Latina and Latino state legislators in the 2001 legislative sessions in California and Texas and made four important findings:

- Both Latina and Latino representatives were well aware of the multiple constituencies that they simultaneously represent. In the case of Latina representatives, it was their district constituency, women, and Latinos. Latino representatives saw themselves as simultaneously representing their district constituents and Latinos more broadly speaking.
- There were no systematic differences in the propensity of Latina and Latino representatives to serve on influential committees or to serve as chairs of committees.
- The way in which both Latina and Latino representatives advocated on behalf of Latino interests was tempered by the political context of the state. Although gender differences here were minimal, there were noticeable differences by state. California legislators tended to speak much more in terms of a California agenda to advocate on behalf of Latino interests. Texas representatives tended to work more with outside advocacy groups.
- Latina representatives in Texas seemed to identify more strongly with their interests as women than did their fellow female representatives in California.

Future Research

In their review of the state of research on Chicanas and Latinas in political science, Sierra and Sosa-Riddell stated that the "challenge [to political science] is to uncover the multidimensional nature of gender and ethnic politics through research that involves a wide array of theoretical and methodological approaches" (1994, 311–12). We offer four general areas where we think it best for such future work to focus.

First, every effort must to be made to expand the available public opinion data on Latinas in American politics. The last major social scientific survey of Latino public opinion occurred in 1989 with the LNPS. Since that time, millions more Latinos have come to populate the United States, their diversity in country of origin continues to grow, and the geographical dispersion of Latinos throughout all regions of the country expands at rates inconceivable in 1989. The 2002 Current Population Survey (CPS) estimated that 38.8 million Latinos lived in the United States. This is 16.4 million more Latinos than lived in the United States in 1990.

The 2002 CPS also found that although the largest subgroup of Latinos are still persons of Mexican origin at 66.9 percent, the second largest grouping is composed of persons with origins in Central and South America at 14.3 percent. Puerto Ricans now compose only 8.6 percent of the Latino population, and people of Cuban origin only 3.7 percent. Interestingly, those who describe themselves as "Other

Hispanic" are a full 6.5 percent of Latinos; African American–Hispanics are estimated to compose 2 percent. Additionally, the ten states with the highest percentage of Latino growth from 1990 to 2000 were North Carolina (394 percent), Arkansas (337 percent), Georgia (300 percent), Tennessee (278 percent), Nevada (217 percent), South Carolina (211 percent), Alabama (208 percent), Kentucky (173 percent), Minnesota (166 percent), and Nebraska (155 percent).

Our previous understandings of how gender provides a useful analytical lens through which to understand public opinion, political participation, and especially leadership must be updated to reflect the current reality that is Latina and Latino life in the United States. Recent surveys conducted by the Pew Hispanic Center have done much to add to our knowledge of Latinos in the United States. Although half of the respondents in these surveys are Latinas, there has been no systematic analysis of their views relative to Latino men. To this end, a group of political scientists secured major funding to implement the Latino National Survey (LNS), which was recently completed. The design developed for this study included the first-ever state-stratified samples allowing meaningful comparisons of Latinas and Latinos across states. Questions specific to Latinas—such as one's family, work, politics, and immigration—composed one important subdivision of the survey questionnaire.

Second, consistent with Montoya (1986), we also think it important that future research not only focus on identifying systematic differences between Latinas and Latino men; it is just as important to determine if the predictors of patterns of belief and behavior are consistent across these two groups. Lack of differences in voting rates or partisanship, for example, may mask different underlying structures of interest, experience, and socialization that could be key to developing gender-informed strategies to influence Latinas and Latino men to vote, run for office, engage in civic participation, or understand their interests within the current party system. In not pursuing gender-specific hypotheses related to underlying values and belief structures, scholars and activists may largely misunderstand Latina political behavior. It is not so much that theories point to important gender-based differences in all areas of public opinion and behavior, but greater theory development and empirical testing will better allow us to know when gender matters, when it does not, and why.

Third, the rich work on the role of Latinas in organizational activity must be continued. The insight that scholars who have an exclusive focus on traditional political activities (such as voting and office holding) are likely to undervalue, if not miss entirely, the consistent presence that Latinas have played in much civic activity is still relevant. The critical leadership role of Latinas in many organizations must continue to be further documented. However, this research must also focus on understanding not just the types of civic activity in which Latinas have engaged, but also the policy effect these actions have had. For example, has community-based organizational activity been most successful at *protesting* and *preventing* the implementation of public policies or have they been equally successful at getting *new* legislation enacted at local, state, and national levels? This is a very important distinction that is not currently made in many studies of organizational activity and leadership. Any assessment of policy effect must face challenges of measurement, especially the selection of measurement criteria. Moreover, studies should examine what the relationship is between Latina organizational leadership and organizational longevity. Are Latinas better than Latino men not only at contributing to organizational success at specific moments in time, but also at helping community-based organizations exist over the longer term?

Additionally, many of the most noted national Latino advocacy organizations, including the National Council of La Raza (NCLR) and the Mexican American Legal Defense and Educational Fund (MALDEF), have recently appointed Latinas to be their new leaders. Why were these women chosen? Was gender seen as an important asset that these highly professionalized, and often money-driven, interest groups need to survive organizationally and to be influential politically? Organizational studies will be well served by expanding the analytical richness of the gendered lens through which such research is conducted.

Finally, we think that the increased Latina success in attaining formal elective office must be linked explicitly with insights provided by writings and scholarship on women and politics, Latina feminism, intersectionality, and especially Latina intersectionality. Research on gendered institutions finds that women face significant challenges in building on their increased presence to attempt to transform institutions to become more able to respond to the legitimate interests of groups, such as women, who have been historically underrepresented in formal political institutions (Acker 1990; Steinberg 1992; Kathlene 1994; Kenney 1996; Rosenthal 2000).

A very important distinction is made in this literature between reform efforts that have the consequence of simply allowing some women elected officials to hold positions of power and transformative efforts that try to change important dimensions of how political institutions do their work to make them more responsive to the interests of historically underrepresented groups. Other research finds that many women elected officials bring distinct interest perspectives and leadership styles to legislative arenas (Kathlene 1989; Acker 1992; Thomas 1994; Tamerius 1995; Sparks 1997; Rosenthal 2000; Carroll 2001; Walsh 2002; Jeydel and Taylor 2003).

It may be the case that Latina intersectionality will force Latina legislators to face even greater barriers to their success within the masculanized and racialized institutions that all legislatures tend to be (Crenshaw 1989, 1997). Research suggests that this is the case for African American women legislators (Darling 1997; Barrett 2001; Smooth 2001; Hawkesworth 2003). The intersectionality of Latina representatives, however, could provide them with a unique, and richer, set of strategic options to pursue the building of coalitions of interest and the legislator support needed to credibly advocate on behalf of a multiplicity of interests simultaneously (Segura 1986; Anzaldua 1987).

As women, Latina representatives may have a greater propensity to develop participatory, deliberative processes of consensus building (Acker 1992; Hardy-Fanta 1993) and may be equally committed to introduce and support legislation that serves both women and Latinos generally, as Edith Barrett (2001) has found for African American women state legislators. If this is the case, are Latina legislators pursuing distinct coalition-building strategies that have greater likelihood of legislative enactment because they can, legitimately, solicit the simultaneous support, for example, of the Latino Caucus and the Women's Caucus? No doubt institutional characteristics like committee structure, partisanship, and legislative leadership will set parameters for any such strategic effort (Swers 2002; Hawkesworth 2003).[4] Might not the unique intersectionality of Latina legislators position them as more ideal leaders, relative to Latino men, of policy development and advocacy that serve the long-term interests of their multiple constituencies? If they are successful, the benefits could be substantial not just to women and Latinos, but to our entire system of governance as well by enhancing what James Mansbridge describes as the "social meaning of 'ability to rule' and . . . the attachment to the polity of the group" (1999, 628). Researchers should examine this prescriptive potential of Latina intersectionality with all the analytical resources available in the social sciences.

One group of scholars is currently pursuing the first-ever national survey of Latina and Latino state legislators. This project is entitled the National Latina/o State Legislator Survey and is sponsored by the National Association of Latino Elected and Appointed Officials (NALEO). Luis R. Fraga, Valerie Martinez-Ebers, Ricardo Ramírez, and Linda Lopez are now analyzing the data from this survey that examines the representational roles, policy agendas, coalition-building strategies, and policy successes of Latina and Latino state legislators.

Preliminary findings based on this survey suggest that gender-based differences are very much influenced by important institutional characteristics like partisanship, legislative decision rules, and the strengths of women's and Latino caucuses. Again, state specific comparisons should help to distinguish between what aspects of representational style and effect are gender-based and which are primarily driven by institutional parameters. The increasing presence of Latinas in all levels of elective office, but especially in the Congress and state legislatures, makes this research absolutely essential.

Without a doubt the study of Latino politics will be analytically richer with a focus on the role of Latinas within it. Latino politics has never operated without significant Latina participation and leadership. Recent research suggests that this reality will become even more common given trends in voting, civic participation, and especially office holding. It may be the case that the most dramatic developments in Latino politics regarding both strategy and effect will be driven far more by the actions of Latinas as leaders and decisionmakers than by those of Latino men. It is certainly the responsibility of the research community to document, analyze, and understand how and why this may be the case.

Notes

1. Modern roles were based on responses to questions regarding whether women should sacrifice their careers to help their husbands by taking care of household chores and children, whether women in public office were more capable than men in public office during times of crisis, and whether women will be better off if they stay home and raise families (See Montoya 1996, 262).

2. Below we will discuss a number of case study findings indicating a long tradition of Latinas in leadership roles in community-based organizations.

3. These data are taken from annual NALEO reports. The figures were calculated simply by comparing 1990 data to that reported for 2002.

4. For an excellent discussion of the prescriptive potential provided by a full understanding of Latina intersectionality, see Aída Hurtado (1996).

PART 4

Latino Political Representation

Is There a Latino Dimension to Voting in Congress?

Rodolfo Espino

Evaluations of Democracy through the Analysis of Legislative Voting

The importance of legislative bodies to democratic systems cannot be overstated, as it is within such bodies that the "will of the people" ideally rests and is exercised. The extent to which the United States' federal legislative body, the U.S. Congress, is a miniature replica of American society — measured not just in physical appearance but also in policy behavior — allows us to assess the quality of representation afforded to the American people.

According to a pure delegate model of representation, the will of Congress ought to be completely congruent with the will of the people in the body politic. Majoritarian models of democracy posit that the will of the people is conveyed to members of Congress through elections, and as many congressional scholars have noted, elections are the mechanism that drives the behavior of members of Congress (Mayhew 1974). In winner-take-all elections and in a majority-rules institution, we ought to expect that the will of the people, expressed during congressional elections, will subsequently be followed by elected representatives through the votes those representatives cast on behalf of their constituents.

Therefore, it is not surprising that the process by which most political scientists choose to evaluate the quality of representation in Congress is through the votes that we observe representatives casting. If the voting of representatives is not the most important mechanism to evaluate the quality of representation, it certainly is the most visible and symbolic. One vote by a single representative symbolizes the votes for the thousands of citizens whom that legislator represents.

Certainly, voting is not the only way in which representatives provide representation to constituents, nor should it be the only way in which we evaluate the quality of congressional representation (Tate 2003). Representatives relish opportunities for constituency casework, ranging from helping elderly constituents track down Social Security checks to obtaining flags that have flown over the U.S. Capitol. Members of Congress also provide an abundance of extended remarks on the floor of Congress to demonstrate to their constituents that they are working on their behalf. Legislators will also spend much of their time out of the public eye providing more representation by drafting and editing legislation (Hall 1996), which is admittedly the primary purpose of any legislative body.

Nevertheless, casting a vote in Congress remains the primary critical test for any analysis of the quality of congressional representation. Votes cast by members of Congress not only have policy consequences but also serve as the mechanism by which representatives signal to their constituents what they stand for; it is the primary activity legislators have to communicate with their constituents back home (Kingdon 1989).

Race and Representation in Congress

Having noted that most assessments of congressional representation are based on the analysis of legislators' votes, scholars thus reach conclusions about American representative democracy based on how congressional representatives cast their votes. The aggregate outcome of votes allows us to make deductions about the structure of Congress (Krehbiel 1991; Weingast and Marshall 1988; Cox and Mc-Cubbins 1993; Gilligan and Krehbiel 1987, 1990; Poole and Rosenthal 1997; Patterson and Caldeira, 1988; Singh 1998), while the individual outcome of votes allow us to deduce how representatives define themselves to their constituents back home (Mayhew 1974; Fenno 1978; Kingdon 1989; Swain 1995; Canon 1999b; Tate 2003).

From either vantage point, scholars interested in race and representation want to examine the outcome of these votes to see the extent to which the will of minority groups, such as African Americans or Latinos, are subsequently being expressed in Congress. Some suggest that Congress, as an institution based on geographic representation and majoritarian rules, will rarely allow for the will of American minority groups to be expressed (Guinier 1994, 1995)—although there are notable instances in congressional history when the interests of minority groups have been successfully advocated (such as through the Civil War amendments, the Civil Rights Acts of the 1880s, the Civil Rights Act of 1964, and the Voting Rights Act of 1965 and its amendments in 1975).

However, these legislative victories for minorities arguably occurred because they were not only congruent with the will of minority Americans but also because the majority of white Americans shared the same sentiments, thus allowing the legislation to pass. Furthermore, there are more infamous examples in congressional history in which the interests of minority Americans were subsumed to the benefit of white Americans, such as the three-fifths compromise, the Missouri Compromise, the alien land law, and race-based immigration policies. These serve as examples demonstrating that Congress, like the rest of American society, has never been able to escape controversies over race and ethnicity and why Lani Guinier (1994, 1995) argues that the only way to guarantee that the will of minorities is incorporated in congressional legislation is to alter the rules of the institution.

Such proposals for change are so far-reaching and radical that they are not foreseeable in the near future. Nevertheless, to a certain extent, we have seen changes adopted inside and outside of Congress that changed the institution as a whole. Some of the internal reforms have been attempts to temper the power of the majority party in Congress (Binder 1996) or efforts to increase committee power as another way to mitigate against majority tyranny (Gamm and Shepsle 1989; King 1997). While such institutional reforms were not designed to enhance the political power of racial minorities, such reforms have allowed African American and Latino representatives to wield extraordinary influence over the legislative process. For instance, during the years of Democratic Party control, the ability of many minority representatives to accrue high levels of seniority allowed them to achieve senior positions both in the party and in committee.

Yet, the most direct way of increasing the probability of success of minority agendas in Congress is to increase the number of minority representatives in Congress. Such attempts have been made both inside and outside of Congress. One notable instance occurred during the 103rd Congress, when representatives of U.S. territories, who were all African American or Latino representatives, were granted voting rights on the House floor (see Canon and Espino 2002). Outside of Congress, other attempts at reform have been made to increase minority representation in Congress by increasing the probability of electoral success for African American and Latino candidates. State legislatures, state and federal courts, and the Department of Justice have worked in tandem to do this through the creation of majority-minority districts.

The creation of majority-minority districts, once a tool to disenfranchise minority Americans, has been used in recent decades to enfranchise them by increasing levels of minority descriptive representation. The underlying logic of this effort was that minority representatives are the best representatives of minority Americans. In fact, history had shown that the absence of African American representatives to Congress following the period of "Redemption" in the South allowed an all-white Congress to forgo any concerns about minority interests. This suggests that Congress possesses a "conscience" (Clay 1992) as long as minority representatives are present in its halls.

There has been considerable debate over the extent to which increasing levels of minority descriptive representation through the creation of majority-minority districts actually increases the overall level of substantive representation for minorities (Grofman, Griffin, and Glazer 1992; Swain 1995; Lublin 1997; Cameron, Epstein, and O'Halloran 1996; Hero and Tolbert 1995; Kerr and Miller 1997; Thernstrom and Thernstrom 1997; Lublin 1999; Epstein and O'Halloran 1999b). The weight of the evidence presented by various camps as to the level of substantive minority presentation in Congress largely rests on the individual voting behavior of representatives. The patterns of voting behavior are obtained from interest group scores, such as the Americans for Democratic Action (ADA), the American Conservative Union (ACU), the Leadership Conference on Civil Rights (LCCR), AFL-CIO's Committee on Political Education (COPE), or the National Hispanic Leadership Agenda (NHLA) scores, or the canonical Poole-Rosenthal NOMINATE (Nominal Three-Step Estimation) scores. The interest group scores are simply the percentage of votes in agreement with the respective advocacy group's position on selected pieces of high-profile legislation. The first and second dimension Poole-Rosenthal scores are the ratings of legislators on liberal-conservative and civil rights scales, respectively, which are computed from the voting patterns of representatives on all nonunanimous roll-call votes, regardless of the profile of the vote.

Aside from the obvious concerns over selection bias in the use of limited versus unlimited samples of roll-call votes, it is remarkable that for the high stakes placed on such debates over the extent to which descriptive minority representation translates into substantive minority representation, few researchers pay careful attention to the construction of these legislators' voting scores. Poole-Rosenthal NOMINATE scores are largely held as the gold standard measure of representatives' overall ideological position. Yet, a large majority of the studies on race and representation use focused interest group scores as measures of support for African American or Latino interests in Congress. The reasons are that the first dimension NOMINATE scores largely measure an overall liberal-conservative dimension. The second dimension NOMINATE scores, while perhaps measuring a racial dimension, are no longer as significant predictors of voting patterns as are the first dimension scores. Therefore, those interested in the representation of minority interests will often turn to scores compiled by interest groups that seek to ascertain support for minority interests, such as scores compiled by the National Hispanic Leadership Agenda (NHLA).

These interest group scores are typically the percentage of times each legislator votes for the preferred position of the interest group for an average of ten to twenty key roll-call votes selected by the group. The use of such particularized interest group scores as measures of support for Latinos or African Americans is not inherently wrong. However, the resulting implication of the use of such scores ought to be more carefully considered. Presumably, researchers only use fewer than 1 percent of all roll-call votes cast in a session of Congress to measure levels of substantive minority representation; if votes constituting more than 1 percent of a select group of votes are used, then researchers will not find any distinctive dimensions to congressional voting other than the influence of political parties.

We would conclude that of all the myriad issues that Congress considers, fewer than 1 percent of these issues are of relevance to minority Americans. Furthermore, because the canonical NOMINATE scores fail to detect any other significant dimension other than the partisan dimension, we are left to conclude that this provides the empirical evidence necessary to support this reasoning. To date, no known research has systematically tested whether this is a valid assumption to make. Researchers interested in race and representation would be well served to reexamine this justification and understand more fully how the ideological measures from spatial voting models are derived—and whether modifications to such models might lead us to conclude that there is a significant racial dimension to congressional voting patterns outside of a sample of select roll-call votes. In the next section, I turn to such a brief overview of the traditional spatial model of legislative voting.

The Spatial Model of Congressional Voting

Nearly every spatial model of legislative voting, such as the Poole-Rosenthal model, relies heavily on the logic of the Euclidean spatial voting model developed by Otto Davis, Melvin Hinich, and Peter Ordeshook (1970). The traditional model in which actors are assumed to have quadratic utilities in their preferences has been rigorously proven and tested since it was first introduced to political science (Enelow and Hinich 1984; Platt, Poole, and Rosenthal 1992). This spatial model of legislative voting patterns has been hailed as the most accurate way to theorize and study legislators' preferences. Furthermore, the simplicity of the Euclidean model has strong intuitive appeal for researchers seeking to make singular conclusions of how representatives routinely make decisions on policies presented to them.

In a strictly unidimensional world of preferences, we can conceive of a single line with polar opposite positions at each end of this line. We can then classify any single issue and any single individual along this single dimension. When a particular issue arises for consideration by a legislative body, there are two positions legislators can choose—either supporting or opposing the issue. The positions of support or opposition are each aligned at different points along this single dimension. In the language of formal spatial modelers, each legislator will derive the greatest utility from choosing the position closest to his or her own unique position on this dimension. A critical assumption, of course, is that legislators are utility maximizers. Given the drive for reelection (Mayhew 1974) and the way in which legislators weigh votes carefully in order to be able to explain their position to constituents back home (Kingdon 1989), this is not too stringent of an assumption.

This in itself is intuitive and easy to understand. Difficulties arise not because of the simple logic of the model but rather in estimating this model with real data. Consider the House of Representatives, where we have 435 representatives, and a typical session of Congress, where each representative casts about one thousand votes for various bills and amendments. Because the "ideal points" for votes and "ideal points" for representatives are all unidentified parameters to be estimated, the actual computation required is substantial even for a relatively simple, single-dimension model.

To explain this further, let us substitute the number of representatives and votes with the letters i and j, respectively. Keep in mind that any vote is a binary choice between yea or nay.[1] And let us define the vote outcomes we observe with the letter y. So, if we want to know how the ith legislator cast her vote on the jth bill, we would write this simply as y_{ij}. Now let us define, y_{ij} in slightly greater detail. In the Euclidean model, the assumption is that legislator i will derive utility from either voting yea or nay on vote j. Let us define the utility for legislator as U_i, the yea position on vote j as ζ_j and the nay position on vote j as ψ_j.

Assuming a utility maximizing world of legislators where these utilities are quadratic over each of the two possible outcomes, each legislator will vote yea or nay based on whichever of those positions is going to give him or her the greatest sense of benefit. We assume that whenever $U_i(\zeta_j)$ is greater than $U_i(\psi_j)$, we will observe $y_{ij} = 1$ if we code yea votes equal to a value of 1. We would observe $y_{ij} = 0$ (that is, a nay vote) if the value of $U_i(\psi_j)$ is greater than $U_i(\zeta_j)$. This can be expressed in the following equation:

$$y^*_{ij} = U_i(\zeta_j) - U_i(\psi_j) \tag{1}$$

We do not directly observe y^*_{ij}. Rather, this serves as the latent measure of the distance between the two positions on each vote for each legislator. When y^*_{ij} is positive, we observe a yea vote, and when it is negative, we observe a nay vote.

How are the "ideal" positions of each legislator defined? These simply are those values that define the utility legislator i derives from voting yea or nay. That is, again assuming quadratic utilities in the Euclidean world, this utility is the squared combination of where a legislator is positioned along a dimension and where the vote choice is positioned along the same dimension, or to vote yea on vote j the utility is simply

$$U_i(\zeta_j) = -(x_i - \zeta_j)^2 \tag{2}$$

and to vote on nay vote j, the utility derived would be defined as

$$U_i(\psi_j) = -(x_i - \psi_j)^2 \tag{3}$$

Whichever of these two was the highest value would be the position the legislator would take.

If we were simply theorists, we would stop here. However, empiricists who then go on to apply the model to real-world data will note that in the imperfect world of human behavior, such a model does not perfectly predict the actual vote outcomes we observe. To account for this error, empiricists have to add an error term to the equation, because human beings may not be utility maximizing every single time. Rather than completely reject the notion that legislators are always rational beings, legislators might have incomplete information to accurately choose the maximizing position.

Returning to the latent variable equation and substituting error terms into the utility equations for both the yea and nay positions, we would then have a model as follows:

$$y^*_{ij} = (-(x_i - \zeta_j)^2 + \eta_{ij}) - (-(x_i - \psi_j)^2 + v_{ij}) \tag{4}$$

where η_{ij} and v_{ij} account for the random error associated in choosing the ideal position. We can assume these error terms have a bivariate normal distribution and are independent and identically distributed (i.i.d.) across legislators and votes.[2] With these assumptions, we can define the variance of each vote j as $\sigma_j^2 = V(\eta_{ij}) - 2Cov(\eta_{ij}, v_{ij}) + V(v_{ij})$ and combine the two error terms into a single value of ε_{ij}, where $\varepsilon_{ij} = (v_{ij} - \eta_{ij})/\sigma_j$. With substitution, we then get

$$y^*_{ij} = 2(\zeta_j - \psi_j)x_i + \zeta_j^2 - \psi_j^2 + \varepsilon_{ij} \qquad (5)$$

and can substitute into the above equation to simplify it further so that:

$$\beta_j = 2(\zeta_j - \psi_j) \text{ and } \alpha_j = \zeta_j^2 - \psi_j^2$$

which results in:

$$y^*_{ij} = \beta_j x_i - \alpha_j + \varepsilon_{ij} \qquad (6)$$

At this point, the above equation ought to look familiar to a linear regression modeler, and given the nature of the variable y_{ij}, it resembles the familiar binary probit or logit models with a hierarchical structure. Yet, this is now finally where the complication arises. With conventional linear regression models, we have data in which we observe both y_{ij} and x_i, which then allows us to estimate the parameters of interests, β_j and α_j. In this model, however, x_1 is an unobserved predictor we still have to estimate. Therefore, this equation is underidentified, and we cannot use methods such as ordinary least squares (OLS) or maximum likelihood estimation (MLE) to estimate the equation.

The only available solution would be to assign values to any one set of unidentified items to identify the other items (Londregan 2000) or to use some form of iterative imputation to simultaneously estimate the unidentified items. The former approach may impose more assumptions than most researchers would be comfortable doing. The latter approach, however, requires significant computing power. With the increasing availability of computing power, though, this problem is less of an issue today.

For instance, Poole and Rosenthal use an iterative imputation algorithm to circumvent this "missing data" problem, which allows them to produce the well-known NOMINATE scores. To use the particular algorithm, they have to make the identifying restriction that ideal points of legislators roughly fall in the range of [1,1]. Recently, Simon Jackman (2000; 2001) and Andrew Martin and Kevin Quinn (2002) have shown that this missing data problem can be resolved through Bayesian estimation methods and that unlike NOMINATE scores, Bayesian estimation can also produce measures of uncertainty of the ideal point estimates for legislators, x_i, and legislation, y_{ij}.

Up to this point, I have refrained from discussing the dimensionality of this Euclidean model. Adding dimensions does not alter the logic of identifying y_{ij} and x_{ij}. What does change, however, is the number of parameters to be estimated (an identical set of equations for each dimension to be estimated) and the ability to easily distinguish the parameters in any one dimension from parameters in other dimensions.

In their thorough analysis of nearly every single roll call in congressional history with such a spatial model, Keith Poole and Howard Rosenthal (1997) found that voting in Congress is largely explained by a single dimension—one that is tied to economic redistribution. To be more precise, Poole and Rosenthal (1991) first presented findings in which they found that only 1.5 dimensions exist. While a second dimension adds significantly in some congresses, the second dimension is clearly less important than the first (232). They found that this second dimension only dominates significantly in a handful of nineteenth-century sessions of Congress and only one session during the 1960s. Overall, this second dimension typically only accounts for an additional 3 percent of the voting patterns in Congress compared to 80 percent for the first dimension.

It is the second dimension that has been of greatest interest to scholars interested in race and representation. Poole and Rosenthal (1991) termed this second dimension an internal party conflict dimension or a regional conflict dimension. In subsequent analysis, Poole and Rosenthal (1997) further confirmed the occasional appearance of this second dimension in congressional voting and showed that it is largely tied to controversy related to civil rights. Yet overall, and especially in recent sessions of Congress, they found that issues related to this second dimension have been all but completely subsumed within the primary liberal-conservative dimension in recent congresses.

The disappearance of this second dimension does not necessarily mean that race-related issues no longer play an important role in how representatives make their voting decisions. Rather, it means that while such issues may continue to be important, they are no longer distinguishable from the single economic redistribution dimension. Such a second dimension is presumably distinguishable from the liberal-conservative redistribution dimension only on a handful of votes—and hence is why many researchers measuring minority representation limit their focus to this handful of votes.

As a result of detecting only a single primary dimension via NOMINATE scores, we might simply conclude that minority representatives are best categorized as being more or less liberal (that is, more or less supportive of redistributive policies). The conclusion most scholars subsequently reach is that minority representatives provide better substantive representation the more liberal they are.

However, we know that a new breed of racial politics has emerged in the last quarter of the twentieth century (Kinder and Sears 1981) that has also brought about a new way in which race is represented by members of Congress (Canon 1999b; Fenno 2003). Furthermore, many spatial voting models have searched for patterns in voting data in seemingly atheoretical ways; what might be more accurate is that the many researchers searching for patterns in legislative voting data have not had their theoretical concerns focused on issues of race and representation.

Recent advancements in the Bayesian estimation of spatial voting models now make it possible to more easily apply substantive information about the ways in which we suspect race will emerge in legislative voting patterns. Specifically, scholars interested in race and representation suspect that race does play a role in legislators' voting decisions. The Bayesian estimation of spatial voting models allows us to incorporate such information to tap any of the dimensions we believe should exist given our substantive prior beliefs—much in the same way that scholars using interest group scores are bringing substantive prior beliefs to their assessments of representation by limiting their focus to only those votes deemed to be substantively important.

It is this Bayesian method of estimation detailed in Jackman (2000, 2001) that I use to estimate a spatial voting model for representatives in the U.S. House during the 108th Congress, with a specific focus on whether a dimension of support or opposition to Latino interests can be identified beyond the traditional liberal-conservative dimension. The ability to identify other dimensions in roll-call voting via Bayesian estimation is not a mere exercise in methodological techniques. Rather, the ability to accurately identify multiple dimensions in congressional roll-call voting requires strong theoretical justification on the part of researchers using such methods.

Specifically, to reduce the complexity of a model with more than one dimension, researchers will often have to add "prior" information to the data that will guide the model estimation. Essentially, this can be thought of as a researcher telling his computer, "Based on what I know, I have some prior beliefs about the way the world works, so look for this particular structure to the data with this particular level of precision." This not only allows for the algorithm to solve the equation but also allows researchers to test how well informed their prior beliefs actually are.

In fact, after detailing the ways in which Bayesian simulation can be applied to estimating the ideal points in multiple dimensions for legislators and bills in the U.S. Congress, Jackman (2001) writes, "Priors need not play a mere technical role. Researchers with interests in, say, trade, foreign policy, or environmental policy can specify informative priors for the discrimination parameters of key roll-call votes; in an extremely crude way, this is how interest group ratings get constructed."

These priors effectively "prelabel" one or more of the dimensions presumed to underlie the roll calls. Analysis can then proceed entirely consistent with the spatial voting model but incorporating the researchers' prior beliefs about the dimensions underlying the policy space. Researchers might then investigate what other roll calls discriminate with respect to these dimensions, which may be helpful in better understanding legislative politics more generally.

Is There a Latino Dimension in Congressional Voting? An Application to the 108th Congress

In this section I present some findings about the dimensions in congressional roll-call voting observed in the 108th Congress. I have entered into this discussion by suggesting that the ways in which members of Congress process information about racial issues in their decision-making is different today than it used to be, much as we have seen a transformation in the processing of racial issues in the general American public. Furthermore, I also have suggested that previous spatial models of voting may have not been correctly searching under the right stones. The question we are then presented with is how we ought to conduct such searches that will accurately capture what many scholars of race and representation believe has existed all along.

To begin to address this, we must first ask whether issues in Congress are even being addressed of relevance to minority Americans, such as Latinos, to make this endeavor worthwhile. Examination of legislation and debate in recent sessions of Congress suggests that such issues are being considered. Because of these debates, we are led to believe that there is at least some dynamic to congressional decision-making that makes a focus on Latinos potentially useful. As many scholars and pundits find that the concerns of Latinos defy easy classification in the unidimensional American policy space (for example, socially conservative but economically liberal), we might take this as further evidence that a unique Latino dimension to legislative voting might emerge.

The question then is under what conditions might we expect the emergence of such a dimension in the modern U.S. Congress. Poole and Rosenthal (1997) make a strong case that a single dimension explains nearly every vote decision in nearly every single session of Congress. However, others (Koford 1989) have suggested that this is an artifact of their methodological technique and that the case for only a single dimension to congressional voting has been overstated. Recently, Jackman (2001) demonstrated that the use of Bayesian simulation to estimate the parameters in the traditional spatial voting model permits the incorporation of theoretical beliefs into model specification that will enhance the ability of researchers to detect other underlying dimensions in congressional voting patterns.

Poole and Rosenthal (1997) and Jackman (2001) indicate that the circumstances under which other dimensions will emerge are those instances where the primary liberal-conservative dimension does not predict voting preferences. Such circumstances include the debate over civil rights for American minorities that divided northern and southern Democrats in the 1960s. Other instances could be debate over interventionist or isolationist foreign policies that split the political parties (Jackman 2001).

The question before us is how to search for a Latino dimension to voting. In his methods for uncovering an alternate dimension to voting patterns, Jackman (2001) notes that he used substantive information from votes that were not as accurately explained in the primary liberal-conservative dimension. Such a method, though, will not be as likely to uncover a Latino dimension to roll-call voting because it is prone to detect dimensions that divide *both* Democrats and Republicans.

In the debate over civil rights legislation in the 1960s, we saw that such issues were more likely to divide Democrats than Republicans. Since the Democrats are the party in Congress with a racial "conscience" (Clay 1992) because of their African American and Latino members, we might expect that this conscience is more likely to be raised within the Democratic Party. That is, the very votes on which the "conscience" of the Democratic Party is raised by its minority members might be the very same votes on which the Republican Party is more unified than ever in opposition.

Therefore, to detect a Latino dimension to voting in Congress, I look to votes in which the Democrats are fractured in their voting cohesiveness. I assume that such votes are indicative of another dimension to voting in Congress and assign priors to the Gibbs sampler in the Bayesian simulations that these particular votes are indicative of this other dimension. Furthermore, I look to votes that divided highly along partisan lines as informative of the first dimension—the liberal-conservative dimension. Specifically, for this analysis I use all roll-call votes in which there was more than 2.5 percent opposition, which provides a total of 756 votes. I also look only at representatives who had at least a 50 percent attendance record in voting, which brings my sample of legislators to 431.

As a first attempt, I estimate a single-dimension spatial voting model in which I run the Gibbs sampler for 250,000 iterations and thin every 100th iteration. "Good" starting values are important for convergence toward the "true" parameter values. For this first attempt, I simply set the starting values for representatives' ideal points to -1 for Democrats and $+1$ for Republicans. I specified noninformative priors for the parameters of $N(0,1)$.[3] Both Raftery-Lewis and Geweke convergence diagnostics suggest convergence is achieved a couple thousand iterations into the sample.

Discarding the first 10 percent of the iterations from this sample as "burn-in," 82 percent of the variance in the legislators' ideal points from this sample is explained by representatives' partisan affiliation.[4] This is not surprising, but it does suggest that there is a nontrivial amount of variation in roll-call voting records that is not explained by this first dimension. This opens the possibility of the existence of a second dimension to roll-call voting in this session of Congress.

Starting values and informative priors for the parameters to be estimated are critical even for a simple single-dimension spatial model of roll-call voting. Starting values and priors are, therefore, even more critical when estimating a model with more than one dimension. To estimate a two-dimensional spatial voting model for this session of Congress, I retain the same sample of legislators and votes used to estimate the simple single-dimension model. For starting values for legislators' ideal points in both dimensions, I use values obtained from a principal-components factor analysis—a method used by Poole and Rosenthal (1997) to provide starting values for their estimates of legislators' ideal points. Starting values for the bill-specific parameters are all set to zero. Noninformative priors are used for legislators' ideal points (e.g., $N(0,1)$). However, I assign priors to the bill parameters for both the first and second dimensions.

To assign priors on the first dimension, I searched for votes in which the Republicans and Democrats voted in 99 percent opposition to each other—that is, votes in which there was very little overlap between Democrats and Republicans. This generated a total of 114 roll-call votes. For those votes, I assigned priors on the first dimension discrimination parameters of 2, if the majority position was Republican, or −2, if the majority position was Democratic, and a variance of 0.1. On these same votes, I assigned noninformative priors for the second dimension parameters and the bill-specific intercept (e.g., $N(0,1)$).

For the priors on the second dimension (i.e., the Latino dimension I hope to find), I searched for votes on which the Democratic representatives were less than 55 percent unified and on which the Congressional Hispanic Caucus (CHC) was at least 95 percent unified. This generated a sample of twenty-one votes. On these roll-call votes, I assigned vague priors on the discrimination parameters for the first dimension and then assigned priors of 2 and variance .1 for the second dimension. For all other roll-call votes, vague priors ($N(0,1)$) were set for all bill-specific parameters. The Gibbs sampler sampled from the posterior density of this data to generate 500,000 samples and only every 100th iteration was retained for the final analysis. Discarding the first half of the iterations as a burn-in leaves a final sample of 2,501 iterations on which I conduct a preliminary analysis of roll-call voting of the dimensionality of voting in the 108th House of Representatives.

Figure 11.1 plots the ordered ideal points and 95 percent confidence intervals for each of the 431 representatives in the estimated first dimension of this spatial voting model. The confidence intervals surrounding the representatives' ideal points show that there are statistically significant differences between representatives at each end of this dimension to roll-call voting. Similarly, figure 11.2 plots the ordered

FIGURE II.I
Representative ideal points in the 1st dimension, 108th Congress, all votes

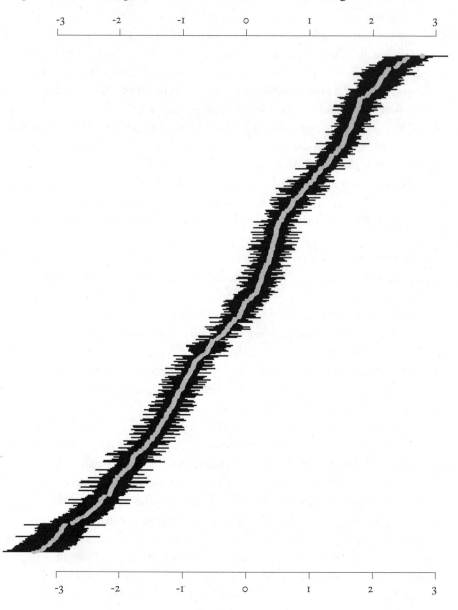

FIGURE 11.2
Representative ideal points in the 2nd dimension, 108th Congress, all votes

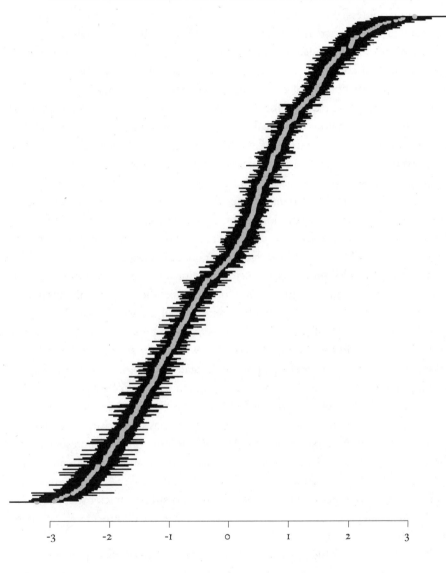

ideal points and confidence intervals for each of the representatives in the second dimension. Here, too, can be seen the statistically significant difference between representatives at the low and high ends of this dimension.

Does this second dimension correspond to a "Latino dimension" to roll-call voting in Congress? As it turns out, membership in the CHC only accounts for 2 percent of the variance in this second dimension, which is only slightly less than the 5 percent of the variance that partisan affiliation explains in this dimension. A greater cause for concern is the fact that partisan affiliation now only explains 42 percent of the variation of roll-call voting in the first-dimension ideal points, which runs counter to the strong empirical evidence years of research have provided on the strong partisan nature of roll call-voting in modern sessions of Congress. An examination of Raftery-Lewis and Geweke convergence diagnostics shows moderate convergence problems for the majority of representatives in the first dimension and even more severe convergence problems for the majority of representatives in the second dimension. This demonstrates that in such analyses of roll-call voting, researchers ought to be very cautious in closely examining convergence of the Markov Chain Monte Carlo (MCMC) sampler even when representatives' ideal points show significant difference from each other for both dimensions.

Substantively, the problems in this estimation of a two-dimensional spatial model demonstrate that the introduction of additional dimensions can complicate the analysis and detrimentally affect the estimation of the well-known first, partisan dimension of roll call-voting in Congress. These problems can be alleviated by reparameterization of the model, perhaps, with better starting values or more informative priors on the parameters to be estimated. However, the most obvious problem lies in the number of representatives and the number of votes to which this two-dimensional model is being applied. Congress considers a wide range of issues (e.g., environment, taxation, armed forces) that may only arise on a handful of roll-call votes. Further, members of the House of Representatives represent a wide array of geographic areas (e.g., South, Northeast, West) and types of congressional districts (e.g., urban, rural) that, undoubtedly, influence the voting behavior of representatives; but the relevance of some of these district characteristics may only become relevant on a handful of roll-call votes, such as the closure of military bases in a handful of districts.

To address this problem, I rerun the two-dimensional spatial voting model on *only* those twenty-one votes identified earlier as those votes in which the Democratic Caucus is split and the CHC is unified. Noninformative priors ($N(0,1)$) for the model parameters are used. Starting values in the first dimension are set to -1 for Democrats and $+1$ for Republicans. Starting values in the second dimension are set to -1 for members of the CHC and $+1$ for everyone else. As before, the

FIGURE II.3
Representative ideal points in the 1st dimension, 108th Congress, CHC votes

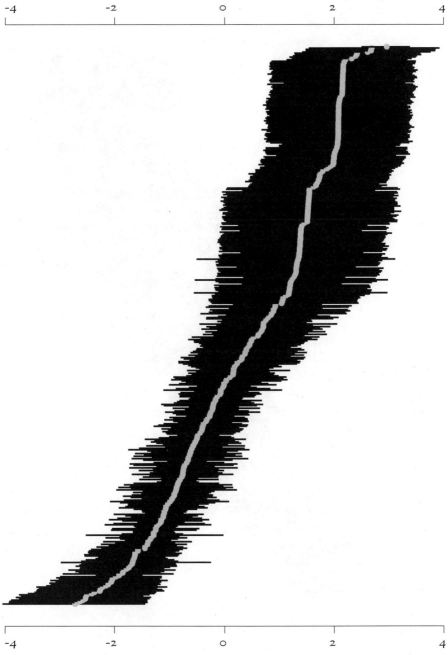

FIGURE II.4
Representative ideal points in the 2nd dimension, 108th Congress, CHC votes

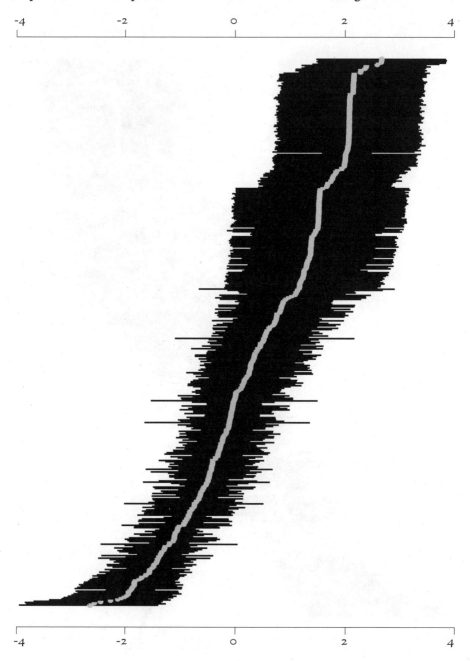

Gibbs sampler is run for 500,000 iterations and thinned every 100th iteration to provide a sample of 5,001 iterations.

Figures 11.3 and 11.4 plot the ideal points for all 431 representatives in the sample derived from these twenty-one votes, respectively. Although similar to the pattern of ideal points plotted in figures 11.1 and 11.2, these sets of ideal points for representatives were not only obtained from a MCMC sample with desirable convergence properties, but, more important, the first dimension of ideal point estimates corresponds to the well-known partisan dimension driving roll-call voting in Congress, with approximately 64 percent of the variance in this first dimension being explained by representatives' partisan affiliation, with positive values representing conservative ideal points and negative values representing liberal ideal points.

The second-dimension ideal points derived from this constrained sample of roll-call votes slightly corresponds to both representatives' partisan affiliation and membership in the CHC. These two characteristics jointly account for just 5 percent of the variation in this second dimension, with CHC membership separately accounting for approximately 2 percent of this variance. While seemingly not significant, this is variability in roll-call voting *after* accounting for the strong partisan dimension to voting in Congress, and the explanatory power of CHC membership is just 50 percent less in this second dimension than in the stronger first dimension.

Unlike figures 11.1 and 11.2, these ideal point estimates in figures 11.3 and 11.4 reflect much more uncertainty for representatives at the positive ends for both dimensions. This is largely a function of the small set of votes (twenty-one) that produced these ideal point estimates. Increased certainty can be obtained with more iterations of the MCMC sampler.

Although partisanship does explain some variability in the second dimension, it does not fully explain members' voting patterns in this second dimension. An interesting question, naturally, is how does race and partisanship correspond to this second dimension? Further, who are those members who are noticeably different from their partisan colleagues on this second dimension? While not fully answering that question in this paper, table 11.1 lists the average ideal point estimates for

TABLE 11.1
Average ideal point estimates

	1st dimension	*2nd dimension*
Latino Democrats	−.860 (.527)	−.451 (.930)
Non-Latino Democrats	−.793 (.528)	−.117 (.914)
Latino Republicans	.618 (.415)	−.104 (.418)
Non-Latino Republicans	.703 (.525)	.152 (.890)

TABLE 11.2
Furthest left on "Latino dimension"

Representative (state, party)	2nd dimension
Kolbe (R-AZ)	−2.641
Dingell (D-MI)	−2.611
Kirk (R-IL)	−2.557
Feeney (R-FL)	−2.446
Neal (D-MA)	−2.268
Tauscher (D-CA)	−2.134
Serrano (D-NY)	−2.064
Green (R-WI)	−2.006

both dimensions for representatives by party and ethnicity. Note that on the second dimension (i.e., the Latino dimension), both Latino Democrats and Latino Republicans are further to the left on this dimension than their non-Latino counterparts, although the difference of means test is only statistically significant for Latino Democrats.

Table 11.2 lists those representatives who are farthest to the left on this second dimension. Given the average position of the CHC, scores to the left on this dimension could be inferred to be points more in line with the agenda of the CHC, whereas scores to the right would be considered further away from the ideal CHC position. Table 11.2 shows Democrats and Republicans to be equally well represented at the far end of this dimension. In fact, the representative farthest to the left on this dimension is Jim Kolbe, a Republican from Arizona, who represents a district with a significant and growing Latino population. Interestingly, only one member of the CHC is found to the far left on this dimension—Jose Serrano, a Democrat from New York, who is known for being one of the most liberal members of the CHC.

Table 11.3 shows those members who are the farthest to the right on the second dimension. Here we see a larger contingent of Democrats than Republicans on the far right of this scale. Interestingly, we see one member of the CHC, Charlie Gonzalez of Texas, included in this list of representatives. Charlie Gonzalez represents the district long represented by his father, Henry B. Gonzalez, a founding member of the CHC but an individual who often drew the ire of Latino political activists for being too conservative in their view. Perhaps even more interesting is the fact that two members of the Congressional Black Caucus, Artur Davis of Alabama and Bennie Thompson of Mississippi, are also among the legislators with the most conservative position on this "Latino dimension." Another point worth noting is that all but two of the members in table 11.3 come from Southern

TABLE 11.3
Furthest right on "Latino dimension"

Representative (state, party)	2nd dimension
Taylor (R-NC)	2.665
Tanner (D-TN)	2.661
Peterson (R-PA)	2.656
Thompson (D-MS)	2.606
Gonzalez (D-TX)	2.581
Lantos (D-CA)	2.385
Davis (D-AL)	2.380

states. These findings open the door for future inquiries to explore whether there is a black-brown divide within the Democratic Party's "conscience" and whether representatives from the South are exhibiting a new, unique dimension to voting, perhaps in response to the rapid increases in the Latino population through the Southern United States.

Conclusion and Future Frontiers

One of the goals for this piece was to demonstrate that methods seemingly devoid of any focus on issues of race and politics can be used by scholars interested in such issues to uncover findings overlooked by scholars whose primary focus is more in the development of such methods. It was my attempt here to apply such recent developments in the estimation of spatial voting models to look for new patterns in congressional voting.

The preliminary findings confirm what other scholars have already known for some time about congressional voting patterns—the parties reign supreme. Nevertheless, many with more of a substantive—rather than methodological—interest in voting and representation have strongly believed that more than one dimension exists in congressional decision making, as Clausen (1973) noted many years earlier. It is those with more substantive interests in voting, race, and representation who should strive to apply their substantive theoretical focus to the advancement and modification of those methods.

In the results presented here, I made an initial attempt to uncover an alternate dimension to the liberal-conservative dimension. When looking across *all* roll call votes, partisanship is, not surprisingly, the driving force behind representatives' voting behavior. The attempt to estimate a second dimension actually can complicate ideal point estimation in a troubling way. While advances in political methodology make more tools available to political scientists, these tools, in themselves, do not change the fact that the majority of roll-call votes are partisan in nature.

When limiting the examination of roll-call votes to a theoretically interesting set of votes, particularly those votes in which members of the CHC break from their Democratic colleagues, one is able to detect the emergence of a second dimension to roll-call voting—a dimension we can label as a "Latino interests" dimension. It is appropriate to ask what is gained by applying a computationally intensive technique such as Markov Chain Monte Carlo estimation to a preselected set of roll-call votes. Are we not doing anything more than identifying a set of votes to produce particular outcomes much in the way that interest groups select key roll-call votes? The answer is yes; however, unlike interest group ratings, ideal point estimates generated via Bayesian estimation have the advantages of providing more continuous measures of ideology, allow us to explore multiple dimensions in roll-call votes, and allow us to reflect the uncertainty in the ideological positions of representatives.

With respect to the "Latino dimension" identified in this piece, it remains to be seen how much this second dimension is detected in past and, more important, future sessions of Congress. Furthermore, the results here should not suggest that this is the only alternate dimension in congressional voting. Future work might take the new developments in spatial voting model estimation to once again examine the question of dimensionality in congressional voting and see whether the second dimension uncovered in this essay is less significant than other dimensions. In addition, future work should explore this with respect to the "electoral connection"—namely, to what extent are these second-dimension scores being driven by characteristics of representatives, their districts, and the electoral environment?

Notes

1. For simplicity, we will not consider abstentions as a third possible choice right now.

2. It is in the actual estimation of the error terms, and particularly the distributive assumptions made, where many spatial voting models diverge.

3. Even such basic starting values as these for the representative ideal points are critical for convergence. In the instance, where I did not specify these starting values, Raftery-Lewis Inflation diagnostics suggested moderate convergence problems (Raftery-Lewis Inflation values greater than 1.5 and less than 5) for approximately one-third of the representatives and severe convergence problems (Inflation values greater than 5) for approximately five representatives.

4. Bernard Sanders (Ind-VT) is excluded from this calculation.

Latino Representation in Congress

To What Extent Are Latinos Substantively Represented?

Jason P. Casellas

O NE OF THE FUNDAMENTAL concepts in the study of Congress is that of representation. Political scientists have tried to understand the many ways members of Congress represent their constituents.[1] In the United States, the representation of Latinos by Latinos, as well as African Americans by African Americans, has been dismal.[2] In terms of overall numbers, African Americans and Latinos still do not have an equal proportion of representatives in Congress when juxtaposed to their respective populations. For example, in the early 1990s, California's population was 35 percent Latino, yet Latinos held only 6 percent of the congressional seats (Grofman and Davidson 1992).[3] In addition, African Americans outnumber Latinos in Congress two to one and in state legislatures three to one. Nevertheless, redistricting changes in 2002—accompanied by the steady growth of Latino populations—increased the number of Latinos in these offices and will likely do so in the future. Such issues are particularly important given the salience of the immigration policy debate. How Congress and the president choose to deal with immigration will have a special effect on Latino politics, and eventually Latino representation.

Relatively little research has explored Latino representation in the U.S. Congress, however. In an effort to fill this research gap, this essay goes beyond the simple discussion of legislator numbers to assess the extent to which Latino legislators vote differently than do non-Latino legislators. I do this by updating Hero and Tolbert's (1995) study to encompass more roll-call votes and a more systematic measure of ideology.

Representation Defined

What does representation entail? Does it mean that African Americans can only be represented by African Americans? Hanna F. Pitkin introduced two notions of representation: descriptive and substantive. Descriptive (or dyadic) representation involves Latinos having a Latino represent their district, while substantive representation involves a representative of any race or ethnicity voting the way her Latino constituents prefer. By examining districts with similar demographics yet representatives from different races and ethnicities, this dichotomous distinction can be somewhat refined.

Descriptive representation occurs when the representative resembles the represented in some way. If a district were majority Catholic, then a Catholic representative would descriptively represent the district. David Canon (1999a) notes three different values of descriptive representation:

- There exists a distinct value in having role models.
- Descriptive representation is not useful unless linked to substantive representation.
- Modern-day politics extols the value of leaders that "look like America."

Most would agree that descriptive representation is important to a certain extent. Precisely how members of Congress represent their constituents is just as important. James Johnson and Philip Secret (1996) refer to Edmund Burke's theory of representation, which combined "a conception of the focus of representation with a concept of the style of representation."[4] In addition, Hanna Pitkin (1967) argued that Burke's notion of a trustee and delegate style of representation must be combined for genuine representation to occur.

Warren Miller and Donald Stokes (1963) contributed to the literature on representation by searching for the "congruence" in the beliefs of constituents and the way their legislators voted. Hence, policy responsiveness or congruence has become a way to assess the extent to which representation is occurring.

Perhaps the best description of precisely how representatives respond to their constituents is from Richard Fenno's interviews. Fenno's *Home Style* (1978) aptly explores several congressmen's efforts to represent their districts. This aspect of representation is crucial to being able to explain roll-call votes and their implications. Unfortunately, Fenno's research style is expensive and difficult and thus is less ubiquitous than roll-call analysis.

In the area of racial representation, Carol Swain's *Black Faces, Black Interests* is an analysis of how African Americans are represented in Congress. Swain's interviews with African American members of Congress provide insight into the varying styles within the African American community. Her analyses of former representative Mike Espy (D-MS) and Rep. John Conyers (D-MI) show how two different African American members of Congress had to respond to their districts in order to secure reelection. Swain's fundamental thesis—that African Americans would be better served by electing Democratic members of Congress, regardless of race—has been a controversial one. For example, Canon (1999b) notes that Swain does not account for all white representatives with at least a 25 percent African American population in the 103rd Congress. Christian Grose (2002) argues that Swain neglects the importance of African American descriptive representation in terms of yielding substantive representation as measured by pork project allocation and constituency service. For roll-call voting, Grose concedes that Swain is correct in calling for the election of more Democratic legislators as a way to increase African American substantive representation.

Furthermore, Swain's thesis cannot be applied to Latinos for a variety of reasons. Latinos are not politically monolithic, nor are they as strongly partisan as African Americans. It is true that the majority of Latinos identify with the Democratic Party, but a significantly larger percentage of Latinos have been willing to cross party lines in certain elections, such as the 2001 election of Michael R. Bloomberg as mayor of New York City.[5] For example, President George W. Bush received approximately 35 percent of the Latino vote in the 2000 election and about 40 percent in 2004—not a majority, but much better than the low single digits he received from African Americans.

This debate between advocates of different types of representation continues to affect members of the Latino community. Former Congressional Hispanic Caucus (CHC) chairman Rep. Silvestre Reyes (D-TX) indicated his clear support for substantive over descriptive representation. He would rather support incumbent white members of Congress than risk the divisiveness of a primary, perhaps referring to Diana DeGette's 54 percent minority Denver district in which a Latina challenged her in the primary (Wallison and Mercurio 2001). Conversely, Larry Gonzalez of the National Association of Latino Elected Officials (NALEO) believes that the CHC is simply neglecting what should be its apparent goal—the election of more Latinos to Congress.

Research in this area is important, because the results could shed light on what is the most effective way of representing Latino interests. Nevertheless, very little

FIGURE 12.1

Percentage of Latino population in key states, 1950–2000

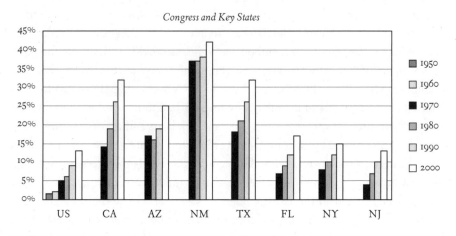

research has been done regarding Latino representation in the U.S. Congress. In addition, some of the research on the representation of racial and ethnic minorities in Congress has not synthesized what we have learned in the field of legislative politics with the contributions of scholars of race and ethnicity.

Some existing work addresses the question of substantive and descriptive representation by examining a collection of approximately fifteen roll call-votes compiled by the Southwest Voter Research Institute (SWVRI) for previous Congresses. Given the population boom of Latinos in just the past few years, more research on this subject using different data is clearly warranted. Figure 12.1 illustrates this growth in a number of key states.

To what extent does having a Latino/a representative make a difference in terms of substantive representation? An analysis of roll-call data can shed light on the differences, if any, among representatives' voting patterns, but it cannot answer the normative question of whether Latino elected officials are essential to advancing a Latino agenda.

Brief History of Latinos in the U.S. House

Before the Voting Rights Act was enacted in 1965, Latinos were hardly represented in the U.S. Congress. Before 1912, only one Latino, California Republican Romualdo Pacheco, had served in the U.S. House. With the exception of New Mexico and Louisiana, no state sent a Latino to Congress between 1912 and 1960

TABLE 12.1

Latino representatives in the U.S. Congress ranked in descending order of Latino population (2002)

Name	District	% Latino	% Black	Party	NHLA Score*
Lucille Roybal-Allard	33-California	86%	4%	Democrat	N/A
Ruben Hinojosa	15-Texas	79%	2%	Democrat	92%
Silvestre Reyes	16-Texas	78%	3%	Democrat	92
Lincoln Diaz-Balart	21-Florida	78%	5%	Republican	67
Grace Napolitano	34-California	72%	2%	Democrat	N/A
Ileana Ros-Lehtinen	15-Florida	71%	5%	Republican	58
Solomon Ortiz	27-Texas	71%	2%	Democrat	92
Luis Gutierrez	4-Illinois	70%	3%	Democrat	96
Charles Gonzalez	20-Texas	67%	6%	Democrat	N/A
Henry Bonilla	23-Texas	66%	1%	Republican	42
Ciro Rodriguez	28-Texas	65%	8%	Democrat	100
Xavier Becerra	30-California	64%	3%	Democrat	96
Jose Serrano	16-New York	63%	36%	Democrat	96
Ed Pastor	2-Arizona	63%	5%	Democrat	100
Loretta Sanchez	46-California	62%	2%	Democrat	83
Hilda Solis	31-California	59%	1%	Democrat	N/A
Joe Baca	42-California	51%	12%	Democrat	N/A
Nydia Velazquez	12-New York	49%	13%	Democrat	88
Robert Menendez	13-New Jersey	47%	13%	Democrat	96

*National Hispanic Leadership Agenda (NHLA) scores begin in 105th Congress (1997–98), and some members of Congress in the table were elected beginning in the 106th or subsequent Congresses. For these members, N/A is noted.

Source: National Journal's *Almanac of American Politics*, 2002.

(Lublin 1997). The CHC began in 1976 through the efforts of Democratic representatives Herman Badillo (NY), Baltasar Corrada (PR), Eligio "Kika" de la Garza (TX), Henry B. Gonzalez (TX), and Edward Roybal (CA).

Compared to the Congressional Black Caucus, the CHC is relatively new and has fewer members. In 1992 and 1994, the number of African American representatives stood at thirty-eight, while the number of Latinos stood at seventeen (Lublin 1997). By today, the number of Latinos in the Congress has increased to nineteen, who are listed in table 12.1. This, of course, partially reflects the rapidly growing Latino population, especially in California, Texas, and Florida. According to the 2000 Census, Latinos constituted approximately 12.6 percent of the U.S. population, and NALEO estimates that 122 (28 percent) of the 435 U.S. House districts have Latino populations that surpass this national average. The Southwest and California clearly have the highest percentages, and Latinos have surpassed African Americans as the largest minority in states like New Jersey and New York. Latinos are also present in greater numbers in the state legislatures as well, as figure 12.2 illustrates.

FIGURE 12. 2

Percentage of Latinos in legislatures and Congress, 1986–2002

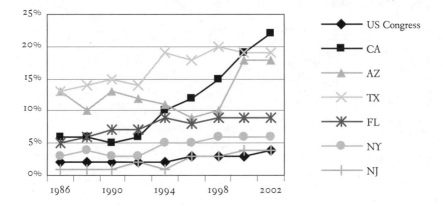

Latino Representation: Earlier Findings

The literature on the question of Latino representation in the U.S. Congress is quite sparse, although several studies have been conducted in the last decade. The earliest work on Latino representation borrowed heavily from previous work on African American representation in the Congress. As such, Latinos were assumed to be a monolithic group and generally more liberal than whites. Susan Welch and John Hibbing (1984) noted that Latino Conservative Coalition scores were more liberal than non-Latino representative scores. This study, however, only studied members from 1973 to 1980. It was not until 1992 that members of Mexican, Puerto Rican, and Cuban heritage were to be simultaneously (descriptively) represented in the Congress. Earlier Latino representatives were Mexican Americans, who are one of the more Democratic Latino groups in the United States.

Rodney Hero and Caroline Tolbert went beyond Welch and Hibbing's (1984) earlier analysis by using Southwest Voter Research Initiative (SWVRI) scores for the 100th Congress to gauge the representation of Latinos and their interests. In this analysis, Hero and Tolbert found that SWVRI scores were not significantly different for Latino and non-Latino representatives. In essence, they found that Latinos benefit from collective representation and that dyadic representation is not evident. Brinck Kerr and Will Miller (1997) responded to this article by arguing that the dyadic representation of Latino interests is present. For them, "dyadic and collective representation can and do occur simultaneously in the political system and, as an analytical matter, should be considered together" (Kerr and Miller 1997, 1071). While exposing some of the methodological problems with the paper, Kerr and Miller did not provide the necessary prescriptions for a better analysis. For example, the SWVRI scores in question are few in number and only cover the 100th Congress. For Hero and Tolbert to conclude based on these data that there is little, direct substantive representation of Latinos is premature.

David Lublin used Poole-Rosenthal Nominal Three-Step Estimation (NOMINATE) scores in his analyses. These scores do a much better job of assessing the political ideology of members of Congress as all votes are included, not just a few select votes (as with Americans for Democratic Action [ADA] and American Conservative Union [ACU] scores). The Poole-Rosenthal scores are also continuously distributed, unlike interest group ratings (Lublin 1997). Lublin interacts Latino population with the party of the representative and finds that Republican members are more conservative when they have higher Latino populations and Democrats are significantly more liberal (Lublin 1997; Canon 1999b). Lublin explains this by noting the differences in which Latino populations Democrats generally represent (Mexican Americans, Puerto Ricans) and which populations Republicans generally represent (Cuban Americans). As Canon (1999b) notes, however, Lublin does not control for these constituency differences within the Latino community (365). Lublin's research provides an improved way of looking at Latino representation; the data are more comprehensive and systematic, which leads to more accurate insights into the nature of Latino representation.

Latino Legislative Behavior: Key Research Questions

After explaining the conditions by which Latinos are elected to state legislatures and Congress, a key question is what difference does it make whether Latinos are elected to Congress and state legislatures? By virtue of being Latino, legislators may care about different issues or more strongly advocate positions on a subset of issues, such as immigration policy. More pointedly, do Latino legislators vote differently from others who represent similar constituencies? Studies of Latino public opinion have shown that Latinos tend to be fiscally liberal and socially conservative.[6] Many Latinos in Congress and legislatures have largely sided with the Democratic Party on votes regarding abortion and gay rights, however. This essay is an attempt to ascertain the extent to which Latinos differ from other representatives in terms of voting behavior.

Data

The data set used in this analysis was organized by David Lublin. It includes Poole-Rosenthal scores and additional population variables. In addition, demographic variables concerning U.S. House districts from the 87th through the 104th Congresses are also included. Poole-Rosenthal scores from the 102nd Congress through the 104th Congress are missing in Lublin's data set, and consequently have been added to provide for a useful analysis. Missing data in this data set are usually coded as a period. The key variable in this data set is a dummy variable for Latino representative. Lublin's data set also includes the necessary population figures for these districts, including racial and ethnic background, median family income, and urban population. This data set is the most updated and comprehensive available for studying Latino representation.

The dependent variable is the Poole-Rosenthal ideology scores. Regression analysis is used to analyze these scores relative to the ethnicity of the representative and the population of Latinos in House districts. Unfortunately, this data set does not separate citizens from noncitizens, which could pose a problem for interpretation. Recall that previous studies (Hero and Tolbert 1995) used the SWVRI scores as the dependent variable to assess Latino representation. Poole-Rosenthal scores can help as an additional measure. Since Hero and Tolbert use data from the 100th Congress, the first regression analysis tabulates Poole-Rosenthal scores for that Congress alone. Hero and Tolbert used a threshold of at least 5 percent Latinos in a given district to reduce the number of representatives in the sample, which is why the number of observations is 127 instead of 435. This is the baseline of comparison to determine whether Latino substantive representation is present, as during the 100th Congress the national Latino percentage hovered around 5 percent.

Latino Legislative Behavior: Findings

In the 100th Congress, the findings of Hero and Tolbert coincided with my findings. The SWVRI scores, albeit limited, were apparently correlated with the Poole-Rosenthal ideology scores, which are the most comprehensive data available. (See table 12.2)

Table 12.3 involves the same dependent and explanatory variables, but it does so over the period of the 87th through 104th congresses, again using districts with at least 5 percent Latino population. In Model A, which does not include a variable

TABLE 12.2
**Effect of Latino representative and percentage
Latino on Poole-Rosenthal score for 100th
Congress**

Explanatory variables	Model 1A	Model 1B
Latino representative	−.106	−.073
	(.099)	(.132)
Percentage Latino in district	—	−.001
		(.003)
Percentage urban	−.005*	−.005
	(.002)	(.003)
Percentage African American	−.007*	−.008*
	(.002)	(.002)
Median family income	−3.65e-06	−6.16e-06
	(8.12e-06)	(.000)
Political party	−1.28*	−1.29*
	(.063)	(.063)
Constant	1.15*	1.19*
	(.199)	(.224)
Adjusted R-squared	.859	.859
N	127	127

* $p < 0.05$

for Latino district population percentage, the coefficient of −.109 is statistically significant for Latino representative. This indicates that Latino representatives are more likely to be on the liberal side of the spatial Poole-Rosenthal score than are non-Latinos. In addition, all of the other explanatory variables except percentage of African Americans are statistically significant.

In Model B, when the percentage of Latinos in the district is added into the regression, the results are virtually the same. Most important, the variable for Latino representative remains significant, although the percentage of African Americans in the district becomes statistically significant, while median family income loses its statistical significance. The new finding in this regression is that the percentage of Latinos in a district is not statistically significant. Hero and Tolbert were correct in asserting that we find little evidence of direct, substantive representation of Latinos over this time period. African Americans, by contrast, have experienced more substantive representation over this time period. In both models, political party remains the most highly significant variable.

TABLE 12.3

Effect of Latino representative and percentage Latino on Poole-Rosenthal score for 87th–104th Congress using districts with at least 5% Latino population

Explanatory variables	Model 2A	Model 2B
Latino representative	$-.110^*$	$-.126^*$
	(.026)	(.049)
Percentage Latino in district	—	$-.000$
		(.000)
Percentage urban	$-.004^*$	$-.005^*$
	(.000)	(.000)
Percentage African American	.001	$-.004^*$
	(.000)	(.001)
Median family income	1.63e-06	-8.47e-07
	(4.82e-07)	(7.88e-07)
Political party	$-.508^*$	$-.615^*$
	(.011)	(.022)
Constant	.558*	.084*
	(.016)	(.062)
Adjusted R-squared	.51	.50
N	3447	1472

$^*p < 0.05$

Table 12.4 shows regression results for all House districts, not just those districts with at least 5 percent Latino population. The Latino representative variable is still statistically significant, and the directions of the other explanatory variables stay virtually the same (although the percentage of African American and median family income become statistically significant). Most important, the percentage Latino variable remains statistically insignificant in Model 3B.

While these data do not address normative concerns, it is nonetheless important to entertain some of these issues. There is no question that Latinos suffer from a lack of descriptive representation in all levels of government. To what extent is it important that Latinos be represented by other Latinos? Is it the case that more Latinos in Congress will contribute to greater political involvement among Latinos? For African Americans, Claudine Gay (2001a) has concluded that more African Americans in Congress only rarely contributes to greater political involvement among African American constituents. Stacey Gordon and Gary Segura (2002) conclude their analysis of California's Latino population by finding that the collective representation of Latinos in the legislature had an overall positive effect on

TABLE 12.4
Effect of Latino representative and percentage Latino on Poole-Rosenthal score for 87th–104th Congress using all House districts

Explanatory variables	Model 3A	Model 3B
Latino representative	−.239*	−.185*
	(.034)	(.052)
Percentage Latino in district	—	−.001
		(.001)
Percentage urban	−.004*	−.004*
	(.000)	(.001)
Percentage African American	−.004*	−.006*
	(.000)	(.001)
Median family income	2.43e-06*	3.27e-06*
	(4.44e-07)	(5.80e-07)
Political party	−.002*	−.002*
	(.001)	(.001)
Constant	.275*	.215*
	(.015)	(.022)
Adjusted R-squared	.12	.11
N	6814	6814

* $p < 0.05$

the Latino population's overall evaluation of government. Whether these findings can be generalized to non-Mexican Latinos and nationwide is a question that deserves additional research. In addition, my analysis shows that the percentage of Latinos in House districts does little to affect ideology scores. While this does not prove the nonexistence of Latino substantive representation, it is safe to conclude that substantive representation of Latino interests is not at the same level as that of African Americans.

Future research in this area may take different forms. For example, Katherine Tate has used data from a 1996 national telephone survey of African Americans to determine how this group feels about the way in which it is represented. This line of research may be applied to the study of Latino representation to determine the extent to which African Americans and Latinos differ in their approaches to representation.

Another promising and necessary line of research is to study the extent to which redistricting has affected and will affect the representation of Latino interests. David Canon's work on this subject, as well as David Lublin's research, must be updated to reflect the latest increases in the Latino population. A comprehensive study is needed solely on the issue of Latino representation, and this to date has not been done within political science.

Moreover, scholarly research on this subject must be informed by the analysis of those members of Congress who do serve substantial Latino populations. Much in the same way Carol Swain was able to connect with African American members of Congress for her research, the need is great for scholarship that engages Latino members of Congress as well as Anglo representatives who represent heavily Latino districts, such as Howard Berman (D-CA). The analysis of roll-call votes, while in many ways instructive, must be supplemented by the myriad of different ways that constitute representation.

Conclusion

Now that Latinos are the largest minority group in the United States, scholarship that examines their representation is urgent. The first issue that needs to be addressed is what has been termed descriptive representation. That is, what accounts for the Latino presence (or lack of presence) in state legislatures and Congress? In 1990, the California legislature included seven Latinos. Today, the same legislature has twenty-six Latinos in both the Assembly and Senate. Is it just the growth of Latino voters that explains this substantial increase, or are Latinos being elected from more heterogeneous districts?

The second challenge is to examine the difference, if any, that Latino legislators make in how they vote and how they represent their constituents. Roll-call voting patterns from the Congress and state legislatures should be analyzed using a variety of dependent variables. Representation involves more than how members vote on bills; off the floor activities, such as bill sponsorships and funding for Hispanic Serving Institutions, should also be examined in state legislatures and Congress.

To date, no systematic study on the nature of Latino representation in state legislatures and Congress has been conducted. Latino representation must be studied taking into account the contributions of legislative scholars in the areas of representation, accountability, incumbency advantage, and decision making (Arnold 1990; Fenno 1978; Cox and Katz 1996; Kingdon 1984). Moreover, the work on Latino representation in the areas of public opinion and social capital must not be neglected in this research (de la Garza, DeSipio, Garcia, and Falcon 1992; Garcia 2001). In addition, great strides in the study of African American representation must also be taken into account, including the works of Swain (1995), Canon (1999b), and Lublin (1997).

Notes

1. See Fenno (1978), Arnold (1990), Swain (1995), and Kingdon (1984).

2. In the political science literature, the use of the term Latino is preferred to Hispanic. As such, I will abide by convention here. In addition, the term Latino or Latinos will refer to males and females of Cuban, Mexican, Puerto Rican, or other Spanish-speaking descent.

3. California's Latino population statistic includes citizens as well as noncitizens.

4. Johnson and Secret (1996) found that African American members of Congress were much more concerned with local interests, while Latino members were focused on national representation. They postulated that the explanation is the much weaker descriptive representation of Latinos in the U.S. Congress.

5. Bloomberg received 50 percent of the Latino vote in his 2001 victory.

6. See Kaiser Foundation study for more details. The majority of Hispanics of all backgrounds (Cubans, Mexican Americans, and Puerto Ricans) believe in a larger role for government, yet are opposed to abortion and gay rights legislation.

Delegation or Political Mobilization?

Latino Access to the Bureaucracy

Eric Gonzalez Juenke

THIS ESSAY EXPLORES a simple question, "Where do Latino legislators and bureaucrats come from?" More precisely, after controlling for the obvious relationship between Latino population characteristics and the demographics of public officials, I examine whether Latino legislators "cause" the emergence of Latino bureaucrats, or whether a reverse process is at work. As a racial minority group's population grows larger over time, individuals gain access to public jobs that had previously been denied to them; they become police officers, postal workers, soldiers, administrators, and teachers. Members of these minority groups also begin to win elective seats on city councils, state legislatures, and local school boards. The difference between these two types of jobs—one bureaucratic and the other legislative—is central to one of the key discussions in political science: whether political control flows from elected officials to appointed bureaucrats, or whether control over policy works in the opposite direction (see Bendor and Moe 1985; Calvert, McCubbins, and Weingast 1989; Moe 1995; West 1995; Epstein and O'Halloran 1999a; Whittington and Carpenter 2003). Fundamental to these questions of policy control is the concept of representation: who represents a minority group's interests—the appointed bureaucrat or the elected legislator? Does one type of representation lead to the other, and how does this representative political control operate over time?

For a number of reasons, I explore these questions by looking at education policy. First, education is a highly salient issue in the Latino community. If one is looking for minority policy influence over time, it is prudent to begin with a policy area that is important to group members. Secondly, the U.S. education system is very decentralized, allowing low-resource groups and individuals to enter the local legislature and bureaucracy more easily than in other policy areas; the amount of minority representation in education is much greater than what would be expected in more centralized policy areas. Thirdly, education is an area crucial to the socialization of new groups. That is, apart from its issue salience, public education is one of the main mechanisms through which new groups interact with government. It is here where a group's political, social, and economic future is created and lost. If a representation gap exists in public education, the effects can, over time, manifest themselves in many other domains.

This essay is fairly straightforward. By looking at a large number of government units (school districts in Texas), I examine whether one type of representation (bureaucratic or legislative) can explain the other *over time.* First, I explore how various scholars define representation and separate the roles of the different branches of government in representing citizens. After covering these theoretical underpinnings, I begin to discuss why it is advantageous to study minority education policy at the school district level. In this section I speak to the specific characteristics of education policy and, in particular, school boards, that lend themselves to appropriate tests of the hypotheses. Next, I clarify the hypotheses and describe the data that will be used to carry out the tests. I then show how using time-series analysis increases the empirical power of the causality tests. I conclude by placing this study within a broad theoretical context, that of legislative and bureaucratic representation.

A secondary theme of this essay is the examination of multiple parts of the policy process at the same time. I make the general argument that Latino scholars must persist in looking at what happens to "representation" as it moves from one level of government to another. By analyzing legislative representation (or any other type of representation) alone, we risk missing important pieces of the puzzle, thereby introducing bias into our substantive conclusions. Thus, representation takes on much more meaning than what happens in a legislature. The essay should therefore be read as a focused look at an important issue in Latino politics as well as a commentary on the state of the field and an example of where it is headed.

Bureaucratic and Legislative Representation

Representation is the key goal of democratic governments, but the meaning of representation is contingent on whether one is speaking about the legislature, the judiciary, or the bureaucracy. Racial and ethnic minorities can, in practice, be represented by each branch of government at different times, making a full concep-tualization difficult in a system of separated powers. Scholars have grappled with a precise depiction of the representational process for centuries but have relatively few concrete answers, not only in normative terms but also within a positive frame-work (Dunn 1999, 316). Which branch plays the legitimate (legal) representational role for political minorities? The labyrinth of the modern separated powers system, in conjunction with a changing racial and ethnic demographic in the United States, makes the search for a clear answer much more challenging.

Researchers who study only the legislative process when examining Latino rep-resentation are missing pieces of the story. By ignoring the implementation of policy in the bureaucracy, scholars disregard the outputs and outcomes of government, the actual effects (or noneffects) of legislative intent. The power of the minority bureau-crat to legitimately "represent" minority constituencies is debatable, but nonetheless potentially powerful (Thompson 1978; Krislov and Rosenbloom 1981; Fraga, Meier, and England 1986; Selden, Brudney, and Kellough 1998). Because of this, scholars talk about descriptive (or passive) and substantive (or active) representation in the legislature and bureaucracy in similar terms. A legislator or bureaucrat is said to descriptively represent a minority group if they share distinct physical traits (Pit-kin 1967; Welch and Hibbing 1984; Selden, Brudney, and Kellough 1998; but see Mansbridge 1999). Substantive representation, conversely, speaks to the passing of legislation or the implementation of policies that benefit minority constituencies (Welch and Hibbing 1984; Hero and Tolbert 1995). These two facets of represen-tation can be mapped onto the bureaucratic and legislative aspects of government. The goal of this essay is to examine whether descriptive representation in the leg-islature leads to descriptive and substantive representation in the bureaucracy, or whether this process works oppositely, from the bureaucracy to the legislature.

The focus here is on the representation of Latino policy interests in the local legislature and bureaucracy. As with many policy areas, a mix of elected and non-elected officials "represent" the interests of students and parents. Elections hold school board members accountable to the public (Manin, Przeworski, and Stokes 1999), but this allows untrained, uninformed citizens to control local policy. Rela-tive to district administrators and teachers, many of whom have been in the system ten to twenty years, the average school board member is at a distinct disadvantage (Tucker and Zeigler 1980; Bolland and Redfield 1988; Dunn 1999). Bureaucrats have experience, expertise, information advantages, and most important, discre-tion (Moe 1995; Brehm and Gates 1997; Fredrickson and Smith 2003). The decen-tralized nature of the U.S. education system allows for individuals who have little to no experience with education to win legitimate control over these bureaucratic "experts."

In the case of the education bureaucracy, we know that the majority of Latinos enter the system as teachers, not school board members or administrators. Here they gain expertise, learn about standard operating procedures, and seek more control over the policy process. Most districts like to "grow" their administrators at home, offering training programs and incentives to administrators to work their way up the bureaucracy within the district. This is particularly crucial to underrepresented groups like Latinos, who typically lack the resources for the education and experience required of administrative work. Secondly, there is both anecdotal and case study evidence that many current school board members were themselves district administrators and teachers (Carr 2003). If this process of moving up from street-level positions to managerial positions to legislative ones is correct, then the idea that Latino school board members are recruiting and hiring more Latino bureaucrats in response to clientele demand may be the exception rather than the rule. Thirdly, Latino teachers can use their ability to shirk and sabotage when faced with supervisors they do not want. In a sense, these agents can use their influence to "shop" for a principal (the principal-agent "principal") until they find one who shares their preferences. This bottom-up theoretical process is examined in this essay.

The resulting conflict between legislators and bureaucrats is wrought with tension. Teachers and administrators who have spent their entire careers determining what is best for students come face to face with less-qualified (but more "legitimate") political masters (the public, as represented by the school board) (Tucker and Zeigler 1980; and see Fiorina 1981; McCubbins, Noll, and Weingast 1989; Moe 2002). When a new racial or ethnic group enters the system with different needs and preferences than those of the majority, the decision about what is best for these students is often left up to majority representatives (either in the legislature or the bureaucracy). For Latinos, this has historically spelled disaster. Most of the discrimination against Latino students in the areas of ability tracking, discipline, college preparation, testing, bilingual education, and special education assignment has come at the hands of Anglo-majority school boards, administrators, and teachers (Meier and Stewart 1991b; Martinez-Ebers, Fraga, Lopez, and Vega 2000; Weiher 2000). Because of this, many Latino parents and voters who wish to reduce the education gap between Latinos and other racial groups use race and ethnicity as a voting cue to select representatives who will deliver resources to their minority constituency (Pomper 1966; Eisinger 1980; Engstrom and McDonald 1981; Bullock 1984; Lieske and Hillard 1984; Arrington and Watts 1991; McCrary 1999).

The legislature and the bureaucracy offer two different kinds of representation. Dan Wood and Richard Waterman (1994) point out that the longer tenure of bureaucratic agents (along with their other organizational advantages) allows them to ride out "policy churn" (Hess 1999) and legislative fads. Their discretion can oftentimes be used to buffer the public system from legislative shocks (Wood and Waterman 1994, 127). In this sense, the bureaucracy can become an advocate for minority groups that are not being represented by the legislature (Herbert 1974; Romzek and Hendricks 1982; Thielemann and Stewart 1996; Weiher 2000). Latinos who are being ignored by elected district officials (whose constituency is often the median, majority Anglo voter) may find their policy preferences represented by Latino administrators and teachers in the school. Latino teachers often discipline and track Latino students differently than Anglo teachers do (Meier and Stewart 1991b, 16–18). Also, Latino bureaucrats can be advocates for policy change in their interaction with the school board, forcing elected officials to choose between the desires of the voting majority and the expertise of district employees (Herbert 1974; Tucker and Zeigler 1980; Romzek and Hendricks 1982; Chubb and Moe 1990).

An alternative perspective suggests that the bureaucracy can be *less* representative of minority populations than locally elected school boards. Oftentimes, public organizations move slowly in terms of "responsiveness," because they are not held accountable to the public through elections (Dahl 1971; Manin, Przeworski, and Stokes 1999; Przeworski, Stokes, and Manin 1999). Because legislators are accountable to the public every few years in elections, it is possible that legislative representation may precede a bureaucratic response. Latino legislators may enter the policy process and push for more bilingual education programs, seek a greater emphasis on the recruitment of Latino teachers and administrators, and even advocate the hiring of a Latino superintendent to lead the district in a new direction. Under this scenario, the legislature is more responsive because of its accountability to the public (and perhaps because of electoral mechanisms that favor the election of minority candidates). These different conceptions of representation mirror the discussion between political control and bureaucratic representation scholars (Moe 1995; Brehm and Gates 1997; Krause 1999; Fredrickson and Smith 2003).

Causal Direction and Policy Influence

The current study stems directly from previous work on the bureaucratic outcomes of school board elections (Meier et al. 2005; Meier and Gonzalez Juenke 2005). These studies demonstrate that ward elections (single member district elections) produce more Latino school board members, and more important, that these Latino legislators are associated with the hiring of Latino administrators and teachers. The findings suggest a "top-down" flow of policy control.

Underpinning these results is a theory that borrows logic from the median voter

FIGURE 13.1
"Top-down" political control

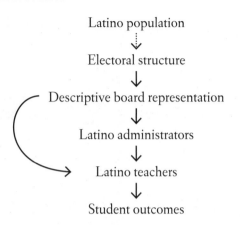

Latino population
↓
Electoral structure
↓
Descriptive board representation
↓
Latino administrators
↓
Latino teachers
↓
Student outcomes

theorem. The electoral structure (ward vs. at large) creates incentives for candidates and office holders in response to different minority and majority constituencies. The institutional structure induces Latino school board members to *behave* differently, depending on which system was used to select them. Latinos elected by at-large systems will not feel the need to push as hard for Latino policy outcomes, while those elected using ward systems have the ability (or face the constraint) to be greater advocates for Latino policy preferences. By bringing in more Latino administrators (superintendents, principals, assistant principals, and so forth), these districts are also associated with more Latino teachers (all else equal). Finally, the work connects the presence of Latino teachers to a number of student-outcome indicators, finding that in most cases, the presence of Latino teachers benefits Latino students (Meier et al. 2005; Meier and Gonzalez Juenke 2005).

Figure 13.1 presents the theoretical story of this previous research. Political control flows from institutional mechanisms to *elected* officials, then to *unelected* bureaucrats, and then down to the clientele. The cross-sectional design of these previous studies provides suggestive evidence of top-down, institutional explanations for the hiring of Latinos in the bureaucracy and also for increased Latino student performance. Thus, the answer to the question, "Where do Latino legislators and bureaucrats come from" is apparently answered: Latino legislators appear to come (disproportionately) from ward electoral structures, and Latino bureaucrats come from policy change at the school board level that seeks to recruit more Latino administrators and teachers to the district.

The cross-sectional analysis does not tell the whole story, however. Perhaps Latino school board members do not come from the general public but are instead

FIGURE 13.2
"Bottom-up" policy influence

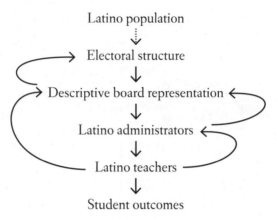

Latino population

Electoral structure

Descriptive board representation

Latino administrators

Latino teachers

Student outcomes

former teachers or administrators with preferences that differ from those of the public. In a different scenario, Latinos could also win a legislative seat with only the support of district teachers and administrators (Moe 2002). In this scenario, the democratic process is turned on its head. Unelected bureaucrats select and control their political masters, giving them almost complete influence over the direction of district policy. Figure 13.2 tells this version of the story. Here, political control flows upward, from the expertise and information of the bureaucratic agents to the choice of elected officials and even, perhaps, the choice of electoral structure.

To test for these effects, we need to analyze observations across space *and* time. The research question can now be restated in this way—"Who came first, Latino legislators or Latino bureaucrats?" Thus, the research design *must* involve data over time. This allows us to demonstrate whether legislators create opportunities for the advancement of minority bureaucrats or whether bureaucrats help create opportunities for Latino elected officials. This is an important question for researchers from many fields, including representation scholars, implementation scholars, and political control theorists.

A study by Kenneth Meier and Kevin Smith (1994) looks at the causal question in the Florida education system between the years 1980 and 1989, finding that African American representation works in *both* directions. The presence of African American bureaucrats increases legislative representation in later years, and the presence of African American legislative representation, in turn, increases the likelihood of African Americans in the bureaucracy. This study provides a good template for how to conduct similar research using a larger sample for a different racial group—Latinos. The importance of the present work, however, is that it is theoretically situated between two divergent perspectives concerning representation. Also, the explosive growth of the U.S. Latino population over the last decade makes the current examination much timelier and provides a greater amount of variation on the variables of interest.

Ideally, we would like to measure the preferences of legislators, the public, and bureaucrats in each district over time. Lacking this survey data, it becomes prudent to use indicators of these phenomena. Keeping in line with the research that generated the questions in this essay, I observe the presence or absence of Latinos in the school board, bureaucracy, and clientele in each school district in Texas. This process provides a limited but powerful look at who shows up first in the policy system and what the effects of this representational presence are for Latinos in the other branches of government. Using proxy measures of Latino preferences affects the interpretation of the results, as well as the strength of the evidence that can be presented, but this is a first attempt at testing the competing theories and will provide an indication of what further data analysis may tell us.

Student Outcomes

The district level of analysis is crucial to questions of representation, because this is where local education policy is made, and this is the level at which elections are conducted. School board elections are ubiquitous in the United States, providing a rich, if often ignored, data source. These boards are filled using a multitude of rules (at large, modified at large, by ward, cumulative voting, partisan, nonpartisan, and so forth), creating a great deal of variation in the amount of Latino representation we will observe across districts and across states. Secondly, it is at the district (not school) level where we observe the effects of the interaction of district and school administrators to create programs for Latino students and to bring more Latino teachers to the district. Lastly, I examine district data because this is the primary entity held accountable for student and school performance. It is here where the state aggregates its command of the education system, so it is here where we should look for indicators of policy change.

The theoretical discussion suggests the following hypotheses:

Top-down

H_1 As Latino representation increases on the school board, we will observe an increase in Latino administrative representation, all else equal.

H_{1A} As Latino representation increases on the school board, we will observe an increase in Latino teacher representation, all else equal.

Bottom-up

H_2 As Latino administrative representation increases, we will observe an increase in Latino school board representation, all else equal.

H_{2A} As Latino teacher representation increases, we will observe an increase in Latino school board representation, all else equal.

Control Hypotheses

H_3 As the percentage of Latino students increases, Latino representation on the school board and in the bureaucracy will increase, all else equal.

H_4 As the percentage of potential Latino voters increases, Latino school board representation will increase, all else equal.

H_5 As income and education increase, Latino legislative and bureaucratic representation will increase, all else equal.

Data and Methods

The data are generated by school districts in Texas. This state is one of the primary political arenas in which Latinos have fought to gain representation, and it presents a good test case for the phenomena under investigation. It is here where we would expect Latinos to have made the largest gains in the legislative and bureaucratic domains. In Texas school districts, Latino bureaucratic and school board representation average around 10 percent during the 1990s (see table 13.1 for descriptive statistics of the data). The period under investigation is the 1990s because the data are available and because it is during this period that the Latino population saw substantial increases.

The variables of interest, and the source of data for each, include the following:

SCHOOL BOARD REPRESENTATION: The percentage of Latinos on the school board. Data obtained from the Project for Equity, Representation, and Governance (PERG), the National Association of Latino Elected Officials (NALEO), and the U.S. Census Bureau.

ADMINISTRATIVE REPRESENTATION: The percentage of Latino superintendents, assistant superintendents, principals, and assistant principals in the district. Data obtained from PERG and the Texas Education Agency.

TEACHER REPRESENTATION: The percentage of Latino teachers. Data obtained from PERG, the Texas Education Agency, and the National Center for Education Statistics (Common Core Data).

TABLE 13.1
Descriptive statistics

Variable	Obs	Mean	Std. dev.	Min.	Max.
% Latino teachers ('93)	1046	7.40	17.31	0	96.5
% Latino teachers ('99)	1103	9.56	19.46	0	100
Change in teachers	1042	1.26	3.60	−16.7	35.3
% Latino admin. ('93)	1029	7.66	20.85	0	100
% Latino admin. ('99)	1013	8.88	22.02	0	100
Change in admin.	1000	1.22	9.04	−83.3	100
% Latino on board ('93)	1041	8.73	20.77	0	100
% Latino on board ('99)	1014	8.41	19.95	0	100
Change on board	1013	−.381	15.30	−100	71.43
% Latino students ('93)	1046	25.38	26.66	0	100
% Latino students ('99)	1103	28.11	27.28	0	100
Change in Latino students	1042	2.26	4.04	−20.7	29.3
% Latino population ('00)	1013	22.59	23.98	0	99
% Latino noncitizens ('00)	1008	19.05	14.85	0	100
% Latinos below poverty ('00)	1008	25.33	15.28	0	100
% Latinos w/h.s. dipl. ('00)	1004	48.27	19.16	0	100
District enrollment ('99)	1015	3,756	11,371	19	210k

STUDENT CHARACTERISTICS: Percentage of Latino student enrollment. Data obtained from the National Center for Education Statistics (Common Core Data).

POPULATION CHARACTERISTICS: Percentage of Latino voting age population, average family income, and average educational attainment. Data obtained from the National Center for Education Statistics (School District Demographics).

TIME FRAME: The years 1993 to 1999. The pool encompasses over one thousand school districts for the seven-year period. The pool for the present analysis includes just the first and last years of the time frame.

The analysis proceeds in two steps. To get a picture of the changes from 1993 to 1999, a variant of the Granger causality test will be performed on one variable at a time while controlling for the other factors (Gujarati 2003, 696–702; Greene 2003, 592–93).[1] We want to know if the presence of Latinos in one area of the policy process at time t-6 will lead to greater representation in other branches at time t. After accounting for the amount of Latino representation we would expect, given our control variables at time t, I include a *lagged* explanatory variable to see if it can explain any of the remaining variation.

The entire data pool is not used because the breadth (over one thousand districts) is far bigger than the depth of the pool (seven years of data), and it would be impractical to look for *time* effects in such a data set. This is a theoretical as well as an empirical difficulty. The nature of Latino legislative representation may require the presence of only one or two members on a school board to significantly transform district policy. More than this, these members may need to retain their legislative seats for a number of years before substantial policy change is realized. Thus, from year to year, Latino representation may not vary, even though the effects of this sustained Latino presence may begin to appear. If one of the policy outcomes is the yearly increase of Latino administrators and teachers, then the process will look autoregressively bureaucratic in nature (bureaucratic representation at time t will look like it came from t-1, when in fact it came from legislative representation at time t-6). A data set that covers a longer period of time would help attenuate this problem. At present, I account for this difficulty by excluding the intervening years and using a model that accounts for potential spuriousness.

Ideally, we would want data from as far back as possible to look for effects across time, but the data availability for Latino administrators in Texas limits the set to the 1993–94 school year. This data limitation, however, is quite helpful for testing the theory at hand. The 1990s was a period of population expansion for Latinos across the country, and particularly in Texas. The Latino student population in the average district increases from 25 percent to 30 percent in this short time period, and Latino representation in the legislature and bureaucracy show similar increases on average (see table 13.1 for more information on these changes).

Thus, the models use data from 1993, near the beginning of this expansion, to explain what we observe in 1999. For example, in the first model (which corresponds with H_1), teacher representation in 1999 is a function of teacher representation in 1993, school board representation in 1993, and the other control variables for 1999. We would expect the percentage of Latino teachers in 1993 to dominate the equation, but the hypothesis states that school board representation should also be a significant predictor. By comparing the results of the different empirical models, we can get a good indication of the direction of the causality (Gujarati 2003). If school board representation in 1993 predicts teacher representation in 1999, but teacher representation in 1993 does *not* explain school board representation in 1999, we have (preliminary) evidence of "top-down" causality. The same comparison method can be used for the other hypotheses. It is just as likely that the analyses will reveal "bottom-up" influences from the bureaucracy to the legislature, and it is also possible that effects will be found in both directions. That is, as Meier and Smith (1994; see also, Krause 1999) argue, perhaps representation is a two-way street, with bureaucrats increasing the opportunities for legislators, and legislators in turn increasing the likelihood of greater bureaucratic representation.

Results and Analysis

I use OLS regression to estimate the models and I include a dummy variable to indicate when the school board is majority Latino. This binary variable is interacted with Latino representation on the board to test for the majority power of Latino boards. Because substantive policy change is more likely to occur when Latinos make up a majority of the legislature, this interaction should detect any effects. These two variables also control for the diminishing returns effect in districts that are already heavily represented by Latinos in both the bureaucracy and the legislature in 1993.

Table 13.2 presents the results of four regressions representing the tests of hypotheses one through three; they are presented side by side for ease of comparison. Coefficient magnitude estimates are not of primary interest in these models because of the presence of the lagged dependent variables. Instead, I am interested in comparing the significance of the explanatory variables across models. The lagged dependent variables create extremely tough tests for the other variables because (it is expected) they will explain the majority of the variation in the dependent variable. If the included bureaucratic (or respectively, legislative) variable significantly explains any of the remaining variation, we have some evidence of causality.

TABLE 13.2

Testing for causes of Latino representation, 1993–1999

	% Latino teachers	% Latino admin.	Model 1 % Latino school board	Model 2 % Latino school board
Independent variables				
% Latino admin. (1993)	—	0.787**	—	0.288**
% Latino teachers (1993)	0.881**	—	0.423**	—
% Latino board members (1993)	0.004**	0.115*	0.148**	0.11 [0]
Interaction				
Latino majority board (1993)	10.83 [0]	−7.54	—	—
% Latino on majority board (1993)	−0.115 [0]	0.024	—	—
Overall effect of interaction	positive	none	—	—
Number of cases	1004	990	1003	989
R^2	0.97	0.85	0.65	0.66
F	1573**	323.78**	55.34**	56.00**

** $p < 0.01$ * $p < 0.05$ [0] $p < 0.10$
Note: All models estimated using STATA 7 with Huber-White robust standard errors.

To interpret the results, we begin by looking at column one. Here, the percentage of Latino teachers in the district in 1999 is a function of the percentage of Latino teachers in 1993 (note the large amount of explained variance), the percentage of Latinos on the school board in 1993, the presence of a Latino majority on the board, and an interaction of this majority dummy with Latino board representation in 1993.[2] As anticipated, the percentage Latino teacher variable dominates the results. The Latino board representation variable, however, is also positive and significant despite the presence of the lagged dependent variable. Further, the majority Latino dummy and the interaction term are both significant (using a one-tailed test) and combine for an additional positive effect on the Latino teacher percentage in 1999. The evidence suggests that districts with greater Latino school board representation in 1993 are associated with more Latino teachers in the district in 1999, all else equal. Secondly, in districts with a majority-Latino school board, the association is significantly larger. Comparing the subsequent columns in this manner provides some leverage on questions of directional influence.

In column two, the percentage of Latino administrators in 1999 is explained by the percentage of Latino administrators in 1993, the percentage of Latino board membership, and the other control variables. The lagged dependent variable performs as expected, positively and significantly and explaining most of the variation. Similar to column one, the board representation variable is significant and positive, although the majority dummy and the interaction term do not significantly add to the model. Again, in the presence of extremely strong controls, increases in the percentage of Latinos in the legislative body are associated with more Latino administrative bureaucrats, all else equal.

Columns three and four present the respective tests for the "bottom-up" hypotheses. Remarkably, the results support this perspective as well. After controlling for the amount of legislative representation in 1993, both the percentage of Latino teachers (column three) and the percentage of Latino administrators (column four) are positively and significantly associated with school board representation in 1999. The results, in combination with those presented in columns one and two, suggest that the process of influence is multidirectional. During the time period under study, legislative representation at time t-6 is associated with bureaucratic representation at time t, and (vice versa) bureaucratic representation at time t-6 is associated with legislative representation at time t.

In light of these results, we are interested in untangling the process further. One way of doing this is to look at the amount of bureaucratic and legislative *change* that occurs in each school district over the six-year period. Table 13.3 reports the results of a preliminary look at these models of change. As explained above, school board representation may work differently than bureaucratic representation because it

TABLE 13.3
Explaining changes in Latino representation, 1993–1999

	Change in % Latino teachers	Change in % Latino administrators	Change in % Latino school board
Independent variables			
% Latino admin. (1993)	0.029	—	0.039
Change in % Latino admin. (93–99)	0.051*	—	0.052
% Latino teachers (1993)	—	0.107	−0.332
Change in % Latino teachers (93–99)	—	0.411*	−0.339
% Latino board members (1993)	−0.029	−0.157	—
Change in % Latino board (93–99)	−0.022	−0.069	—
Consistent board presence	1.489**	3.87*	—
Number of Cases	989	989	989
R^2	0.23	0.05	0.05
F	17.23**	2.43**	2.04*

$^{**}\,p < 0.01$ $^{*}\,p < 0.05$ $^{0}\,p < 0.10$
All models estimated using STATA 7 with Huber-White robust standard errors.

may require a sustained Latino presence in the legislature to bring about bureaucratic change. One way to capture this consistent Latino presence in the legislature is to distinguish those districts that had Latino board representation in both 1993 and 1999 from those that had inconsistent (or no) representation during this time. While these models are preliminary, they demonstrate how this type of (representational-directional) causal analyses could proceed in the future.

The three columns in Table 13.3 can be compared with each another as was done using the results from Table 13.2. In the presence of strict controls, we are trying to explain the representational *change* across time from a top-down or a bottom-up perspective. In column one, the change in the percentage of Latino administrators from 1993 to 1999 positively and significantly explains the change in Latino teachers during this same time.[3] Changes in Latino board representation, however, do *not* significantly explain any of the variation. This is notable until we look at the result for the "consistent Latino school board" dummy variable. This result suggests that, in terms of predicting Latino teacher change, there is a significant and substantial difference between those districts that had a consistent Latino presence on the school board and those that did not. The results for Latino administrator change in column two support this "top-down" influence. After controlling for other factors, including the change in the percentage of Latino teachers, a consistent Latino board presence is significantly associated with substantial Latino administrative increases. Finally, in column three, the results show that neither type of bureaucratic change has a significant effect on the amount of legislative change across districts.

Taken together, the evidence in table 13.3 seems to support a unidirectional, top-down perspective of change. This conclusion is tempered by the small amount of explained variance in each of the models and by the understanding that the school board and bureaucratic *change* measures represent different types of variation. It is much more difficult to explain changes in legislative representation (which is purposefully designed to fluctuate across time as a result of scheduled elections) than changes in bureaucratic representation (which is generally additive across time). Bureaucrats do not need to reapply (and compete) for their jobs every two or three years. Once present in a district, Latino teachers and administrators typically increase their numbers or hold onto them (this is in part why they are so important to the policy process). Therefore, the evidence in table 13.3 is suggestive rather than conclusive.

Taken as a whole, the evidence in tables 13.2 and 13.3 combine to present a complicated causal process that needs to be examined with better tools. I undertake these methodological difficulties elsewhere (Gonzalez Juenke 2005), but the evidence here supports other work in this area. Latino representation occurs in both the legislature and the bureaucracy. Latino administrators and (particularly) teachers are crucial elements to Latino school board representation. These bureaucratic variables function apart from the typical democratic (that is, sociodemographic) characteristics, and in fact turn democracy on its head. Latino bureaucrats, these unelected experts who are ostensibly under the control of more-legitimate political masters in the legislature, have been shown to have an improbable amount of influence on determining who these masters will be.

Discussion

Representation is a tricky concept in a democracy with separated powers. Democracy is identifiable mainly through the ability of its citizens to choose representatives in competitive and fair elections. Whatever happens after the election is supposed to be corrected through the electoral process again at a later time. The bureaucracy, the administrative state, is largely accountable to these chosen representatives and thus theoretically has no independent representational purpose. As political control scholars contend, elected officials create institutional mechanisms that monitor and control bureaucratic activity. But the unelected official's expertise and information advantages create a more-difficult system of political control than the ideal democratic form.

Public administration and public policy scholars have consistently found evidence of an active and representational role for the bureaucracy. Unelected officials use their organizational and clientele knowledge to shift policy away from legislative intent whenever it serves their preferences and when they have the discretion to do so. Sometimes this policy drift can benefit groups that are underrepresented at the ballot box, and at other times it can severely hinder minority policy outcomes. The tension between these two possibilities marks a clear opportunity for researchers to seek evidence of these processes in a variety of settings.

The public education setting is an excellent policy area to observe potential "top-down" or "bottom-up" causal mechanisms because of its issue salience and its decentralized nature in the United States. As one of the most decentralized policy processes, the capability of bureaucrats to influence local legislators is substantial. If we do not find bottom-up effects in this particular area, it is hard to imagine that they exist in many others. In conjunction with this, I focus on minority group preferences and outcomes over time because they allow us to observe how new preferences and resource needs work their way through the policy process from beginning to end.

Returning to the opening question ("Where do Latino legislators and bureaucrats come from?"), we can see how the method employed here leads to some preliminary answers. Policy control in Texas school districts in the 1990s seems to flow in both directions. That is, bureaucratic representation appears to be an important factor in Latino legislative representation, and school board representation is consistently associated with bureaucratic representation. The lack of conclusive evidence should not be discouraging.

The results inform future analysis in important ways. Legislative representation is fundamentally different than bureaucratic representation, both theoretically and empirically. Thus, further analysis should take into account the feedback process uncovered here, with an eye toward teasing out the dynamic electoral processes that characterize legislative representation. The results in table 13.3 suggest that it is representational *stability*, not variation, that promotes significant bureaucratic change.[4] In turn, it appears that bureaucratic representation at both the street level and administrative level serve as significant precursors to a Latino representational presence.

The data and tests displayed here do not go far enough. A longer time period, and data from more states, would provide a better picture of the complex underlying causal process. These data are currently being collected for a number of states with growing Latino populations. The tests will be improved by focusing on representational change and modeling the entire process (testing for, and including, different lag lengths of each of the variables once a longer time period is established). The key lesson here is that both time and space need to be examined by representation and bureaucracy scholars in order to untangle the process by which minority preferences are turned into policy. It is also clear that Latino legislative success and Latino bureaucratic outcomes are inextricably tied together and must be examined together to get a complete picture of how minority preferences are represented and transformed into policy outcomes over time.

Notes

1. Traditional endogeneity tests like Vector Auto Regression (VAR), Seemingly Unrelated Regressions (SEM), or Structural Equation Modeling (SUR), and to an extent traditional Granger causality tests, are not equipped to handle these kinds of situations (Greene 2003, 592–93; Gujarati 2003, multiple chapters). I explain why below. Please see Gonzalez Juenke (2005) for a more thorough set of empirical tests concerning this problem.

2. Controls for percentage of Latino students, Latino population percentage of the district, noncitizen percentage, percentage of Latinos with a high school diploma, and the total district enrollment are included in all of the models. All of the controls perform as expected; they are excluded from the presentation because of space considerations (and their coefficients are not critical to the causal analysis). Full results are available from the author.

3. Lagged dependent variables cannot be used as controls in these models because they are used to construct the dependent (change) variables. All other controls remain in the models.

4. A finding that adds a new element to the conversation over "safe districts" and their over-all effects on minority policy change (de la Garza and DeSipio 1997; Swain 1993).

¡Muéstreme el Dinero!

Assessing the Linkage between Latino School Superintendents and English-Language Learner Program Resources

Nick A. Theobald

A GROWING BODY of research finds that bureaucratic representation improves outcomes for represented clientele. Increases in minority teachers lead to improvements in minority student performance (Meier, Wrinkle, and Polinard 1999), police forces with more women are more responsive to rape allegations (Meier and Nicholson-Crotty 2002), representative Equal Employment Opportunity Commission (EEOC) offices are more responsive to minority complaints (Hindera 1993), and minority Federal Housing Administration (FHA) loan applicants are more likely to receive loans from FHA offices with minority employees (Selden 1997). All of these works suggest that improved outcomes are a function of active representation. That is, minority bureaucrats are using discretion in their roles to act on behalf of minority clientele. Missing in this literature, however, is direct evidence that improved outcomes are a function of active representation (see Lim 2006), and of what role, if any, upper-level administrators play in actively representing minority clientele.

To address these issues, this study will examine how resources are generated for English-language Learner (ELL) programs. Specifically, this study addresses the question of whether representation by Latino school superintendents increases the level of resources available for these programs. Given that these programs almost exclusively serve Latino students and that Latinos exhibit high levels of support for these programs (de la Garza 1992; Krashen 1996; Shin 2000), the questions posed here are of great importance for the study of Latino politics.

And while not the focus of this study, this research also speaks to electoral representation. Two studies (Robinson 2002; Leal and Hess 2000) have found that Latino representation on school boards affects ELL program resources, yet they come to opposite conclusions regarding the nature of the effect. I present a complete model of representation, including both electoral and bureaucratic measures of representation, and address measurement issues in both studies. The research presented in this essay shows that Latino representation by both elected and non-elected officials leads to increased resources for limited-English-proficient (LEP) students, an important and rapidly growing subpopulation of Latino students.

Representation and Bilingual Education

An Ideal Policy for the Study of Bureaucratic Representation

As several authors have noted (Saltzstein 1979; Thompson 1976; Meier 1993), part of the difficulty in assessing linkages between passive and active representation is finding a policy where there is a clear distinction in policy preferences associated with race, or a policy that largely affects one group. One such policy area, however, pertains to programs geared for LEP students. These programs include bilingual, ESL (English as a Second Language), and structured immersion programs. In this policy area, policy preferences vary by race, and there are asymmetrical benefits for one group, Latinos.

Admittedly, there is some debate concerning support for bilingual education by Latinos. Opponents of bilingual education argue that Latinos do not support bilingual education (see Krashen 1996). Instead, they claim that Latinos are in favor of programs that help ESL students quickly acquire English skills, such as with structured immersion programs. Ron Unz, the person behind Proposition 227 in California, often cited polls that indicated 81 percent of Latinos favor English immersion programs over bilingual programs.

Stephen Krashen (1996) argues that polls that indicate Latinos are against bilingual education frame bilingual education with a negative bias. These surveys tend to frame bilingual programs as teaching Spanish instead of being a method for English acquisition. Although not all Latinos believe that LEP students need to maintain their native language, there is nearly unanimous agreement that LEP students need to learn English. Any survey questions, then, that frame bilingual programs as hindering English-language acquisition will likely lead to responses indicating disfavor for these programs. However, without a negative bias in the question, there is clear support for bilingual education among the Latino community (de la Garza 1992; Krashen 1996; Shin 2000). The strong support for bilingual education within the Latino community makes this a suitable policy for assessing the linkage between passive and active representation.

Latino organizations have also actively promoted bilingual programs at all levels of government. The Mexican American Youth Organization (MAYO) organized dozens of school boycotts throughout Texas during the late 1960s to call for the end of discrimination against Mexican American students (Navarro 1995; Shockley 1974). Also central in their demands was a call for bilingual and bicultural programs that recognized both the language and culture of Mexican Americans. The Mexican American Legal Defense and Educational Fund (MALDEF) offered legal aid to protesting students and testified at state and federal legislative hearings about the importance of bilingual education for serving the needs of LEP children (San Miguel 1987; Navarro 1998, 1995; Blanton 2004). The League of United Latin American Citizens (LULAC), once a supporter of English-only instruction for LEP students, actively lobbied Congress to resist calls by bilingual education opponents to relax restrictions on funds available through the Bilingual Education Act and reserve these funds for programs that used the students' native language (Moran 1988; San Miguel 2004; Kaplowitz 2003).

Latino legislators, at both the state and federal levels, have sponsored, promoted, and protected bilingual programs. In 1969, Carlos Truan and Joe Bernal, two of the few Latino legislators in the Texas statehouse at the time, sponsored a bill that decriminalized bilingual education in Texas (San Miguel 1987; Blanton 2004). Four years later, Truan played a pivotal role in passing legislation that required bilingual education for LEP children in Texas. He also testified at hearings for the passage of the 1968 Bilingual Education Act (BEA), Title VII of the Elementary and Secondary Education Act, arguing that the BEA would "help many Mexican-Americans become good taxpayers instead of tax-eaters" (cited in Kaplowitz 2003, 209). Joseph Montoya of New Mexico, the only Mexican American U.S. senator at the time, cosponsored the 1974 Senate reauthorization of the BEA (Schneider 1976). The reauthorization placed a restriction on Title VII funds, requiring funded programs to use and develop LEP students' native language and also stipulated that funded programs promote biculturalism. Montoya, who was also bilingual, felt that children "who enter school with the ability to speak a language other than English have an educational asset which should be built upon, not discarded or destroyed" (cited in Schneider 1976, 49). During subsequent reauthorizations of the BEA, the Congressional Hispanic Caucus consistently pushed for more Title VII funds and supported restrictions on the BEA requiring that funded programs use LEP students' native language (Moran 1988; Ovando 2003).

Even if Latinos did not have a strong preference for bilingual programs, it is still reasonable to expect that they would be more likely to support devoting resources toward programs for LEP students, whether the resources are for bilingual, ESL, or structured immersion programs. This is because ELL programs largely serve Latino students. Nationwide, 74 percent of all LEP students are Latino (Feinberg 2002) and data from Texas show that 92 percent of LEP students are Latino. This policy area's asymmetric consequences for Latinos, along with clear differences in policy preferences, make it an ideal policy for the study of representation.

Of course, in order for this policy area to be appropriate for the study of bureaucratic representation, bureaucrats must be able to exercise some discretion over the policy area. Although decisions regarding resource levels for bilingual education are constrained by federal, state, and local elected bodies, educational bureaucracies still exercise control over program resources. Superintendents, in particular, not only make decisions regarding the level of resources devoted toward bilingual programs, but they also advise school boards on budgetary matters (Norton 1996).

In addition to having discretion over decisions regarding resources for this policy area, organizational influences in the public school systems should enhance the likelihood of active representation by superintendents. Past work has argued that organizational socialization produces upper-level managers with neutral preferences in regard to representing certain groups (Thompson 1976; Meier and Nigro 1976; Downs 1967; Meier and Nigro 1976). Current research, however, has found evidence that race and gender are significant predictors of policy preferences for executives in state and federal administrations (Brudney, Herbert, and Wright 2000; Dolan 2002). Kenneth Meier (1993) argues that active representation is enhanced in organizations that value representation, such as by hiring minorities as advocates for minority interests. Given that certain states, including Texas, and the federal government mandate educational performance levels by race, it is reasonable to expect that school systems represent the type of organization that values minority interests, which could, in turn, enhance the likelihood of active representation by upper-level managers.

Three studies of school administrators support the argument that school systems are conducive to active representation by upper-level management. D. Mann (1974) found that principals and superintendents often felt they needed to be responsive to demands by constituent groups. Hugh Scott's (1990) study of African American superintendents found that along with valuing traditional bureaucratic roles, African American superintendents felt that they "must commit their expertise to the eradication of racism and the rectification of socioeconomic inequities" and should "identify with Black-directed endeavors to resolve the problems and needs of Black Americans in a racist society" (168). Finally, in her study of three Latina superintendents, Flora Ida Ortiz (2000) found these superintendents felt they were appointed, in part, to represent the needs of Latino students. Of course, the studies mentioned above only measure attitudinal differences. The research presented here seeks to assess whether attitudinal differences produce different policy outputs.

Evidence of Linkages

Anecdotal evidence suggests that Latino superintendents are sensitive to the Latino community's demands for addressing the needs of LEP children. After the Crystal City Revolt of 1970, the new school board president, José Angel Gutiérrez, offered the Crystal City School District superintendent position to Angel Noel González. González accepted the offer and in the process became one of the first Latino superintendents in Texas (González 1999). In a 1999 interview, González noted that before assuming the position, he researched the list of demands set forth by MAYO, with particular attention to the demand of creating bilingual-bicultural programs (González 1999). He acknowledged that at the time he was not familiar with bilingual programs, nor was he familiar with research on the topic, stating that his perception of bilingual education was "teaching children in their native language while you teach them English . . . it was totally that," with little understanding about "how much time you have to spend on, on native language instruction for them to be able to learn and the whole idea of learning" (González 1999, 36). Regardless of his knowledge or attitude about bilingual education, he met the demands of MAYO and set up bilingual-bicultural programs in the district and aggressively pursued federal grants for bilingual programs that were made available through the 1968 Bilingual Education Act. In 1973, González exceeded the demands of the walkout participants by making Spanish the official language of the district alongside English (Navarro 1998; González 1999).

While not the primary focus of her study, Valentina Bali (2003) finds that bureaucratic representation has affected the implementation of Proposition 227. The primary focus of her study is how electoral support, the percentage of voters in a district who voted for Proposition 227, affected the implementation of the proposition. Although Proposition 227 called for an end to bilingual education, schools could receive special waivers to continue bilingual programs. In addition to studying electoral influence on the application and implementation of these special waivers, she also included the race of the superintendent and percentage of Latino principals in her models. For these variables, she found that the presence of Latino bureaucrats increased the likelihood of districts continuing their bilingual programs.

Bubba Polinard, Robert Wrinkle, and Thomas Longoria (1990) analyzed the effect of bureaucratic representation in schools and found that Latino representation benefited Latino students. In regard to bilingual education, they found that the ratio of percentage of Latinos in bilingual programs over the percentage of Latinos in the overall student population decreased as representation increased. Although this type of representation ratio makes sense for certain policy outcomes, such as disciplinary actions or assignments for gifted programs, it is unclear what it means in this case. A decrease in their representation ratio could be a function of placing more non-Latinos in bilingual programs, as would occur in systems with two-way bilingual education or an increase in the percentage of Latinos in a district, which was not properly controlled for in their models.

Two other studies (Robinson 2002; Leal and Hess 2000) assessed the effect of electoral representation, in the form of Latino representation on school boards, on bilingual program resources. Both studies find that school board representation affects bilingual program resources but arrive at different conclusions regarding the nature of this relationship. David Leal and Frederick Hess's study suggests that LEP students benefit from representation, finding a positive relationship between representation and resources, but Scott Robinson finds that LEP students receive fewer resources under systems with representation. Not only do his results conflict with Leal and Hess, but his study also is controversial, because it suggests that representation is harmful for the represented.

There are fundamental modeling and measurement differences in both studies, which likely produce the difference in results. Instead of modeling per-pupil bilingual program expenditures for LEP students, Leal and Hess use bilingual program expenditures for all pupils as their dependent variable. Although they control for bilingual program enrollment, their results could still be a function of overall enrollment in districts. Furthermore, their study was limited to fifty-six school districts, meaning that a few large districts could easily be driving these results. Robinson (2002) argues that studies of representation do not properly account for the institutional nature of representation and presents an interactive model, interacting need with representation, to address this shortcoming in the literature. His empirical model, however, seriously misrepresents need. Robinson uses the number of Latino students to represent need even though most Latino students speak English. The appropriate measure of need for ELL assistance is the number of children classified LEP. Both studies also suffer from a serious omission, the influence of the superintendent. As mentioned above, superintendents make funding decisions, including funding decisions for ELL programs. Any attempt to link school board representation with resources, then, must at least control for superintendent influence.

The research presented here advances the study of representation in this policy area by addressing the gaps in the research addressed above. First, I avoid the potential of an ecological fallacy that plagues most studies of bureaucratic representation. These studies use aggregate levels of passive representation to predict an individual-level theory. By studying the decision of an individual, the superintendent, I avoid the ecological fallacy problem. Also, I simultaneously assess the effect of both electoral and bureaucratic representation. Finally, I use Robinson's model of representation, interacting both electoral and bureaucratic representation with actual need.

Data and Methods

Sample

The sample for this analysis consists of all Texas school districts with at least twenty LEP students from the 1995–1996 school year until the 1999–2000 school year, which represents about half of all Texas school districts. Texas requires districts with twenty or more LEP students in a single grade to offer ELL programs. Some districts, then, are required to offer resources toward LEP students, while other districts are not. Because of this, the decision to distribute resources toward LEP students differs between districts under state mandate and those that are not. Ideally, a dummy variable would be included for districts under this mandate, but there are no data available on whether a district falls under this mandate.[1]

Data for this analysis come from four sources. Information on district finance, teachers, principals, superintendents, and LEP students comes from the Texas Education Agency (TEA). Latino school board membership comes from the National Association of Elected Latino Official (NALEO) and Kenneth Meier, Eric Juenke, Robert Wrinkle, and J. L. Polinard. (2003). Finally, data on the Latino population in the school district come from the 2000 U.S. Census.

Dependent Variables

Although the TEA maintains records on bilingual and ESL program expenditures, I do not use these data for two reasons. First, expenditure figures reported by the TEA do not distinguish between bilingual and ESL programs. Variations in costs should be, in part, a function in variation in program types, both between bilingual and ESL programs and between the many different types of bilingual programs (Prince and Hubert 1994). Not enough data are available to completely control for the variation in expenditures caused by program variation. Second, and most important, from examining the data, it is clear that the reporting standards vary dramatically both across districts and across years within districts. Some districts report ten-fold increases in bilingual program expenditures from one year to the next, while the number of LEP students remains relatively stable from one year to the next.

Because of these concerns, the analyses conducted here assess the effect of representation on bilingual and ESL teacher assignments. Although funds for bilingual and ESL programs are not solely a function of teacher salaries, teacher salaries should represent an overwhelming majority of bilingual and ESL program expenditures (Robinson 2002). Also, the TEA keeps track of both the number of bilingual and ESL certified teachers. This allows me to assess whether there is a differential effect of representation between bilingual and ESL teacher assignments. Several models of representation, then, are examined in this study. The first two models assess the effect of representation on assignment of both bilingual and ESL teachers. Subsequent models assess whether there is a differential effect from representation on the assignment of teachers for each type of ELL program.

Teacher assignment to ELL programs is modeled as both ELL teacher totals and as percentage of teachers. The models predicting total bilingual and ESL teachers assess the effects of resources and representation on the level of resources available for LEP students. The models using percentage of teachers who are in bilingual and/or ESL programs, conversely, capture trade-offs along with responses to resources and representation. Districts can represent LEP students by hiring more bilingual teachers or ESL teachers while simultaneously hiring more teachers for other programs. In this case, representation would affect total numbers of ELL teachers but not the percentages of teachers in ELL programs. In a constrained environment, though, I would expect that addressing the need of one group, through teacher allocations, would come at a cost to other groups. By modeling both ELL teacher total and percentages, I can both assess if representation occurs and whether it occurs through the reallocation of resources.

The final four models separate bilingual and ESL teachers. Models 3 and 4 assess the effect of representation on the count of certified bilingual teachers and the percentage of teachers who are bilingual certified. Models 5 and 6 assess the effect of representation on the count of certified ESL teachers and the percentage of teachers who are ESL certified.

The distribution of teacher totals is heavily skewed. Because of this, the totals were logged. Several districts reported no bilingual or ESL teachers, so a 1 was added to the teacher totals before they were logged. The same natural log transformations were performed on independent variables that were represented as counts—number of LEP students, number of Latino principals, and student enrollment. These variables are discussed below.

Independent Variables

I expect bilingual and ESL teacher assignments to be a function of need, representation, political demand/resources, and financial resources. Need is measured by the logged total of LEP students in a district for the total teacher models and the percentage of students classified LEP for the models predicting the percentage of teachers in bilingual and ESL programs.

Representation is measured by the percentage of school board members who are Latino and whether the superintendent is Latino. In addition to the main effects, both the Latino school board representation and Latino superintendent representation measures are interacted with need. Evidence of representation would be apparent if the interactions are significant and positive in the bilingual and ESL teacher totals models. For the models of teacher percentages, positive interactions would also suggest that representation is occurring, and that it is occurring through the transfer of resources from other programs toward bilingual education.

Political demand/resources are measured using the percentage of the voting population that is Latino and the number or percentage of principals who are Latino. The Latino population can exert pressure on school boards, superintendents, and principals. As the Latino population increases, so should the demand for policy outputs favorable toward the Latino population, in this case resources for LEP students. Superintendents and school board members can also use the Latino population as a political resource when implementing certain policies. As noted above, districts with larger Latino populations should be more amenable to diverting resources toward bilingual education programs. The Latino population can also act as a resource for hiring qualified teachers. Although not all bilingual teachers are Latino, Latinos would be more likely to speak both Spanish and English. This measure of political resource comes from the 2000 Census, thus it is constant across the years in this analysis.

Latino principals represent potential demand for bilingual education within an agency. If Latino principals favor bilingual education more than other principals, then as the number or percentage of Latino principals in a district increases, so should the demand for bilingual education within districts. Latino principals can also be pivotal in hiring and retaining qualified teachers, thus acting as a resource for ELL programs.

The financial resources of a district are measured by the percentage of district funds from local sources. As district wealth increases, usually as a function of increased property wealth, so does the availability of funds for schools. Conversely, districts with low levels of property wealth receive more of their funds from state and federal resources. Even though the state and federal governments compensate for low levels of local resources, poorer districts still lag behind in revenue totals (Wood and Theobald 2003). Districts with greater local revenue can afford to hire more teachers, regardless of program type. There should therefore be a positive relationship between financial resources and teacher totals, but not necessarily a relationship between financial resources and percentage of ELL teachers.

In addition to the four sets of independent variables mentioned above, a variable for district size was included to control for economies of scale. District size is measured by using logged student enrollment figures.

Method

Each model is estimated as a pooled time series. All models use an estimator that corrects for unit influence by year. Tobit regression is used for all the models, because all the dependent variables are censored.

Findings

Table 14.1 presents the findings, with columns one and three showing the findings for the models combining both bilingual and ESL teachers. Model 1 predicts total number of bilingual and ESL teachers, while Model 2 predicts the percentage of teachers who are bilingual or ESL. First, looking at resources, the models show a positive effect on both the total number of ELL teachers and the percentage of ELL teachers for the percent voting age Latino variable. The same positive relationship exists for the percentage Latino principal variable across both models. The effect of local revenue differs across the two models. For the ELL teacher total model, there is a positive relation, while there is a negative relationship between local revenue and percentage of ELL teachers. This indicates that as local revenue goes up, we would expect to see more ELL teachers, but we would also expect to see even more general, special, or gifted education teachers.

In regard to electoral representation, the results here indicate that Latino representation on school boards leads to districts being more responsive to LEP student needs, as indicated by the positive and significant coefficient for the interaction variable. Holding all else equal, a district with more Latino school board representatives allocates more ELL teachers toward LEP students. That is, more teachers are allocated per LEP district as representation goes up. Looking at Model 2, it

TABLE 14.1
Regression results

	1 Total ELL teachers	2 Percent ELL teachers	3 Total bilingual teachers	4 % bilingual teachers	5 Total ESL teachers	6 % ESL teachers
LEP need	0.526 (0.016)*	0.316 (0.012)*	1.022 (0.047)*	0.286 (0.023)*	0.351 (0.019)*	0.199 (0.012)*
% Latino school board	−0.012 (0.002)*	−0.030 (0.007)*	0.010 (0.006)*	−0.020 (0.013)	−0.013 (0.003)*	0.016 (0.007)*
Latino SB × need	0.002 (0.000)*	0.001 (0.000)*	−0.001 (0.001)	0.001 (0.000)*	0.002 (0.000)*	−0.001 (0.000)*
Latino superintendent	−0.885 (0.163)*	−1.139 (0.440)*	−0.383 (0.427)	−1.866 (0.809)*	−0.331 (0.193)	0.821 (0.460)
Latino sup. × need	0.106 (0.025)*	0.034 (0.015)*	0.045 (0.063)	0.070 (0.025)*	0.004 (0.030)	−0.082 (0.015)*
Latino principals	0.156 (0.026)*	0.026 (0.005)*	−0.091 (0.063)	0.038 (0.009)*	0.179 (0.030)*	−0.018 (0.005)*
% Latino pop over 18	0.004 (0.001)*	0.026 (0.006)*	0.018 (0.003)*	0.083 (0.013)*	−0.005 · (0.001)*	−0.001 (0.006)
% Local revenue	0.002 (0.000)*	−0.011 (0.003)*	0.001 (0.001)	−0.002 (0.006)	0.003 (0.001)*	0.013 (0.003)*
Enrollment	0.243 (0.018)*	1.032 (0.050)*	0.329 (0.055)*	2.691 (0.106)*	0.175 (0.021)*	−0.593 (0.053)*
Constant	−2.712 (0.102)*	−8.034 (0.434)*	−8.081 (0.338)*	−28.275 (1.003)*	−1.547 (0.121)*	5.639 (0.454)*
Observations	2836	2836	2836	2836	2836	2836

Standard errors in parentheses
* $p < 0.05$

appears that representation occurs through the shifting of resources. As representation increases, so does the percentage of teachers allocated to ELL programs, which implicitly implies that fewer resources are available for other programs. This finding supports Leal and Hess's finding that electoral representation leads to greater resources for represented groups.

In addition to evidence of electoral representation, the results also present evidence of bureaucratic representation. Even when controlling for electoral representation, I find a positive effect when there is bureaucratic representation as indicated by the positive and significant coefficient for the interaction variable. This is a similar pattern to that for electoral representation, such that districts with Latino superintendents allocate more ELL teachers in response to need. They also devote a

FIGURE 14.1
Logged ELL teacher totals and need

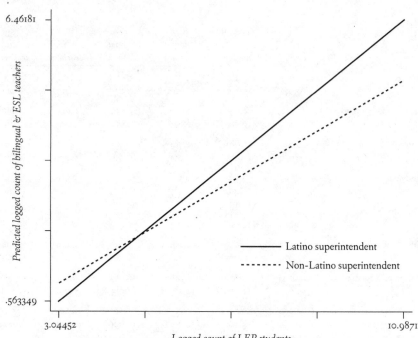

Logged count of LEP students

greater proportion of teachers to ELL programs in response to need. Furthermore, this finding offers strong evidence of active representation. With school board representation, part of the effect could be non-Latino board members responding to Latino representation. There is only one superintendent in a district; so barring any uncontrolled spurious correlation, this finding can be attributed to policy decisions made by Latino superintendents.

Figures 14.1 and 14.2 show the effect of representation by graphing the predicted values for both total and percentage models respectively as a function of need. Figure 14.1 shows that the model predicts that for districts with small numbers of LEP students and a Latino superintendent, these districts are predicted as having fewer ELL students. Since these are results from logged variables, the graph is misleading. The actual crossover point is at approximately one hundred LEP students, and below that there is a small difference in expected ELL teacher totals. Figure 14.2 shows that not only are districts with Latino representation expected to be more responsive to need, but districts with Latino superintendents are also expected to have a greater proportion of ELL teachers at all levels of need.

Columns three and four show the results for models predicting bilingual teacher

FIGURE 14.2
Percentage of ELL teachers and need

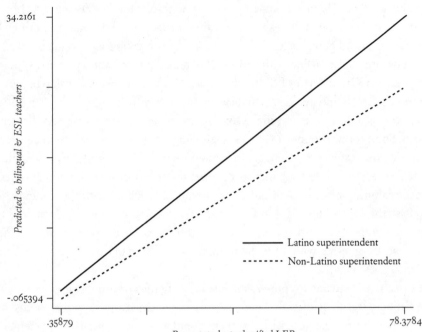

Percent students classified LEP

totals and percentages. Increasing the percentage of voting-age Latinos leads to increases in both bilingual teacher totals and percentage of bilingual teachers. The percentage of Latino principals variable is only significant in model 4, the percentage of bilingual teachers model. There is no evidence of a local revenue dynamic in either of these models.

In regard to electoral representation, the results are mixed. For the bilingual teacher total model, there is a positive and significant main effect for school board representation, but the coefficient for the interaction term is not significant. This indicates that although districts with representation are expected to have more bilingual teachers, there is no evidence that they are more responsive to changes in need. For the percentage bilingual teacher model, though, the main effect of representation is not significant. There is a positive and significant interaction effect, thereby indicating that electoral representation leads to greater proportions of resources being devoted to bilingual education.

Bureaucratic representation also produces mixed results. Unlike the model predicting both bilingual and ESL teacher totals, there is no evidence of an effect for representation on bilingual teacher totals. Model 4, though, predicts that districts with Latino superintendents are more likely to devote a greater percentage of teachers to bilingual education in response to changes in need.

The last two columns in table 14.1 show the results for models 5 and 6. In regard to resources, the models show a positive effect for local revenue on both ESL teacher totals and percentages. The results for Latino voting-age population indicate a negative relationship with ESL teacher totals. As for Latino principals, there is a positive relationship for ESL teacher totals, but a negative relationship between Latino principals and percentage of teachers who are ESL certified.

Looking at the interaction effects for electoral representation, it appears that representation produces opposite effects depending on how resources are measured, mirroring the results for the effect of Latino principals. Specifically, representation increases responsiveness for increasing ESL totals but decreases responsiveness to redistributing resources toward ESL programs. Coupled with the findings for models 1 through 4, this suggests that Latino representation is more likely to lead to bilingual program resources relative to ESL resources. As the proportion of bilingual teachers goes up with representation, the proportion of teachers who are ESL certified goes down.

Finally, bureaucratic representation is only significant in model 6, the model predicting percentage of ESL teachers. Districts with Latino superintendents are less responsive to changes in LEP student populations in regard to the percentage of ESL teachers. Once again, coupled with the results presented above, bilingual program resources appear to be favored over ESL program resources in districts with representation.

Conclusions

The findings here suggest that public organizations with representation at the top do behave differently than those without representation. Specifically, Latino superintendents appear to be both distributing more resources toward LEP students and diverting these resources from other education programs. Past research suggested that this was unlikely to occur because of organizational and political constraints. The main reason cited for lack of active representation by those at the top of public organizations is that the process of achieving upper-level management positions creates neutral bureaucrats, at least in regard to representation. However, as I argued above, socialization in public schools should enhance the linkage between passive representation and active representation. If top-level managers are appointed with the expectation of representing minority interests, then we should expect to find evidence of bureaucratic representation from organizations headed by minorities.

Of course, finding such linkages is difficult, especially when attempting to connect passive representation by upper-level managers with policy outcomes for represented groups. As noted above, outcomes may be affected by several factors, such as behavioral responses by nonminority bureaucrats or minority clientele. It is also likely that a necessary condition for improved outcomes as a function of upper-level representation is street-level representation. Given that street-level representation is related to upper-level representation, empirical models of representation will most likely produce null results. By looking at outputs that are a direct function of upper-level management decisions, in this case ELL program resources, I avoid the problems of attempting to link representation with outcomes. Thus, I am able to make stronger inferences regarding active representation, because the outputs studied here are not prone to behavioral responses by clientele, nor are these inferences prone to problems of ecological inference.

The results here offer strong evidence of active representation. Specifically, Latino superintendents devote more resources toward LEP students. There also appear to be differences in program types offered for LEP students in systems with Latino superintendents. That is, the ratio of bilingual to ESL teachers appears to increase in systems with Latino superintendents. Polls show that Latinos are more likely to prefer bilingual programs over ESL or immersion programs (Krashen 1996; Shin 2000). The results here suggest that Latino superintendents are able to implement these preferences in the schools they administer.

In addition, the results presented here show a positive effect for electoral representation. That is, Latino school board members appear to produce more resources for the Latino students served by these programs. This directly contradicts Robinson's findings that "bilingual education is controversial, and in districts with Hispanic school board members, its opponents appear to be winning" and that "Representation, in this case, manifests itself as a rejection of the targeted program" (Robinson 2002, 61). However, his measurement for need did not match actual need, so his damning conclusion regarding the affect of representation is not supported. In response to Robinson, I would argue that even though bilingual education is controversial and divisive, Latinos in positions of both elected and appointed authority appear to be winning in this important policy area.

Note

1. Not all districts with twenty LEP students are under state mandate to offer bilingual programs, as it is likely that these students are distributed across several grades. The data on district LEP enrollment and bilingual and ESL teachers show that most districts with LEP enrollment

figures between twenty and thirty (82 percent) have bilingual or ESL teachers. Only 35 percent of districts with LEP enrollment between one and twenty have any bilingual or ESL teachers. The cut point of twenty LEP students, then, creates a sample where an overwhelming majority of districts have either been required to offer resources or have at least made the decision to offer ELL programs.

PART 5

The Future of Latino Politics Research

We've Come a Long Way, but Not Far Enough

Assessing the Status of Latinos and Latino Politics in Political Science

Valerie Martinez-Ebers and Manuel Avalos

IN HIS PREFACE to *Latinos and the Political System*, Chris Garcia (1988) observed that scholarly recognition of Latino politics "has lagged behind their recognition by the popular media, practicing politicians, and those involved in marketing" (ix). More than fifteen years later, it is tempting to simply say that his assessment is still accurate. We are still more likely to read about Latinos in major city newspapers than we are in mainstream political science journals, and we are more likely to hear from politicos—as opposed to political scientists—about the significance of Latino participation. However, to overlook completely the progress made in terms of Latino representation and scholarship minimizes the important efforts of many people (including the contributions of the editors and authors of this publication). With this in mind, we more carefully assess the status of Latinos and Latino politics in political science. First we examine the Latino presence in the discipline and the influence of related scholarship. We then discuss strategies for greater success in these areas.

In addition, this edited volume showcases research by many scholars of Latino politics who are relatively new to the field. Key to the future production of good research on Latinos is the continual entry of Latino scholars into the profession. This essay explores the efforts being made to increase the number of Latino faculty members and to promote the visibility of them and their work.

Positive Developments in the Latino Presence in Political Science

The serious shortage of Latino political scientists in relation to their numbers in the U.S. population was first reported in 1970 by an American Political Science Association (APSA) ad hoc committee. This committee was highly critical of the discipline for its failure to attract and retain Mexican Americans and also for the absence of political research on their community. At the time of the report, there were around 8 million Mexican Americans residing in the United States but only two with doctorates in political science. Moreover, both men had left academe for more favorable employment with the U.S. government (Ad Hoc Committee on Mexican Americans in the Profession 1970).

Similar findings were reported in 1991. Citing an average of fewer than three Latino(a)s per year graduating with doctorates in political science and a serious shortage of journal articles on Latino politics, Manuel Avalos concluded that "the situation of Latino(a)s in these areas has not significantly improved in the last twenty years" (1991, 245).

Today, Latinos continue to be severely underrepresented in political science relative to their population numbers, but we also see modest growth in the Latino presence along every dimension examined.[1] More Latinos are going to college and attending graduate school than ever before (Carnevale 1999), but there have been only minimal gains in the percentages of political science graduate students and PhDs who are Latino/a (+ 1 percent and + .04 percent, respectively. See table 15.1).

However, the presence of Latina/o faculty in political science departments has more than doubled, from 1.3 percent to 2.4 percent. Similar increases in Latina/o representation occurred in the membership and leadership ranks of the leading professional organization, the APSA.

Perhaps the most encouraging development is the significant increase in the number of scholars specializing in Latino Politics. The APSA first included "Latino politics" on its list of academic specialized fields of interest that members provide on their membership applications in 1993. In an organization with more than eight thousand members, only twenty-five people included Latino politics as one of their specialized fields in the *1994–1996 APSA Directory of Members.* In 2004, 186 members reported Latino politics as one of their specialized fields (Bronson 2004).

A greater Latino presence is also reflected in institutional changes and program building at both national and regional levels. There are permanent standing committees on the status of Latina/os in the profession established by both the APSA and the Western Political Science Association (WPSA). The status committees, in cooperation with the Latino Caucus in Political Science (organized in 1998),

TABLE 15.1
Latino representation in political science, 1991 and 2001

Latinos as (number of Latinos/total number)	1991	2001
Percentage of U.S. population	10	12.5
Percentage of students in political science graduate programs	5 (977/19401)	6 (1220/20345)
Percentage of PhDs in political science	2.5 (150/5943)	2.9 (295/10247)
Percentage of all full- and part-time political science faculty members	1.3 (123/9835)	2.4 (264/11180)
Percentage of APSA membership	.8 (75/8894)	2.3 (313/13164)
Percentage of APSA graduate student membership	NA[a]	4 (39/992)
Number of APSA executive council members/officers	1	3

Note: Figures derived from data published by U.S. Census Bureau, Ethnic and Hispanic Statistics Branch, Population Division; Commission on Professionals in Science and Technology; American Political Science Association; and National Opinion Research Center.
[a] While no data are available for 1991, we do know that in 1997 Latino/a graduate students were only 1.2 percent of the APSA graduate student membership.

hold business meetings and sponsor workshops, panels, and receptions at annual meetings of the associations. The number of sponsored events and the level of participation have increased over the years. The caucus has gradually evolved from a friendly agreement among twenty-five like-minded individuals to a formal organization with a constitution and bylaws, elected officers, and membership dues. The size of the membership fluctuates between forty-five and sixty members. Most recently, a number of Latino politics scholars met at the 2004 Midwest Political Science Association meeting to form an MPSA Latino Caucus and to discuss the establishment of a new Latino status committee.

The primary objective of the caucuses and the status committee is to increase Latino representation and visibility in the profession. They also seek to expand the dialogue and the dissemination of information related to Latino politics scholarship. To accomplish these goals, three initiatives are ongoing: (1) the Fund for Latino Scholarship, (2) the Latino Politics Scholarship Pre-Conference Workshop, and (3) the Latino Outreach Program, or "Road Show." These programmatic efforts are going fairly well.

The Fund for Latino Scholarship, established in 1999 to support Latino politics research and to promote the recruitment and retention of Latino/a political scientists, reached its endowment level of $40,000 by 2001 and currently has pledges in excess of $57,000. In 2003, sufficient proceeds from the fund existed to begin awarding annual travel grants to graduate students and tenure-track professors. Meanwhile, caucus and status committee leaders are approaching private foundations with the hope of significantly increasing the fund's endowment.

For the past six years, the WPSA Status Committee has hosted the highly successful Latino Politics Scholarship Pre-Conference Workshop in conjunction with the WPSA annual meeting. The longer, half-day format allows for extended discussions of both academic and applied topics. It also provides the opportunity for better networking and socialization for students and junior faculty members. Strong positive feedback and growing attendance has led to discussion of an additional workshop to include interested persons who can only attend the national APSA meeting.

The Latino "Road Show," or Outreach Program, was originally conceived in the fall of 1999. The plan was to have faculty volunteers visit schools with significant numbers of Latino undergraduates where the political science program has neither Latina/o faculty members nor faculty members working on topics in Latino politics. The Road Show visit, ideally consisting of two Latina/o faculty members offering two presentations, is designed to give students the opportunity to make valuable connections with Latino faculty members and receive information about the place of Latinos in political science. The principal presentation targets a broad audience of interested undergraduates and includes an introduction to Latino politics as well as some basic information about options for careers in political science. Road Show faculty members also discuss choosing a graduate school, funding opportunities, the differences between political science and policy programs, and the challenges and opportunities for Latinos who take this path. The second presentation for graduate students and faculty members focuses on current research in Latino politics as well as strategies and resources for greater minority student recruitment and retention (Martinez-Ebers, Avalos, Fanta, Lopez, Segura, and Schmidt 2000).

To date, the Road Show has visited only five campuses. Thus far, the feedback has been consistently favorable, but the Road Show obviously is an ambitious initiative. It requires extensive cooperation, planning, and resource commitment on the part of both Latino faculty volunteers and the receiving or host political science departments. This would be much easier to accomplish if the program had financial underwriting, but efforts to secure financial backing have been unsuccessful. The APSA Status Committee continues its efforts to find a Road Show sponsor. Interestingly, the number of schools expressing an interest in hosting a Road Show has not been as high as one might expect, given the circumstances of Latino underrepresentation previously detailed. It is probably too early to judge the Road Show's contributions, but the lack of funding and limited interest may result in the eventual demise of the program.

Problems in the Latino Presence

The good news concerning Latino gains in the profession is dampened by several problems, including the central fact that the increase in Latino representation has never kept pace with Latino growth in the general population. Unless this pattern is reversed, significant change in the proportion of Latino political scientists will never occur — and it is more likely that the gap in representation will increase. The latter point highlights the need to greatly improve current efforts to recruit and retain Latino political science students.

Recruitment and Retention

Admission officers on many college campuses make special efforts to enroll Latino students. Yet, there are no reported efforts on the part of political science departments or the professional associations to recruit Latino undergraduate majors. There are no data available on the numbers of Latino undergraduate majors, so we have no information regarding the most likely pool of potential Latino graduate students.

Departmental efforts to attract Latino graduate students vary considerably. Many departments make no special effort, while some programs offer generous financial support to qualifying Latino students. A few departments that have Latino faculty members will occasionally send their faculty members to personally recruit at schools with large Latino student populations. Fifty graduate departments use the Minority Identification Project, an APSA-sponsored minority student database, to identify qualified Latino students (Brintnall and Lopez 2004). Unfortunately, the database is limited to only the student information provided by fifty core schools. Moreover, there are no data collected on the number of Latino students contacted by the graduate departments or their recruitment success rate.

The only association-sponsored recruitment program, besides the previously referenced Minority Identification Project, is the Ralph Bunche Summer Institute (RBSI). RBSI was exclusively for African Americans until 2000, when it was officially expanded to also include Latinos and Native Americans. RBSI is a wonderful opportunity for select minority undergraduates to get early exposure to graduate studies in political science. The program allows approximately fifteen students to attend Duke University for five weeks. The experience includes taking classes, attending lectures, meeting graduate recruiters, and preparing for the Graduate Record Exam. However the design of the program limits annual participation to only a handful of Latino students at a time when they are only 6 percent of those in graduate programs. If the goal is to significantly expand the pipeline of Latino students, RBSI does not appear to be the most effective use of the limited resources spent on recruitment.

A growing body of research identifies factors that contribute to the retention and successful completion of graduate programs by minority students, including mentoring relationships with faculty members, academic integration into the department, participation in professional activities of the discipline, a positive institutional climate, strong peer relationships, and generous financial support (Clewell 1987; Brintnall and Lopez 2004).

A survey of APSA Latino graduate student members in 2000 confirms the importance of these factors; 30 percent reported the presence of one or more of these types of support as helpful in their ability to continue or successfully complete their programs. Unfortunately, a significantly higher percentage said they had no mentors (40 percent), and 52 percent said they had experienced or witnessed racial/ethnic discrimination in their program. A total of 55 percent said their financial support was short term or inadequate, or both. More than a quarter of the survey respondents were dissatisfied with their graduate experiences, and 20 percent were thinking of dropping out (Martinez-Ebers et al. 2000). The survey findings do not bode well for the future retention of Latino graduate students, and there are no reported efforts on the part of departments to improve the situation.

The only organized effort to retain underrepresented minority students in political science is the recently modified APSA Minority Fellows Program (MFP). Until 2002, MFP was a select recruitment program, a merit-based competition recognizing up to six outstanding minority students who were applying to doctoral programs. APSA assisted the students in obtaining admission and financial support to pursue their degrees. If an MFP student did not receive financial assistance from other sources equal to or greater than $6,000, APSA provided the student with a one-time grant of $6,000. The modified program now provides each MFP student with that amount regardless of the additional financial assistance they receive. The APSA funds are dispersed to the students in $2,000 allotments of approximately one per year after they complete their first year of graduate school. The MFP is a good program, but it can help only a few Latino students at any given time.

Gender Disparity

Another worrisome development in the Latino presence in political science is the sizable gender imbalance among Latina/o PhDs, especially among tenured faculty members. According to APSA records, a gender balance exists among Latinos and Latinas in graduate programs (51 percent to 49 percent), but the percentage of women drops to 39 percent at the untenured assistant professor level, 18 percent at the associate level, and only 9 percent of full professors. There is only anecdotal information to explain the growing gender disparity, but it suggests that Latinas commonly confront both sexism and racism on their campuses. A less than friendly environment, coupled with the anxiety felt by most untenured faculty members, causes a higher number of Latinas to leave the faculty before the tenure process is completed.

The lower percentage of Latina associate and full professors may result in part from their later entrance into the profession relative to Latino men, but the anecdotal evidence also points to lower promotion rates for Latinas, probably for the same reasons that explain lower promotion rates for women faculty members in general. Women are more likely to teach part-time and at community college campuses. They also are less likely than male faculty members to pursue activities leading to full professor status, such as concentrated research and writing (Benjamin 1998).

To date, there are no departmental or associational programs that specifically address the retention and promotion problems of Latinas. Latinas, however, are striving to help themselves. For the first time, they held their own exclusive social gathering at the 2004 APSA annual meeting. Besides providing an opportunity for Latinas to network and socialize, they used this women-only meeting to frankly discuss gender issues related to professional development and to exchange information on how to successfully navigate a profession that is still overwhelmingly male. Organizers are hopeful that APSA or another organization will assume sponsorship of the Latina gathering and make it an annual event.

Meanwhile, to encourage and recognize individual efforts to assist both Latina and Latino political scientists, in 2001 the APSA Latino Status Committee established the Adalijsa Sosa-Riddell Latino Mentoring Awards. There are three annual awards given to college faculty members or administrators for extraordinary mentoring of Latino undergraduates, graduate students, and junior faculty members. While mentoring is a very important retention activity, it can be time consuming and has few formal benefits or payoffs on the part of the mentors. It is unlikely that mentoring awards play a significant role in the campaign to recruit and retain Latinos, but they are a positive factor.

The Impact of Latino Politics Scholarship

Looking at the program listings from past meetings of APSA provides some evidence of the incidence and subsequent visibility of Latino politics research. One way to assess the effect of this scholarship on the discipline is to look at publications on the subject in the top-tiered journals of political science. Avalos (1991) conducted the first reported study of the publication of articles on Latino, African American, and gender politics in top-tier political science and sociology journals from 1964 to 1988. Looking at the *American Political Science Review (APSR)*, the *American Journal of Political Science (AJPS)*, the *Journal of Politics (JOP)*, and the *Western Political Quarterly (WPQ* was later renamed the *Political Research Quarterly*, or *PRQ)*, Avalos identified only eleven articles on Latino Politics. Ten of these eleven articles were in *WPQ*, and the remaining one was in *JOP*. In contrast, twenty Latino/Hispanic-focused articles were published during this period in sociology journals.[2]

Admittedly, articles on other related topics—such as African American politics, race/ethnicity politics, or women and politics—were also published in very small numbers in the top political science journals. In each of the four journals examined, the total number of articles published on Latinos, African Americans, race/ethnicity, and/or gender politics topics never exceeded more than 3 percent over the twenty-five year period.

Since 1988, much has changed on the political landscape with regard to the political importance of Latinos in the United States. During the decade of the 1990s, the Latino population grew by 57.9 percent—from 22.4 million in 1990 to 32.8 million in 2000—or 12.5 percent of the population. Conservative population projections estimate that by 2040 Latinos will be 25 percent of the population in the United States. The increased demographic changes have also increased the attention of the two major political parties on the Latino electorate (de la Garza and DeSipio 2004). Both the Democratic and Republican parties courted the Latino electorate in 2000, and it was anticipated that the Latino electorate would become more significant in the 2004 election, especially in potential swing states such as Arizona and Florida.

We also find an increase in national and regional political science conference panels and papers focusing on a wide range of topics dealing with Latinos in American politics, such as political incorporation, voting behavior, representation, coalition building, reapportionment, and other issues involving gender, transnational politics, and immigration. Much of this research attempts to incorporate the study

TABLE 15.2
Total number of articles on Latino politics and related topics in the top-tier journals in political science from 1964 to 2003

Topics	AJPS	APSR	JOP	PRQ	Total
Latino politics	4	0	2	14	20
African American politics	17	12	26	21	76
Women and politics	24	13	25	77	139
Race and ethnic politics	21	15	28	21	85

of Latino politics within traditional paradigms and theories in American politics, political theory, gender politics, and international political economy.

Despite the increase in scholarship activity at professional meetings, very little headway has been made in the publication of Latino politics articles. Data in table 15.2 extends the Avalos study by adding articles published from 1988 to 2003. Over the last fifteen years, only nine additional articles were published on Latino topics in *AJPS, JOP, APSR* and *PRQ*. Since 1964, articles published on Latino politics are fewer than 1 percent of the almost 1,450 articles per journal published over the thirty-nine year period. The single greatest increase in articles occurred in *AJPS* (four).

Significantly, three of the four *AJPS* articles were published during the three-year editorship of Kenneth J. Meier in the mid 1990s. Meier is a Latino politics scholar and also is the only member of the Latino Caucus to ever serve as a journal editor. His notable success in acquiring and publishing Latino politics research underscores the critical importance and necessity of individual effort to make a difference in the discipline.

Strategies for Increased Success

Our assessment of the Latino presence in the discipline and the influence of Latino politics scholarship shows that some progress, albeit limited, has been made. It also reveals continued limitations and potential problems for the future that must be addressed if we want our numbers in political science to better reflect the population and our work to become an important part of the mainstream of political knowledge. In other words, we have further to go and more to do, and we must adopt strategies for increased success. There are several strategies that should be adopted. Some require institutional support but many rely only on the actions of committed individuals.

Institutional Strategies

It is difficult to recruit Latino undergraduate majors to graduate school when we do not know how many of them there are or where they are located. We must persuade APSA or the regional political science associations to commit to the systematic collection of information on Latino majors in political science. Ideally, the information could be obtained for all minority undergraduate majors, and this effort might qualify for financial support from the U.S. Department of Education, the National Science Foundation, or a variety of private foundations. Similar information also needs to be collected on Latino graduate students. Once their location is known, we can better conduct individual retention efforts.

When the severity of Latino underrepresentation in political science reflects a less than one to sixty ratio, the situation calls for a recruitment strategy that casts the widest net possible. Institutional programs that recruit only a few students per year should be abandoned in favor of initiatives that attempt to connect with as many students as possible.

For instance, APSA should be encouraged to expand the Minority Identification Program. With an improved database (following the strategy described above), APSA could devote more effort to increasing the number of participating graduate schools and to establishing reporting requirements so we know exactly where and how many students are contacted and what transpires after the contact.

Almost two years ago, APSA began a three-year trial virtual-mentoring program. Given the established importance of relationships with faculty members and peers in the retention of Latino students, APSA needs to make its mentoring program permanent and to expand the program's services and activities. APSA also needs to work with regional associations and departments to disseminate information about the availability of mentoring to all graduate students and junior faculty members.

The Latino Road Show has both a recruitment and retention function. It also facilitates the dissemination of Latino politics research. Best of all, it has the potential to reach a large number of Latino students and previously uninformed faculty members. APSA and the regional associations should support the Road Show concept. They could help this program in a variety of ways, such as by providing direct financial support and/or helping to solicit funding from other sources. They also could provide administrative and/or marketing assistance.

Individual Strategies

Recognizing that much of what is published in refereed journals is a function of what is submitted for publication (Lineberry 2000; Patterson, Bailey and Martinez 1987), the most direct strategy for increasing the effect of Latinos and related research is for each of us to increase the number of papers we submit to top-tier political science journals. Individuals should continue submitting their papers to every possible journal until they are accepted. We also should pursue repeat or revised submissions whenever possible. As the old saying goes, "Don't take no for an answer."

With the understanding that Latinos and Latino politics scholars are more inclined to see the importance of research on Latino topics and also to provide positive critiques, another related strategy is for each of us to increase our service as paper reviewers for the journals. Individuals should contact every top-tier journal and volunteer their reviewing services. Every time we are given the opportunity to review Latino articles, we need to respond in a timely fashion and provide thorough and constructive reviews.

Almost every year there is an editorship opportunity at one of the major journals. Latino faculty members and those who study Latino politics, if they are tenured and working at research universities, should follow Ken Meier's example and apply for that journal editorship. Whoever is the first Latino to serve in this capacity can make both substantive and symbolic contributions to the professional development of Latino political scientists everywhere.

Increasing the number of Latino PhDs is the first step toward improving Latino representation in the discipline, and we cannot rely on institutions or others to do this for us. Each of us should take personal responsibility for recruitment and retention by first seeking out talented Latino undergraduates and encouraging them to pursue studies in political science. This means mentoring these students and persuading them to apply to graduate school. Also, each of us should be mentoring Latino graduate students. If there is no graduate program in our department or no Latino students, we still can be long-distance mentors to Latino students or junior faculty members on other campuses. If each of us would take the responsibility for mentoring one student and encouraging or assisting one junior faculty member, we could have more influence on the Latino presence in the discipline than all the current institutional efforts put together.

Finally, intellectual influence within the discipline often is measured by both research productivity and the relative contribution to the major fields of study. Based on historical exclusion from the mainstream of the discipline as well as shared interests in the study of Latino politics, Latinos have chosen to follow the example of other marginalized groups in political science by organizing and separating ourselves within the professional associations—as through our caucus and status committee events and through the establishment and subsequent activities of the APSA organized section of Race, Ethnicity, and Politics. While this has facilitated our level of comfort and degree of influence within the associations and led to the development of professional networks, friendships, and collaborative projects among those who study Latino politics and race and politics in general, it has not facilitated integration of our work into the major fields of study. To increase the intellectual influence of our work outside the subfield of Latino politics, we should probably spend more effort both talking to, and collaborating with, scholars outside of our Latino groups. This could be accomplished by increasing our individual participation in conference panels sponsored by other groups and by developing collaborative research projects with non-Latinos who are studying similar research questions in other fields of political science.

Conclusions

Despite the problems identified, and our sober assessment of the level of individual effort required for solving them, we remain optimistic about the future, primarily because the Latino *community* is stronger in the profession than ever before.[3] For this reason we expect the behavior of Latino political scientists to be influenced by perceptions of group interests. We trust that individuals will step up and follow the strategies that we identify. Meanwhile, the Latino leaders within our profession—including the association officers and members of the caucus and status committees—must use their organizational influence to persuade the associations to take the required actions.

Another reason for our optimism is the confidence that we share with the other authors in this volume that Latino politics research is significant and worth pursuing. A quick perusal of the essays contained in this book reveals the quality, variety, timeliness, and sophistication of current Latino politics scholarship. It clearly deserves recognition by the mainstream in political science.

Notes

1. We feel obligated to qualify our assessment because no data were available on Latino undergraduate majors in political science.

2. Our thanks to Sue Phelps, journal and periodicals librarian at Texas Christian University, for providing this count of sociology articles.

3. Our definition of Latino *community*—that is, the group(s) of Latino and non-Latin people tied together by Latino cultural values and practices as well as by similar experiences, goals, and/or substantive interests—is adapted from John Garcia (2003).

What Don't We Know and Why Don't We Know It

One Research Agenda in Latino Politics

Kenneth J. Meier

OBSERVING THE RICH ARRAY of research in this volume and being aware of the changing demographics of the United States suggests we are on the verge of an explosion in scholarship on Latino politics. The number of scholars in the field exceeds any definition of a critical mass. The range of methods and substantive specialties runs virtually the full gamut of political science. A new national Latino political survey with the capacity to analyze large numbers of Latino respondents in multiple states was recently completed. As might be expected, the political landscape is changing even faster than political science is. Latinos are now the largest minority population in the United States; more Latinos are participating in politics, running for office, and serving in elected and appointed positions than ever before.

Even with the dramatic increase in scholars and research opportunities, however, resources are not unlimited. Professional hubris suggests that by a strategic application of our resources we can make faster progress by targeting areas that pose major theoretical puzzles or topics that have not received much scholarly attention. This essay is one person's proposal for a scholarly agenda in Latino politics; it reflects the biases and interests of that person. One such bias is my belief that we need to consciously think about these broader issues and be strategic about building our field. In some future world perhaps there will be sufficient resources and scholars to simply let a thousand flowers bloom. Until that time, we should always ask "where will our research efforts matter the most?"

American Politics Is Latino Politics

Mainstream political science, particularly the field of American politics, has frequently ignored the work in Latino politics. A significant portion of our effort has been focused on getting major journals and associations to recognize the value of Latino politics as a field of study. In many cases our claim is that Latino politics is an increasingly important part of American politics and merits study in its own right. Let me suggest that we cease being petitioners and begin being missionaries, in short that we take the offensive in this battle. Our message should be that the literature in Latino politics not only greatly informs the study of American politics, but it also provides leverage on important theoretical questions of mobilization, representation, and democracy. To illustrate, because Latinos are an emerging minority, the study of Latino representation provides an excellent research opportunity for all students of representation. Scholars can track the evolution of the representation linkages from institutions with no representation to those that have well-established representatives with substantial clout. Latinos provide significantly more variation, and with ongoing immigration will continue to do so, on variables likely to affect the linkages between elites and masses. Similar arguments could be made about political participation, coalition formation, and institution building. A full understanding of representation, or any other area in American politics, is more likely to the degree that Latino politics is explicitly part of the study.

Political Behavior

Political behavior, broadly defined, has occupied the bulk of the time of Latino scholars. The essays in this book and other work indicate that much has been done. Three areas of political behavior appear to be exceptionally promising for future research — identity, context, and heterogeneity.

Substantial work has been done on Latino identity and whether a pan-Latino identity exists. The diversity of Latino experiences as they correlate with national origins has long been a specter haunting the empirical study of Latino political behavior, calling into question whether Latino politics can be studied generically or whether studies must be focused on Mexican Americans, Hondurans, or some other more homogeneous group. Theory and qualitative evidence in this case radically outstrips our current data sets. Even those existing data sets that oversample Latinos rarely permit analysis beyond the common trichotomy of Mexican American, Puerto Rican, and Cuban.

The new national Latino political survey will provide additional leverage on the multiple Latino groups with its large oversamples in key states. Although the survey will provide only a one-time snapshot for a set of communities that are rapidly changing, it does offer the potential to structure future research in systematic ways. It might be worthwhile to assume that the array of Latino identities has a limited number of dimensions and that the individual Latino communities could be located among these limited dimensions. Some of these dimensions, such as liberalism or foreign policy, are immediately obvious, but others are not.

This project requires the interaction of theoretical scholars working on identity politics (see essays by Márquez and Jones-Correa) and empirical scholars who study attitudes and behavior. In political science in general, the theoretical work in identity politics is complex and highly nuanced, while empirical work in behavior is reductionist. The literature in Latino politics has similar characteristics. While the empirical work will never have the rich detail that characterizes the theoretical work simply because identities at the individual level can have infinite variation, it can provide some general empirical classifications. By being able to specify, for example, a Dominican identity in a limited set of empirical dimensions, scholars can then actually use the broader identity categories in smaller surveys to assign "identities" to individual respondents. Research might then be able to hypothesize that a given mix of Latino populations should produce a set of Latino attitudes or behaviors that differ in predictable ways. The application to the comparative study of U.S. cities or states should be obvious.

Combining identity theory and empirical analysis in this manner is one way that Latino politics scholarship can move beyond the dummy variable approach to analysis where Latino status is just another variable included in the model. A second way is to interpret Latino status as a lens that shapes how other factors contribute to whatever behavior is being studied. We know, for example, that education affects political participation by Latinos just as it does for Anglos; but an equally interesting question is whether the influence of education on participation is the same for Latinos as it is for Anglos in similar situations. By using Latino simply as a dummy variable, we can determine if the intercept for Latinos is different from the intercept for Anglos; but we cannot tell if the slopes are fundamentally different. An extensive literature on human capital economics examines the interaction of race or gender with numerous other factors in determining income or similar outcomes. Such a literature often focuses on whether, for example, Latinos receive the same income benefit from an additional year of education that Anglos do. This literature could serve as a methodological guide for work in Latino politics.

One lesson of identity theory for political behavior is that individuals have multiple identities and the salience of the individual identities varies by time and context. The Luis Ricardo Fraga and Sharon Navarro essay illustrates how the complexity of gender and Latino ethnicity interact for legislators. We should expect similar, complex patterns to exist for other types of representatives (executives, bureaucrats, interest group leaders, and so forth) as well as for mass publics. This set of identities is also likely to interact with other identities such as that of immigrant, naturalized citizen, upward mobile professional, and so forth (see the Jones-Correa essay).

The essays by Matt Barreto and Ricardo Ramírez illustrate that context plays a significant role in Latino political behavior just as it does for Anglos and other groups (Huckfeldt and Sprague 1992, Leighley 2001). Their work essentially shows how the presence of Latino elected officials and candidates feeds back into the electoral process and stimulates greater political participation. Such work is only just starting to tap the role that context plays in Latino politics.

One exciting opportunity for context-related work is to take advantage of the natural experiment that is provided by the U.S. states. As an illustration, Latino politics in both California and Texas is essentially Mexican American politics, yet the political parties have created a context for Latino issues that clearly has ramifications for how Latinos will be incorporated into the political system. In California, the Republican Party has decided that immigration will be a hot-button issue and that the electorate should be polarized on this dimension. The party has essentially foreclosed the possibility of Latinos being able to play the role of a swing electoral group in California politics; in such cases only turnout, not how Latinos actually vote, will matter. In contrast, the Texas Republican Party has actively sought to cultivate Latino voters, playing down the immigration issue and eschewing policies that prohibit the provision of government services to immigrants. The different contexts clearly have implications for coalitional behavior, political mobilizations, and representational strategies.

The Texas-California comparison is by no means the most extreme. The exceptionalism of New Mexico, with its long history of Latinos in political power and its cleavages based on primacy versus recency of arrival, and that of Florida, driven by the large but very localized Cuban community, are two even more disparate cases. Taking advantage of such natural experiments requires generating sufficient cases in individual states to conduct systematic analysis. At the mass behavior level, the new national Latino political survey, with its large oversamples in several states, has great promise. The National Latino Education Project (see essays by Rocha and Gonzalez Juenke) has sufficient cases for analysis by the states with the largest Latino population, especially given its commitment to future survey efforts to supplement its 2001 and 2004 samples. Building individual state data sets over time to examine policy areas or to investigate state-level representational issues also has promise.

The heterogeneity of the Latino population is much like the weather; everyone talks about it, but no one ever does anything about it. Few data sources actually recognize this heterogeneity; I know of no state or local database on education that makes any finer distinction than Latino for a classification. At the same time, there are ways to use the 2000 Census categories, however flawed they might be, simply because they permit self-identification with separate Latino nationality groups. There are well-accepted measures of heterogeneity of groups, such as the Blau dissimilarity index, that can be used to measure the relative homogeneity of a population. My own unpublished analysis of Latino school board representation indicates that Latino population heterogeneity is a significant factor in reducing the level of Latino representation. Similar efforts could be done with any other aggregate type of database that relies on political jurisdictions such as cities, counties, or states. If the proposed alliance (between identity politics and political behavior) is successful in classifying the various groups along a limited set of dimensions, the actual calculation of heterogeneity and its effects might become even simpler.

Such cross-jurisdictional analysis might even address the question as to whether it is heterogeneity per se or the actual composition of individual Latino nationality groups that matter. One hypothesis might be that it is the actual divisions among the Latino groups (e.g., attitudinal differences or cultural differences between Guatemalans and Nicaraguans) rather than the distribution among all groups that will matter in terms of crafting pan-Latino coalitions or pan-Latino identities.

Political Institutions

The legislature is the most studied institution in Latino politics, perhaps not surprising, because it is the most studied institution in American politics generally. The literature has focused on two specific legislative institutions, the U.S. Congress and local school boards, with somewhat different results. Whether Latino representation matters in the U.S. Congress is subject to some dispute, given the collinearity between Latino representation and the Democratic Party (Hero and Tolbert 1995). Even with that high level of overlap, the essay by Rodolfo Espino indicates the emergence of a distinct pattern of Latino representation on roll-call votes. In contrast, at the school district level, Latino substantive representation has been demonstrated in numerous studies over an extended period of time (see essays by Rocha and Gonzalez Juenke and the citations therein), and the agenda in this literature has moved to an examination of factors that enhance or restrict the quality of Latino representation (see Meier et al. 2005).

There are two obvious opportunities posed by this literature, one empirical and one theoretical. The empirical opportunity is to move the study of representation to state legislatures or city councils. Both provide more cases and more variation than provided by the U.S. Congress and have the advantage of having jurisdiction over more than a single policy area. In particular, research on school districts appears to indicate that Latino majority status in a legislature generates a significantly different representation process than does Latino minority status regardless of size of minority (Gonzalez Juenke 2004). Movement to state legislatures or city councils provides a check to determine if this finding is specific to school boards or generalizable. Theoretically, the interesting question is why representation always matters in school boards and is so difficult to find in the U.S. Congress. My own hypothesis is that this is a function of legislative size and that small group dynamics, especially in a nonpartisan context, provide a more inclusive process that permits individual members of the legislature to be more effective (Meier 2005). While that hypothesis fits the data, it has not been subjected to systematic tests nor has it been examined in the context of any rival hypotheses.

My own favorite institution to receive additional attention in Latino politics is, of course, the bureaucracy. The literature on representative bureaucracy has examined when and under what conditions demographic representation in the bureaucracy produces policy benefits for the represented group (see Keiser et al. 2002). Latino representative bureaucracy remains a puzzle in comparison to the literature on African American representation and gender representation. African American substantive representation has been found in school districts (Meier, Stewart, and England 1989), the Equal Employment Opportunity Commission (EEOC, Hindera 1993), and the Farmer's Home Administration (FmHA, Selden 1997). Substantive representation for gender has been found in school districts (Keiser et al. 2002), child support enforcement (Wilkins and Keiser forthcoming), and police forces (Meier and Nicholson-Crotty 2006; but not for African Americans. See Wilkins and Williams 2005). Latino representation, in contrast, has only been found in school districts and specifically was not found in the EEOC and only in some cases in the FmHA (Selden 1997, 105).

An explicit theory that applies gender to representative bureaucracy (Keiser et al. 2002) specifies the conditions where bureaucrats are likely to be representative. Theoretical application of this theory to Latinos and bureaucracy would likely generate additional cases and contribute both to the literature on Latinos and the literature on bureaucratic politics. We have numerous agencies that collect information on the ethnic distribution of services delivered, and agencies are required by law to keep information on the ethnic distribution of their employees (some of which is public record, and even that which is not can often be gathered directly via survey). Linking these two sets of data can tell us a great deal about Latinos and representative bureaucracy.

Political executives, whether elected or appointed, offer additional opportunities to study Latinos and political institutions. At the national level, of course, these opportunities are limited, given the few Latinos that have held high-level administrative posts. At the state and local level, opportunities are plentiful. Nick Theobald demonstrates how Latino superintendents play a role in shaping the educational experience of Latino students via action in regard to language instruction. Latinos have achieved significant representation among school superintendents and city mayors generating the variance needed to address questions of executive politics. Structural variation provides an additional dimension to the puzzle, because chief executives might be either elected or appointed and there are obvious hypotheses about representation pressures, given whether an official is elected or appointed.[1]

A final promising area of institutional study is nonprofit organizations. Any casual student of Latino politics in urban areas is well familiar with the incredible array of nonprofit and private self-help organizations that serve the Latino community. These organizations provide instruction in English, information on citizenship requirements, job training, day care, home mortgages, charter schools, and a variety of other services. What accounts for the density of these institutions across urban areas or how such institutions facilitate the political incorporation of Latinos are fruitful areas for additional research.

Public Policy

Policy issues relevant to the Latino communities include virtually every public policy. Within political science, however, public policy studies that focus on Latinos or incorporate Latinos in a significant way are rare other than in education policy. A search of the JSTOR archives in political science since 1990 found only three articles with the key word search "immigration and [Latino or Hispanic]" and all three articles examined public opinion on immigration rather than immigration policy. A similar search found no political science articles on health care, crime, housing, or welfare policy and Latinos. This search does not mean that no political science work on Latinos and these public policies exists in these journals, only that these key words do not appear in the title or the abstract.[2]

To be sure, much public policy research in regard to Latinos occurs in other disciplines such as economics or sociology or in the public policy journals. Even recognizing that literature, one can still contend that Latinos and public policy are significantly understudied. In addition, that literature tends to be narrowly focused on programs (that is, how does Head Start affect Latino students?) and generally omits any consideration of the politics of public policy.

The education studies within political science provide a template for expanding the literature on Latinos and public policy. First, in those studies that examine public policy as a dependent variable, the education literature focuses on how Latino elected representatives and access to bureaucratic positions affect the adoption of public policies that should benefit Latinos (more-equitable ability grouping, larger bilingual education programs, and so forth. See Meier and Stewart 1991b). Second, public policy is often treated as an independent variable to determine what the effect of such policies might be on Latino student performance on a variety of dimensions. Both of these questions are directly relevant in other public policy areas.

The interesting political questions concerning Latinos and education policy are far from exhausted. The National Latino Education Study database, with information on the eighteen hundred largest school districts in the United States, has surveyed school districts in 2001 and 2004 on a variety of education questions (see Leal, Martinez-Ebers, and Meier 2004). The size of the database permits examination of the educational access of Latino students in a variety of contexts, from states where Latinos have long been numerous to areas where their growth is recent and exponential. Even more potential is found in the area of higher education, where the number of studies has been minuscule in comparison to those at the K-12 level (see Hicklin forthcoming).

Which public policies offer the best opportunities for a scholar willing to dig out original data and craft a new research agenda? Health policy is an especially promising area, given that health policy systems collect large amounts of data on access to health care or health outcomes and that these data are frequently reported by race and ethnicity. Within the health policy community, health disparities are a major policy issue reflecting the policy dilemma in the United States of high health care costs and poor health outcomes in terms of infant mortality, immunization, and rates of preventable diseases. Given that health disparities appear to mirror disparities in political power, investigating how politics affects health outcomes appears tailor-made for a political scientist.

Of particular interest in health policy might be the Behavior Risk Factor Surveillance System, billed as the largest continuing phone survey in existence. The Behavior Risk Surveys contact large samples within each of the states and ask about such risky behaviors as cigarette and alcohol consumption, driving without seat belts, dietary habits, and other items. A second set of these surveys examines risky behaviors that include drug and alcohol use by high school students. The Centers for Disease Control and Prevention permits analysis of the individual-level data, and sufficient state levels totals now exist for some aggregate analysis to be done.

Crime and criminal justice policy is another promising area, given the general disparate effect of the criminal justice system on low-income individuals and the well-established racial biases (Meier 1994). The normal national databases in this area have some quirks, however, that limit quantitative analysis. The FBI crime statistics collect information by race but not by ethnicity, so that Latinos are grouped with Anglos as white for the calculation of arrest rates. This grouping is interesting, given that incarceration rates (which are collected by a different federal agency) are available by ethnicity as well as race. Local data sets, often archived either via the University of Michigan or through the Bureau of Justice Statistics, frequently have better data by ethnicity. (For example, there are local data sets with information on ethnic profiling of traffic stops. See Wilkins and Williams 2005.)

Given the close linkages between Latinos, immigration, and labor policies, that more political scientists do not examine labor policy is surprising. The United States has frequently used immigration policies to produce cheap labor when needed and to rid itself of labor when it was unneeded. The Bracero program and the forced repatriation of Latinos in the 1930s are classic examples. It is quite clear that a variety of businesses in the United States could not survive economically without access to cheap, immigrant labor (either legal or illegal immigrants). A systematic assessment of the enforcement of immigration law violations on U.S. business would likely make a fascinating study. The politics of working conditions is also a prime topic, given that Latino immigrants are frequently found in industries with dangerous working conditions (poultry production) or exposure to toxic chemicals (agriculture). The politics of minimum wage determinations is also directly relevant. Other labor-related issues include the disposition of Social Security taxes paid by illegal aliens, policies on sending money back to families living in other countries, and the old standby of union organization.

Welfare policy is currently settling into the post-AFDC (Aid to Families with Dependent Children) era of a temporary assistance program. Although we know that race plays a major role in the politics of welfare policy (Lieberman 1998), we do not know a great deal about the role of ethnicity. Efforts by the state of California to restrict welfare payments to immigrants, however, suggest that Latino ethnicity is important also. Other policy questions that might be addressed in regard to Latino politics include the participation of Latinos in the military, how the creation of transportation systems affects Latino migration patterns and thus eventually politics, and Latinos' access to adequate housing.

Theoretical Questions

Empirical theories of Latino politics face a set of interesting questions. Should we build a separate theory of Latino politics that encompasses the unique aspects of the Latino populations? Should we borrow theories from elsewhere, particularly African American politics, to determine if Latinos fit the same pattern? Should we concentrate on broader theories of politics and use Latino studies for leverage on what they can say about politics in general? Each of these is possible. The work in identity theory clearly develops from theories unique to Latino populations; the work on social capital and Latinos (see Manzano essay) uses an Anglo theory to study Latinos (and to challenge the original theory). The reliance of social distance theory (Rocha) uses Latino politics to examine general theories about group interactions.

At the present time, most of this theoretical work is empirical, and we rarely have empirical studies that could contrast these theoretical orientations in the same study. My own bias is for general theories, but I could well be wrong. The question also calls for pure theoretical work that traces out the implications of each of these theoretical orientations for what we study and how we study it.

Conclusion

The basic premise of this essay was that Latino scholars should be strategic about their research agendas. Even with our growing numbers, the number of interesting questions is virtually limitless and our resources are not. Latino politics has a great deal to say that is relevant to the study of political science in general, and scholars should not be hesitant to point out that the failure to systematically study Latino politics will provide nothing more than an incomplete view of U.S. politics. The study of Latino politics provides important leverage in examining major theories of political behavior, institutions, and public policy.

This essay has sketched one view on what the research agenda in Latino politics should be. It was based on intuition and personal interests, and decidedly not any effort to be exclusionary. Other strategies might work equally well, but the important thing is to be strategic in our choices. We Latino politics scholars live in the best of times: We have lots of work to do and interesting questions to study.

Notes

I would like to thank Rudy Espino, David Leal, Chris Olds, René Rocha, and Erica Solis for assistance with this essay. Financial support was provided by the Carlos Cantu Hispanic Education and Opportunity Endowment.

1. In addition to the elected mayor versus appointed city manager, there are states that elect school superintendents rather than appoint them. Some states, such as Alabama, permit the school board to be elected or appointed and the superintendent to be elected or appointed.

2. For example, I have the annoying tendency of using education policy data on Latinos to address questions of representative bureaucracy, public management, or political-bureaucratic relationships. Because the titles and abstracts reflect the theoretical interests in these areas rather than substantive concerns about Latino education, these articles are not picked up by this search process.

References

Aaron, Robert, and Glen Powell. 1982. "Feedback Practices as a Function of Teacher and Pupil Race during Reading Group Instruction." *Journal of Negro Education* 51:50–59.

Abramowitz, Alan I. 1989. "Viability, Electability, and Candidate Choice in a Presidential Primary Election: A Test of Competing Models." *Journal of Politics* 51:977–92.

Achen, Christopher H. 1978. "Measuring Representation." *American Journal of Political Science* 22:475–510.

Acker, Joan. 1992. "From Sex Roles to Gendered Institutions." *Contemporary Sociology* 21:565–69.

———. 1990. "Hierarchies, Jobs, Bodies: A Theory of Gendered Organizations." *Gender and Society* 4:139–58.

Acosta-Belen, Edna. 1986. *The Puerto Rican Woman: Perspective on Culture, History, and Society.* New York: Praeger.

Acuña, Rodolfo. 1984. *A Community under Siege: A Chronicle of Chicanos East of the Los Angeles River, 1945–1975.* Los Angeles, CA: Chicano Resources Center, UCLA.

———. 1972. *Occupied America: The Chicano's Struggle toward Liberation.* San Francisco: Canfield Press.

Ad Hoc Committee on Mexican Americans in the Profession. 1970. "Report of the APSA Committee." *PS: Political Science and Politics* 3:739.

Ahrari, Mohammed E. ed. 1987. *Ethnic Groups and U.S. Foreign Policy.* New York: Greenwood Press.

Alba, Richard D., and Victor Nee. 2003. *Remaking the American Mainstream: Assimilation and Contemporary Immigration.* Cambridge, MA: Harvard University Press.

Aldrich, John H., John L. Sullivan, and Eugene Borgida. 1989. "Foreign Affairs and Issue

Voting: Do Presidential Candidates 'Waltz before a Blind Audience?'" *American Political Science Review* 83:123–41.

Alex-Assensoh, Yvette. 2002. "Social Capital, Civic Engagement and the Importance of Context." In *Social Capital: Historical and Theoretical Perspectives on Civil Society*, edited by Scott McLean, David Schultz, and Manfred Steger, 203–17. New York: Columbia University Press.

Ambrecht, Biliana, and Harry Pachón. 1974. "Ethnic Political Mobilization in a Mexican American Community: An Exploratory Study of East Los Angeles 1965–1972." *The Western Political Quarterly* 27:500–519.

Anderson, Benedict. 1994. "Exodus." *Critical Inquiry* 20:314–27.

Anzaldua, Gloria. 1987. *Borderlands/La Frontera: The New Mestiza*. San Francisco: Aunt Lute Books.

———. 1990. *Making Face/Making Soul: Haciendo Caras*. San Francisco: Aunt Lute Books.

Arce, Carlos H. 1979. *Mexican Origin People in the United States: The 1979 Chicano Survey*. [Computer file.] Ann Arbor: University of Michigan Survey Research Center.

Arnold, R. Douglas. 1990. *The Logic of Congressional Action*. New Haven, CT: Yale University Press.

Arrington, Theodore S., and Thomas Gill Watts. 1991. "The Election of Blacks to School Boards in North Carolina." *Western Political Quarterly* 44:1099–1105.

Arteaga, Luis. 2000. "Are Latinos Pro-Democrat or Anti-Republican? An Examination of Party Registration and Allegiance in the 2000 Election and Beyond." San Francisco: Latino Issues Forum.

Arvizu, John R., and F. Chris Garcia. 1996. "Latino Voting Participation: Explaining and Differentiating Latino Voting Turnout." *Hispanic Journal of Behavioral Sciences* 18: 104–28.

Ashbaugh, Carolyn. 1976. *Lucy Parsons: American Revolutionary*. Chicago: Charles H. Kerr Publishing Company.

Avalos, Manuel. 1991. "The Status of Latinos in the Profession: Problems in Recruitment and Retention." *PS: Political Science and Politics* 24:241–46.

Ayala, Louis J. 2000. "Trained for Democracy: The Differing Effects of Voluntary and Involuntary Organizations on Political Participation." *Political Research Quarterly* 53:99–115.

Azize, Yamila, ed. 1987. *La Mujer en Puerto Rico*. Rio Piedras, PR: Ediciones Huracan.

Baca Zinn, Maxine. 1975. "Chicanas: Power and Control in the Domestic Sphere." *De Colores* 2:19–31.

Bai, Matt. 2004. "The Multilevel Marketing of the President." *New York Times Magazine*, April 25, 43.

Bali Valentina. 2003. "Implementing Popular Initiatives: What Matters for Compliance?" *Journal of Politics* 65:1130–46.

Barr, Alwyn. 1995. *Black Texas: A History of African-Americans in Texas 1528–1995*. Norman: University of Oklahoma Press.

Barrera, Mario. 1979. *Race and Class in the Southwest*. South Bend, IN: University of Notre Dame Press.

Barreto, Matt, and Jose A. Muñoz. 2003. "Reexamining the 'Politics of In-between': Political Participation among Mexican Immigrants in the United States." *Hispanic Journal of Behavioral Sciences* 25:427–47.

References

Barreto, Matt, Gary M. Segura, and Nathan Woods. 2004. "The Mobilizing Effect of Majority-Minority Districts on Latino Turnout." *American Political Science Review* 98:65–76.

Barrett, Edith J. 2001. "Black Women in State Legislatures: The Relationship of Race and Gender to the Legislative Experience." In *The Impact of Women in Public Office*, edited by Susan J. Carroll, 185–204. Bloomington: Indiana University Press.

Basch, Linda, Nina Glick Schiller, and Christina Szanton Blanc. 1994. *Nations Unbound: Transnational Projects, Postcolonial Predicaments, and the Deterritorialized Nation-State.* Amsterdam: Gordon and Breack.

Bean, Frank, and Marta Tienda. 1987. *The Hispanic Population of the United States.* New York: Russell Sage Foundation.

Bendor, Jonathan, and Terry Moe. 1985. "An Adaptive Model of Bureaucratic Politics." *American Political Science Review* 79:755–74.

Benjamin, Ernst. 1998. "Disparities in the Salaries and Appointments of Academic Women and Men: An Update of the 1988 Report of Committee W on the Status of Women in the Academic Profession." www.aaup.org/AAUP/issues/women/menwomenpay.htm

Berry, Jeffery M. 1999. "The Rise of Citizen Groups." In *Civic Engagement in American Democracy*, edited by Theda Skocpol and Morris P. Fiorina, 367–93. Washington, DC: Brookings Institution Press.

Betancur, John J., and Douglas C. Gills, eds. 2000. *The Collaborative City: Opportunities and Struggles for Blacks and Latinos in U.S. Cities.* New York: Garland Publishing.

Binder, Norman E., Jerry L. Polinard, and Robert D. Wrinkle. 1997. "Mexican American and Anglo Attitudes toward Immigration Reform: A View from the Border." *Social Science Quarterly* 78:324–37.

Binder, Sarah A. 1996. "The Partisan Basis of Procedural Choice: Allocating Parliamentary Rights in the House, 1789–1990." *American Political Science Review* 90:8–20.

Blackwelder, Julia Kirk. 1984. *Women of the Depression; Caste and Culture in San Antonio, 1929–1939.* College Station: Texas A&M University Press.

Blanton, Carlos Kevin. 2004. *The Strange Career of Bilingual Education in Texas, 1836–1981.* College Station: Texas A&M University Press.

Block, Carolyn. 1993. "Lethal Violence in the Chicago Latino Community." In *Homicide: The Victim/Offender Connection*, edited by Anna Wilson, 267–343. Cincinnati, OH: Anderson Publishing Company.

Bloom, Jack M. 1987. *Class, Race, and the Civil Rights Movement.* Bloomington: Indiana University Press.

Bobo, Lawrence, and Frank D. Gilliam. 1990. "Race, Sociopolitical Participation, and Black Empowerment." *American Political Science Review* 84:377–94.

Bobo, Lawrence, and Vincent L. Hutchings. 1996. "Perceptions of Racial Group Competition: Extending Blumer's Theory of Group Position to a Multiracial Social Context." *American Sociological Review* 61:951–72.

Bolland, John M., and Kent D. Redfield. 1988. "The Limits to Citizen Participation in Local Education: A Cognitive Interpretation." *Journal of Politics* 50:1033–46.

Bonilla-Santiago, Gloria. 1988. *Organizing Puerto Rican Migrant Farm Workers: The Experience of Puerto Ricans in New Jersey.* New York: Peter Lang.

Bowers, Jake. 2004. "Does Moving Disrupt Campaign Activity?" *Political Psychology* 21: 525–43.

Boyer, Richard O., and Herbert M. Morias. 1974. *Labor's Untold Story.* 3rd Edition. New York: United Electrical, Radio and Machine Workers of America.

Bradshaw, Benjamin, David Johnson, Derral Cheatwood, and Stephen Blanchard. 1998. "A Historical Geographical Study of Lethal Violence in San Antonio." *Social Science Quarterly* 79:863–78.

Brady, Henry, Sidney Verba, and Kay Lehman Schlozman. 1999. "Prospecting for Participants: Rational Expectations and the Recruitment of Political Activists." *American Political Science Review* 93:153–68.

Brehm, John, and Scott Gates. 1997. *Working, Shirking, and Sabotage: Bureaucratic Response to a Democratic Republic.* Ann Arbor: University of Michigan Press.

Brehm, John, and Wendy Rahn. 1997. "Individual-Level Evidence for the Causes and Consequences of Social Capital." *American Journal of Political Science* 41:999–1023.

Brians, Craig Leonard. 1997. "Residential Mobility, Voter Registration, and Electoral Participation in Canada." *Political Research Quarterly* 50:215–27.

Brintnall, Michael, and Linda Lopez. 2004. "Minority Programs Review." Memorandum to the APSA Administrative Committee, March 1.

Brischetto, Robert, and Rodolfo de la Garza. 1983. *The Mexican-American Electorate: Political Participation and Ideology.* Austin, TX: The Center for Mexican American Studies and the Southwest Voter Research and Education Project.

Bronson, Sylvia. 2004. Electronic communication with APSA Program Operations Associate, August 13.

Browning, Rufus P., Dale Rogers Marshall, and David H. Tabb. 1984. *Protest Is Not Enough: The Struggle of Blacks and Hispanics for Equality in Urban Politics.* Berkeley: University of California Press.

Brudney, Jeffrey L., F. Ted Herbert, and Deil S. Wright. 2000. "From Organizational Values to Organizational Roles: Examining Representative Bureaucracy in State Administration." *Journal of Public Administration Research and Theory* 10:491–512.

Bullock, Charles S. 1984. "Racial Crossover Voting and the Election of Black Officials." *Journal of Politics* 46:238–51.

Butler, Katherine I., and Richard W. Murray. 1991. "Minority Vote Dilution Suits and the Problem of Two Minority Groups: Can a 'Rainbow Coalition' Claim the Protection of the Voting Rights Act?" *Pacific Law Journal* 21:623–76.

Cain, Bruce, and D. Roderick Kiewiet. 1985. "Ethnicity and Electoral Choice: Mexican American Voting Behavior in the 30th Congressional District." In *The Mexican-American Experience: An Interdisciplinary Anthology,* edited by Rodolfo de la Garza, Frank Bean, Charles Bonjean, Ricardo Romo, and Rodolfo Alvarez, 213–27. Austin: University of Texas Press.

———. 1984. "Ethnicity and Electoral Choice: Mexican American Voting Behavior in the California 30th Congressional District." *Social Science Quarterly* 65:315–27.

———. 1987. "Latinos and the 1984 Election: A Comparative Perspective" In *Ignored Voices: Public Opinion Polls and the Latino Community,* edited by Rodolfo de la Garza, 47–62. Austin, TX: Center for Mexican American Studies.

Cain, Bruce E., D. Roderick Kiewiet, and Carole Uhlaner. 1991. "The Acquisition of Partisanship by Latinos and Asian Americans." *American Journal of Political Science* 35:390–422.

REFERENCES

Caldeira, Gregory A., Aage R. Clausen, and Samuel C. Patterson. 1990. "Partisan Mobilization and Electoral Participation." *Electoral Studies* 9:191–204.

Caldeira, Gregory A., Samuel C. Patterson, and Gregory A. Markko. 1985. "The Mobilization of Voters in Congressional Elections." *Journal of Politics* 47:490–509.

California Opinion Index. 2000. *A Digest Examining . . . California's Expanding Latino Electorate.* San Francisco: The Field Institute.

Calvert, Randall L., Matthew McCubbins, and Barry Weingast. 1989. "A Theory of Political Control and Agency Discretion." *American Journal of Political Science* 33:588–611.

Cámara Fuertes, Luis Raúl. 2004. *The Phenomenon of Puerto Rican Voting.* Gainseville: University Press of Florida.

Cameron, Charles, David Epstein, and Sharyn O'Halloran. 1996. "Do Majority-Minority Districts Maximize Substantive Black Representation in Congress?" *American Political Science Review* 90:794–812.

Campbell, Angus, Philip Converse, Warren Miller, and Donald Stokes. 1960. *The American Voter.* New York: Wiley.

Canon, David T. 1999a. "Electoral Systems and the Representation of Minority Interests in Legislatures." *Legislative Studies Quarterly* 24:331–85.

———. 1999b. *Race, Redistricting, and Representation: The Unintended Consequences of Black Majority Districts.* Chicago: University of Chicago Press.

Canon, David T., and Rodolfo Espino. 2002. "Vote Switching in the U.S. House of Representatives." Presented at the annual meeting of the American Political Science Association, Boston, MA.

Carnevale, Anthony. 1999. *Education=Success: Empowering Hispanic Youth and Adults.* Princeton, NJ: Educational Testing Service.

Carr, Nora. 2003. "The Toughest Job in America." *American School Board Journal* 46:201–6.

Carroll, Susan J., ed. 2001. *The Impact of Women in Public Office.* Bloomington: Indiana University Press.

Cassel, Carol. 2002. "Hispanic Turnout: Estimates from Validated Voting Data." *Political Research Quarterly* 55:391–408.

Chavez, Jennie V. 1997. "Women of the Mexican American Movement." In *Chicana Feminist Thought,* edited by Alma M. Garcia, 36–38. New York: Routledge.

Chubb, John E., and Terry Moe. 1990. *Politics Markets and America's Schools.* Washington, DC: Brookings Press.

Clausen, Aage. 1973. *How Congressmen Decide: A Policy Focus.* New York: St. Martin's Press.

Clay, William. 1992. *Just Permanent Interests: Black Americans in Congress, 1870–1992.* New York: Amistad Press.

Clewell, Barbara C. 1987. *Retention of Black and Hispanic Doctoral Students.* GRE No. 83–4. Princeton, NJ.

Cole, Beverly P. 1986. "The Black Educator: An Endangered Species." *Journal of Negro Education* 55:326–34.

Coleman, James S. 1988. "Social Capital in the Creation of Human Capital." *American Journal of Sociology* 94:95–120.

Colon, Jesus. 1961. *A Puerto Rican in New York and Other Sketches.* New York: International Publishers.

Congressional Research Service. 1999. "Bilingual Education: An Overview." Washington, DC: Author.

Cornell, Stephen E., and Douglas Hartmann. 1998. *Ethnicity and Race: Making Identities in a Changing World.* Thousand Oaks, CA: Pine Forge Press.

Cox, Gary, and Jonathan N. Katz. 1996. "Why Did the Incumbency Advantage in U.S. House Elections Grow?" *American Journal of Political Science* 40:478–97.

Cox, Gary W., and Matthew D. McCubbins. 1993. *Legislative Leviathan: Party Government in the House.* Berkeley: University of California Press.

Crenshaw, Kimberlè Williams. 1997. "Beyond Racism and Misogyny: Black Feminism and 2 Live Crew." In *Women Transforming Politics,* edited by Cathy J. Cohen, Kathleen B. Jones, and Joan C. Tronto, 541–68. New York: New York University Press.

———. 1989. "Demarginalizing the Intersection of Race and Sex: A Black Feminist Critique of Antidiscrimination Doctrine, Feminist Theory and Antiracist Politics." *University of Chicago Legal Forum,* 139–67.

Cronin, Bruce. 1999. *Community under Anarchy: Transnational Identity and the Evolution of Cooperation.* New York: Columbia University Press.

Crotty, William J. 1971. "Party Effort and Its Impact on the Vote." *American Political Science Review* 65:439–50.

Dahl, Robert. 1971. *Polyarchy: Participation and Opposition.* New Haven, CT: Yale University Press.

———. 1964. *Who Governs? Democracy and Power in an American City.* New Haven, CT: Yale University Press.

Davis, Otto A., Melvin J. Hinich, and Peter C. Ordeshook. 1970. "An Expository Development of a Mathematical Model of the Electoral Process." *American Political Science Review* 64:426–48.

Dawson, Michael. 1994. *Behind the Mule: Race and Class in African-American Politics.* Princeton, NJ: Princeton University Press.

DeConde, Alexander. 1992. *Ehnicity, Race and American Foreign Policy: A History.* Boston: Northeastern University Press.

De Genova, Nicholas, and Ana Y. Ramos-Zayas. 2003. *Latino Crossings: Mexicans, Puerto Ricans, and the Politics of Race and Citizenship.* New York: Routledge.

de la Garza, Rodolfo. 1985. "As American as Tamale Pie: Mexican-American Political Mobilization and the Loyalty Question." In *Mexican-Americans in Comparative Context,* edited by Walker Connor, 227–42. Washington, DC: The Urban Institute Press.

———. 2004. "Latino Politics." *Annual Review of Political Science* 7:91–123.

———. 1997. "Latino Politics: A Futuristic View." In *Pursuing Power,* edited by F. Chris Garcia, 448–56. South Bend, IN: University of Notre Dame Press.

———. 1992. *Latino Voices: Mexican Puerto Rican, and Cuban Perspectives on American Politics.* Boulder, CO: Westview Press.

de la Garza, Rodolfo, and Marissa A. Abrajano, with Jeronimo Cortina. 2002. "Get Me to the Polls on Time: Latino Mobilization in the 2000 Election." Presented at the annual meeting of the American Political Science Association, Boston, MA.

de la Garza, Rodolfo, and Louis DeSipio eds. 2004. *Muted Voices: Latinos and the 2000 Elections.* Lanham, MD: Rowman & Littlefield.

———. 1994. "Overview: The Link between Individuals and Electoral Institutions in Five

Latino Neighborhoods." In *Barrio Ballots: Latino Politics in the 1990 Elections,* edited by Rodolfo de la Garza, Marta Menchaca, and Louis DeSipio, 1–41. Boulder, CO: Westview Press.

———. 1997. "Save the Baby, Change the Bathwater, and Scrub the Tub: Latino Electoral Participation after 20 Years of Voting Rights Act Coverage." In *Pursuing Power: Latinos and the Political System,* edited by F. Chris Garcia, 72–126. South Bend, IN: University of Notre Dame Press.

de la Garza, Rodolfo, Louis DeSipio, F. Chris Garcia, John Garcia, and Angelo Falcon. 1992. *Latino Voices: Mexican, Puerto Rican, and Cuban Perspectives on American Politics.* Boulder, CO: Westview Press.

de la Garza, Rodolfo, Luis Fraga, and Harry Pachón. 1988. "Toward a Shared Agenda." *Journal of State Government* 61:77–80.

de la Garza, Rodolfo, and Myriam Hazan. 2003. *Looking Backward, Moving Forward: Mexican Organizations in the U.S. as Agents of Incorporation and Dissociation.* Claremont, CA: Tomás Rivera Policy Institute.

de la Garza, Rodolfo, Martha Menchaca, and Louis DeSipio eds. 1994. *Barrio Ballots: Latino Politics in the 1990 Elections.* Boulder, CO: Westview Press.

de la Garza, Rodolfo, and Janet Weaver. 1985. "Does Ethnicity Make a Difference: Chicano-Anglo Public Policy Perspectives in San Antonio." *Social Science Quarterly* 66:576–86.

de Leon, Arnoldo. 1989. *Ethnicity in the Sunbelt: A History of Mexican Americans in Houston.* Houston, TX: Mexican American Studies Program.

DeSipio, Louis. 1996. *Counting on the Latino Vote: Latinos as a New Electorate.* Charlottesville: University of Virginia Press.

———. *Immigrant Organization, Civic Outcomes: Civic Engagement Political Activity, National Attachment, and Identity in Latino Immigrant Communities.* University of California Irvine, Center for the Study of Democracy. Working Paper 02–08. http://repositories .cdlib.org/cds/02–08, accessed April 22, 2004.

———. 2000. "Sending Money Home . . . For Now: Remittances and Immigrant Adaptation in the United States." Claremont, CA: Inter-American Dialogue/Tomás Rivera Policy Institute working paper.

———. 2002b. "Sending Money Home . . . For Now: Remittances and Immigrant Adaptation in the United States." In *Sending Money Home: Hispanic Remittances and Community Development,* edited by Rodolfo O. de la Garza and Briant Lindsay Lowell, 157–87. Lanham, MD: Rowman and Littlefield.

DeSipio, Louis, and Rodolfo de la Garza. 2002. "Forever Seen as New: Latino Participation in American Elections." In *Latinos: Remaking America,* edited by Marcelo Suárez-Orozco and Mariela Páez, 398–409. Berkeley: University of California Press.

DeSipio, Louis, Rodolfo de la Garza, and Mark Setzler. 1999. "Awash in the Mainstream: Latinos and the 1996 Elections." In *Awash in the Mainstream: Latino Politics in the 1996 Elections,* edited by Rodolfo de la Garza and Louis DeSipio, 3–45. Boulder, CO: Westview Press.

DeSipio, Louis, Harry Pachón, Rodolfo de la Garza, and Jongho Lee. 2003. *Immigrant Politics at Home and Abroad: How Latino Immigrants Engage the Politics of Their Home Communities and the United States.* Claremont, CA: Tomás Rivera Policy Institute.

Deutsch, Morton. 1985. *Distributive Justice.* New Haven, CT: Yale University Press.

Dolan, Julie. 2002. "Representative Bureaucracy in the Federal Executive: Gender and Spending Priorities." *Journal of Public Administration Research and Theory* 12:353–75.

Domínguez, Jorge. 1994. "Do Latinos Exist?" *Contemporary Sociology* 23:354–56.

Downs, Anthony. 1957. *An Economic Theory of Democracy.* New York: Harper and Row.

———. 1967. *Inside Bureaucracy.* Boston: Little Brown.

Duany, Jorge. 2002. *The Puerto Rican Nation on the Move: Identities on the Island and in the United States.* Chapel Hill: University of North Carolina Press.

———. 1994. *Quisqueya on the Hudson: The Transnational Identity of Dominicans in Washington Heights.* New York: The CUNY Dominican Studies Institute.

Dunn, Delmer D. 1999. "Mixing Elected and Nonelected Officials in Democratic Policy Making: Fundamentals of Accountability and Responsibility." In *Democracy, Accountability, and Representation,* edited by Adam Przeworski, Susan C. Stokes, and Bernard Manin, 297–325. Cambridge, UK: Cambridge University Press.

Dyer, James, Arnold Vedlitz, and Stephen Worchel. 1989. "Social Distance among Racial and Ethnic Groups in Texas: Some Demographic Correlates." *Social Science Quarterly* 70:607–16.

Edwards, Bob, and Michael W. Foley. 1998. "Civil Society and Social Capital beyond Putnam." *American Behavioral Scientist* 42:124–39.

———. 2000. "Much Ado about Social Capital." *Journal of Contemporary Sociology* 30:227–30.

———. 1997. "Social Capital and the Political Economy of Our Discontent." *America Behavioral Scientist* 40:669–78.

Eisinger, Peter K. 1980. *The Politics of Displacement.* New York: Academic Press.

Eldersveld, Samuel J. 1956. "Experimental Propaganda Techniques and Voting Behavior." *American Political Science Review* 50:154–65.

Enelow, James, and Melvin J. Hinich. 1984. *The Spatial Theory of Voting: An Introduction.* Cambridge, UK: Cambridge University Press.

Engstrom, Richard L. 1992. "Modified Multi-seat Election Systems as Remedies for Minority Vote Dilution." *Stetson Law Review* 21:743–70.

Engstrom, Richard L., and Robert B. Brischetto. 1997. "Cumulative Voting and Latino Representation: Exit Surveys in Fifteen Texas Communities." *Social Science Quarterly.* 78.

Engstrom, Richard L., and Michael McDonald. 1981. "The Elections of Blacks to City Councils: Clarifying the Impact of Electoral Arrangements on the Seats/Population Relationship." *American Political Science Review* 75:344–54.

Epstein, David, and Sharyn O'Halloran. 1999a. *Delegating Powers: A Transaction Cost Politics Approach to Policy Making under Separate Powers.* Cambridge, UK: Cambridge University Press.

———. 1999b. "A Social Science Approach to Race, Redistricting, and Representation." *American Political Science Review* 93:187–91.

Escobar, Edward J. 1999. *Race, Police, and the Making of a Political Identity: Mexican Americans and the Los Angeles Police Department, 1900–1945.* Berkeley: University of California Press.

Espiritu, Yen Le. 1992. *Asian American Panethnicity: Bridging Institutions and Identities.* Philadelphia: Temple University Press.

Estrada, Leonardo, F. Chris Garcia, Reynaldo F. Marcias, and Lionel Maldonado. 1981.

"Chicanos in the United States: A History of Exploitation and Resistance." *Daedalus* 110:103–32.

Estrade, Paul. 1987. "Los Clubes Femeninos en el Partido Revolucionario Cubano (1892–1898)." *Anuario del Centro de Estudios Martianos* 10:175–201.

Evans, William, Shelia Murray, and Robert Schwab. 1997. "Schoolhouses, Courthouses, and Statehouses after Serrano." *Journal of Policy Analysis and Management* 16:10–31.

Falcon, Angelo. 1988. "Black and Latino Politics in New York City: Race and Ethnicity in a Changing Urban Context." In *Latinos and the Political System*, edited by F. Chris Garcia, 171–94. South Bend, IN: University of Notre Dame Press.

Farley, Reynolds. 1998. "Presentation to the Race Advisory Board, President's Initiative on Race." http://clinton3.nara.gov/Initiatives/OneAmerica/farley.html.

Feinberg, Rosa Castro. 2002. *Bilingual Education: A Reference Handbook, Contemporary Education Issues*. Santa Barbara, CA: Abc-Clio.

Fenno, Richard F. 2003. *Going Home: Black Representatives and Their Constituents*. Chicago: University of Chicago Press.

———. 1978. *Home Style: House Members in Their Districts*. Boston, MA: Little Brown.

Fiorina, Morris P. 1981. "Congressional Control of the Bureaucracy." In *Congress Reconsidered*, 2nd edition, edited by Lawrence Dodd and Bruce Oppenheimer, 332–48. Washington, DC: Congressional Quarterly Press.

Fischer, Claude S. 2001. "Bowling Alone: What's the Score?" Presented at the American Sociological Association, Anaheim, CA.

Foner, Nancy. 2000. *From Ellis Island to JFK: New York's Two Great Waves of Immigration*. New Haven: Yale University Press.

———. 2001. "Transnationalism Then and Now: New York Immigrants Today and at the Turn of the Twentieth Century." In *Migration, Transnationalization, and Race in a Changing New York*, edited by Hector R. Cordero-Guzman, Robert C. Smith, and Ramon Grosfoguel, 35–57. Philadelphia: Temple University Press.

Fouron, Georges, and Nina Glick-Schiller. 2003. "The Generation of Identity: Redefining the Second Generation within a Transnational Social Field." In *The Changing Face of Home: The Transnational Lives of the Second Generation*, edited by Peggy Levitt and Mary C. Waters, 168–210. New York: Russell Sage Foundation.

Fraga, Luis Ricardo, Valerie Martinez-Ebers, Ricardo Ramírez, and Linda Lopez. 2001. "Gender and Ethnicity: The Political Incorporation of Latina and Latino State Legislators." Presented at the annual meeting of the American Political Science Association, San Francisco, CA.

Fraga, Luis Ricardo, Kenneth J. Meier, and Robert E. England. 1986. "Hispanic Americans and Educational Policy: Limits to Equal Access." *Journal of Politics* 48:850–76.

Fredrickson, H. George, and Kevin B. Smith. 2003. *The Public Administration Theory Primer*. Boulder, CO: Westview Press.

Fuchs, Lawrence. 1990. *The American Kaleidoscope: Race, Ethnicity, and the Civic Culture*. Hanover, NH: Wesleyan University Press.

Gamm, Gerald H., and Kenneth A. Shepsle. 1989. "Emergence of Legislative Institutions: Standing Committees in the House and the Senate, 1810–1825." *Legislative Studies Quarterly* 14:39–66.

Garcia, F. Chris. 1987. "Comments on Papers Presented by the Panel on Latinos and the 1984

Election." In *Ignored Voices: Public Opinion Polls and the Latino Community*, edited by Rodolfo de la Garza, 106–17. Austin, TX: Center for Mexican American Studies.

———, ed. 1988. *Latinos and the Political System*. South Bend, IN: University of Notre Dame Press.

Garcia, Ignacio. 1997. *Chicanismo: The forging of a militant ethos among Mexican Americans*. Tucson: University of Arizona Press.

———. 1989. *United We Win*. Albuquerque: University of New Mexico Press.

Garcia, John A. 2000. "Coalition Formation: The Mexican-Origin Community and Latinos and African Americans." In *Immigration and Race: New Challenges for American Democracy*, edited by Gerald Jaynes, 255–75. New Haven, CT: Yale University Press.

———. 2001. "Does Social Capital Work for Latinos and Political Participation?" Presented at the annual meeting of the American Political Science Association, San Francisco, CA.

———. 2003. *Latino Politics in America: Community, Culture, and Interests*. Lanham, MD: Rowman & Littlefield.

———. 1997. "Political Participation: Resources and Involvement among Latinos in the American Political System." In *Pursuing Power: Latinos and the Political System*, edited by F. Chris Garcia, 44–71. South Bend, IN: University of Notre Dame Press.

Garcia, John A., and Carlos H. Arce. 1988. "Political Orientations and Behaviors of Chicanos: Trying to Make Sense out of Attitudes and Participation." In *Latinos and the Political System*, edited by F. Chris Garcia, 125–51. South Bend, IN: University of Notre Dame.

Garcia, John, and Rodolfo de la Garza. 1985. "Mobilizing the Mexican Immigrant: The Role of Mexican-American Organizations." *Western Political Quarterly* 38:551–64.

Garcia, John A., and Sylvia Manzano. 2001. "Mass Capital: Social Capital Accumulation and Political Engagement among Latinos." Presented at the annual meeting of the Western Political Science Association, Las Vegas, NV.

Garcia, Mario. 1989. *Mexican Americans: Leadership, Ideology, and Identity*. New Haven, CT: Yale University Press.

García-Bedolla, Lisa. 2000. "They and We: Identity, Gender, and Politics among Latino Youth in Los Angeles." *Social Science Quarterly* 81:106–21.

Gay, Claudine. 2001a. "The Effect of Black Congressional Representation on Political Participation." *American Political Science Review* 95:589–602.

———. 2001b. "The Effect of Minority Districts and Minority Representation on Political Participation in California." San Francisco: Public Policy Institute of California.

Gerber, Alan S., and Donald P. Green. 2000. "The Effects of Canvassing, Direct Mail, and Telephone Contact on Voter Turnout: A Field Experiment." *American Political Science Review* 94:653–63.

Gershtenson, Joseph. 2003. "Mobilization Strategies of the Democrats and Republicans, 1956–2000." *Political Research Quarterly* 56:293–308.

Giles, Michael, and Marylin Dantico. 1982. "Political Participation and Neighborhood Social Context Revisited." *American Journal of Political Science* 26:144–49.

Giles, Michael W., and Arthur S. Evans. 1985. "External Threat, Perceived Threat, and Group Identity." *Social Science Quarterly* 66:50–66.

Gilligan, Thomas, and Keith Krehbiel. 1990. "Asymmetric Information and Legislative Rules with a Heterogeneous Committee." *American Journal of Political Science* 34:531–64.

———. 1987. "Collective Decision-Making and Standing Committees: An Informational Rationale for Restrictive Amendment Procedures." *Journal of Law, Economics, and Organization* 3:287–335.

Gimpel, James, and Karen Kaufmann. 2001. "Impossible Dream or Distant Reality? Republican Efforts to Attract Latino Voters." Washington, DC: Center for Immigration Studies.

Ginsberg, Benjamin. 1986. *The Captive Public: How Mass Opinion Promotes State Power.* New York: Basic Books.

Glazer, Nathan, and Daniel Patrick Moynihan. 1975. *Ethnicity, Theory and Experience.* Cambridge, MA: Harvard University Press.

Glick Schiller, Nina. 1999. "Transmigrants and Nation-States: Something Old and Something New in the U.S. Immigrant Experience." In *The Handbook of International Migration,* edited by Charles Hirschman, Philip Kasinitz, and Josh DeWind, 94–119. New York: Russell Sage Foundation.

Glick Schiller, Nina, Linda Basch, and Cristina Szanton Blanc. 1995. "From Immigrant to Transmigrant: Theorizing Transnational Migration." *Anthropological Quarterly* 68: 48–63.

———. 1992 *Toward a Transnational Perspective on Migration: Race, Class, Ethnicity, and Nationalism Reconsidered.* New York: New York Academy of Sciences.

Gomez-Quiñones. Juan. 1994. *Mexican American Labor, 1790–1990.* Albuquerque: University of New Mexico Press.

González, Angel N. 1999. *Interview.* Available from http://libraries.uta.edu/tejanovoices/transcripts/TV_029.html, accessed December 22, 2006.

Gonzalez, Arturo 2002. *Mexican Americans and the U.S. Economy: Quest for Buenos Dias.* Tucson: University of Arizona Press.

Gonzalez Juenke, Eric. 2005. *Minority Influence on Public Organization Change.* Unpublished PhD diss., Department of Political Science, Texas A&M University.

Gonzalez-Baker, Susan. 1996. "Su Voto, Su Voz: Latino Political Empowerment and the Immigration Challenge." *PS: Political Science and Politics* 29:465–69.

Gordon, Milton M. 1964. *Assimilation in American Life. The Role of Race, Religion, and National Origins.* New York: Oxford University Press.

Gordon, Stacy B., and Gary M. Segura. 2002. "Looking Good . . . Feeling Good! Assessing Whether Dyadic and Collective Descriptive Representation Enhances Latino Efficacy." Presented at annual meeting of the American Political Science Association, Boston, MA.

Gosnell, Harold. 1927. *Getting Out the Vote.* Chicago: University of Chicago Press.

———. 1935. *Negro Politicians: The Rise of Negro Politics in Chicago.* Chicago: University of Chicago Press.

Graman, Kevin. 2004. "Hispanic Organization Plans Coalition with NAACP." *The Spokesman-Review,* March 11.

Grasmuck, Sherri, and Patricia Pessar. 1991. *Between Two Islands. Dominican International Migration.* Berkeley: University of California Press.

Graves, Scott, and Jongho Lee. 2000. "Ethnic Underpinnings of Voting Preference: Latinos and the 1996 U.S. Senate Election Texas." *Social Science Quarterly* 81:227–36.

Greeley, Andrew. 1997. "Coleman Revisited: Religious Structures as a Source of Social Capital." *American Behavioral Scientist* 40:587–94.

References

Greene, William H. 2003. *Econometric Analysis: 5th Edition*. New York: Prentice Hall.

Grofman, Bernard. 1993. "Voting Rights in a Multi-ethnic World." *Chicano-Latino Law Review* 13:15–37.

Grofman, Bernard, and Chandler Davidson, ed. 1992. *Controversies in Minority Voting: The Voting Rights Act in Perspective*. Washington, DC: The Brookings Institution.

Grofman, Bernard, Robert Griffin, and Amihai Glazer. 1992. "The Effect of Black Population on Electing Democrats and Liberals to the House of Representatives." *Legislative Studies Quarterly* 17:365–79.

Grofman, Bernard, and Lisa Handley. 1989. "Minority Population Proportion, and Black and Hispanic Congressional Success in the 1970s and 1980s." *American Politics Quarterly* 17:436–45.

Grose, Christian. 2002. "Beyond the Vote: A Theory of Black Representation in Congress." Presented at annual meeting of the American Political Science Association, Boston, MA.

Guarnizo, Luis Eduardo. 2001. "On the Political Participation of Transnational Migrants: Old Practices and New Trends" In *E Pluribus Unum? Contemporary Historical Perspectives on Immigrant Political Incorporation*, edited by Gary Gerstle and John Mollenkopf, 213–63. New York: Russell Sage Foundation.

Guinier, Lani. 1995. "The Representation of Minority Interests in Congress." In *Classifying by Race*, edited by Paul Pierson, 21–49. Princeton, NJ: Princeton University Press.

———. 1994. *The Tyranny of the Majority: Fundamental Fairness in Representative Democracy*. New York: Free Press.

Guinier, Lani, and Gerald Torres. 1999. "Critical Race Theory Revisited." *Nathan I. Huggins Lectures*. Cambridge, MA: Harvard University.

Gujarati, Damodar. 2003. *Basic Econometrics*. 4th edition. Boston: McGraw-Hill.

Gutierrez, David G. 1995. *Walls and Mirrors: Mexican Americans, Mexican Immigrants, and the Politics of Ethnicity*. Berkeley: University of California Press.

Gutiérrez, José Ángel. *Jose Angel Gutierrez Papers. 1959–1990*. MS24, UTSA Archives and Special Collections, Library, University of Texas at San Antonio.

Hajnal, Zoltan, and Taeku Lee. 2006. "Out of Line: Immigration and Party Identification among Latinos and Asian Americans." In *Transforming Politics, Transforming America: The Political and Civic Incorporation of Immigrants in the United States*, edited by Taeku Lee, Karthick Ramakrishnan, and Ricardo Ramírez, 129–50. Charlottesville: University of Virginia Press.

Hall, Richard L. 1996. *Participation in Congress*. New Haven, CT: Yale University Press.

Hamilton, Dona Cooper, and Charles V. Hamilton. 1997. *The Dual Agenda: Race and Social Welfare Policies of Civil Rights Organizations*. New York: Columbia University Press.

Hamilton, Nora, and Norma Stolitz Chinchilla. 2001. *Seeking Community in a Global City: Guatemalans and Salvadorans in Los Angeles*. Philadelphia: Temple University Press.

Hancock, Elia. 1971. "La Chicana, Chicano Movement and Women's Liberation." *Chicano Studies Newsletter* (February-March) 1:1–6.

Handlin, Oscar. 1973[1951]. *The Uprooted*. 2nd edition. Boston: Little, Brown.

Haney-Lopez, Ian. 2003. *Racism on Trial: The Chicano Fight for Justice*. Cambridge, MA: Harvard University Press.

Hanushek, Eric A. 1996. "School Resources and Student Performance." In *Does Money Mat-*

ter? *The Effect of School Resources on Student Performance and Adult Success,* edited by Gary Burtless, 43–73. Washington, DC: Brookings Institution Press.

Hardy-Fanta, Carol. 1993. *Latina Politics, Latino Politics: Gender, Culture, and Political Participation in Boston.* Philadelphia: Temple University Press.

———. 2000. "A Latino Gender Gap? Evidence from the 1996 Election." *Milenio* 2. February. South Bend, IN: Inter-University Program for Latino Research.

Hawkesworth, Mary. 2003. "Congressional Enactments of Race-Gender: Toward a Theory of Race-gendered Institutions." *American Political Science Review* 97:529–50.

Hedges, Larry V., and Rob Greenwald. 1996. "Have Times Changed? The Relation between School Resources and School Performance." In *Does Money Matter? The Effect of School Resources on Student Performance and Adult Success,* edited by Gary Burtless, 74–92. Washington, DC: Brookings Institution Press.

Henry, Charles P. 1980. "Black-Chicano Coalitions: Possibilities and Problems." *Western Journal of Black Studies* 4:202–32.

Herberg, Will. 1955. *Catholic—Protestant—Jew.* New York: Doubleday & Co.

Herbert, Adam W. 1974." The Minority Administrator: Problems, Prospects, and Challenges." *Public Administration Review* 34:556–63.

Hero, Rodney E. 1998. *Face of Inequality: Social Diversity in American Politics.* New York: Oxford University Press.

———. 1992. *Latinos and the US Political System: Two Tiered Pluralism.* Philadelphia: Temple University Press.

———. 2003. "Social Capital and Racial Inequality in America." *Perspectives on American Politics* 1:113–22.

Hero, Rodney E., F. Chris Garcia, John Garcia, and Harry Pachón. 2000. "Latino Participation, Partisanship, and Office Holding." *PS: Political Science and Politics* 33:529–34.

Hero, Rodney E., and Caroline J. Tolbert. 1995. "Latinos and Substantive Representation in the U.S. House of Representatives: Direct, Indirect, or Nonexistent?" *American Journal of Political Science* 39:640–52.

Hess, Frederick M. 1999. *Spinning Wheels: The Politics of Urban School Reform.* Washington, DC: Brookings Institution Press.

Hess, Frederick M., and David L. Leal. 1997. "Minority Teachers, Minority Students, and College Matriculation: A New Look at the Role-Modeling Hypothesis." *Policy Studies Journal* 25:235–48.

Hicklin, Alisa. Forthcoming. "The Effect of Race-Based Admissions in Public Universities: Debunking the Myths about Hopwood and Proposition 209." *Public Administration Review.*

Highton, Benjamin. 2000. "Residential Mobility, Community Mobility, and Electoral Participation." *Political Behavior* 22:109–20.

Highton, Benjamin, and Raymond Wolfinger. 2001. "The Political Implications of Higher Turnout." *British Journal of Political Science* 31:179–92.

Hindera, John J. 1993. "Representative Bureaucracy—Imprimis Evidence of Active Representation in the EEOC District Offices." *Social Science Quarterly* 74:95–108.

Hinich, Melvin J., and James M. Enelow. 1981. *The Spatial Theory of Voting: An Introduction.* Cambridge, UK: Cambridge University Press.

Hispanic Market Facts. 2003. http://mobile-media.com/library/Latino_More_Facts.pdf

Hochschild, Jennifer, and Reuel Rogers. 2000. "Race Relations in a Diversifying Nation." In *New Directions: African Americans in a Diversifying Nation*, edited by James Jackson, 45–85. Washington, DC: National Planning Association.

Honig, Emily. 1996. "Women at Farah Revisited: Political Mobilization and Its Aftermath among Chicana Workers in El Paso, Texas, 1972–1992." *Feminist Studies* 22:425–52.

Hood, M. V., III, Irwin L. Morris, and Kurt A Shirkey. 1997. "'Quédate o Vente!': Uncovering the Determinants of Hispanic Public Opinion toward Immigration." *Political Research Quarterly* 50:627–47.

Hotelling, Harold. 1929. "Stability in Competition." *The Economic Journal* 39:41–57.

Hritzuk, Natasha, and David. K. Park. 2000. "The Question of Latino Participation: From an SES to a Social Structural Explanation." *Social Science Quarterly* 81:151–66.

Huckfeldt, Robert, Jeffrey Levine, William Morgan, and John Sprague. 1999. "Accessibility and the Political Utility of Partisan and Ideological Orientations." *American Journal of Political Science* 43:888–911.

Huckfeldt, Robert, and John Sprague. 1992. "Political Parties and Electoral Mobilization: Political Structure, Social Structure, and the Party Canvass." *American Political Science Review* 86:70–86.

Huntington, Samuel P. 1997. "The Erosion of American National Interests." *Foreign Affairs* (September/October), 28–49.

———. 2004. "The Hispanic Challenge." *Foreign Policy* (March/April), 30–45.

Hurtado, Aída. 1996. *The Color of Privilege: Three Blasphemies on Race and Feminism.* Ann Arbor: The University of Michigan Press.

Ignatiev, Noel. 1995. *How the Irish Became White.* New York: Routledge.

Itzigsohn, Jose. 2000. "The Hispanic Challenge." *Foreign Policy* (March/April), 30–45.

Jackman, Simon. 2000. "Estimation and Inference Are Missing Data Problems: Unifying Social Science Statistics via Bayesian Simulation." *Political Analysis* 8:307–32.

———. 2001. "Multidimensional Analysis of Roll Call Data via Bayesian Simulation: Identification, Estimation, Inference, and Model Checking." *Political Analysis* 9:227–41.

Jackson, Brian O., Elizabeth R. Gerber, and Bruce E. Cain. 1994. "Coalitional Prospects in a Multi-racial Society: African-American Attitudes toward Other Minority Groups." *Political Research Quarterly* 47:277–94.

Jackson, Robert A. 1996. "A Reassessment of Voter Mobilization." *Political Research Quarterly* 49:331–49.

Jacobson, Matthew Frye. 1998. *Whiteness of a Different Color: European Immigrants and the Alchemy of Race.* Cambridge, MA: Harvard University Press.

Jenkins, J. Craig. 1985. *The Politics of Insurgency. The Farm Worker Movement in the 1960s.* New York: Columbia University Press.

Jenkins, Richard. 1996. *Social Identity.* New York: Routledge.

Jennings, James. 1997. "Blacks and Latinos in the American City in the 1990s: Toward Political Alliances or Social Conflict?" In *Pursuing Power: Latinos and the Political System*, edited by F. Chris Garcia, 472–78. South Bend, IN: University of Notre Dame Press.

———. 1994. *Blacks, Latinos, and Asians: Status and Prospects for Activism.* Westport, CT: Praeger.

———, ed. 1992. *Race, Politics, and Economic Development.* New York: Verso.

Jeydel, Alana, and Andrew J. Taylor. 2003. "Are Women Legislators Less Effective? Evidence from the U.S. House in the 103rd–105th Congress." *Political Research Quarterly* 56:19–27.

Johnson, James B., and Philip E. Secret. 1996. "Focus and Style: Representational Roles of Congressional Black and Hispanic Caucus Members." *Journal of Black Studies* 26:245–73.

Johnson, Martin, Robert M. Stein, and Robert Wrinkle. 2003. "Language Choice, Residential Stability, and Voting among Latino Americans." *Social Science Quarterly* 84:412–24.

Joint Center for Housing Studies. 2001. "The State of the Nation's Housing." Cambridge, MA: Author. Available at: www.jchs.harvard.edu/publications/son2001/text/SON2001.pdf

Jones-Correa, Michael. 1998. *Between Two Nations: The Political Predicament of Latinos in New York City.* Ithaca, NY: Cornell University Press.

———. 2001a. "Institutional and Contextual Factors in Immigrant Citizenship and Voting." *Citizenship Studies* 5:41–56.

———. 1995. "New Directions for Latinos as an Ethnic Lobby in U.S. Foreign Policy." *Harvard Journal of Hispanic Policy.*

———. 2003. "The Study of Transnationalism among the Children of Immigrants: Where We Are and Where We Should Be Headed." In *The Changing Face of Home: The Transnational Lives of the Second Generation,* edited by Peggy Levitt and Mary Waters, 221–41. New York: Russell Sage Foundation.

———. 2001b. "Under Two Flags: Dual Nationality in Latin America and Its Consequences for Naturalization in the United States." *International Migration Review* 35:997–1029.

Jones-Correa, Michael, and David L. Leal. 1996. "Becoming Hispanic: Secondary Panethnic Identification among Latin American-Origin Populations in the United States." *Hispanic Journal of Behavioral Sciences* 18:214–54.

Kaiser Foundation. 2000. *National Survey on Latinos in America.* Questionnaire and Toplines. The Washington Post/Kaiser Family Foundation/Harvard University Survey Project. No. 3023. Menlo Park, CA: Kaiser Family Foundation.

Kamasaki, Charles, and Raul Yzaguirre. 1995. "Black-Hispanic Tensions: One Perspective." *Journal of Intergroup Relations.* Winter: 17–40.

Kaplowitz, Craig Allen. 2003. "A Distinct Minority: Lulac, Mexican American Identity, and Presidential Policymaking, 1965–1972." *Journal of Policy History* 15(2):192–222.

Kapur, Devesh. 2001. "Diasporas and Technology Transfer." Background Paper for the Human Development Report.

Kasinitz, Philip, John Mollenkopf, and Mary Waters. 2003. "Transnationalism and the Children of Immigrants in Contemporary New York." In *The Changing Face of Home: The Transnational Lives of the Second Generation,* edited by Peggy Levitt and Mary Waters, 96–122. New York: Russell Sage Foundation.

Kathlene, Lyn. 1994. "Power and Influence in State Legislative Policymaking: The Interaction of Gender and Position in Committee Hearing Debates." *American Political Science Review* 88:560–76.

———. 1989. "Uncovering the Political Impacts of Gender: An Exploratory Study." *Western Political Quarterly* 42:397–421.

Kaufmann, Karen M. 2003. "Cracks in the Rainbow: Group Commonality as a Basis for Latino and African-American Political Coalitions." *Political Research Quarterly* 56:199–210.

Kearney, Michael. 1991. "Borders and Boundaries of the State and Self at the End of Empire." *Journal of Historical Sociology* 4:52–74.

References

Keiser, Lael R., Vicky Wilkins, Kenneth J. Meier, and Catherine Holland. 2002. "Lipstick and Logarithms: Gender, Institutional Context and Representative Bureaucracy." *American Political Science Review* 96:553–64.

Kennedy, Peter. 2003. *A Guide to Econometrics.* 5th Edition. Cambridge, MA: MIT Press.

Kenney, Sally J. 1996. "New Research on Gendered Political Institutions." *Political Research Quarterly* 49:445–66.

Kerr, Brinck, and Will Miller. 1997. "Latino Representation, It's Direct and Indirect." *American Journal of Political Science* 41:1066–71.

Key, V. O., Jr. 1949. *Southern Politics in State and Nation.* New York: Vintage.

Kinder, Donald R., and David O. Sears. 1981. "Prejudice and Politics: Symbolic Racism versus Racial Threats to the Good Life." *Journal of Personality and Social Psychology* 40:414–31.

———. 1985. "Public Opinion and Political Behavior." In *Handbook of Social Psychology.* 3rd edition, edited by Gardner Lindzey and Elliot Aronson. New York: Random House.

King, David C. 1997. *Turf Wars: How Congressional Committees Claim Jurisdiction.* Chicago: University of Chicago Press.

Kingdon, John W. 1984. *Agendas, Alternatives, and Public Policies.* New York: Longman Press.

———. 1989. *Congressmen's Voting Decisions,* 3rd Edition. Ann Arbor: University of Michigan Press.

Koford, Kenneth. 1989. "Dimensions in Congressional Voting." *American Political Science Review* 83:949–62.

Kohpahl, Gabriele. 1998. *Voices of Guatemalan Women in Los Angeles.* New York: Garland Publishing.

Kramer, Gerald. 1970. "The Effects of Precinct-level Canvassing on Voter Behavior." *Public Opinion Quarterly* 34:560–72.

Krashen, Stephen D. 1996. *Under Attack: The Case against Bilingual Education.* Culver City, CA: Language Education Associates.

Krause, George. 1999. *A Two-Way Street: The Institutional Dynamics of the Modern Administrative State.* Pittsburgh, PA: University of Pittsburgh Press.

Krehbiel, Keith. 1991. *Information and Legislative Organization.* Ann Arbor: University of Michigan Press.

Krislov, Samuel, and David H. Rosenbloom. 1981. *Representative Democracy and the American Political System.* New York: Praeger.

Kuklinski, James H., and Gary M. Segura. 1995. "Endogeneity, Exogeneity, Time, and Space in Political Representation." *Legislative Studies Quarterly* 20:3–22.

Ladd, Everett C. 1996. "The Data Just Don't Show Erosion of America's 'Social Capital.'" *Public Perspective* 7:5–22.

Landry, Bart. 1987. *The New Black Middle Class.* Berkeley: University of California Press.

Leal, David L. 2002. "Political Participation by Latino Non-Citizens in the United States." *British Journal of Political Science* 32:353–70.

Leal, David L., and Frederick M. Hess. 2000. "The Politics of Bilingual Education Expenditures in Urban School Districts." *Social Science Quarterly* 81:1064–72.

Leal, David L., Valerie Martinez-Ebers, and Kenneth J. Meier. 2004. "The Politics of Latino Education: The Biases of At-Large Elections." *Journal of Politics* 66:1224–44.

Leighley, Janet E. 1990. "Social Interaction and Contextual Influences on Political Participation: *American Politics Quarterly* 18:450–75.

———. 2001. *Strength in Numbers? The Political Mobilization of Racial and Ethnic Minorities.* Princeton, NJ: Princeton University Press.

Levi, Margaret. 1996. "Social and Unsocial Capital." *Politics and Society* 24:44–55.

Levitt, Peggy. 2002. "The Times that Change: Relations to the Ancestral Home over Life Cycle." In *The Changing Face of Home: The Transnational Lives of the Second Generation,* edited by Peggy Levitt and Mary Waters. New York: Russell Sage Foundation.

———. 2001. *The Transnational Villagers: Dominicans in Boston.* Berkeley: University of California Press.

Levitt, Peggy, and Nina Glick Schiller. 2004. "Conceptualizing Simultaneity: A Transnational Social Field Perspective on Society." *International Migration Review* 38:1002–39.

Levitt, Peggy, and Mary Waters, eds. 2003. *The Changing Face of Home: The Transnational Lives of the Second Generation.* New York: Russell Sage Foundation.

Lewis, I. A. 1987. "Muted Voices—Problems in Polling." In *Ignored Voices: Public Opinion Polls and the Latino Community,* edited by Rodolfo de la Garza. Austin, TX: Center for Mexican American Studies.

Lieberman, Robert C. 1998. *Shifting the Color Line.* Cambridge, MA: Harvard University Press.

Lieberson, Stanley. 1980. *A Piece of the Pie: Blacks and White Immigrants since 1880.* Berkeley: University of California Press.

Lieberson, Stanley, and Mary C. Waters. 1990. *From Many Strands: Ethnic and Racial Groups in Contemporary America.* New York: Russell Sage Foundation.

Lien, Pei-te. 1998. "Does the Gender Gap in Political Attitudes and Behavior Vary across Racial Groups?" *Political Research Quarterly* 51:869–94.

———. 1994. "Ethnicity and Political Participation: A Comparison between Asian and Mexican Americans." *Political Behavior* 16:237–64.

Lieske, Joel, and Jan William Hillard. 1984. "The Racial Factor in Urban Elections." *Western Political Quarterly* 37:545–63.

Light, Ivan Hubert, and Steven J. Gold. 2000. *Ethnic Economies.* San Diego, CA: Academic Press.

Lim, Hong-Hai. 2006. "Representative Bureaucracy: Rethinking Substantive Effects and Active Representation." *Public Administration Review* 66:193–204.

Lineberry, Robert. 2000. "Letter from the Editor." *Social Science Quarterly* 81:1.

Linz, Juan J., and Alfred Stepan. 1996. *Problems of Democratic Transition and Consolidation: Southern Europe, South America, and Post-Communist Europe.* Baltimore, MD: Johns Hopkins University Press.

Londregan, John. 2000. "Estimating Legislator's Preferred Points." *Political Analysis* 8:35–56.

Long, J. Scott. 1997. *Regression Models for Categorical and Limited Dependent Variables.* Advanced Quantitative Techniques in the Social Sciences. Volume 7. Thousand Oaks, CA: Sage Publications.

Long, J. Scott, and Jeremy Freese. 2001. *Regression Models for Categorical Outcomes Using Stata.* College Station, TX: Stata Press.

Lopez-Garza, Marta. 1986. "Toward A Reconceptualization of Women's Economic Activities: The Informal Sector in Urban Mexico." In *Chicana Voices: Intersections of Class, Race, and Gender,* edited by Teresa Cordova, 66–76. Austin, TX: Center for Mexican American Studies.

Lovrich, Nicholas. 1974. "Differing Priorities in an Urban Electorate: Service Priorities among Anglo, Black and Mexican-American Voters." *Social Science Quarterly* 55:704–17.

Lowell, B. Lindsay, and Rodolfo de la Garza. 2000. "The Developmental Role of Remittances in US Latino Communities and in Latin American Countries" Final report to the Inter-American Dialogue: http://www.thedialogue.org/publications/pdf/lowell.pdf.

Lublin, David. 1997. *The Paradox of Representation: Racial Gerrymandering and Minority Interests in Congress.* Princeton, NJ: Princeton University Press.

———. 1999. "Racial Redistricting and African-American Representation: A Critique of 'Do Majority-Minority Districts Maximize Substantive Black Representation in Congress?'" *American Political Science Review* 93(2): 183–86.

Lublin, David, and Katherine Tate. 1992. "Black Office Seeking and Voter Turnout in Mayoral Elections." Presented at the annual meeting of the American Political Science Association, Chicago, IL.

Maciel, David, and Isidro Ortiz, eds. 1996. *Chicanas/Chicanos at the Crossroads.* Tucson: University of Arizona Press.

MacManus, Susan, Charles Bullock III, and Barbara Grothe. 1986. "A Longitudinal Explanation of Political Participation Rates of Mexican American Females." *Social Science Quarterly* 67:604–12.

Mahler, Sarah J. 1995. *Salvadorans in Suburbia: Symbiosis and Conflict.* Boston: Allyn and Bacon.

Manin, Bernard, Adam Przeworski, and Susan C. Stokes. 1999. "Introduction." In *Democracy, Accountability, and Representation,* edited by Adam Przeworski, Susan Stokes, and Bernard Manin, 1–26. Cambridge, UK: Cambridge University Press.

Mann, D. 1974. "Politics of Representation in Educational Administration." *Education and Urban Society* 6:297–317.

Mansbridge, Jane. 1999. "Should Blacks Represent Blacks and Women Represent Women? A Contingent 'Yes.'" *Journal of Politics* 61:628–57.

Marbut, Robert G. 2004. "Un Nuevo Dia? Republican Outreach to the Latino Community in the 2000 Campaign." In *Muted Voices: Latinos and the 2000 Elections,* edited by Rodolfo de la Garza and Louis DeSipio, 61–83. Lanham, MD: Rowman & Middlefield.

Márquez, Benjamin. 2003a. "Bankrolling Mexican American Political Organizations: Corporate and Foundation Sponsorship of Racial Politics." *Social Service Review* 77:329–46.

———. 2003b. *Choosing Issues Taking Sides: Mexican American Organizations and Identity Politics.* Austin: University of Texas Press.

———. 1993. *LULAC: The Evolution of a Mexican American Political Organization.* Austin: University of Texas Press.

———. 1998. "Mobilizing for Environmental and Economic Justice: The Politics of Environmental Justice in Mexican American Neighborhoods." *Capitalism, Nature, Socialism* 9:43–65.

Martin, Andrew D., and Kevin M. Quinn. 2002. "Dynamic Ideal Point Estimation via Markov Chain Monte Carlo for the U.S. Supreme Court, 1953–1999." *Political Analysis* 10:134–53.

Martinez, Romero. 1996. "Latinos and Lethal Violence: The Impact of Poverty and Inequality." *Social Problems* 43:131–46.

Martinez-Ebers Valerie, Manuel Avalos, Carol Hardy Fanta, Linda Lopez, Gary Segura, and

Ron Schmidt Sr. 2000. "An Update on the Status of Latinos y Latinas in Political Science: What the Profession Should Be Doing." *PS: Political Science and Politics* 34:898–901.

Martinez-Ebers, Valerie, Luis Fraga, Linda Lopez, and Arturo Vega. 2000. "Latino Interests in Education, Health and Criminal Justice Policy." *PS: Political Science and Politics* 33:547–54.

Marx, Anthony W. 1998. *Making Race and Nation: A Comparison of South Africa, the United States, and Brazil*. New York: Cambridge University Press.

Massey, Douglas S. 1999. "Why Does Immigration Occur? A Theoretical Synthesis." In *The Handbook of International Migration: The American Experience*, edited by Charles Hirschman, Philip Kasinitz, and Joshua DeWind, 34–52. New York: Russell Sage Foundation.

Massey, Douglas S., Jorge Durand, and Nolan Malone. 2002. *Beyond Smoke and Mirrors: Mexican Immigration in an Era of Economic Integration*. New York: Russell Sage Foundation.

Massey, Douglas S., and Kristin E. Espinoza. 1997. "What's Driving Mexico-US Migration? A Theoretical, Empirical and Policy Analysis." *American Journal of Sociology* 102:939–99.

Mayhew, David R. 1974. *Congress: The Electoral Connection*. New Haven, CT: Yale University Press.

McClain, Paula D. 1993. "The Changing Dynamics of Urban Politics: Black and Hispanic Municipal Employment-Is There Competition?" *Journal of Politics* 55:399–414.

McClain, Paula D., and Albert K. Karnig. 1990. "Black and Hispanic Socioeconomic and Political Competition." *American Political Science Review* 84:535–45.

McClain, Paula, Niambi Carter, Victoria DeFrancesco, J. Kendrick, Monique Lyle, Shayla Nunnally, Thomas Scotto, Jeffrey Grynaviski, and Jason Johnson. 2003. "What's New about the New South? Race, Immigration, and Intergroup Relations in a Southern City." Presented at the annual meeting of the American Political Science Association, Philadelphia, PA.

McClurg, Scott. 2003. "Social Networks and Political Participation: The Role of Social Interaction in Explaining Political Participation." *Political Research Quarterly* 56:448–64.

McCrary, Peyton. 1999. "The Dynamics of Minority Vote Dilution: The Case of Augusta, Georgia, 1945–1986." *Journal of Urban History* 25:199–225.

McCubbins, Matthew, Roger G. Noll, and Barry R. Weingast. 1989. "Structure and Process, Politics and Policy: Administrative Arrangements and the Political Control of Agencies." *Virginia Law Review* 75:431–82.

McWilliams, Carey. 1949. *North From Mexico: The Spanish-Speaking People of the United States*. Philadelphia, PA: J. B. Lippincott Company.

Meier, Kenneth J. 1993. "Representative Bureaucracy: A Theoretical and Empirical Exposition." *Research in Public Administration* 2:1–35.

———. 2005. "School Boards and the Politics of Education Policy: Downstream Consequences of Structure." In *The Politics of Democratic Inclusion*, edited by Christina Wolbrecht and Rodney E. Hero, 238–56. Philadelphia: Temple University Press.

Meier, Kenneth J., and Eric Gonzalez Juenke. 2005. "Electoral Structure and the Quality of Representation on School Boards." In *Besieged: School Boards and the Future of Education Politics*, edited by William Howell, 199–227. Washington, DC: Brookings Press.

Meier, Kenneth J., Eric Gonzalez Juenke, Robert D. Wrinkle, and J. L. Polinard. 2005.

"Structural Choices and Representational Biases: The Post-election Color of Representation." *American Journal of Political Science* 49:758–69.

———. 2003. "Structural Choices and Representational Biases: What You See May Not Be What You Get." Paper presented at the national meeting of the Midwest Political Science Association, Chicago, IL.

Meier, Kenneth J., Paula McClain, Robert D. Wrinkle, and Jerry L. Polinard. 2004. "Divided or Together?: Conflict and Cooperation between African Americans and Latinos." *Political Research Quarterly* 57:399–409.

Meier, Kenneth J., and Jill Nicholson-Crotty. 2002. "Gender, Representative Bureaucracy, and Law Enforcement: The Case of Sexual Assault." Paper presented at the annual meeting of the American Political Science Association, August 29–September 1, Boston, MA.

———. 2006. *Public Administration Review* 66(6): 850–60.

Meier, Kenneth J., and Lloyd G. Nigro. 1976. "Representative Bureaucracy and Policy Preferences." *Public Administration Review* 69:458–70.

Meier, Kenneth J., Laurence J. O'Toole Jr., and Sean Nicholson-Crotty. 2003. "Democracy and Political Control of the Bureaucracy." Manuscript.

Meier, Kenneth J., and Kevin B. Smith. 1994. "Representative Democracy and Representative Bureaucracy: Examining the Top-Down and Bottom-Up Linkages." *Social Science Quarterly* 75:790–803.

Meier, Kenneth J., and Joseph Stewart. 1991a. "Cooperation and Conflict in Multiracial School Districts." *Journal of Politics* 53:1123–33.

———. 1991b. *The Politics of Hispanic Education.* Albany: State University of New York Press.

Meier, Kenneth J., Joseph Stewart, and Robert England. 1989. *Race, Class, and Education: The Politics of Second Generation Discrimination.* Madison: University of Wisconsin Press.

Meier, Kenneth J., Robert D. Wrinkle, and Jerry L. Polinard. 1999. "Representative Bureaucracy and Distributional Equity: Addressing the Hard Question." *Journal of Politics* 61:1025–39.

Melendez, Miguel. 2003. *We Took to the Streets: Fighting For Latino Rights.* New York: St. Martin's Press.

Melendez, Edwin, Clara Rodriguez, and Janis Barry Figueroa eds. 1991. *Hispanics in the Labor Force: Issues and Policies.* New York: Plenum Press.

Meyerson, Harold. 2004. "Front-Porch Campaign." *L. A. Weekly* 20 August, 20.

Michelson, Melissa R. 2002. "Getting Out the Latino Vote: How Door-to-Door Canvassing Influences Voter Turnout in Rural Central California." Presented at the annual meeting of the Western Political Science Association, Long Beach, CA.

Miller, Lawrence W., Jerry L. Polinard, and Robert D. Wrinkle. 1984. "Attitudes toward Undocumented Workers: The Mexican-American Perspective." *Social Science Quarterly* 65:482–94.

Miller, Warren, and Donald Stokes. 1963. "Constituency Influence in Congress. *American Political Science Review* 57:45–56.

Moe, Terry. 2002. "Political Control and the Power of the Agent." Presented at the conference Controlling the Bureaucracy, College Station, Texas A&M University.

———. 1995. "The Politics of Structural Choice." In *Organization Theory: From Chester*

Barnard to the Present and Beyond, edited by Oliver E. Williamson, 116–53. New York: Oxford University Press.

Montejano, David. 1987. *Anglos and Mexicans in the Making of Texas, 1836–1986.* Austin: University of Texas Press.

Montoya, Lisa J. 2000. "Gender and Citizenship in Latino Political Participation." Presented at the Conference on Latinos in the 21st Century: The Research Agenda. David Rockefeller Center for Latin American Studies, Harvard University, Cambridge, MA.

———. 1997. "Investigating Latino Gender Differences in Political Participation." Presented at the annual meeting of the American Political Science Association, Washington, DC.

———.1996. "Latino Gender Differences in Public Opinion: Results from the Latino National Political Survey." *Hispanic Journal of Behavioral Sciences* 18:255–76.

Montoya, Lisa J., Carol Hardy-Fanta, and Sonia Garcia. 2000. "Latina Politics: Gender, Participation, and Leadership." *PS: Political Science and Politics* 33:555–61.

Mooney, Patrick H., and Theo J. Majka. 1995. *Farmers' and Farm Workers' Movements: Social Protest in American Agriculture.* New York: Twayne Publishers.

Moore, Richard, and Louis Head. 1994. "Building a Net That Works: SWOP." In *Unequal Protection,* edited by Robert Bullard, 191–206. San Francisco, CA: Sierra Club Books.

Moraga, Cherrie, and Gloria Anzaldua. 1984. *This Bridge Called My Back: Writings by Radical Women of Color.* Berkeley, CA: Third Woman Press.

Moran, Rachel F. 1988. "The Politics of Discretion: Federal Intervention in Bilingual Education." *California Law Review* 76 (6):1249–1352.

Morawska, Ewa. 2001. "Immigrants, Transnationalism, and Ethnicization: A Comparison of the Great Wave and the Last." In *E Pluribus Unum? Contemporary and Historical Perspectives on Immigrant Political Incorporation,* edited by Gary Gerstle and John Mollenkopf, 175–212. New York: Russell Sage Foundation.

Muñoz, Carlos. 1989. *Youth Identity, Power.* New York: Verso.

Muñoz, Carlos, and Charles Henry. 1986. "Rainbow Coalitions in Four Big Cities: San Antonio, Denver, Chicago, and Philadelphia." *PS: Political Science and Politics* 19:598–609.

Myrdal, Gunnar. 1944. *An American Dilemma: The Negro Problem and Modern Democracy.* New York: Harper & Row.

Nagel, Joane. 1996. *American Indian Ethnic Renewal: Red Power and the Resurgence of Identity and Culture.* New York: Oxford University Press.

National Telecommunications and Information Administration (NTIA). 1998. "Falling through the Net II: New Data on the Digital Divide." Washington, DC: U.S. Department of Commerce.

National Telecommunications and Information Administration (NTIA). 1999. "Falling through the Net: Defining the Digital Divide." Washington, DC: U.S. Department of Commerce.

National Telecommunications and Information Administration (NTIA). 2000. "Falling through the Net: Toward Digital Inclusion." Washington, DC: U.S. Department of Commerce.

Navarro, Armando. 1998. *The Cristal Experiment: A Chicano Struggle for Community Control.* Madison: University of Wisconsin Press.

———. 1995. *Mexican American Youth Organization: Avant-Garde of the Chicano Movement in Texas.* 1st edition. Austin: University of Texas Press.

REFERENCES

Navarro, Sharon Ann. 2002. "Las Mujeres Invisibles/The Invisible Women." In *Women's Activism and Globalization: Linking Local Struggles and Transnational Politics,* edited by Nancy Naples and Manisha Desai, 83–98. New York: Routledge.

Nelson, Candace, and Marta Tienda. 1997. "The Structuring of Hispanic Ethnicity: Historical and Contemporary Perspectives." In *Challenging Fronteras,* edited by Mary Romero, Pierrette Hondagneu-Sotelo, and Vilma Ortiz, 7–29. New York: Routledge.

Newton, Kenneth. 1997. "Social Capital and Democracy." *American Behavioral Scientist* 40:575–86.

Nie, Norman H., Jane Junn, and Keneth Stehlik-Barry. 1996. *Education and Democratic Citizenship in America.* Chicago: University of Chicago Press.

Nieto, Consuelo. 1974. "The Chicana and the Women's Rights Movement: A Perspective." *Civil Rights Digest* 6:36–42.

Nieto-Gomez, Anna. 1973. "The Chicana: Perspectives for Education." *Encuentro Femenil* 1:34–61.

Nissen, Beth. 2000. "Campaigning with a Spanish accent: Courting the Latino vote." http://www.cnn.com/2000/ALLPOLITICS/stories/08/16/latino.voters.

Norton, M. Scott. 1996. *The School Superintendency: New Responsibilities, New Leadership.* Boston, MA: Allyn and Bacon.

Orozco, Manuel. 2003. "Remittances and Markets: New Players and Practices" Claremont, CA: Inter-American Dialogue and the Tomás Rivera Policy Institute. http://www.thedialogue.org/publications/Remittances_and_Markets.htm.

Ortiz, Flora Ida. 2000. "Who Controls Succession in the Superintendency? A Minority Perspective." *Urban Education* 35:557–66.

Ovando, Carlos Julio. 2003. "Bilingual Education in the United States: Historical Development and Current Issues." *Bilingual Research Journal* 27(1):1–24.

Pachón, Harry. 1999. "California Latino Politics and the 1996 Elections: From Potential to Reality." In *Awash in the Mainstream,* edited by Rodolfo de la Garza, and Louis DeSipio, 167–89. Boulder, CO: Westview Press.

———. 1998. "Latino Politics in the Golden State: Ready for the 21st Century?" In *Racial and Ethnic Politics in California,* edited by Byran Jackson and Michael Preston, 411–38, Berkeley: Institute for Governmental Studies, University of California.

Pachón, Harry, and Lourdes Arguelles, with Rafael González. 1994. "Grass-Roots Politics in an East Los Angeles Barrio: A Political Ethnography of the 1990 General Election." In *Barrio Ballots: Latino Politics in the 1990 General Election,* edited by Rodolfo de la Garza, Marta Menchaca, and Louis DeSipio, 137–60. Boulder, CO: Westview Press.

Pachón, Harry, Matt A. Barreto, and Frances Marquez. 2004. "Latino Politics Comes of Age: Lessons from the Golden State." In *The Latino Electorate in 2000,* edited by Rodolfo de la Garza and Louis DeSipio, 84–100. Boulder, CO: Westview Press.

Pachón, Harry, and Louis DeSipio. 1992. "Latino Elected Officials in the 1990s." *PS: Political Science and Politics* 25:212–17.

———. 1988. *The Latino Vote in 1988.* NALEO Background Paper #7. Washington, DC: NALEO Educational Fund.

Pachón, Harry, Rodolfo O. de la Garza, and Adrian D. Pantoja. 2000. "Foreign Policy Perspectives of Hispanic Elites." In *Latinos and U.S. Foreign Policy,* edited by Rodolfo O. de la Garza and Harry P. Pachón, 21–42. New York: Rowman and Littlefield Publishers.

Padilla, Felix. 1985a. *Latino Ethnic Consciousness*. South Bend, IN: University of Notre Dame Press.

———. 1985b. "On the Nature of Latino Ethnicity." In *The Mexican-American Experience*, edited by Rodolfo de la Garza, Frank Bean, Charles Bonjean, Ricardo Romo, and Rodolfo Alvarez, 332–45. Austin: University of Texas Press.

Page, Benjamin. 1987. "Comment: Why Polls Matter and Why Latinos Are Ignored." In *Ignored Voices: Public Opinion Polls and the Latino Community*, edited by Rodolfo de la Garza, 42–46. Austin, TX: Center for Mexican American Studies.

Page, Benjamin, and Robert Y. Shapiro. 1992. *The Rational Public: Fifty Years of Trends in Americans' Policy Preferences*. Chicago, IL: University of Chicago Press.

Pantoja, Adrian D., Ricardo Ramirez, and Gary M. Segura. 2001. "Citizens by Choice, Voters by Necessity: Patterns in Political Mobilization by Naturalized Latinos." *Political Research Quarterly* 54:729–50.

Pantoja, Adrian D., and Gary Segura. 2003. "Fear and Loathing in California: Contextual threat and Political Sophistication among Latino Voters." *Political Behavior* 25:265–86.

Pantoja, Adrian D., and Nathan D. Woods. 1999. "Latino Voter Turnout in Los Angeles County: Did Interest Group Efforts Matter?" *American Review of Politics* 20:141–62.

Pardo, Mary. 1990. "Mexican American Grassroots Community Activists: 'Mothers of East Los Angeles.'" *Frontiers* 11:1–7.

———. 1998. *Mexican American Women Activists: Identity and Resistance in Two Los Angeles Communities*. Philadelphia: Temple University Press.

———. 1997. "Mexican American Women Grassroots Community Activists: Mothers of East Los Angeles." In *Pursuing Power: Latinos and the Political System*, edited by F. Chris Garcia, 151–68. South Bend, IN: University of Notre Dame Press.

Patterson, Samuel, Michael Bailey, and Valerie Martinez. 1987. "Report of the Managing Editor of the American Political Science Review, 1986–87." *PS: Political Science and Politics* 20:450–55.

Patterson, Samuel C., and Gregory A. Caldeira. 1983. "Getting Out the Vote: Participation in Gubernatorial Elections." *American Political Science Review* 77:675–89.

Paul, Pope John, II. 1995. *The Gospel of Life: The Encyclical Letter on Abortion, Euthanasia, and the Death Penalty in Today's World*. New York: Times Books.

Perez, Lisando. 1986. "The Cuban Population in the United States." *The Annals of the American Academy of Political Science* 485:126–37.

Perez-Firmat, Gustavo. 2000. *Next Year in Cuba: Coming of Age in America*. Houston, TX: Scrivenery Press.

Pesquera, Beatriz M., and Denise Segura. 1993. "There Is No Going Back: Chicanas and Feminism." In *Chicana Critical Issues*, edited by Norma Alarcon and Mujeres Activas en Letras y Cambio Social, 95–115. Berkeley, CA: Third World Woman Press.

Pessar, Patricia R. 1995. *A Visa for a Dream. Dominicans in the United States*. Boston, MA: Allyn and Bacon.

Pitkin, Hanna F. 1967. *The Concept of Representation*. Berkeley: University of California Press.

Pitti, Stephen J. 2003. *The Devil in Silicon Valley: Northern California, Race, and Mexican Americans*. Princeton, NJ: Princeton University Press.

Piven, Frances Fox, and Richard A. Cloward. 1977. *Poor People's Movements: Why They Succeed, How They Fail*. New York: Pantheon Books.

REFERENCES

Platt, Glenn, Keith T. Poole, and Howard Rosenthal. 1992. "Directional and Euclidean Theories of Voting Behavior: A Legislative Comparison." *Legislative Studies Quarterly* 17:561–72.

Polinard, Jerry L., Robert D. Wrinkle, and Tomas Longoria. 1990. "Education and Governance, Representational Links to Second Generation Discrimination." *Western Political Quarterly* 43:631–46.

Polinard, Jerry L., Robert D. Wrinkle, Tomas Longoria, and Norman E. Binder. 1994. *Electoral Structure and Urban Policy, Impact on Mexican American Communities.* Armonk, NY: M. E. Sharpe.

Pomper, Gerald. 1966. "Ethnic and Group Voting in Nonpartisan Municipal Elections." *Public Opinion Quarterly* 30:79–97.

Poole, Keith, and Howard Rosenthal. 1997. *Congress: A Political-Economic History of Roll Call Voting.* New York: Oxford University Press.

———. 1991. "Patterns of Congressional Voting." *American Journal of Political Science* 35: 228–78.

Popkin, Samuel. 1991. *The Reasoning Voter.* Chicago: University of Chicago Press.

Portes, Alejandro. 2003. "Conclusion: Theoretical Convergences and Empirical Evidence in the Study of Immigrant Transnationalism." *International Migration Review* 37:874–92.

———. 1999. "Conclusion: Toward a New World Order: The Origins and Effect of Transnational Activities." *Ethical and Racial Studies* 22:463–78.

Portes, Alejandro, and Robert L. Bach. 1985. *Latin Journey.* Berkeley: University of California Press.

Portes, Alejandro, and Patricia Landolt. 1996. "The Downside of Social Capital." *The American Prospect* 26:18–21.

Portes, Alejandro, and Ruben Rumbaut. 1996. *Immigrant America: A Portrait.* Berkeley: University of California Press.

———. 2001. *Legacies: The Story of the Immigrant Second Generation.* Berkeley: University of California Press.

Prince, Cynthia D., and John A. Hubert. 1994. "Measuring the Cost of Bilingual Education." *Journal of Educational Issues* 13:121–35.

Przeworski, Adam, Susan Stokes, and Bernard Manin, eds. 1999. *Democracy, Accountability, and Representation.* Cambridge, UK: Cambridge University Press.

Pulido, Laura. 1996. *Environmentalism and Economic Justice: Two Chicano Struggles in the Southwest.* Tucson: University of Arizona Press.

Putnam, Robert. 2000. *Bowling Alone.* New York: Simon and Schuster Press.

———. 1993. *Making Democracy Work: Civic Traditions in Modern Italy.* Princeton, NJ: Princeton University Press.

Pyle, Amy, Patrick McDonnell, and Hector Tobar. 1998. "The Latino Vote: Voter Participation Doubled Since '94 Primary." *Los Angeles Times,* June 4:A1.

Quiñónez, Naomi H. 2002. "Re(Riting) the Chicana Postcolonial: From Traitor to 21st Century Interpreter." In *Decolonial Voices,* edited by Arturo J. Aldama and Naomi H. Quiñónez, 129–51. Bloomington and Indianapolis: Indiana University Press.

Rahn, Wendy M., John Brehm, and N. Carlson. 1999. "National Elections as Institutions for Generating Social Capital." In *Civic Engagement in American Democracy,* edited by Theda Skocpol and Morris Fiorina, 111–60. Washington, DC: Brookings Institution Press.

Ramírez, Ricardo. 2002a. "The Changing California Voter: A Longitudinal Analysis of Latino

Participation." Presented at the annual meeting of the Midwest Political Science Association, Chicago, IL.

———. 2002b. "Getting Out the Vote: The Impact of Non-Partisan Voter Mobilization Efforts in Low Turnout Latino Precincts." Presented at the annual meeting of the American Political Science Association, Boston, MA.

———. 2005. "Giving Voice to Latino Voters: A Field Experiment on the Effectiveness of a National Nonpartisan Mobilization Effort." *The Annals of the American Academy of Political and Social Science* 601:66–84

Ramos, Jorge. 2004. *The Latino Wave: How Hispanics Will Elect the Next American President.* New York: HarperCollins Publishers Inc.

Ricourt, Milagros, and Ruby Danta. 2003. *Hispanas de Queens: Latino Panethnicity in a New York City Neighborhood.* Ithaca, NY: Cornell University Press.

Robinson, Chauncy. 2002. "Can African Americans and Hispanics form a Coalition in Atlanta?" *Mundo Hispanico* 23:59.

Robinson, Randall N. 1999. *The Debt: What America Owes to Blacks.* New York: Dutton.

Robinson, Scott E. 2002. "Rules, Roles, and Minority Representation: The Dynamics of Budgeting for Bilingual Education in Texas." *State Politics and Policy Quarterly* 2:52–65.

Rodrigues, Helena, and Gary Segura. 2003. "Attitudinal Underpinnings of Black-Brown Coalitions: Latino Perceptions of Commonality with African-Americans and Anglos." Presented at the annual meeting of the Midwest Political Science Association, Chicago, IL.

Rodriguez, Clara. 1993. "Puerto Rican Circular Migration: Revisited." *Latino Studies Journal* 93–113.

Roediger, David R. 1999. *The Wages of Whiteness: Race and the Making of the American Working Class.* New York: Verso.

Romzek, Barbara S., and J. Stephen Hendricks. 1982. "Organizational Involvement and Representative Bureaucracy: Can We Have It Both Ways?" *American Political Science Review* 76:75–82.

Rosenstone, Steven, Roy L. Behr, and Edward H. Lazarus. 1984. *Third Parties in America.* Princeton, NJ: Princeton University Press.

Rosenstone, Steven J., and John M. Hansen. 1993. *Mobilization, Participation, and Democracy in America.* New York: Macmillan.

Rosenthal, Cindy Simon. 2000. "Gender Styles in State Legislative Committees: Raising Their Voices in Resolving Conflict." *Women and Politics* 21:21–45.

Ruiz, Vicki L. 1987. *Cannery Women/Cannery Lives.* Albuquerque: University of New Mexico Press.

Rumbaut, Ruben. 2003. "Severed or Sustained Attachments? Language, Identity and Imagined Communities in the Post-Immigrant Generation." In *The Changing Face of Home: The Transnational Lives of the Second Generation,* edited by Peggy Levitt and Mary Waters, 43–95. New York: Russell Sage Foundation.

Rumbaut, Ruben, and Alejandro Portes. 2001. *Ethnicities: Children of Immigrants in America.* Berkeley: University of California Press.

Saltzstein, Grace Hall. 1979. "Representative Bureaucracy and Bureaucratic Responsibility—Problems and Prospects." *Administration & Society* 10:465–75.

San Miguel, Guadalupe, Jr. 2001. *Brown, Not White: Integration and the Chicano Movement in Houston.* College Station: Texas A&M University Press.

———. 2004. *Contested Policy: The Rise and Fall of Federal Bilingual Education in the United States, 1960–2001.* Denton: University of North Texas Press.

———. 1986, 1987. *Let All of Them Take Heed: Mexican Americans and the Campaign for Education Equality in Texas, 1910–1981.* College Station: Texas A&M University Press.

———. 1987. "The Status of Historical Research on Chicano Education." *Review of Educational Research* 57(4):467–80.

Santiago, Esmeralda, and Joie Davidow. 1998. *Christmas: Favorite Latino Authors Share Their Holiday Memories.* New York: Knopf.

Schlesinger, Arthur. 1998. *The Disuniting of America, Reflections on a Multicultural Society.* New York: W. W. Norton and Company.

Schneider, Susan Gilbert. 1976. *Revolution, Reaction, or Reform: The 1974 Bilingual Education Act.* New York: Las Americas.

Scott, Hugh J. 1990. "Views of Black School Superintendents on Black Consciousness and Professionalism." *Journal of Negro Education* 59:165–72.

Segal, Adam. 2004. *Bikini Politics: Covering Only the Essential Parts of the Body Politic.* Baltimore, MD: Hispanic Voter Project, Johns Hopkins University.

———. 2003. *The Hispanic Priority: The Spanish Language Television Battle for the Hispanic Vote in 2000 U.S. Presidential Election.* Baltimore, MD: Hispanic Voter Project, Johns Hopkins University.

———. 2006. *Total Spanish-language TV Spending by Market in the 2004 Presidential Election.* Baltimore, MD: Hispanic Voter Project, Johns Hopkins University.

Segura, Denise A. 1986. "Chicanas and Triple Oppression in the Labor Force." In *Chicana Voices: Intersection of Class, Race, and Gender,* Teresa Cordova, 47–65. Albuquerque: University of New Mexico Press.

———. 1988. "Familism and Employment among Chicanas and Mexican Immigrant Women." In *Mexicana at Work in the United States,* edited by Margarita Melville. La Jolla, CA.: Mexican American Studies Program.

Segura, Gary, Denis Falcon, and Harry Pachón. 1997. "Dynamic of Latino Partisanship in California: Immigration, Issue Salience, and Their Implications." *Harvard Journal of Hispanic Politics* 10:62–80.

Segura, Gary, F. Chris Garcia, and Rodolfo de la Garza. 1999. *Social Capital and the Latino Community.* Claremont, CA: Tomás Rivera Policy Institute.

Segura, Gary M., Harry Pachón, and Nathan Woods. 2001. "Hispanics, Social Capital, and Civic Engagement." *National Civic Review* 90:85–96.

Selden, Sally Coleman. 1997. *The Promise of Representative Bureaucracy: Diversity and Responsiveness in a Government Agency, Bureaucracies, Public Administration, and Public Policy.* Armonk, NY: M. E. Sharpe.

Selden, Sally Coleman, Jeffrey L. Brudney, and J. Edward Kellough. 1998. "Bureaucracy as a Representative Institution: toward a Reconciliation of Bureaucratic Government and Democratic Theory." *American Journal of Political Science* 42:717–44.

Serrano, Basilio. 1999. "Rifle, Canon, y Escopeta: A Chronicle of the Puerto Rican Student Union." In *The Puerto Rican Movement: Voices from the Diaspora,* edited by Andrés Torres and José E. Velázquez, 124–43. Philadelphia: Temple University Press.

Shain, Yossi. 1999. *Marketing the American Creed Abroad, Diasporas in the U.S. and Their Homelands.* Cambridge, UK: Cambridge University Press.

Shaw, Daron, Rodolfo de la Garza, and Jongho Lee. 2000. "Examining Latino turnout in 1996: A Three-State Validated Survey Approach." *American Journal of Political Science* 44:338–46.

Shin, Fay H. 2000. "Parent Attitudes toward the Principles of Bilingual Education and Their Children's Participation in Bilingual Programs." *Journal of Intercultural Studies* 21:93–99.

Shirley, Dennis. 1997. *Community Organizing for Urban School Reform*. Austin: University of Texas Press.

Shockley, John S. 1974. *Chicano Revolt in a Texas Town*. Notre Dame, IN: University of Notre Dame Press.

Sierra, Christine Marie, Teresa Carrillo, Louis DeSipio, and Michael Jones-Correa. 2000. "Latino Immigration and Citizenship." *PS: Political Science and Politics* 33:535–40.

Sierra, Christine Marie, and Adaljiza Sosa-Riddell. 1994. "Chicanas as Political Actors: Rare Literature, Complex Practice." *National Political Science Review* 4:297–317.

Singh, Robert. 1998. *The Congressional Black Caucus: Racial Politics in the U.S. Congress*. Thousand Oaks, CA: Sage Publications.

Skerry, Peter. 1993. *Mexican Americans: The Ambivalent Minority*. Cambridge, MA: Harvard University Press.

Skocpol, Theda. 1999. "Advocates without Members: The Recent Transformation of American Civic Life." In *Civic Engagement in American Democracy*, edited by Theda Skocpol and Morris Fiorina, 461–509. Washington, DC: Brookings Institution Press.

Smith, Michael Peter. 1994. "Can You Imagine? Transnational Migration and the Globalization of Grassroots Politics." *Social Text* 39:15–33.

Smith, Michael Peter, and Luis Guarnizo. 1998. *Transnationalism from Below*. New Brunswick, NJ: Transaction Publishers.

Smith, Rogers M. 1997. *Civic Ideals: Conflicting Visions of Citizenship in U.S. History*. New Haven, CT: Yale University Press, 1997.

Smooth, Wendy G. 2001. *African American Women State Legislators: The Impact of Gender and Race on Legislative Influence*. PhD diss. University of Maryland.

Sobel, Richard. 1993. "From Occupational Involvement to Political Participation." *Political Behavior* 15:339–53.

Solorzano-Torres, Rosalia. 1987. "Female Mexican Immigrants in San Diego County." In *Women on the U.S.-Mexico Border: Responses to Change*, edited by Vicki L. Ruiz and Susan Tiano, 41–59. Boston: Allen & Unwin.

Sonenshein, Raphael J. 1986. "Biracial Coalition Politics in Los Angeles." *PS: Political Science and Politics* 19:582–90.

———. 1989. "The Dynamics of Biracial Coalitions: Crossover Politics in Los Angeles." *Western Political Quarterly* 42:333–53.

———. 2003. "Post-Incorporation Politics in Los Angeles." In *Racial Politics in American Cities*, 3rd edition, edited by Rufus Browning, Dale Rogers Marshall, and David H. Tabb, 51–76. New York: Longman.

Sonenshein, Raphael J., and Susan Pinkus. 2002. "The Dynamics of Latino Political Incorporation: The 2001 Los Angeles Mayoral Election as Seen in *Los Angeles Times* Exit Polls." PS: Politics and Political Science 35:67–74.

Sosa, Lionel. 2004. "Communicating to the Latino Voter: What Works, What Doesn't." Presented at the conference *From Rhetoric to Reality: Latino Politics in 2004*. Claremont, CA: The Tomás Rivera Policy Institute.

Sparks, Holloway. 1997. "Dissident Citizenship: Democratic Theory, Political Courage, and Activist Women." *Hypatia* 12:74–110.

Squire, Peverill, Raymond E. Wolfinger, and David P. Glass. 1987. "Residential Mobility and Voter Turnout." *American Political Science Review* 81:45–65.

Steinberg, Ronnie J. 1992. "Gender on the Agenda: Male Advantage in Organizations." *Contemporary Sociology* 21:576–81.

Steinberg, Stephen. 2001. *The Ethnic Myth: Race, Ethnicity, and Class in America.* Boston: Beacon Press.

Stimson, James A. 1990. *Public Opinion in America: Moods, Cycles, and Swings.* Boulder, CO: Westview Press.

Swain, Carol M. 1993, 1995. *Black Faces, Black Interests: The Representation of African-Americans in Congress.* Cambridge, MA: Harvard University Press.

Swers, Michele L. 2002. *The Difference* Women *Make: The Policy Impact of Women on Congress.* Chicago: University of Chicago Press.

Takao Ozawa v. United States. 260 U.S. 178 (1922).

Takash, Paule Cruz. 1993. "Breaking Barriers to Representation: Chicana/Latina Elected Officials in California." *Urban Anthropology* 22:325–60.

Tamerius, Karin L. 1995. "Sex, Gender, and Leadership in the Representation of Women." In *Gender Power, Leadership and Governance,* edited by Georgia Duerst-Lahti and Rita Mae Kelly, 93–112. Ann Arbor: University of Michigan Press.

Tarrow, Sidney. 1996. "Making Social Science Work across Space and Time: A Critical Reflection on Robert Putnam's Making Democracy Work." *American Political Science Review* 90:389–97.

Tate, Katherine. 1999. "African Americans and Their Representatives in Congress: Does Race Matter?" Irvine, CA: UC Irvine Center for the Study of Democracy Working Paper.

———. 2003. *Black Faces in the Mirror: African Americans and Their Representatives in the U.S. Congress.* Princeton, NJ: Princeton University Press.

———. 1993. *From Protest to Politics: The New Black Voters in American Elections.* Cambridge, MA: Harvard University Press.

Tedin, Kent T., and Richard W. Murray. 1981. "Dynamics of Candidate Choice in a State Election." *Journal of Politics* 43:435–55.

Tedin, Kent L., and Richard W. Murray. 1994. "Support for Biracial Political Coalitions among Blacks and Hispanics." *Social Science Quarterly* 75:772–89.

Teixiera, Ruy A. 1992. *The Disappearing American Voter.* Washington, DC: Brookings Institution.

Thernstrom, Stephen, and Abigail Thernstrom. 1997. *American in Black and White: One Nation Indivisible.* New York: Simon and Schuster.

Thielemann, Gregory S., and Joseph Stewart Jr. 1996. "A Demand-Side Perspective on the Importance of Representative Bureaucracy: AIDS, Ethnicity, Gender, and Sexual Orientation." *Public Administration Review* 56:168–73.

Thomas, Sue. 1994. *How Women Legislate.* New York: Oxford University Press.

———. 1991. "The Impact of Women on State Legislative Policies." *Journal of Politics* 53:958–76.

Thompson, Frank J. 1978. "Civil Servants and the Deprived: Socio-political and Occupational

Explanations of Attitudes toward Minority Hiring." *American Journal of Political Science* 22:325–47.

———. 1976. "Minority-Groups in Public Bureaucracies—Are Passive and Active Representation Linked." *Administration & Society* 8:201–26.

Torres, Andres. 1998. "Introduction: Political Radicalism in the Diaspora, The Puerto Rican Experience" In *The Puerto Rican Movement, Voices from the Diaspora*, edited by Andres Torres and Jose E. Velazquez, 1–22. Philadelphia: Temple University Press.

Torres, Andres, and Jose E. Velazquez, eds. 1999. *The Puerto Rican Movement: Voices from the Diaspora*. Philadelphia: Temple University Press.

Torres, David L. 1990. "Dynamics behind the Formation of a Business Class: Tucson's Hispanic Business Elite." *Hispanic Journal of Behavioral Sciences* 12:25–49.

Torres, María de los Angeles. 1999. *In the Land of Mirrors: Cuban Exile Politics in the United States*. Ann Arbor: University of Michigan Press.

Torres-Saillant, Silvio. 1989. "Dominicans as a New York Community: A Social Appraisal." *Punto 7 Review: A Journal of Marginal Discourse* 2:7–25.

Trueba, Enrique (Henry). 1999. *Latinos Unidos: From Cultural Diversity to the Politics of Solidarity*. Lanham, MD: Rowman & Littlefield.

Tucker, Harvey and Harmon Zeigler. 1980. *Professionals Versus the Public: Attitudes, Communication, and Response in School Districts*. New York: Longman Press.

Ueda, Reed. 2002. "An Early Transnationalism? The Japanese American Second Generation of Hawaii in the Interwar Years." In *The Changing Face of Home: The Transnational Lives of the Second Generation*, edited by Peggy Levitt and Mary Waters, 33–42. New York: Russell Sage Foundation.

Uhlaner, Carole J. 1989. "Relational Goods and Participation: Incorporating Sociability into a Theory of Rational Action." *Public Choice* 62:253–85.

Uhlaner, Carole, Bruce Cain, and D. Roderick Kiewiet. 1989. "Political Participation of Ethnic Minorities in the 1980s." *Political Behavior* 11:195–231.

Uhlaner, Carole and F. Chris Garcia. 2002. "Latina Public Opinion." In *Understanding Public Opinion*, edited by Barbar Norrander and Clyde Wilcox. Washington DC: Congressional Quarterly Press.

U.S. Immigration and Naturalization Service. 1992. *Statistical Yearbook of the Immigration and Naturalization Service*. Washington, DC: U.S. Government Printing Office.

United States v. Wong Kim Ark. 169 I/S/ 649 (1898).

United States v. Bhagat Singh Thind. 261 U.S. 204 (1923).

Uslaner, Eric E. 1999. "Democracy and Social Capital." In *Democracy and Trust*, edited by Mark E. Warren. Cambridge, UK: Cambridge University Press.

Valdez, Armando. 1987. "An Assessment of Data Resources on Latinos in the United States." In *Ignored Voices: Public Opinion Polls and the Latino Community*, edited by Rodolfo de la Garza, 174–94. Austin, TX: Center for Mexican American Studies.

Vélez-Ibáñez, Carlos, and Anna Sampaio, eds. 2002. *Transnational Latina/o Communities: Politics, Process, and Cultures*. Lanham, MD: Rowman and Littlefield.

Verba, Sidney, Kay Lehman Scholzman, and Henry E. Brady. 1995. *Voice and Equality: Civic Voluntarism in American Politics*. Cambridge, MA: Harvard University Press.

Vertovec, S. 1999. "Conceiving and Researching Transnationalism. *Ethnic and Racial Studies* 22:347–62.

Vidal, Mirta. 1971. "New Voice of La Raza: Chicanas Speak Out." *International Socialist Review* 7:31–33.

Vigil, Ernesto B. 1999. *The Crusade for Justice: Chicano Militancy and the Government's War on Dissent.* Madison: The University of Wisconsin Press.

Vila, Pablo. 2000. *Crossing Borders, Reinforcing Borders: Interpellations, Metaphors, and Narrative Identities on the US-Mexico Frontier.* Austin: University of Texas Press.

Walker, Kenneth. 1965a. "Manuela Solis and Emma Tenayucca: A Tribute." In *Chicana Voices: Intersections of Class, Race, and Gender,* edited by Teresa Cordova, 95–115. Austin, TX: Center for Mexican American Studies.

———. 1965b. "The Pecan Shellers of San Antonio and Mechanization." *Southwestern Historical Quarterly* 69:44–58.

Wallison, Ethan, and John Mercurio. 2001. "Caucus' Move Could Limit Hispanic Gains." *Roll Call* (April 23).

Walsh, Katherine Cramer. 2002. "Enlarging Representation: Women Bringing Marginalized Perspectives to Floor Debate in the House of Representatives." In *Women Transforming Congress,* edited by Cindy S. Rosenthal, 370–96. Norman: University of Oklahoma Press.

Warren, Christopher L., John F. Stack Jr., and John G. Corbett. 1986. "Minority Mobilization in an International City: Rivalry and Conflict in Miami." *PS: Political Science and Politics* 19:626–35.

Warren, Mark R. 2001. *Dry Bones Rattling: Community Building to Revitalize American Democracy.* Princeton, NJ: Princeton University Press.

———. 1987. "The Hollow Realignment: Partisan Change in a Candidate-Centered Era." *Public Opinion Quarterly* 51(1): 58–74.

Weiher, Gregory. 2000. "Minority Student Achievement, Passive Representation and Social Context in Schools." *Journal of Politics* 62:886–95.

Weingast, Barry, and William Marshall. 1988. "The Industrial Organization of Congress—or, Why Legislatures, Like Firms, Are Not Organized as Markets." *Journal of Political Economy* 96:132–63.

Welch, Susan 1990. "The Impact of At-Large Elections on the Representation of Blacks and Hispanics." *Journal of Politics* 52:1050–76.

Welch, Susan, and John R. Hibbing. 1984. "Hispanic Representation in the U.S. Congress." *Social Science Quarterly* 65:328–35.

Welch, Susan, and Lee Sigelman. 1992. "A Gender Gap among Hispanics? A Comparison with Blacks and Anglos." *Western Political Quarterly* 45:181–99.

West, William. 1995. *Controlling the Bureaucracy: Institutional Constraints in Theory and Practice.* London: M. E. Sharpe.

Whitby, Kenny. 2000. *The Color of Representation: Congressional Behavior and Black Interests.* Ann Arbor: University of Michigan Press.

Whittington, Keith, and Daniel Carpenter. 2003. "Executive Power in American Institutional Development." *PS: Political Science and Politics* 36:495–513.

Wilkins, Vicky, and Lael R. Keiser. Forthcoming. "Linking Active and Passive Representation by Gender: The Case of Child Support Enforcement." *Journal of Public Administration Research and Theory.*

Wilkins, Vicky, and Brian N. Williams. 2005. "Black or Blue: Racial Profiling and Representative Bureaucracy." Paper presented at the Eighth National Public Management Research Conference, University of Southern California, October 1–2.

Williams, Norma. 1990. *The Mexican American Family: Tradition and Change*. Dix Halls, NY: General Hall.

Wilson, William J. 1996. *When Work Disappears*. New York: Alfred A. Knopf.

Winant, Howard. 1995. "Race: Theory, Culture, and Politics in the United States Today." In *Cultural Politics and Social Movements*, edited by Marcy Darnovsky, Barbara Epstein, and Richard Flacks, 174–88. Philadelphia: Temple University Press.

Wolfinger, Raymond E. 1965. "The Development and Persistence of Ethnic Voting." *American Political Science Review* 59:896–908.

Wolfinger, Raymond, and Steven J. Rosenstone. 1980. *Who Votes?* New Haven, CT: Yale University Press.

Wong, Janelle. 2006. *Democracy's Promise: Immigrants and American Civic Institutions*. Ann Arbor: University of Michigan Press.

Wood, B. Dan, and Nick Theobald. 2003. "Political Responsiveness and Equity in Public Education Finance." *Journal of Politics* 65:718–38.

Wood, B. Dan, and Richard Waterman. 1994. *Bureaucratic Dynamics: The Role of Bureaucracy in a Democracy*. Boulder, CO: Westview Press.

Woodson, Carter G. 1933. *The Mis-Education of the Negro*. New York: The Associated Publishers.

Wrinkle, Robert D. 1991. "Understanding Intra-ethnic Attitude Variations: Mexican Origin Population Views of Immigration." *Social Science Quarterly* 72:379–87.

Wrinkle, Robert, Joseph Stewart, Jerry Polinard, Kenneth Meier, and John Arvizu. 1996. "Ethnicity and Nonpolitical Participation." *Hispanic Journal of Behavioral Sciences* 18:142–53.

Zahniser, Steven. 1999. *Mexican Migration to the United States: The Role of Migration Networks and Human Capital Accumulation*. New York: Garland Publishing.

Zamora, Emilio. 1993. *The World of the Mexican Workers in Texas*. College Station: Texas A&M University Press.

Zavella, Patricia. 1987. *Women's Work & Chicano Families*. Ithaca, NY: Cornell University Press.

Contributors

Manuel Avalos is currently the Associate Vice Provost for Research and Faculty Development and the Associate Director of the Hispanic Research Center at Arizona State University (ASU) at the West campus. He is also an Associate Professor of Political Science in the Department of Social and Behavioral Sciences at ASU West campus. He received his doctoral degree in political science at the University of New Mexico and did postdoctoral work at the Center for Mexican-American Studies at the University of Texas at Austin. His current research focuses on questions of racial inequality in the Americas and the political representation and incorporation of the Latino electorate at the state, local, and national level. He is currently working on the completion of an analysis of the effect of the Latino vote on the 2004 presidential election, with special emphasis on Arizona and an analysis of the effect of the passage of Proposition 200 in the 2004 election, which requires: (1) proof of citizenship when registering to vote; (2) ID at polling places; (3) proof of immigration status when applying for state public welfare benefits. His publications have appeared in *Sociological Perspectives, Harvard Journal of Hispanic Policy,* and *Policy Studies Journal,* as well as articles in edited volumes by Roberto de Anda, *Chicanas and Chicanos in Contemporary Society,* and in Rodolfo de la Garza and Louis DeSipio, *Ethnic Ironies, Awash in the Mainstream: Latino Politics in the 1996 Elections,* and *Muted Voices: Latino Politics in the 2000 Elections.*

Matt A. Barreto is an Assistant Professor of Political Science at the University of Washington (UW) and a member of the Washington Institute for the Study of Ethnicity and Race (WISER). He received his PhD in political science from the University of California, Irvine, in 2005. His research examines the political participation of racial and ethnic minorities in the United States and has been published in the *American Political Science Review, Political Research Quarterly, Social Science Quarterly, Urban Affairs Review,* and other peer-reviewed journals. He specializes in Latino and immigrant voting behavior and teaches courses on racial and ethnic politics, Latino politics, voting and elections, and American politics. Part of his research agenda also includes public opinion and election surveys, including exit polling methodology. He is also an affiliated faculty member in the Center for Statistics and the Social Sciences (CSSS) at the University of Washington. Beyond UW, he has been an affiliated research scholar with the Tomás Rivera Policy Institute (TRPI) since 1999 and with the Center for the Study of Los Angeles since 2002. In 2004 he was a coauthor of the TRPI/Washington Post/Univision National Survey of Latino Voters, and in 2005 he was coprincipal investigator of the CSLA Los Angeles mayoral election exit poll.

Jason P. Casellas is an Assistant Professor of Government at the University of Texas at Austin. He received his PhD in politics from Princeton University in 2005. His research and teaching interests include Latino politics and congressional politics. He has been the recipient of numerous grants and fellowships, including a Horowitz Foundation for Social Policy Grant, a Woodrow Wilson Fellowship, a Princeton President's Fellowship, a Ford Motor Company Fellowship, and an American Political Science Association Fellowship.

Louis DeSipio is an Associate Professor in the Department of Political Science and the Chicano/Latino Studies Program at the University of California, Irvine (UCI). He is the author of *Counting on the Latino Vote: Latinos as a New Electorate* (1996, University Press of Virginia) and the coauthor, with Rodolfo O. de la Garza, of *Making Americans/Remaking America: Immigration and Immigrant Policy* (1998). He is also the author and editor of a seven-volume series on Latino political values, attitudes, and behaviors. The most recent volume in this series, *Muted Voices: Latinos and the 2000 Elections,* was published in 2004. His research focuses on Latino politics, on the process of political incorporation of new and formerly excluded populations into U.S. politics, and on public policies such as immigration, immigrant settlement, naturalization, and voting rights. He served as Interim Director of the University of Illinois at Urbana-Champaign Latina/Latino Studies Program from 1999 to 2002 and the Acting Director of the UCI Chicano/Latino Studies Program in 2004. He serves as Graduate Director in the UCI Department of Political Science and Undergraduate Adviser in the Chicano/Latino Studies Program.

Rodolfo Espino is an Assistant Professor at Arizona State University. He received his BA from Luther College and his MA and PhD from the University of Wisconsin-Madison. His primary research and teaching interests are in the fields of minority politics, political behavior, and political methodology. His dissertation focused on the Congressional Hispanic Caucus and Latino representation in Congress, specifically on how institutional and electoral forces both hinder and facilitate the representation of Latinos. This work received the American Political Science Association award for the best dissertation on race and politics. He is presently engaged in a number of research projects, some of which include an examination of Latino political empowerment, the campaign rhetoric of Latino candidates and Spanish-language political campaign ads, and the political behavior of whites in response to Latinos. Aside from research on Latino politics, he is also conducting work that examines bias in survey item response, the effect of civic education on political participation, and the political participation of language-minority Americans.

Luis Ricardo Fraga is Associate Vice Provost for Faculty Advancement, Director of the Diversity Research Institute, Russell F. Stark University Professor, and Professor of Political Science at the University of Washington, Seattle. He has published widely in scholarly journals and edited volumes. His primary interests are urban politics, politics of race and ethnicity, educational politics, and voting rights policy. He is coeditor of *Ethnic and Racial Minorities in Advanced Industrial Democracies* (1992). He is currently completing two book manuscripts: *The Changing Urban Regime: Toward an Informed Public Interest,* a history of the political incorporation of Latinos in San Antonio city politics from 1950 to 1990, and *Missed Opportunities: The Politics of Schools in San Francisco,* an examination of the implementation of a desegregation consent decree from 1983 to 2003. He is a past president of the Western Political Science Association and has served on the Executive Council of the American Political Science Association (APSA). He was appointed in 2002 by the president of the APSA to serve on its Standing Committee on Civic Engagement and Education. He received a number of teaching and advising awards at Stanford, including the Rhodes Prize for Excellence in Undergraduate Teaching (1993), the Dinkelspiel Award for Distinctive Contributions to Undergraduate Education (1995), the Allan V. Cox Medal for Faculty Excellence Fostering Undergraduate Research (1997), the Faculty Award from the Chicano/Latino Graduating Class (1993, 1996, 1997, 1999, 2000, 2001), the Undergraduate Faculty Adviser of the Year Award (2001), and the Associated Students of Stanford University Teaching Award (2003). He was also given the Adaljiza Sosa-Riddell Award for Exemplary Mentoring of Graduate Latina/o Students by the Committee on the Status of Latinos y Latinas in the Profession of the American Political Science Association (2001) and this same award for mentoring junior faculty (2004). In 2003–2004, he was a Fellow at the Radcliffe Institute for Advanced Study, Harvard University, working on a study entitled "Gender and Ethnicity: The Political Incorporation of Latina and Latino State Legislators," based on the first-ever nationwide survey of all Latina/o state legislators in the United States. He is one of six principal investigators on the Latino National Survey (LNS), the first-ever sixteen-state stratified survey of Latinos in the United States. This project received $1.25M in support from major foundations and universities and was completed in 2006.

Eric Gonzalez Juenke is an Assistant Professor of Political Science at the University of Colorado at Boulder. His current research examines how racial minorities turn their preferences into policy in the face of institutional constraints, entrenched majority interests, and policy incrementalism. His other research interests include the effects of minority representation in legislative and bureaucratic institutions, policy change, interinstitutional interactions over time, and the cross-national analysis of education. He received his BS (1999) and MA (2002) in political science from the University of North Texas, and his PhD (2005) from Texas A&M University.

Rodney E. Hero is the Packey J. Dee Professor of American Democracy and is Chair of the Department of Political Science at the University of Notre Dame. He specializes in U.S. democracy and politics, especially as viewed through the analytical lenses of Latino and ethnic/minority politics, state/urban politics, and federalism. He has published a number of research articles on these topics. His book, *Latinos and the U.S. Political System: Two-tiered Pluralism* (1992), received the American Political Science Association's Ralph J. Bunche Award ("best scholarly work in political science published in the previous year which explores the phenomenon of ethnic and cultural pluralism"). He also authored *Faces of Inequality: Social Diversity in American Politics* (1998),

325

which was selected for the American Political Science Association's Woodrow Wilson Foundation Award ("best book published on government, politics, or international affairs"). He is also coauthor of *Multiethnic Moments: The Politics of Urban Education Reform* (2006) and author of *Racial Diversity and Social Capital: Equality and Community in America* (2007).

Michael Jones-Correa is an Associate Professor of Government and Director of American Studies at Cornell University. He taught at Harvard University as an Assistant and Associate Professor of Government from 1994 to 2001 and has been a visiting fellow at the Woodrow Wilson Center for International Scholars 2003–2004 and a visiting scholar at the Russell Sage Foundation 1998–99. He is the author of *Between Two Nations: The Political Predicament of Latinos in New York City* (1998) and the editor of *Governing American Cities: Inter-ethnic Coalitions, Competition and Conflict* (2001). He has also written more than a dozen articles and book chapters on, among other things, the diffusion of racial restrictive covenants, religion and political participation, Latino identity and politics, the role of gender in shaping immigrant politics, dual nationality, immigrant naturalization and voting, and Hispanics as a foreign policy lobby. He is currently completing a book examining the implications of increasing racial/ethnic diversity in suburbia and is engaged in two additional projects: one on the renegotiation of ethnic relations in the aftermath of civil disturbances in New York, Los Angeles, Miami, and Washington, D.C., and the other the analysis of a national and state-by-state survey of Latinas in the United States, completed in 2006. His research and teaching interests include, among other things, immigrant politics and immigration policy, minority politics and interethnic relations in the United States, and urban and suburban politics.

David L. Leal is an Associate Professor of Government at the University of Texas at Austin. His research interests include Latino political opinion and behavior, public policy, and state and local politics. He has published over two dozen articles in journals such as *Journal of Politics, British Journal of Political Science, Political Research Quarterly, American Politics Quarterly, Political Behavior, PS: Political Science and Politics, DuBois Review, Armed Forces & Society, Social Science Quarterly, Policy Studies Journal, Urban Affairs Review,* and *Educational Policy.* He is also the author of *Electing America's Governors* (2006). He was an American Political Science Association (APSA) Congressional Fellow from 1998 to 1999 and a Spencer/National Academy of Education Post-Doctoral Fellow from 2002 to 2004. He received a PhD in political science from Harvard University in 1998. He is currently a member of the APSA Task Force on Religion and American Democracy and the editorial boards of *American Politics Research* and *Social Science Quarterly.*

Sylvia Manzano completed her PhD in 2004 at the University of Arizona. The essay in this volume is derived from her dissertation, which examines social capital and Latino political behavior. Her research interests also include immigration and urban politics. Currently she is an Assistant Professor in the Political Science Department at Texas A&M University.

Benjamin Márquez is a Professor of Political Science at the University of Wisconsin, Madison. His research interests include social movements, urban politics, and minority politics. His published work examines the relationship between race, political power, social identities, and public and political incorporation. He is the author of *Power and Politics in A Chicano Barrio: A Study of Mobilization Efforts and Community Power in El Paso* (1985), *LULAC: The Evolution* *of a Mexican American Political Organization* (1993), and numerous articles on Latino politics. His most recent book, *Mexican-American Political Organizations: Choosing Issues, Taking Sides* (2003) won the 2004 Best Book Award by the Race, Ethnicity and Politics (REP) section of the American Political Science Association. His current research project is an analysis of race and identity in Texas electoral politics from 1950 to the present.

Valerie Martinez-Ebers is an Associate Professor at Texas Christian University. She specializes in public policy analysis, race and politics, and survey research. She typically teaches courses on education policy; race, ethnicity, and politics; civil liberties and political tolerance; American and Texas government; and research methods in political science. While much of her research focuses on the consequences of school choice reform and other educational policies, she is also interested in the political incorporation and representation of Latinos. Her latest research project is a national survey of the political attitudes and behaviors of Latinos and other minority groups in the United States. Her most recent research has appeared in the *Journal of Politics, Phi Delta Kappan,* and *PS: Political Science and Politics.*

Kenneth J. Meier, Distinguished Professor of Political Science and the Charles H. Gregory Chair in Liberal Arts at Texas A&M University, is Professor of Public Management at the Cardiff University School of Business in Wales. A former editor of the *American Journal of Political Science,* he has eclectic research interests that cover a wide range of subfields in political science, including a long-standing research interest in questions of race, equity, and democratic inclusion. He is currently directing a study of the politics of educational equity using the eighteen hundred largest school districts in the United States.

Sharon A. Navarro is an Assistant Professor of Political Science at the University of Texas at San Antonio. She received her PhD from the University of Wisconsin and teaches American government and politics; ethnic politics, urban politics; Latino politics; culture and history; comparative politics-Latin America; politics of race, class, and gender; identity politics; U.S.-Mexico politics; women and politics; and minority politics. Her publications include book chapters, a journal article in *Latin American Politics and Society,* and a coedited volume, *Latino Americans and Political Participation* (2004). She is also the coauthor of the forthcoming *Latina Trailblazers.*

Adrian D. Pantoja is an Associate Professor of Political Science and Chicano Studies at Pitzer College. He received his PhD and MA from Claremont Graduate University and BA from the University of San Francisco. His research interests are in the areas of Latino political behavior and public opinion, as well as the fields of immigration and ethnic/racial politics. His research has appeared in a variety of journals, including *Political Research Quarterly, Political Behavior, Social Science Quarterly,* and edited volumes. He is currently working on a number of projects relating to the Dominican diaspora, transnational ties, and immigration. His interest in immigration and transborder politics stem from having spent his childhood living less than a mile from the Rio Grande in El Paso, Texas.

Ricardo Ramírez is an Assistant Professor in the Department of Political Science and the Program in American Studies and Ethnicity at the University of Southern California. His research interests include state and local politics, political behavior, and the politics of race and ethnicity, especially as they relate to participation, mobilization, and political incorporation. He is coeditor (with Taeku Lee and Karthick Ramakrishnan) of *Transforming Politics, Transforming America: The Political and Civic Incorporation of Immigrants in the United States.* (University of Virginia Press 2006) His other writings include coauthoring "Citizens by Choice, Voters by Necessity: Patterns in Political Mobilization by Naturalized Latinos" (with Adrian Pantoja and Gary Segura), "Giving Voice to Latino Voters: A Field Experiment on the Effectiveness of a National Non-Partisan Mobilization Effort," and "Are Naturalized Voters Driving the Latino Electorate? Measuring the Impact of IRCA on Latino Voting in California" (with Matt Barreto and Nathan Woods). His current projects include field experiments on the effects of elite mobilization efforts of Latino voters and on the role of residential mobility and race/ethnicity on patterns of mobilization during the 2004 presidential election.

René R. Rocha is Assistant Professor of Political Science at the University of Iowa. He received his BA from the University of Texas–Pan American and his PhD from Texas A&M University. His current research projects include the study of how residential context influences Latino politics and an assessment of the competition or cooperation between African Americans and Latinos in electoral and policy areas (focused on education policy).

Helena Alves Rodrigues is an Academic Advisor at the University of Arizona. She received her PhD in political science from the University of Iowa in June 2005. She specializes in Latino politics, and her dissertation is entitled "Building Bridges or Blockades? Latinos and Coalitions with African-Americans." In addition to Latino politics, her interests are in minority politics, including African American political behavior and public opinion, and intergroup relations among minority groups in the United States.

Gary M. Segura is an Associate Professor of American Politics at the University of Washington. He received his PhD in American politics and political philosophy from the University of Illinois in 1992 and previously taught at the University of California, Davis; Claremont Graduate University; and the University of Iowa. His work focuses on issues of political representation and currently is focusing on the accessibility of government and politics to America's growing Latino minority, as well as a book-length project on the links between casualties in international conflict and domestic politics. Among his most recent publications are "The Mobilizing Effect of Majority-Minority Districts on Latino Turnout" in the *American Political Science Review;* "War Casualties, Policy Positions, and the Fate of Legislators" in *Political Research Quarterly*; "Racial/Ethnic Group Attitudes toward Environmental Protection in California: Is 'Environmentalism' Still a White Phenomenon?" in *Political Research Quarterly*; and "Earth Quakes and After Shocks: Race, Direct Democracy, and Partisan Change," in the *American Journal of Political Science.* Earlier research has appeared in the *Journal of Politics, Political Behavior, Legislative Studies Quarterly, Social Science Quarterly*, the *National Civic Review*, the *Harvard Journal of Hispanic Policy*, the *Journal of Conflict Resolution*, and *Rationality and Society*, and his work has, on three occasions, been funded by the National Science Foundation.

Nick A. Theobald is a lecturer in the Department of Political Science at Cal Poly San Luis Obispo. His research includes work on educational accountability, bilingual education, state finance, bureaucratic representation, and organizational theory.

Index

abortion, 225; attitudes on, 35–37, 39, 156
active representation, 249, 263. *See also* substantive representation
administrative positions, competition over, 169
administrators, Latino, 166, 263; as determinant of teachers, 172; growth in, 246; hired by school boards, 167; principals, 257, 261; as a source of school board members, 235. *See also* school superintendents
affirmative action, 31, 68; attitudes on, 156; and coalitions, 162; competition over, 152
African American(s), 46, 75; mayors, 67; participation of, 75; school superintendents, 252; voters, 70. *See also* coalitions
age: and home country electoral engagement, 115; of Latinos, 91; and participation, 113
"air war" campaigns, 91–92
Alabama, 191
American Jews, 52
American National Election Study, 29, 33
American Political Science Association, 268
American politics, as Latino politics, 281
American Voter, The, 70

amnesty, for undocumented immigrants, 147
Anglo representatives, in Latino districts, 230
Anglos, as preferring to coalesce with Latinos, 155, 171
anti-immigrant initiatives, 68, 77
Arizona, 181
Arkansas, 191
Asian Americans, 47, 58; immigration of, 47
assimilation: and ethnic voting, 71; and identity formation, 18; of immigrants, 51; problems with models of, 19; theories of, 44; varying by national origin, 19
assisted suicide, attitudes on, 35–37, 156
at-large elections, 165; and Latinas, 179–80
attentiveness to politics, and mobilization, 100
attitudes, versus actions on coalitions, 146–49. *See also* public opinion, Latino

Badillo, Herman, 223
balseros, 58
Barrio Defense Committee, 184
Bayesian estimation methods, 204–6, 218

RACE, ETHNICITY, AND POLITICS

Louis DeSipio
Counting on the Latino Vote: Latinos as a New Electorate

Sheila L. Croucher
Imagining Miami: Ethnic Politics in a Postmodern World

Bernard Grofman, editor
Legacies of the 1964 Civil Rights Act

Gary M. Segura and Shaun Bowler, editors
Diversity in Democracy: Minority Representation in the United States

Taeku Lee, S. Karthick Ramakrishnan, and Ricardo Ramírez, editors
Transforming Politics, Transforming America: The Political and Civic Incorporation of Immigrants in the United States

Erica Frankenberg and Gary Orfield, editors
Lessons in Integration: Realizing the Promise of Racial Diversity in American Schools

Rodolfo Espino, David L. Leal, and Kenneth J. Meier, editors
Latino Politics: Identity, Mobilization, and Representation